Corporate Management Ecosystem in Emerging Economies

Fred A. Yamoah • Adnan ul Haque
Editors

Corporate Management Ecosystem in Emerging Economies

Global Perspectives

palgrave
macmillan

Editors
Fred A. Yamoah
Department of Management, School of Business, Economics and Informatics
Birkbeck, University of London
London, UK

Adnan ul Haque
Faculty of Business
Yorkville University Toronto
ON, Canada

ISBN 978-3-031-41577-7 ISBN 978-3-031-41578-4 (eBook)
https://doi.org/10.1007/978-3-031-41578-4

This Palgrave Macmillan imprint is published by the registered company Springer Nature Switzerland AG.
The registered company address is: Gewerbestrasse 11, 6330 Cham, Switzerland

Paper in this product is recyclable.

Contents

Notes on Contributors

Salwani Affandi possesses a Master of Arts in Finance from the University of Wales Bangor, United Kingdom in 2009. She is currently employed at the Universiti Teknologi MARA, Malaysia since September 2010. Her main role involves teaching undergraduate students in various finance courses like personal financial planning, investment analysis, banking operations, and financial statement analysis. She is also active in university and international research publications. Her research interests include bank lending, capital adequacy, and the performance of Malaysian commercial and Islamic banks. She has written and published several articles on this subject in the Scopus/WoS/ERA indexed journals. In addition, she has undertaken research on corporate finance subjects, including the capital structure and performance of numerous Malaysian industry sectors. She presented her work at international conferences such as the Terengganu International Business and Economics Conference. She earned the Best Paper Award in two times she attended the conference. In addition, she also received a prize for Best Paper at the National Finance and Management Conference (NAFMAC 2019).

Mahyudin Ahmad is an associate professor at the Faculty of Business and Management, Universiti Teknologi MARA (UiTM) Perlis Branch. He holds PhD in Economics from University of Leicester, United Kingdom. His research interests are in the field of Applied Economics, particularly in economic growth & development, mostly with empirical applications using panel data and spatial analysis. He has published more 20 empirical papers, such as in International Journal of Finance & Economics, Economic Change and Restructuring, Journal of Policy Modeling, Margin Journal of Applied Economics, Economies, International Journal of Social Economics, and New Zealand Economic Papers, to name a few. He has been invited to become internal and external examiner for several master's and PhD students in the field of economics and finance at UiTM and Universiti of Karachi, Pakistan. He also acts as a referee for more than 50 pre-published manuscripts submitted to more than 20 top-indexed journals. He has been invited to conduct numerous panel data and spatial analysis workshops to academic staff and postgraduate students at Accounting Research Institute UiTM Shah Alam, UiTM Pahang, UiTM Johor, UiTM Perlis, UiTM Kedah, UiTM Melaka, Universiti Utara Malaysia, Universiti Malaysia Sarawak, and Universitas Airlangga, Indonesia.

Nizam Ahmat is a Senior Lecturer at the Faculty of Business, Economics and Social Development, Universiti Malaysia Terengganu since December 2016. In 1998, he has graduated with a Bachelor of Management Technology from Malaysia's University Technology of Malaysia. Then, in 2006, he received his master's degree in economics from the National University of Malaysia. He then obtained his Ph.D in Economics from the National University of Malaysia in 2015. His research interest focuses on financial economics, the economy of transportation, economic modeling and applied Econometrics. Until now, he has 20 journal articles to date that are listed in SCOPUS, Web of Science (SSCI, ESCI), Excellent Research Australia (ERA), and MyCite as authors, corresponding authors and co-authors. He has connections with researchers in local universities and industries in Malaysia, also in Indonesia and Ghana, from various fields of expertise such as Financial, Environment, Transportation, mathematical science, and Econometrics. Besides journal publications, he has received 5 research grants totaling RM138, 610 as principal investigator and co-researcher.

Tahmina Akhter is a professor in the Yorkville University's BBA program. She received her PhD from the University of Waterloo and a second M.Sc. from the Toronto Metropolitan University, both in Applied Mathematics. Before moving to Canada, she was working as an Assistant Professor of Mathematics in the University of Asia Pacific, Dhaka, Bangladesh. She also worked as a sessional instructor and a post-doctoral fellow, in the Applied Mathematics department of the University of Waterloo. Dr. Akhter's research interests span a wide range of topics, including Statistical Analysis and Model, Pharmacokinetics, Mathematical Medicine, and Fluid Dynamics. Beyond her passion for research and academia, Tahmina is known for her enthusiasm in motivating and inspiring others. She takes every opportunity to support and encourage those around her. This passion for motivating others has influenced her commitment to both teaching and research, making her an influential and dedicated figure in the field.

Fadli Fizari Abu Hassan Asari is currently a senior lecturer in the Faculty of Business and Management at UiTM Perlis Branch, Arau Campus, Malaysia. He received his bachelor's degree in economics from Universiti Malaya. Later, he obtained his master's degree in economics from the same university. His career at three different universities as well as in three different positions, sparked interest in him to pursue a PhD in a topic related to academic affairs. Thus, he successfully completed his PhD journey from Universiti Malaysia Terengganu. His niche areas are Microeconomics, Behavioral Economics, Education Economics, Environmental Economics, Love Economics, and Creativity & Innovation. He dreams that one day, he and his family members will become professors.

Kwasi Awuah-Werekoh is a PhD and a Director, Finance, Ghana Maritime Authority, Accra, Ghana.Dr. Kwasi Awuah-Werekoh is a highly proactive and self-motivated person with strong business and analytical abilities. He is an enthusiastic, reliable and team player with a flexible approach to understanding new and demanding tasks at the workplace. He has strong professional, practical and research knowledge and experience in various disciplines. He is a Chartered Management Accountant (CIMA) with a B.Sc. Computer Science (Kwame Nkrumah University of Science and Technology, Ghana), Post Graduate Diploma in Education (University of Cape Coast, Ghana), MBA Finance (University of

Leicester, UK), MSc International Accounting (Anglia Ruskin University, UK) and PhD in Accounting and Finance (University of Birmingham, UK). Dr. Awuah-Werekoh has worked and lectured at various institutions both in Ghana and in the UK, notably working as lecturer at the Ghana Institute of Management & Public Administration (GIMPA) and the City of London Business College. Kwasi has consultancy experience with the African Development Bank (AfDB).

Shamsul Amri Baharuddin is a Malaysian academic and scientist, specializing in social science and social anthropology. He is the founding director of the Institute of Ethnic Studies (KITA), Universiti Kebangsaan Malaysia (UKM), founded in 2007. In 2010, the Ministry of Higher Education selected him as a Distinguished Professor. He was appointed Deputy Chairman of the National Council of Professors in 2010 and Chairman in 2019. In April 2018, he was invited to become a Fellow of the Malaysian Academy of Sciences (ASM). In February 2019, he was appointed as a UNESCO Chair holder in "social practice in intercultural communication and community cohesion." In 2020, he was appointed Unity Advisor to the Ministry of National Unity.

Joseph Dankwah is a PhD and a Business Development and Sales Manager, TechnipFMC Ghana Limited, Accra, Ghana. Dr. Joseph Dankwah is an Eminent Member and "supply chain subject matter expert" of Chartered Institute of Supply Chain Management, Ghana. Educated at both University of Cape Coast and Takoradi Technical University, Ghana, Dr. Dankwah pursued his graduate studies at the KNUST, Ghana. He obtained Doctor of Business Administration and Master of Applied Business Research from Swiss Business School SBS, Zurich, Switzerland. Dr. Dankwah has over twenty (20) years' experience in Procurement and Supply Chain Management as well as business development across different industries such as upstream Oil & Gas, Mining and Transport Operations. Dr. Joseph Dankwah had previously worked with Tullow Ghana Limited as the Contracts & Procurement Lead. Prior to joining Tullow Oil PLC. Currently, at TechnipFMC, Dr. Joseph Dankwah is a Business Development & Sales Manager for Ghana and Ivory Coast based in Ghana. He is also an Adjunct Lecturer at the Pentecost University Ghana.

Clement Dodoo (PhD) is a Group Director, Integration & Remedial Management, Equity Group Holdings PLC, Nairobi, Kenya. Dr. Dodoo has been in the banking since 1994 and has experience in Project Review & Management, Relationship Management, Credit, Risk Management, Business Development and General & Change Management. As Regional Risk Manager for the then East & Southern Africa Region of the Ecobank Group from 2007 to early 2009, he held oversight supervision responsibilities in Rwanda, Burundi, Zambia, Kenya, Malawi and Uganda. Clement is currently a Group Director of Integrations with Equity Group Holdings Limited, the parent company of Equity Bank, East and Central Africa's largest bank. He holds a Doctorate degree in Business Administration (2020) from the Swiss Business School, Master of Applied Business Research from the Swiss Business School, a Master of Business Administration and Bachelor of Arts (Hons) Degree in Economics from the University of Ghana, Legon and a Certificate in Contemporary Management from the Nobel International Business School. Accra.

Riffat Faizan holds a Doctor of Business Administration from Royal Academy of Economics and Technology in Switzerland. She has over decade experience in Academic teaching (nationally and internationally). As a professional researcher, she has numerous papers published in Scopus/ABS/ impact factor Journals. She had a privilege of chairing sessions and presenting as keynote speaker at international conferences. Also have two-decade experience in networking, logistic operations and managing corporate clients in Canada and worldwide. She also has expertise in building international teams and works on a core value of reliability and integrity to work across diverse cultures and regions.

Ireneus Gundona (PhD) is a Managing Partner, Consumer Insights Consult Ltd, Accra, Ghana. Dr. Gundona is the founder and managing director of Consumer Insights Consult—a leading market and social research firm in sub-Saharan Africa. He has actively participated within the Market and Social Research space across sub-Saharan Africa for close to two decades, exercising leadership and responsibility over diverse teams and projects of significant financial accountability. Dr. Gundona is Director and Chairman at Tangkama Company Limited (dba Tangkama), Board Chair for BI Microfinance, Akayet Mining & Supply Services and

Akayete Hotel. He holds a Doctor of Business Administration from Swiss Business School Zurich, Switzerland, and an MSc in Marketing and Business Management from the University of Bedfordshire, UK. He is a member of ESOMAR and doubles and served as the country representative for Ghana. A founding member of GHAMRA, an affiliate member of the Market Research Society, UK and an associate member of the Chartered Institute of Marketing, Ghana.

Irfan ul Haq is an independent researcher with over two decades experience in effective and efficient managements of projects. He has worked on national and international projects with diverse groups across the globe. He holds PMP Certification and received distinction in MBA from Anglia Ruskin University, UK. His research area focuses on Entrepreneurship, project management, stress, and sustainable practices.

Adnan ul Haque holds a Doctor of Business Administration (DBA) in Organizational Behaviour from the University of Wales Trinity Saint David, United Kingdom. He specializes in gender related occupational stress through a cultural lens. He received Best PG Research Student Award from University of Sunderland, London in MBA-HRM, distinction in PGD in Business and Management, ATHE, London and diploma in Research and Leadership, University of Copenhagen, Denmark. He earned his Management and Sciences distinctions at Public Administration Department for his MPA in HRM and his BPA (Hons) from the University of Karachi. Dr. Haque is a Business and Management lecturer, Senior Researcher, Session Chair and Keynote Presenter at various international conferences and external PhD examiner for universities across the globe. He has been a Corporate Trainer for Stress Management and Professional Development at MNCs and HR consultant for IT and Logistic firms in the UK, Canada, and Pakistan. His research interest includes organizational behaviour, human resources management, sustainability, Industry 4.0, knowledge hiding, occupational stress, supply chain management, innovative work behaviour, and leadership styles. He has a specialization in the Occupational stress and have published several research articles and presented keynotes in international conferences on the subject matter (varying stressors at workplace). He also serves as an editor for books and special issues (i.e., IGI, Springer, and

Sustainability).Adnan ul Haque, DBA, Faculty of Business, Yorkville University, Canada, ahaque@yorkvilleu.ca

Fauziah Abu Hasan is a Professor at the Faculty of Business, Economics and Social Development, Universiti Malaysia Terengganu. Her research area focuses on Economic Development. Her interests currently are in healthcare economics, labour and gender in equality.

Muhammad Imran is a PhD, currently he is working as international senior lecturer in School of Business Management, Universiti Utara Malaysia, Malaysia. Furthermore, he is affiliated with department of project and operations management, institute of business management and administrative sciences, the Islamia university of Bahawalpur, Pakistan as assistant professor since 2019. Apart from academic experience, he has published around 40 research papers in various indexed national and international journals. His research interest are SMEs, Industry 4.0, human resource management, occupational health and safety, risk management, supply chain and operations management.

Nurul Liyana Mohd Kamil is a Senior Lecturer in Human Resource Management and Organisational Behaviour, Faculty of Business and Economics, Universiti Malaya, Malaysia. She currently serves as a Postdoctoral Visiting Fellow at the Department of Management at the London School of Economics and Political Science (LSE) in the United Kingdom. She obtained a PhD in Human Resource Management from Universiti Sains Malaysia. Her research interests mainly in leadership, work engagement, innovation, and employees' work performance. She is the Associate Editor for Institutions and Economies and a Membership Officer of the Asia Pacific Academy for Psychosocial Factors at Work. She has received various accolades, including the Universiti Malaya's Excellent Service Award (2023). Her most recent publications have appeared in a variety of Scopus and WOS journals, including Journal of Social Service Research, PLoS ONE, International Journal of Public Administration, and many others. Nurul's profile can be viewed at https://umexpert.um.edu.my/nurulliyana.html.

Henri Kouam is the Deputy Managing Director at Prima Finance and Investment, a challenger Microfinance bank in Cameroon. He is equally the founder of a new Association—the Economic Policy Institute (EPI), that seeks to improve the quality of Economic Policy in Cameroon. He holds an MBA with a Finance Major from Cardiff Metropolitan University. He was previously an economist at the Nkafu Policy Institute between 2020 and 2022. and was the Lead Researcher for Africa on the Demographic Dividend, a project sponsored by the Bill and Melinda Gates Foundation. He is a NATO consultant for Africa, with experiences ranging from Sterlinxglobal, a UK-based e-commerce tax company, to Benzinga, a market intelligence firm based in the United States. He is a contributor to the UK-based Economist Intelligence Unit (EIU).

John Ampontuah Kumah is a PhD and MP/Deputy Minister of Finance and Economic Planning, Accra, Ghana. Dr. Kumah, Esq is the Member of Parliament for Ejisu, in the Ashanti Region and deputy Minister of Finance in charge of wealth creation in Ghana. He is a Lawyer and an Entrepreneur with over 15 years' experience. Some of his past roles include CEO for National Entrepreneurship and Innovation Programme, managing partner of Aduaprokye Chambers, founder of Majak Associates Ltd. He holds a Doctorate in Business Innovation from Swiss Business School in Switzerland and a Masters in Applied Business Research, from the same School. In 2009, he had an Executive Masters degree in Business Administration (Finance), from Ghana Institute of Management and Public Administration. He holds a Bachelor of Arts degree in Economics with Philosophy, a Bachelor of Art Degree (Law) LLB from University of Ghana and Professional Law Certificate from the Ghana School of Law in 2013.

Nor Isma Liyana Binti Hasran received her Bachelor's and Master of Economics from the Department of Economics, Faculty of Business, Economics and Social Development, Universiti Malaysia Terengganu, Malaysia. Her research interest is Financial Economics, International Trade, Macroeconomics and Islamic Financial Economics.

Suriyani Muhamad graduated from the University of Malaya (B. Econs), MSc (London School of Economics) and PhD (University of Manchester). She is a Professor at the Faculty of Business, Economics and Social Development, Universiti Malaysia Terengganu. Her research area focuses on Economic Development. Her interests currently are in healthcare economics, labour and gender, specifically on women's issues.

Mohd Nasir Nawawi is a Senior Lecturer at the Faculty of Business, Economics and Social Development, Universiti Malaysia Terengganu. He received her Bachelor of Economics and Master of Economics from National University of Malaysia and PhD in Economics from Universiti Utara Malaysia. His research interests focus on Environmental Economics and Development Economics. To date, He has published 12 journal publications indexed in SCOPUS, Web of Science (SSCI, ESCI), Excellent Research Australia (ERA) and MyCite and has published 12 chapters in books with various Publishing. He is a member of the Malaysian Social Science Association.

Ayesha Nida is a research scholar at Institute of Business Management and Administrative Sciences, The Islamic University of Bahawalpur, Pakistan. She has earned MBA from same institute and now working as Relationship Manager at Bank. She is involved in different research projects related to business management. Her interest is in marketing, consumer behavior, sustainable practices, and Industry 4.0.

Wan Noor Azreen Wan Mohamad Nordin graduated with a Bachelor of Science Administration from Universiti Teknologi MARA and a Master of Public Administration from Universiti Malaya, Malaysia. She is currently a graduate research assistant under Malaysia's Fundamental Research Grant Scheme and pursuing a doctoral degree in organizational behaviour at the Faculty of Business and Economics, Universiti Malaya. Her research focuses mainly on innovative work behaviour, leadership, autonomy, and organizational citizenship behaviour in the public and service sector. Her publications are currently being reviewed in Scopus and WoS journals.

Genevieve Pearl Duncan Obuobi is a Lead Consultant, Tarragon Edge Ltd, Accra, Ghana. Dr. Genevieve is a multiple award winner in Banking, Leadership and a light bearer for African Women. She is listed among the 100 most impactful change makers in Africa by HAG 2023 and listed in the 40 most influential female leaders in Ghana 2020. She is a Customer Experience Strategist, Corporate Trainer and an SME consultant with passion for gender financing and youth leadership. She is currently the Lead Consultant of Tarragon Edge. She worked with Fidelity Bank Ghana Limited were she managed flag ship branches. Her expertise is in personal and team development, leadership, customer experience, writing and management consulting. Dr. Genevieve is an alumnus of the Swiss Business School Zurich, Switzerland where she earned her Doctorate in Business Administration, and the University of Ghana, Legon where she attained Masters Degree and GIMPA. She is also a business consultant certified by CEIBS, Shanghai, Cranfield Management—UK and Harvard.

Maxim Rakov is a professor at Yorkville/Algoma University with a Master's Degree in Strategic Foresight and Innovation, specializing in marketing and sustainability. Bringing along 15 years of experience in international organizations and global companies, Maxim has honed his leadership skills, guiding organizations toward sustainable futures. His career spans significant roles in academia and industry, focusing on Sustainability and Business Innovations. As an educator, he encourages critical thinking and real-world application of theoretical concepts, shaping future leaders in his field. Actively involved in professional societies, Maxim regularly contributes to conferences and workshops, staying at the cutting edge of his discipline.

Jumadil Saputra is a PhD holder and works as a senior lecturer in the Department of Economics, Faculty of Business, Economics, and Social Development, Universiti Malaysia Terengganu, Malaysia. He has published 257 articles Scopus/ WoS indexed. As a lecturer, he has invited as a speaker in numerous universities, the examiner (internal and external), the reviewer for article journal and proceeding, the conference committee, journal editorial board, and others. He is a professional member of the International Business Information Management Association (IBIMA), Ocean Expert: A Directory of Marine and Freshwater Professional, and Academy for Global Business Advancement (AGBA). He awarded the best paper at the conference and excellent staff. His research areas are Quantitative Economics (Microeconomics, Macroeconomics, and Economic Development), Econometrics (Theory, Analysis, and Applied), Islamic Banking and Finance, Risk and Insurance,

Takaful, i.e., financial economics (Islamic), mathematics and modeling of finance (Actuarial).

Ali Sher is a Professor of Business Administration at Yorkville University. He received his PhD in Engineering Management with a concentration in Information & Process Engineering and MS in Computer Science from George Washington University. He earned his M.Sc. from University of Peshawar and BSc in Mathematics and Statistics from Edwardes College Peshawar. He taught Business courses at both undergraduate and graduate level at different universities including Business Information Systems, Data Analysis, Business Decision Analysis, Statistical Analysis for Management, Operations Management, and e-Commerce, etc. Dr. Sher's research interests lie in the areas of Online Learning and Big Data. He has published in prominent peer-reviewed journals including International Technology Management Review, Journal of Interactive Learning, and Journal of Online Learning and Teaching. Prior to joining Yorkville University, Dr. Sher taught at the business schools of University of New Brunswick, George Mason University, Rochester Institute of Technology, and DeVry University. Earlier in his career, he worked for the World Bank, and International Finance Corporation, Washington DC where he was responsible for developing and managing financial information systems for the worldwide emerging market stock database clients.

Negar Sohaee is a highly accomplished and dedicated educator with a profound commitment to empowering students through education. With a DBA and MBA in Management, she currently serves as a Professor at Yorkville University, specializing in Human Resource Management, Development, and Organization Behavior. Nikki joined the faculty in 2018 and has held various positions, including Instructor, Associate Professor, and Professor. Aside from her academic achievements, Nikki has over six years of industry experience in management and business development across the Middle East, the USA, and Canada. Transitioning to academia in 2015, she brings a wealth of practical knowledge to her teaching. Her approach to education goes beyond imparting knowledge; she aims to instill life lessons and empower students to succeed. Her research interests focus on Preparing the Workforce for AI Integration, identifying critical employability competencies. As a respected member of the Ontario Campus Curriculum Committee, she takes a leadership role in guiding faculty members in Human Resource Management courses.

Muhammad Najit Sukemi is a Senior Lecturer at the Faculty of Business, Economics and Social Development, Universiti Malaysia Terengganu since 2003. He received her Bachelor of Economics in 2001, Master of Economics in 2003 and PhD in Economics at the National University of Malaysia in 2021. His research interests focus on economic development, Islamic Economics and Finance, Economics Modelling and ethnicity. To date, He has published 10 journal publications indexed in SCOPUS, Web of Science (SSCI, ESCI), Excellent Research Australia (ERA) and MyCite and has published 11 chapters in books with various Publishing. He is a member of the Malaysia Consumer and Family Economy Association and Malaysian Social Science Association.

Nor Fatimah Che Sulaiman is a Senior Lecturer at the Faculty of Business, Economics and Social Development, Universiti Malaysia Terengganu since 2018. She received her Bachelor of Economics in 2011 from Yokohama National University, Japan. She received her Master of Science in Economics in 2014 from Universiti Malaysia Terengganu. She then received her PhD in Economics at the National University of Malaysia in 2018. Her research interest is focused on inclusive economic development. This field of research requires a detailed understanding of human and community development. To date, she has published 16 journal publications indexed in SCOPUS, Web of Science (SSCI, ESCI), Excellent Research Australia (ERA) and MyCite and has published 9 chapters in books with Emerald Group Publishing. She has connections with researchers from various fields of expertise such as engineering, hydrology, food science, mathematical science, and statistics in universities and industries in Malaysia, also in Japan. Besides journal and book publications, she has received eight research grants with total amount of RM698,610 as principal investigator and co-researcher.

Sheikh Ahmad Faiz Sheikh Ahmad Tajuddin is a lecturer at the Faculty of Business and Management, Universiti Sultan Zainal Abidin, Malaysia.

He completed his PhD in Economics from Universiti Malaysia Terengganu. He has Master of Commerce from University of Queensland and Bachelor of Economics from International Islamic University Malaysia. His research area focuses on Economic Development and his research interests include labour economics and policies.

Arif Toor has extensive teaching experience in the filed of management and business studies. He has taught business and accounting courses universities in Canada, the UK, and the Middle East. He has a PhD from the University of Toronto and manages his training consultancy business in Downtown Toronto. He is a firm believer in participatory learning that is student-centered.

Fred A. Yamoah is a Reader in Sustainability. He serves as Chair for both MSc Marketing Online Programme and UN's Principles of Responsible Management Education (PRME) at Birkbeck—University of London. He has previously served as a Sustainability Expert Panel Member for the British Council's Newton Fund Grant Review Panel, Commonwealth Scholarship Academic Adviser and African Academy of Sciences Post-Doctoral Grants Reviewer. Fred is currently a topic Editor 'Sustainable Food' for MDPI Sustainability Journal and Sustainability Co-Editor for the Annual Review of Social Partnership. He has numerous sustainability, business ethics, circular economy and sustainable consumption and ethical marketing-related research papers rated as internationally excellent and world leading. These include publications in world ranked journals such as the European Journal of Operational Research, International Journal of Production Economics, Technological Forecasting and Social Change, Resources, Conservation and Recycling, International Marketing Review, Journal of Environmental Management, Environmental Management, The International Food and Agribusiness Management Review, British Food Journal, Journal of Business Ethics, Computers in Human Behaviour, Journal of Cleaner Production, Studies in Higher Education, Economic and Industrial Democracy and Journal of Business Research. Fred is a Co-author of 'Contemporary Retail Marketing in Emerging Economies' 2022 Palgrave Macmillan publication and three book chapter contributions in *The Role of Government and Consumer Behaviour. Perspectives on Consumer Behaviour: Theoretical*

Aspects and Practical Applications, Springer, Cham (2020); *Incorporating Sustainability in Management Education—An Interdisciplinary Approach*, Palgrave Macmillan (2019) and *Developing Skills for Business Leadership, Chartered Institute of Personnel and Development (2014).*

Fred A. Yamoah Ph.D., School of Business, Economics and Informatics, Birkbeck—University of London, UK, f.yamoah@bbk.cu.uk

Azlina Zid (PhD) is a senior lecturer in the Department of Sport Management at the Faculty of Sports Science and Recreation, Universiti Teknologi MARA (UiTM), Shah Alam. She received a Bachelor of Science in Finance from Oklahoma City University USA in 1997 and Master of Science in Physical Education from Universiti Putra Malaysia in 2002. She received her PhD in Accounting Management from Universiti Kebangsaan Malaysia in 2017. Her research activities are on Sports Management, Financial Management and Accounting Management. She has published a few articles in journals and seminar proceeding such as the Malaysian Journal of Sports Science and Recreation (MJSSR), Current Psychology (WoS), Environment Behaviour Proceedings Journal (Wos), Journal of Positive School Psychology (Scopus) and Social Sciences and Humanities (MJSSH). She also has produced A-Z Guide for Sports Research book (2020) as a guideline for undergraduate students to prepare for their research projects and Prosedur Operasi Standard [SOP]: Rekreasi Luar Kebangsaan (2022). She also has been granted a few industries grants for scientific research.

List of Figures

Innovation Management in the Public Sector: How Leaders Oversee Employees' Innovative Work Behaviour?

Challenges and Implications of Cryptocurrencies, Central Bank Digital Currencies, and Electronic Money

On the Prospects of Sustainable Tourism in Bangladesh

Impact of Bank's Customer Relationship Management on Customer Satisfaction and Loyalty of SMEs: The Moderating Role of Advisory Services and Capacity Building

Identifying the Global Demand for Cross-Border Higher Education of Malaysian Public Universities

Business Schools and Their Connections with the Labour Market: An Exploratory Analysis of Pakistani Public Universities

The Reasons Behind Imbalanced Ecosystem of Latin America: A Comprehensive Systematic Review

List of Tables

A Framework for Understanding Agribusiness Stakeholders Decision-Making Dynamics in the Pesticide Industry of Pakistan

Innovation Management in the Public Sector: How Leaders Oversee Employees' Innovative Work Behaviour?

On the Prospects of Sustainable Tourism in Bangladesh

Impact of Bank's Customer Relationship Management on Customer Satisfaction and Loyalty of SMEs: The Moderating Role of Advisory Services and Capacity Building

Factors Affecting the Success of Product/Service Innovation Among SMEs in Ghana: The Moderating Role of Functional Diversity and Strategic Alignment

Is Interest Rate an Effective Instrument for Controlling Inflation and Its Effect on Investment Activities in Developing Countries?

Assessing the Impact of Customer Engagement on Brand Performance: The Mediating Role of Customer-Based Brand Equity (CBBE)

The Impact of Economy Affirmative to Wealth Distribution Among Ethnic Groups in Malaysia

The Reasons Behind Imbalanced Ecosystem of Latin America: A Comprehensive Systematic Review

Introduction to Corporate Management Ecosystem

Adnan ul Haque and Fred A. Yamoah

1 Introduction

Undoubtedly, human progress in science and technology has produced many rewards and benefits, but it has also adversely impacted both the natural and business ecosystems globally. Thus, sustainable practices are essential requirements of the time. Several studies have confirmed the critical role of the ecosystem in the modern era (Adner & Kapoor, 2010; Kapoor & Lee, 2012; Meyer et al., 2005; Pierce, 2009; Teece, 2007), especially in the fields of innovation, sustainability, and management of technology. However, different authors in the literature have defined it

A. ul Haque (✉)
Faculty of Business, Yorkville University, Toronto, ON, Canada
e-mail: ahaque@yorkvilleu.ca

F. A. Yamoah
Department of Management, School of Business, Economics and Informatics, Birkbeck, University of London, London, UK
e-mail: f.yamoah@bbk.ac.uk

F. A. Yamoah, A. ul Haque (eds.), *Corporate Management Ecosystem in Emerging Economies*, https://doi.org/10.1007/978-3-031-41578-4_1

differently. Hence, there is no single agreed-upon definition of the natural ecosystem (Tsujimoto et al., 2018). A simple definition attributed to the Oxford English Dictionary (2017) is that an ecosystem is "a biological system composed of all the organisms found in a particular physical environment, interacting with it and each other. Also in extended use: a complex system resembling this." In a natural environment, inhabitants interact with one another and as well actively interact with their physical environment. The sustainable ecosystem is the focus of attention among researchers, academics, and practitioners (Kanter, 2017) because the natural world requires a balanced ecosystem for inhabitants to thrive, while imbalanced ecosystems have severe destructive consequences. Therefore, the sustainable ecosystem ensures and promotes the provision and protection of essential resources in the natural setting. Drawing a parallel between the nature and attributes of the natural and business ecosystems, against the backdrop of the continuing expansion of businesses across the globe, the business ecosystem requires equal attention in different forms to contribute to sustainable business management practices. Indeed, a business ecosystem is interconnected—a highly complex network of various stakeholders, organizations, operations, and resources to work in collaboration or compete, while creating invaluable value for all. In other words, to succeed in the complex business environment, companies collaborate to produce innovative ideas, services, and solutions. Thus, sustainable practices are vital components in the due process of business ecosystem. How the corporate management ecosystem in emerging economies of the world is shaping as a promoter and/or inhibitor towards attaining sustainability in the long run is the prime focus of this book.

2 Core Concepts

There is no definition in the literature at hand that can define the corporate management ecosystem. It is the combination of three key terminologies, namely, 'corporate', 'management', and 'ecosystem'. Corporate is an entity pertaining to a united group operating business (Dictionary.com, 2022). It is often a corporation—an entity that is interconnected and interlinked with the processes and systems in the environment while ensuring governance and the management of operations.

Drucker (1963) defined management as the product of effectiveness and efficiency, where "doing things right" is regarded as 'efficiency' while "doing the right things" is considered as 'effectiveness' (cited from Robbins & Coulter, 2012; Hussain et al., 2019). The theme of Drucker's definition is based on "knowledge work" (McGrath & Young, 2019). On the other hand, Fayol defined it as, "to manage is to forecast and to plan, to organize, to command, to co-ordinate and to control" (Prasad & Gulshan, 2011; Hussain et al., 2019). Thus, one could infer that management is the product of effectiveness and efficiency—attainment of impactful practices with no or minimal wastage of resources.

Lastly, an ecosystem is "a biological system composed of all the organisms found in a particular physical environment, interacting with it and each other. Also in extended use: a complex system resembling this" (Oxford English Dictionary, 2017). Thus, the corporate management ecosystem could be defined as processes, practices, entities, and systematic elements/units that are interlinked and interdependent to ensure that the operations and functioning of the organizations remain effective and efficient by reducing the adverse impact on the physical environment. It encompasses the various components and stakeholders that contribute to the strategic direction, decision-making, and overall performance of the corporation. The executives, leaders, management teams, board of directors, partners, investors, regulatory bodies, suppliers, customers, shareholders, and other stakeholders are the key elements of the corporate management ecosystem. All the mentioned elements interact directly or indirectly with each other as well as with their immediate and remote physical environments, affecting and shaping the entire approach and practices of management and outcomes of the corporation. The interaction is dynamic in nature, and thus, clear governance practices, reliable structure, rationale and sound process of decision-making, effective and efficient utilization of resources, collaboration with distinct stakeholders, effective communication, and risk management that places emphasis on the formation of value for distinct stakeholders are the characteristics of effective corporate management.

The scarcity of resources is one of the main drivers for academics, practitioners, planners, authorities, and researchers to understand and manage the corporate management ecosystem while finding ways to adopt sustainable practices. The agenda is to create collective value and optimize the experiences of all stakeholders involved in the governance and management of operations. Marketing has significantly changed over the years because of the current contemporary environment (Yawson & Yamoah, 2022). Similarly, management practitioners have also adopted new strategies and approaches to deal with the dynamics of the environment. Sustainable development is important for managers and marketing practitioners to manage and market their products and services, thus creating the value in social, economic, and environmental sphere. Slaper and Hall (2011) stated that triple bottom line (TBL) includes people (social), profit (economic), and planet (environment) as essential components of the sustainable development framework that primarily focus on the notion of ensuring the present generation's needs are fulfilled while future generations' needs are not sacrificed. In other words, the sustainable consumption of resources by the present generation should not be at the expense of future generations' needs.

Modern management and marketing encompass various perspectives and approaches that have emerged from the unintended consequences of traditional marketing practices, such as the unsustainable impact on the environment. This shift has led to the development of contemporary marketing, which includes relationship marketing and sustainability marketing (Brodie et al., 1997; Coviello et al., 1997). Similarly, contemporary management has driven organization's activities to be more sustainable so that there is optimal utilization of resources (Hussain et al., 2019). Transformational approach, perseverance with scarce resources, sustainable practices, and corporate governance in emerging economies are the core themes of this book. Although these phenomena are experienced in varying modes by different types of economies, this book examines the corporate management ecosystem through a global lens because within the emerging economies, different countries are on different scale of progress. Thus, it offers an in-depth insight into the sustainable ecosystem from a global perspective.

3 Emerging Economies

Emerging economies are the epicenters of growth for global business in the twenty-first century (Yawson & Yamoah, 2022). This trend is driven by the growing market prospects and foreign direct investment attractiveness. Emerging economies as actively changing societies invoke new questions about the future direction for national and global development and equitable economic growth. Therefore, understanding the corporate management ecosystem of emerging economies from governance, marketing, sustainability, ecotourism, innovation management, innovative work behavior, financial infrastructure, and supply chain perspectives is fundamental ingredient for contemporary business management in the globalized economy. Disserting the sources of their economic success alongside existing developmental challenges are worth pursuing. This book's approach is to discuss for context the key attributes of emerging economies—population dynamics, labor and production patterns, employment, and productivity trends, changing demography including a growing middle class, level of international trade engagement, foreign direct investment trajectory, and foreign and local investments potential, among other attributes. The interphase between these attributes and governance, marketing, innovation management, and supply chain research and practice is identified and discussed. Specific emphasis is placed on the selection of emerging economies by looking at the cases of Ghana, Malaysia, Pakistan, Iran, Bangladesh, Turkey, Poland, and Latin American countries, their unique characteristics, and a discourse of the selected cases of governance, marketing, innovation management, financial infrastructure, and ecotourism sustainable practices. These case studies accentuate the distinctiveness of corporate management dynamics in emerging economies that complement existing global corporate management knowledge that is dominated by developed country frameworks. The case studies also cover examples of corporate management research and practice in both local and international companies in the emerging economies.

4 Individual Chapter Analysis

The second chapter discussed the nature and dynamics of the emerging economies. It provides in-depth details of the key ingredients found in the emerging economies. It asserts that the rise to prominence of emerging economies is due to the era of globalization. The rise is not accidental, but a direct result of deliberate acts of planning, investments, and human mobility. The dynamics and nature of emerging economies vary; thus, generalization should not be made. Despite having some common attributes, the civil liberties, freedom of speech, incomplete reforms, political freedom, informal economies, and rule of law vary among emerging economies.

The third chapter examined the oil and gas industry of Ghana to understand the impact of distinct sourcing strategies such as single sourcing, multiple sourcing, and partnership sourcing on the supplier's performance. The evidence from the oil and gas industry of Ghana (emerging economy) confirmed that procurement process plays a pivotal role in the deliverance of on-time deliveries. The supplier's performance is significantly affected by all types of sourcing strategies. The corporate management practices need to be addressed for improving the economic condition of the country.

The fourth chapter provides the details of the effect of the minimum wage on employment in the Malaysian manufacturing sector. Prior to the introduction of the minimum wage in Malaysia, the cheap foreign labor was higher in Malaysia. To discourage foreign workers, the government introduced a minimum wage policy in 2012. However, after a decade of the policy implementation, the present study found that minimum wage has significantly reduced the overall employment in the manufacturing sector. Moreover, employment has reduced because of higher labor cost incurred by the employers, affecting the ecosystem.

The fifth chapter examined the skilled gap existing in the developing countries by investigating the role of international students' mobility in bridging the skills gaps. The competitiveness of the developing countries improves due to the knowledge, skills, and innovative ideas developed by the international students in the advanced economies. The benefits of international student mobility are evident in closing the gaps by improving competitiveness, economic growth, and human capital development in the emerging economies.

The sixth chapter explained the effect of corporate governance variables on the financial performance of banks in Ghana. There is a significant positive relationship between board characteristics and financial performance while firm control moderates positive relationship between board size, composition, foreign ownership, and financial performance. The greater corporate administration is the result of the expansion of money, leading to an increase in the proportion of non-executive directors on the board. The step would bring higher independence and objectivity to decision-making, especially related to the strategy and governance.

The seventh chapter discussed the importance and usage of pesticides in Pakistan as well as the determinants of farmers' protective behavior over the use of pesticides. Theory of planned behavior (TPB) is considered in this study. Results revealed that there is a significant positive impact of knowledge of pesticide use and past health experience with pesticides on the protective behavior. Attitude towards pesticides significantly mediates the relationship. The chapter is informative in creating awareness among farmers about the best sustainable farm practices in emerging economy.

The eighth chapter explored innovation management in the public sector of Malaysia by considering a multilevel analysis of the association between leadership (transformational and transactional) styles and innovative work behavior of employees. The buffering mechanism is job autonomy in this study and results confirmed that self-determination theory is effective in the due process. The job autonomy is affected by neither considered leadership styles. Thus, the corporate management governance should promote the job autonomy to improve the innovative work behavior in the public sector of an emerging economy (Malaysia).

The ninth chapter discussed the impact of cryptocurrencies on the global platform and how emerging economies are viewing it. The challenges characterized by the noble currency are examined along with the tax compliance, data privacy, sound governance, portability, fair competition, and cybersecurity. Moreover, the financial stability risk and economic uncertainties are explored to understand the role of policymakers in finding the right corporate practices.

The tenth chapter provides the details of sustainable tourism practices in Bangladesh. It offers to explain the challenges and opportunities interlined with the tourism industry while promoting sustainable practices in the popular tourist destinations. Bangladesh's tourism sector is promising despite having infrastructural challenges.

The eleventh chapter investigated the impact of customer relationship management on customer satisfaction and loyalty of small and medium-sized enterprises (SMEs). Moreover, the role of advisory bodies and capacity building is considered to assess how it moderates the relationship between loyalty and customer satisfaction. It also recommends strategic approaches that could enable the banks in engaging with the SMEs in proving best corporate management practices.

The twelfth chapter examined the global demand for cross-border higher education during the post-pandemic. The present scenario is evaluated to explain how Malaysia requires bold steps in offering higher public seats for Asian 'glocal' students. It also offers details about the strategic approaches required to mark Malaysia as the major recipient of international students, which would lead to foreign remittances.

The thirteenth chapter considered the secondary sources to explain the reality of business schools of public universities and their connection with the labor market in Pakistan. Majority of the students enrolled in the business program with the hope of finding a better job after graduation. It is evident that most business schools of public universities do not have objectives for their programs on their official website. There is ambiguity in the education sector, further widening the gap between labor market pools and offered education. Moreover, the graduates' success viewed the stronger linkage between his/her institution and different companies providing job opportunities (employers), however, it was not properly incorporated.

The fourteenth chapter investigated the accountability systems of non-governmental organizations (NGOs) in Ghana. The donors and beneficiaries are the main stakeholders for upward and downward accountability. The impact of institutional and environmental pressures has altered the face of NGOs' design as a coping mechanism. Findings revealed that the dominant accountability systems are upward towards donors, while downward accountability is not given significant prominence by NGOs in Ghana because of the absence of donor's commitment. The chapter highlights the corporate management ecosystem practices for legitimately dealing with institutional and environmental pressures.

The fifteenth chapter examined Iran's ecotourism by exploring the challenges in maintained sustainable development practices. Despite having rich historical, cultural, and natural resources, there are significant challenges for ecotourism. The urban development's significance and environmental issues have affected green spaces. The sustainable ecosystem is explained by providing strategies for effective urban management and governance.

The sixteenth chapter considered comparative analysis to examine corporate social responsibility (CSR) in Poland and Russia. It is evident that despite two countries sharing culture and history, the two countries have taken different routes regarding CSR practices. Many companies have taken higher interest in CSR, especially post-pandemic. Russia is struggling with good corporate practices while Poland is reaping the rewards for taking CSR initiatives.

The seventeenth chapter explored the concept of ecotourism by exploring the opportunities and challenges faced by Turkey. It considers the pre- and post-pandemic impact on the sustainable development and natural resource management.

The eighteenth chapter investigated the demand of Asian countries on Malaysian public universities through the application of panel generalized methods of moments (GMM) estimation. Only 40% students enrolled in the Malaysian public university, despite governmental efforts. The gravity model and rate of return theory are employed to understand the phenomenon. The policies are proposed to the Malaysian government and public universities for enrolling higher number of international students. This also explains the corporate practices required to make Malaysia as a key player in the education industry by 2025.

The nineteenth chapter examined the factors that affect the success of product/service innovation among SMEs in Ghana. Moreover, the moderating role of functional diversity and strategic alignment in the relationship between the factors affecting product/service innovation success among SMEs in Ghana has been explored. It is evident that organizational capabilities and product/service characteristics were positively related to innovation success, while competitive environment influenced innovation success negatively. The moderating role of functional diversity and strategic alignment played a significant role in the factors affecting the innovation–success relationship. In addition to that, the positive moderating role of strategic alignment in the relationship between innovation factors and the success of product/service innovation, which gives them a competitive advantage.

The twentieth chapter provides details about the interest rate as an effective instrument for controlling inflation. Rising price levels are also associated with weaker investor confidence. As in the IS–LM model, John Hicks explained that the two-dimensional macroeconomic tool that shows the relationship between interest rates and the assets market. However, there is a debate among researchers about whether interest rate is an effective instrument to control inflation (INFL) in developing countries. This debate is parallel to this research aim to test the effectiveness of interest rates to control inflation in 20 selected developing countries. This study used panel data from 20 developing countries (Bangladesh, Brunei, Chile, China, Colombia, India, Indonesia, Jordan, Laos, Malaysia, Maldives, Mongolia, Myanmar, Nigeria, Pakistan, Philippines, Singapore, Sri Lanka, Thailand, and Vietnam) from 1991 until 2021. The result indicates that the fixed-effect model is the best model. Further, money supply (MS) and exchange rate (EXC) has a significant positive relationship with Foreign Direct Investment (FDI). Meanwhile, interest rate (IR) has no significant relationship with Foreign Direct Investment (FDI). Moreover, Nigeria coefficient of money supply (MS) and exchange rate (EXC) is higher and more efficient than in another 19 selected developing countries. Foreign Direct Investment is affected by Money Supply (MS) and Exchange Rate (EXC) while the Interest Rate (IR) is just mediating effect to Foreign Direct Investment (FDI).

The twenty-first chapter examined the relationship between customer engagement, customer-based brand equity, and brand market performance in the alcoholic bitters industry in Ghana. The study found that customer engagement has a significant positive impact on brand performance, which suggests that actively engaging with customers can contribute to improving a brand's market performance. Additionally, the study identified brand loyalty, brand awareness, and brand association as key factors that mediate the relationship between customer engagement and brand performance, implying that enhancing these customer-based brand equity variables can further strengthen the relationship between customer engagement and brand performance. The study offers the best corporate management practices to improve the economic condition of the country.

The twenty-second chapter explained the impact of economic affirmative distribution among ethnic groups in Malaysia since it is viewed as a conflict resolution mechanism for easing tension among ethnic groups and socio-economic imbalances. The new economic policy (NEP) is reviewed to understand the impact it has while creating an equal distribution of wealth for each group. The equity data was used while employing the autoregressive distributed lag (ARDL) approach. Findings revealed that affirmative action has a significant influence in affecting the distribution of wealth between ethnic groups in the short term and the long term. The study also proves the wealth distribution between ethnic groups was distributed through the growing economy rather than through the acquisition of other ethnic ownership, especially Chinese ethnic ownership was later transferred to the Bumiputera's.

The last chapter examined the ecosystem of the Latin America, specifically focusing on the common challenges. It explores the reasons behind the imbalance between the urban and rural sustainable development. The findings revealed that deforestation, soil erosion, glaciers melting, water scarcity and water pollution, and rise in the sea level are the major five challenges faced by the majority of Latin America. The findings also revealed that there is an imbalanced sustainable development in the Latin America as the emphasis is more on the Urban Green Initiatives (UGI) while rural structural development has been given limited concentration. Moreover, the role of principal actors needs further clarity. Thus, despite an enriched ecosystem, Latin America lags in the development of sustainable ecosystems.

References

Adner, R., & Kapoor, R. (2010). Value creation in innovation ecosystems: How the structure of technological interdependence affects firm performance in new technology generations. *Strategic Management Journal, 31*(3), 306–333.

Brodie, R. J., Coviello, N. E., Brookes, R. W., & Little, V. (1997). Towards a paradigm shift in marketing? An examination of current marketing practices. *Journal of Marketing Management, 13*, 383–406.

Coviello, N. E., Brodie, R. J., & Munro, H. J. (1997). Understanding contemporary marketing: Development of a classification scheme. *Journal of Marketing Management, 13*(6), 501–522. https://doi.org/10.1080/0267257X.1997.9964490

Dictionary.com. (2022). Corporate. Retried from https://www.dictionary.com/browse/corporate.

Drucker, P. F. (1963). *Managing for business effectiveness*. Harvard Business Review. Retrieved from https://hbr.org/1963/05/managing-for-business-effectiveness.

Hussain, N., Haque, A. U., & Baloch, A. (2019). Management theories: The contribution of contemporary management theorists in tackling contemporary management challenges. *Journal of Yasar University, 14*(SI), 156–169.

Kanter, H. (2017). What is a sustainable ecosystem? Synonym. Available at: https://classroom.synonym.com/what-is-a-sustainable-ecosystem-12081802.html.

Kapoor, R., & Lee, J. M. (2012). Coordinating and competing in ecosystems: How organizational forms shape new technology investments. *Strategic Management Journal, 34*(3), 274–296. https://doi.org/10.1002/smj.2010

McGrath, S., & Young, J. E. E. (2019). *Mobilizing global knowledge: Refugee research in an age of displacement*. University of Calgary Press.

Meyer, A. D., Gaba, V., & Colwell, K. A. (2005). Organizing far from equilibrium: Nonlinear change in organizational fields. *Organization Science, 16*(5), 456–473. https://doi.org/10.1287/orsc.1050.0135

Oxford English Dictionary. (2017). *Ecosystem*. Retrieved from https://en.oxforddictionaries.com/definition/ecosystem.

Pierce, L. (2009). Big losses in ecosystem niches: How core firm decisions drive complementary product shakeouts. *Strategic Management Journal, 30*(3), 323–347. https://doi.org/10.1002/smj.736

Prasad, L., & Gulshan, S. S. (2011). *Management principles and practices*. Excel Books.

Robbins, S. P., & Coulter, M. (2012). *Management* (11th ed.). Prentice Hall.

Slaper, T. F., & Hall, T. J. (2011). *The triple bottom line: What is it and how does it work?* Retrieved April 7, 2023, from http://www.ibrc.indiana.edu/ibr/2011/spring/article2.html.
Teece, D. J. (2007). Explicating dynamic capabilities: The nature and microfoundations of (sustainable) enterprise performance. *Strategic Management Journal, 28*(13), 1319–1350. https://doi.org/10.1002/smj.640
Tsujimoto, M., Kajikawa, Y., Tomita, J., & Matsumoto, Y. (2018). A review of the ecosystem concept — Towards coherent ecosystem design. *Technological Forecasting and Social Change*, 136, 49–58. Available at: https://doi.org/10.1016/j.techfore.2017.06.032.
Yawson, D. E., & Yamoah, F. A. (2022). *Contemporary retail marketing in emerging economies: The case of Ghana's supermarket chains.* Palgrave Macmillan.

Emerging Economies: Nature and Dynamics

Fred A. Yamoah and Adnan ul Haque

1 Introduction

The concept of emerging countries or economies or markets dates to the early 1980s but there is no universally agreed definition of an emerging country (Ithurbide & Bellaiche, 2019). Countries earmarked as emerging economies are key global players in the twenty-first century global economy. These emerging economies are characterized by increasing levels of economic growth driven by the adoption of liberalized economic policies that result in stable energy regimes and continually improving economic imperatives and information and communication technology systems. Indeed, Wright et al. (2005) not only acknowledged the rapid changes

F. A. Yamoah (✉)
Department of Management, School of Business, Economics and Informatics, Birkbeck, University of London, London, UK
e-mail: f.yamoah@bbk.ac.uk

A. ul Haque
Faculty of Business, Yorkville University, Toronto, ON, Canada
e-mail: ahaque@yorkvilleu.ca

F. A. Yamoah, A. ul Haque (eds.), *Corporate Management Ecosystem in Emerging Economies*, https://doi.org/10.1007/978-3-031-41578-4_2

taking place in emerging economies but also noted that they are progressively playing an increasingly prominent role in the world economy. The rise to prominence of emerging economies in the global economy is further substantiated by the amount of foreign direct investment (FDI) into these economies that hit a record value of 849 billion USD in 2002 (UNCTAD, 2003). Similarly, there has been an upsurge in emerging economy-related research including pioneering studies such as Hoskisson et al.'s (2000) work on 'Strategy in emerging economies'; the insightful book on 'Doing Business in Emerging Markets' by Cavusgil et al. (2002); and the work on 'Business Strategies in Transition Economies' by Peng (2000), among others. The rise to global prominence of emerging economies has not been accidental but a deliberate act of 'planning', 'investments', and 'mobilization of human endowments of the respective countries (Cavusgil, 2021). The nature of emerging economies is characterized by obvious common features. However, the dynamics within emerging economies showcase distinctive differences with critical implications for corporate management ecosystem practice and research in emerging economies.

2 The Nature of Emerging Economies

Interestingly, countries around the world experiencing such evolving economic transformations, typically described as emerging economies, have received other designations such as 'emerging markets', 'emerging country', and 'emerging market economy' in management studies, particularly in international business research. The extant literature generally refers to an 'emerging economy' (or an emerging country or an emerging market economy or an emerging market) as a market that has some features of an advanced or developed market but does not completely satisfy its requirements and standards (see Yawson & Yamoah, 2022; MSCI, 2014).

Whereas Hoskisson et al. (2000, p. 249) defined emerging economies as 'low-income, rapid-growth countries using economic liberalization as their primary engine of growth', Cavusgil (2021) preferred to describe 'rapidly transforming and liberalizing countries' as 'emerging markets', auspiciously to fall in line with a growing consensus in the contemporary academic and business literature. Additionally, the emerging market economy label has been variously explained. One exemplar description is that an emerging market economy is a middle-income country which is in transition to advanced countries but still incorporates many features of developing countries (Goda & Priewe, 2019, p. 2). Another description of an emerging market economy according to the Corporate Finance Institute – (CFI) (2021, p. 1) is "a country that is in the process of developing its economy to become more advanced; generating low to middle per capita income and rapidly expanding due to high production levels and significant industrialization."

The Corporate Finance Institute (CFI) further indicated that 80 percent of the world's population lives in emerging market economies contributing almost 70 percent of the global gross domestic products. The growing importance of emerging economies is further alluded to by Cavusgil (2021) who indicated that they accounted for 30 percent of the global gross domestic product in 1990 but increased by 12 percent to 42 percent by the year 2021. According to Liu et al. (2021), emerging economies with an estimated 50 percent of the global population are steadily playing a significant role in the global economy relative to their developed country counterparts.

There is an emerging consensus among business researchers that an 'emerging economy' or 'emerging markets' or 'emerging market economy' is a growing economy that is progressively becoming connected with global markets, as it attains some of the key attributes of a developed economy but still retains some distinctive features of a developing economy. It is relevant to recap that developed economies or markets are characterized by resilient economies, consistent economic growth, high gross domestic product, high liquidity figures, openness to overseas investments, and reliable regulatory and legal systems.

According to Yawson and Yamoah (2022, p. 26), an emerging market economy (EME) is a "nation with an economy characterised by low to middle per capita income that is showing all the traits of moving towards becoming a developed one in the due course. Also, emerging market economies can be said to be transitioning from a closed market system to an open market system while developing economic reform programmes."

Therefore, countries depicting similar growth trajectory and economic features across the globe are collectively referred to as emerging economies, with key examples including Argentina, Brazil, China, Ghana, India, Indonesia, Mexico, Poland, South Africa, South Korea, Turkey, Egypt, Iran, Nigeria, Pakistan, Russia, Saudi Arabia, Taiwan, and Thailand. These emerging economies share a characteristic feature of experiencing interconnections with the global economic markets comprising of developed and emerging economies across all regions of the world. They are further characterized by a widening middle class with improving living standards due to steady socio-economic development (Yawson & Yamoah, 2022; Kvint, 2009).

In the 'Two Decades of Management Research on Emerging Economies' paper, Ferreira et al. (2020) provide a historical narrative on academic studies on emerging economies that highlighted notable phases of emerging market research evolution. Firstly, the historical narrative traced the genesis of the phrase 'emerging market' to economist from the World Bank in 1981. The study further indicated that despite the term's World Bank origins, it was after twenty years that the term received considerable global attention—this was behind the backdrop of a Goldman Sachs' report in 2001, that postulated the eminent growth path of emerging economies to become major economies with a focus on the BRICS countries, namely, Brazil, Russia, India, China, and South Africa by the year 2050. Secondly, the study highlighted the remarkable increase in research on emerging economies from the year 2000 onward and the significant focus on institutional theory as a theoretical lens to investigate emerging economies. Other theories that have featured in the research in the context of emerging economies are transaction cost theory, agency theory, resource-based theory covering capabilities, knowledge, and learning perspectives (Hoskisson et al., 2000; Peng et al., 2001; Meyer & Peng, 2004).

The historical narrative of Ferreira et al. (2020) also pointed out that the research interest and the rather dramatic growth in emerging economies research output from the early 2000s were driven by the impetus toward global expansion and internationalization of multinational cooperations in 'promising' emerging economies. Such international growth and expansion strategies to further achieve a global competitive edge necessitated research understanding and its practical implications for global strategies in emerging economy markets. There is also indication that business interactions spearheaded by multinational companies outside emerging economies, alongside increased commercial activities within and among various emerging economies and a significant outward incursion by companies in emerging economies entering developed economies, have all in diverse ways contributed to the growing importance of emerging economies in the global economy, as well as the attendant research interest among researchers.

Wright et al. (2005) indicated that the growth expansion strategy of multinational companies in advanced economies to explore new markets to enhance their competitiveness in emerging economies provided the impetus for the prevailing vibrant role of emerging economies in the global economy. This position reaffirmed a similar assertion earlier by Meyer (2004) that global companies play a vital role in the economic growth and development of many emerging economies across the world. Drawing on the work of Brouthers and Brouthers (2003) on selected countries in Central and Eastern Europe, Wright et al. (2005) further asserted that emerging economies have in one breath become an enterprise 'laboratory' for multinational enterprises (MNEs) to test and refine their respective transactional cost theory (TCT).

Another factor that has been highlighted to have influenced the development and economic activity upsurge in some emerging economies is the survival issues that companies encounter because of environmental uncertainties in many emerging economies. As such, the drive to survive, grow, and expand served as a critical catalyst for ambitious business leaders in emerging economies to improve and maximize the use of their resources as a potent response to these characteristic institutional and market factors associated with emerging economies (Wright et al., 2005; D'Aunno et al., 2000).

An additional factor known to have promoted the increasing prominent role of emerging economies globally is the 'internationalization of emerging economies multinationals' (Ferreira et al., 2020), that is, companies from emerging economies entering developed economies. Cavusgil (2021) confirmed the internationalization trend among emerging economies enterprises and cited examples of these companies including

AB-InBev (Brazil), Sinopec (China), Samsung Electronics (South Korea), and Cemex (Mexico). These companies through the internationalization process mentioned earlier have joined the league of Global 500 companies.

Developed economy entry poses obvious challenges to companies from emerging economies. This notwithstanding, some companies in emerging economies are motivated to pursue a developed market entry strategy to improve their international reputation and competitiveness (Hoskisson et al., 2004; Wright et al., 2005). It is noteworthy that the rise to global economy prominence of emerging economies has also been partly influenced by some companies in emerging economies entering other emerging economies to explore economies of scales. Companies in emerging economies pursing such strategy are deemed to have a competitive advantage over their advanced economy counterparts who tend to lack an understanding of the local institutional structures and market forces at play in emerging economies (Wright et al., 2005).

3 The Dynamics Within Emerging Economies

In an insightful abstract to a discussion paper "on 'How to differentiate emerging countries? New approaches for classification and typology', Ithurbide and Bellaiche (2019, p. 3) asserted that 'once accepted, the idea that the emerging world may behave like a block in period of crises (as the group of advanced countries also does), one must wonder whether one should go beyond that and consider that the emerging world deserves better: the wide divergence between countries, the health of some countries (sometimes better than some advanced countries) simply mean that it does not make sense to view the 'emerging world' as a whole, as a block, but as well-defined, specific and homogeneous subsets." Emerging economies or markets are casually assumed to be a homogenous group of countries (Hoskisson et al., 2000; Ferreira et al., 2020; Cavusgil, 2021). There are no intellectual tensions associated with the notion of a shared commonality among emerging economies with regard to a similar profile for economic reforms implementation, democratic, governance, rule of law, and transparency issues alongside a growing middle class. However, there are distinctive political, social, and cultural and lifestyle differential attributes among emerging economies (Cavusgil, 2021). For example, Ferreira et al. (2020) observed peculiar patterns of transition and transformation in the socio-political arena of the respective emerging economies considered in the study. Additionally, the level of market expansion, performance, and maturity of the various emerging economies are notable distinguishing features between emerging economies (Cavusgil, 2021). This point was further illustrated with the sharp differences between the transformed 'emerged' economies such as Hong Kong, Israel, South Korea, Singapore, and Taiwan that are still referred to as emerging economies and those that have transformed much or experienced stagnation like Egypt, Pakistan, and Nigeria among others.

Cavusgil (2021, p. 3) based on the narrative below in 'Advancing knowledge on emerging markets: Past and future research in perspective', opined that the prominence of emerging markets has not been accidental, but a result of deliberate planning, investments, and mobilization of human endowments of a nation:

The Cavusgil (;2021;, p. 3) narrative: "Key to the rapid economic ascension of most emerging markets are three components: legacy assets, enablers, and outcomes. Legacy assets function as the foundations for economic renewal. countries started their journey towards modernization with such home-grown assets as: cultural cohesion and territorial integrity, idiosyncratic institutions, relational bonds, family conglomerates (or state-owned companies in the case of China and Russia), favourable demographics, and a certain commercial infrastructure. Then, typically through deliberate and sustained implementation, emerging market governments put in place progressive programs that served as enablers of economic transformation. These included: structural reforms, market liberalization, privatization, and strategic investments in select industries. When sustained over a long period, these investments produced handsome dividends for emerging markets. Well recognized by now, these outcomes include: the rise of a robust middle class with substantial disposable income, intensified entrepreneurial activity, urbanization, and sustained economic growth."

In a similar vein, Hoskisson et al. (2000) canvassed the viewpoint that emerging market economies are not the same but heterogenous, even for those emerging economies located in similar geographical areas. They cited Latin America, East Asia, Africa and Middle East, and Central and Eastern Europe, classified as four identifiable classes of geographical regions with emerging economies, that are distinctively different and have followed diverse economic development trajectories. The examples outlined below were drawn on to buttress the point about the dissimilarities between emerging countries from the same geographical regions of the world.

Firstly, Hoskisson et al. (2000) underscore the distinct differences between emerging economies such as Hungary and Poland and countries of the former Soviet Union, which are all located within Central and Eastern Europe. Secondly, they referred to the example of unique and distinct economic transformation pathways followed by the emerging economies of the presently 'independent republics of the former Soviet Union', despite their common antecedent. Thirdly, the obvious differences between previously 'centrally planned economies' in the Far East Asia such as China, Hong Kong, Macau, North Korea, South Korea, Mongolia, Siberia, Taiwan, Brunei, Cambodia, East Timor, Malaysia, Laos, Indonesia, Myanmar, Philippines, Thailand, and Vietnam are highlighted.

In effect, discounting these differences will result in a faulty generalization of emerging economies with respect to their economic evolution and growth trajectory, and their distinct country-level attributes and features for a targeted business and management strategy intervention. Cavusgil (2021, p. 3) provides a concise summary of the similarities and differences between emerging countries, as follows: "most emerging markets adopted similar recipes in their economic transformation, yet they differ greatly in terms of political and social evolution. They have pursued diverse political regimes; some were purely autocratic while others pursued more democratic regimes. In addition, political freedoms, freedom of speech, rule of law, and civil liberties vary widely among them. Such factors as a large informal economy, incomplete reforms, or frequent change of political leadership curtailed progress in some emerging markets."

References

Brouthers, K., & Brouthers, L. E. (2003). Why service and manufacturing entry mode choices differ: The influence of transaction cost factors, risk, and trust. *Journal of Management Studies, 40*, 1179–1204.

Cavusgil, S. T. (2021). Advancing knowledge on emerging markets: Past and future research in perspective. *International Business Review, 30*(2), 101796. https://doi.org/10.1016/j.ibusrev.2021.101796

Cavusgil, S. T., Ghauri, P. N., & Agarwal, M. R. (2002). *Doing business in emerging markets.* Sage.

Corporate Finance Institute. (2021). *Emerging market economy.* Published January 28, 2021. Accessed November 24, 2023, from https://corporatefinanceinstitute.com/resources/economics/emerging-market-economy/.

D'Aunno, T., Succi, M., & Alexander, J. A. (2000). The role of institutional and market forces in divergent organizational change. *Administrative Science Quarterly, 45*, 679–703.

Ferreira, M. P., Reis, N. R., & Pinto, C. F. (2020). Two decades of management research on emerging economies: A citation and co-citation review. *International Studies of Management & Organization, 50*(1), 5–26.

Goda, T., & Priewe, J. (2019). Determinants of real exchange rate movements in 15 emerging market economies. *Center for Research in Economics and Finance (CIEF), working papers*, pp. 19–13.

Hoskisson, R. E., Eden, L., Lau, C. M., & Wright, M. (2000). Strategy in emerging economies. *Academy of Management Journal, 43*(3), 249–267.

Hoskisson, R. E., Kim, H., White, R. E., & Tihanyi, L. (2004). A framework for understanding international diversification by business groups from emerging economies. In M. A. Hitt & J. L. C. Cheng (Eds.), *Theories of the multinational Enterprise: Diversity, complexity, and relevance. Advances in international management* (Vol. 16, pp. 137–163). Elsevier/JAI Press.

Ithurbide, P., & Bellaiche, M. (2019). How to differentiate emerging countries? New approaches for classification and typology. *Amundi Research team*, 3–60.

Kvint, V. (2009). *The global emerging market: Strategic management and economics*. Routledge.

Liu, L. A., Ghauri, P. N., & Cavusgil, S. T. (2021). Doing Business in Emerging Markets, 1–100.

Meyer, K. E. (2004). Perspectives on multinational enterprises in emerging economies. *Journal of International Business Studies, 35*, 259–276.

Meyer, K. E., & Peng, M. W. (2004). Identifying leading theories for research on central and Eastern Europe: Transactions, resources, and institutions. Working paper, Copenhagen Business School and The Ohio State University.

MSCI. (2014). MSCI market classification framework, June 2014.

Peng, M. W. (2000). *Business strategies in transition economies*. Sage.

Peng, M. W., Lu, Y., Shenkar, O., & Wang, D. (2001). Treasures in the China shop: A review of management and organizational research on greater China. *Journal of Business Research, 52*, 95–110.

UNCTAD (United Nations Conference on Trade and Development). (2003). Press release 83. 25 August 25.

Wright, M., Filatotchev, I., Hoskisson, R. E., & Peng, M. W. (2005). Strategy research in emerging economies: Challenging the conventional wisdom. *Journal of Management Studies, 42*(1), 1–33.

Yawson, D. E., & Yamoah, F. A. (2022). Introduction to contemporary retail Marketing in Emerging Economies: Ghana's supermarket chains. In *Contemporary retail Marketing in Emerging Economies* (pp. 1–44). Palgrave Macmillan.

The Effect of Sourcing Strategies on Supplier's Performance in the Upstream Oil and Gas Industry, Ghana

Joseph Dankwah, Fred A. Yamoah, and Riffat Faizan

1 Introduction

The upstream sector of the oil and gas industry is capital-intensive, and the procurement of goods is critical to sustain operations. Procuring goods can be a challenging and time-consuming process, but it is important for companies to have an effective and efficient sourcing strategy in place to mitigate these risks. One approach that companies can take is to build strong relationships with suppliers. By establishing long-term relationships with reliable suppliers, companies can reduce the time and

J. Dankwah
TechnipFMC Ghana Limited, Accra, Ghana

F. A. Yamoah (✉)
Department of Management, School of Business, Economics and Informatics, Birkbeck, University of London, London, UK
e-mail: f.yamoah@bbk.ac.uk

R. Faizan
Faculty of Business, Yorkville University, Toronto, ON, Canada

F. A. Yamoah, A. ul Haque (eds.), *Corporate Management Ecosystem in Emerging Economies*, https://doi.org/10.1007/978-3-031-41578-4_3

effort required to source goods as well as the risk of delays or quality issues. This can be achieved through regular communication, collaboration on product development, and joint planning and forecasting (Okoth et al., 2017). Moreover, companies can use technology to streamline the procurement process. This can involve implementing a digital procurement platform to automate routine tasks such as purchase order creation, invoice processing, and supplier management. By leveraging technology, companies can reduce the time and cost associated with procurement, while also improving accuracy and compliance.

There are a range of strategies that companies can use to improve the efficiency and effectiveness of their procurement processes in the upstream sector of the oil and gas industry. By building strong supplier relationships, leveraging technology, and outsourcing procurement, companies can reduce risk, save time and money, and ensure a reliable supply of goods to support their operations (Slack et al., 2010). There are three key sourcing strategies: single sourcing, multiple sourcing, and partnership sourcing (Slack et al., 2010). Each of these strategies has its own advantages and disadvantages, and the choice of strategy will depend on various factors such as the nature of the goods being procured, the availability of suppliers, and the company's overall procurement goals and objectives. The sourcing strategies adopted by companies can have a significant impact on supplier's performance and the quality of goods supplied, and it is important for companies to carefully consider their sourcing strategies and invest in effective supplier management to ensure business success in the global market space (Okoth, 2011).

It is believed that there is an impact of the emphasis of adopting good procurement process on the supply of the quality of goods, cost contribution, and technology development (Monczka et al., 1998). As per Waters (2004), the procurement activities do not conclude with the time of purchase, however, to the period of product disposal. Subsequently, Okoth et al. (2017) proposed that procurement processes should be viewed as essential in ensuring the fairness and nonappearance of malpractices for sustainable integrity, which supports informed decision-making during supplier selection, based on precise information and expectation of the procurement outcome. At present, organizations are embarking on partnership sourcing, as an approach to procurement that emphasizes collaboration and cooperation between buyers and suppliers with the concept of exchanging information on numerous issues, supplier expansion, and collaboration on new product development. The partnership sourcing approach is favored over the 'arm length' procurement approach (Macbeth & Ferguson, 1994; Lysons & Farrington, 2006; Bailey et al., 2005).

Procurement of goods and services is a significant cost for most businesses, with estimates suggesting that around 70 percent of a business's revenue can be spent on procurement-related expenses. In the upstream oil and gas sector, procurement and supply-related costs can be particularly high. Estimates suggest that procurement and supply-related costs can account for up to 60 percent of exploration and development costs in this sector.

In light of the above statement, this study pursues to examine the effect of sourcing strategies on supplier's performance in Ghana's upstream oil and gas industry, including single sourcing, multiple sourcing, and partnership sourcing.

By examining the relationship between control mechanisms and sourcing strategies, the study can provide guidance on how organizations can effectively manage their procurement processes to achieve their desired outcomes. This can help organizations optimize their procurement strategies and achieve better supplier's performance. Many studies on sourcing strategies tend to focus on the dichotomy between single sourcing and multiple sourcing, as these are two common approaches used by organizations in procurement. Therefore, it is important for studies to also examine the impact of partnership sourcing on supplier's performance and how it compares to single sourcing and multiple sourcing in achieving procurement objectives. The study can provide a more comprehensive understanding of the impact of sourcing strategies on supplier's performance in the Ghana upstream oil and gas industry. By focusing on the impact of sourcing strategies on supplier's performance and the role of control mechanisms in this relationship, the study can provide valuable insights for both academia and practitioners. Additionally, gathering data from 20 upstream oil and gas companies in Ghana can provide a robust sample size and enhance the generalizability of the study's findings.

2 Literature Review

Shih et al. (2004) define the sourcing strategy as the method of choosing the best and most suitable suppliers founded on the suppliers' competences. As per Hahn et al. (1986), the motive for the adoption of various sourcing strategies is to enhance competition. Firms are globally, grappling with question as to how the firm can meet its procurement needs reflected as 'single sourcing'. Moreover, companies try to locate answers to procurement questions such as whether supplies procurement should be through a single, or multiple or should there be collaborative, or partnership arrangements with suppliers where both parties are open to costs and problems. Newman (1989) identifies the critical variances between single sourcing and sole sourcing. On the other hand, multiple sourcing refers to the practice of procuring goods or services from more than one supplier, while dual sourcing specifically refers to the practice of procuring goods or services from two suppliers (Treleven & Schweikhart, 1988). This led to another important notion that is partnership sourcing. Hence, it is important to critically evaluate the concept of partnership sourcing.

Partnership sourcing is a procurement strategy that involves establishing a long-term relationship between a buyer and a supplier, with a focus on collaboration, shared risks and rewards, and mutual benefits. This consists of information sharing, rewards, and risks and that originates with the relationship (Ellram, 1991). In partnership sourcing encourages joint problem solving, continuous improvement, and collective benefit along with transparency of relevant information allocation relatively than seeking a new supplier (Ellram & Edis, 1996; SMMT & DTI, 1994). Nonetheless, how this is linked to supplier control should be examined. Atuahene-Gima et al. (2006) conducted a study using output on supervisee trust and sales performance. The definition of process control is more related to the management of a manufacturing process to ensure that the final product meets specific quality and performance requirements. It involves monitoring and adjusting the process parameters to achieve the desired outcome and minimize variations and defects (Anderson & Oliver, 1987).

The literature review conducted for the study has identified several relevant issues related to the topic being studied. These issues may have been observed in various environments or contexts, and under different conditions or circumstances. One of the issues is supplier selection evaluation in the oil and gas industry (Luzon & El-Sayegh, 2016). Therefore, the fact that the literature review for the study has identified many issues related to the research topic indicates that there is information available on the subject, which can be used to inform the study's design, methodology, and analysis, and to help ensure that the research contributes to the existing body of knowledge in a meaningful way. Moreover, the ethical practices in procurement should also be examined to gain the in-sight. The issue of ethical practices in procurement is an important one, particularly in industries like oil and gas, which have a significant impact on the environment and society, which has been the subject of criticism for its procurement practices. For a study that examines procurement practices in the oil and gas industry, addressing ethical concerns is crucial.

Risk management in procurement sourcing is another vital aspect evident from the critical review of the literature. Effective risk management is essential for successful procurement as procurement is a complex process that involves multiple stakeholders, including suppliers, buyers, and end-users. As per the OECD (2018), procurement function also comprises of risk management. Organizations need to identify and assess the risks associated with their procurement processes and develop strategies to mitigate and manage these risks.

Due to the complex nature of the buyer–supplier relationship, it is unlikely that one single theory can fully explain all the intricacies of this interaction. However, by examining different theories and concepts related to buyer–supplier relationships, researchers can gain a deeper understanding of the dynamics at play and develop a more comprehensive picture of how these relationships work. Moreover, the study can help shed light on the nature of the interaction that takes place between buyers and suppliers and highlight the factors that are critical for building and maintaining successful relationships. Thus, the social exchange theory should be used first to understand the role of supplier's performance as trust theory plays a significant role in supplier's performance (Atuahene-Gima et al., 2006). According to Homans (1958), social exchange theory has emerged from the intersection of multiple disciplines, including sociology, economics, and psychology. The theory proposes that social relationships are based on the exchange of resources and rewards between individuals, and that the success of these relationships depends on the perceived benefits and costs of these exchanges. On the other hand, the transaction cost analysis (TCA) in relation to the supplier's performance needs to be understood. TCA aims to explore how different types of controls, specifically output and process controls, may affect supplier's performance in different sourcing arrangements or relationships. By exploring the impact of different types of controls in different sourcing arrangements, the study aims to provide insights into the factors that are critical for managing supplier's performance effectively. Contextualizing trust, social exchange, and transactional cost analysis theories in sourcing strategies. The study argues that by integrating multiple theoretical perspectives, a better understanding of the factors that contribute to supplier's performance can be achieved, which could lead to improved outcomes for buyers.

The viewpoint of Deming (1986) on single sourcing strategy suggests that building long-term relationships with suppliers can lead to improved supplier's performance. On the other hand, considering the aspect of multiple sources guided by Porter's (1985) viewpoint, which suggests that competition in the marketplace can drive suppliers to improve their performance in order to remain competitive. The study hypothesizes that the threat of losing business and competitive pressure can have a positive impact on supplier's performance. Study hypothesizes that partnership sourcing strategy can lead to greater supplier's performance due to the long-term collaboration and trust that are built between the buyer and supplier. This hypothesis is guided by the viewpoints of Lamming (1993) and Macbeth and Ferguson (1994), who have argued that partnerships between buyers and suppliers can lead to greater efficiency, innovation, and cost savings.

The study aims to address a gap in the literature by investigating the impact of sourcing strategies on supplier' performance in the oil and gas industry in Ghana and exploring the moderating role of supplier controls. The study argues that although there has been some research done on sourcing strategies and supplier's performance in other contexts, such as manufacturing and service industries, there is a lack of research in the oil and gas industry in Ghana. Furthermore, the study aims to contribute to the literature by providing a better understanding of how different sourcing strategies, such as single sourcing and partnership sourcing, impact supplier's performance in the oil and gas industry in Ghana, and how these relationships are moderated by different types of supplier controls. The study aims to address a gap in the literature by investigating the impact of sourcing strategies on supplier's performance in the oil and gas industry in Ghana and exploring the moderating role of supplier controls. Furthermore, the study suggests that previous research has not fully examined the moderating role of supplier controls, such as output and process controls, on the relationship between sourcing strategies and supplier's performance.

3 Research Methodology

The study acknowledges the importance of ontological mediations in understanding social world reality. The study suggests that the development of an organization's sourcing strategies is a social science phenomenon that must be investigated objectively. This suggests that the study adopts a realist ontology, which assumes that social phenomena exist independently of human perception and can be studied objectively through empirical observation and analysis (Bryman & Bell, 2011). The nature of reality is reflected through ontology. This stance highlights the field through facts and knowledge (Dietz, 2006). Therefore, the study's ontology is both objective and subjective. Epistemology is the branch of philosophy concerned with knowledge and belief. The relationship between the truth and the researcher is an important aspect of epistemology. This allowed the researcher to hold a position that allowed them to examine the relationship between sourcing strategy and supplier's performance empirically, which suggests that they believed in the possibility of objective knowledge through empirical methods. The researcher considered the values that were attributed to various aspects of the research together with the data, participants, and the audience to whom the research results were to be reported. The techniques used by the researcher in order to investigate the reality of sourcing strategy and supplier's performance are referred to as methodology (Healy & Perry, 2000). However, for the current study, methodology is founded on the ontological and epistemological assumptions, acknowledging positivists and phenomenological approaches (Ansari, 2015). These perspectives were valuable to attain comprehensive understanding of the phenomenon. The researcher has opted to collecting and analyzing quantitative data. The rational for this approach is that quantitative data can provide a general picture of the research problem (Haque, 2020). It is often believed that the truth regarding the importance of quantitative and qualitative approaches in research lies somewhere between the two extremes.

The sample frame for this study was derived from the population of supply chain staff and end-users in the upstream oil and gas industry. The sample frame includes supply chain managers, contract and procurement managers, contract and procurement leads, senior contract advisors, contract analysts, contract administrators, project managers, engineering managers, operations managers, and engineers. For the current study's research method and questions, both nonprobability and probability sampling techniques have been adopted. The sample of companies chosen was purposively considered from the category to be included. The pre-test respondents were similar to those in the study and were carried out under similar settings. Varimax rotation and component analysis were used for identification of each dimension of the proposed model of single, multiple, partnership sourcing, process control, output control, and supplier's performance (flexibility, reliability, cost, quality, and delivery time) in the oil and gas industry. The quantitative data employed to gain factual truth (Haque et al., 2020). The research adheres to ethical principles ensuring the participants' rights are respected. Informed consent was obtained from the respondents before the questionnaires were administered to them ensuring participants were aware of the purpose of the research and their involvement. Additionally, the confidentiality and anonymity of the participants were assured as the questionnaires did not encompass any information that could trace responses back to specific respondents.

4 Results Findings and Discussions

The sample of companies for the study was purposively considered from the category to include the companies listed below (Table 1).

Descriptive Statistics This analysis allowed the researcher to use graphical and numerical methods to summarize and have a clear understanding of the data collected. According to Jaggi et al. (2018), this analysis helps researchers summarize a multitude of data in a reasonable manner. In using the numerical approach to summarize the data, the mean and standard deviation are calculated. The numerical approach is considered appropriate because it gives precise and accurate information, which is necessary to understand the pattern, dispersion, and distribution and find the central tendency of the data. The descriptive statistics confirmed that the information is accurate.

Data Cleaning The data was assessed to identify and address issues of outliers, missing data, and multicollinearity. The issue of outliers occurs when an observation is seen to be deviating so much from other observations in a sense that it causes suspicion such that observation may be because of other mechanisms other than what is being studied (Barnett & Lewis, 1994; Johnson & Wichern, 2002). This helped us in attaining the specificity. In quantitative study, the occurrence of missing data is common but causes a great deal when not dealt with, as this has an impact on the outcome of the results. Because of their impact on the results of quantitative analysis, some researchers have advised that missing data should be treated before further data analysis continues (Baraldi & Enders, 2010). In this study, the issue of missing data was addressed.

Multicollinearity Test A test of multicollinearity was conducted to find out which predictors were highly correlated. According to Daoud (2017), the presence of multicollinearity is identified when there is a high correlation between two or more independent variables in a regression model.

Table 1 List of considered cases and the justification for selection

S. N.	Companies	Reason
1	Tullow Ghana Ltd.	Core system integrator
2	ENI Ghana Exploration and Production	Core system integrator
3	Aker Energy	Core system integrator
4	Ghana National Petroleum Corporation (GNPC),	Core system integrator
5	MODEC Ghana Ltd.,	Major oil and gas contractors
6	Yinson Production	Major oil and gas contractors
7	Technip FMC Ghana Ltd.,	Oil and gas service companies
8	Baker Huges Ghana Ltd.,	Oil and gas service companies
9	Orsam Oil and Gas Ltd.	Oil and gas service companies
10	Deep Ocean Ghana Ltd.	Oil and gas service companies
11	Aker Solutions Ghana Ltd.	Oil and gas service companies
12	Amaja Tubular Services Ltd.	Oil and gas service companies
13	Swire Adonai Services Ltd.	Oil and gas service companies
14	Dac International Airline Ltd.	Oil and gas service companies
15	PHI Centry Ltd.	Oil and gas service companies
16	Subseas 7 Volta Contractors Ltd.	Oil and gas service companies
17	NOV Oil and Gas Services Ghana Ltd.	Oil and gas service companies
18	GE Oil and Gas Ghana Limited	Oil and gas service companies
19	Maersk RigWorld Ghana Ltd	Oil and gas drilling companies
20	Stena Unicon Offshore Services	Oil and gas drilling companies

These samples were chosen to have a holistic representation of the sector

Exploratory Factor Analysis The quantitative analysis used factor analysis as the main method of analysis for the data. The purpose of conducting factor analysis is said to allow researchers to summarize their data to be able to establish relationships between the factors and identify their patterns for easy identification and interpretation to enhance our understanding of the data for further analysis (Yong & Pearce, 2013). This analysis is important, given that it helps researchers to be able to regroup measurable items into sizable categories with a common variance. This study used the exploratory factor analysis to reveal the intricate pattern by exploring a set of data to test for assumptions (Child, 2006). The exploratory factor analysis is usually referred to as EFA and is used to study several factors that influence variables. It helps the researcher to analyze which of the variables "run parallel" (DeCoster, 1998). The variables that "run parallel" or "go together" are considered the factors that affect the dependent variables (Tucker & MacCallum, 1997). We confirmed the relationship between the factors, and the pattern was identified. The performance of exploratory factor analysis is underscored by some underlying assumptions such that consideration must be given to the existence of multivariate and univariate normality in the dataset (Child, 2006) and the absence of outliers (Field, 2009). It is also assumed that there is a linear relationship between the variables and the factors when determining the factors (Gorsuch, 1983). The analysis also takes into consideration that for a factor to be acceptable, it must have at least three variables. The factor loading of the variables is used to determine how much that variable contributes to the variance of the factor; in this case, a high factor loading is appreciated (Yong & Pearce, 2013). We found higher factor loading.

Correlation Analysis After the factor analysis, a correlation analysis was conducted to find the relationship between the variables. Zaid (2015) explained that correlation is used to compute the degree, extent, strength, and direction of relationship between two variables. It involves quantifying the correlation coefficient that explains the degree or extent to which each of the variables tends to modify along with the changes in the other. In this case, the study finds no correlation between the variables if the correlation coefficient (r) is 0.0. The direction of the relationship between the variables is determined by the (+, -) sign the r value assumes. For instance, the relationship between the variables is considered to be positive if the value of r is found to be +1 and negative if the value of r is found to be −1. At the end of the analysis, the relationship between the variables is found to be positive if it is realized that the value of r is positive. In this case, it means that there is a positive association between the variables and implies that there is a parallel increment among the variables; when one increases, the other will also increase and vice versa. However, if at the end of this analysis, the value of r is found to be negative, this implies that there is a negative association between the variables. This also indicates that when there is an increment in one, the other decreases. The relationship between the variables is considered to be perfect if the value of r is found to be −1 or +1. The extent of strength between the variables is considered to be strong if the value of r is above -0.5 or +0.5 but weak if the value of r is less than -0.5 or +0.5. If the value of r is exactly -0.5 or +0.5, then the relationship is said to be moderate. This analysis does not take into consideration a variable being either a dependent or independent variable. The correlation was confirmed.

Reliability Test Reliability test was conducted on the items used to measure the variables to find out the degree to which when they are used in other tests, they would produce consistent and stable results. To do this the Cronbach alpha (α) of the variables was calculated in the pre-test to find out the reliability of the variables when used in the actual study. The reliability of the instrument was acceptable.

Regression Analysis To test the model and find out the effect of sourcing strategies on supplier's performance, a regression analysis was conducted. The analysis engaged the independent, dependent, and moderating variables to understand the effect of their interactions. It has been indicated by Campbell and Campbell (2008) that regression analysis is used as a technique when a researcher seeks to define the linear association that exists between dependent and independent variables based on the assumption of cause and effect. We confirmed that a regression exists between variables. On this note, this analysis helps the researcher to understand how the variation in one variable causes variation in the other. This is used to predict the causal inference of variables. In this analysis, the coefficient of R^2 determined the fitness of the model.

5 Conclusion and Recommendations

In the upstream oil and gas sector, the procurement of goods is essential to ensure the smooth operation of the industry. This is because the goods procured are often specialized and are required to meet specific design and supply specifications. As such, the procurement process plays a critical role in ensuring that the goods procured meet the required standards and are delivered on time. Additionally, the goods procured are often critical to the production of oil and gas, and any delays or disruptions in the supply chain could have significant impacts on the industry. Therefore, the procurement of goods in the upstream oil and gas sector is considered a vital function, and the goods themselves are often referred to as "critical goods."

The study emphasizes the importance of tracking spending and performance systematically in order to ensure that each investment has a credible chance of bringing value to the country. With the energy transition looming, no objective certificates (NOCs) can no longer afford to take a relaxed approach to resource development. Instead, they must be proactive and focused on delivering results that will benefit the country. By adopting a strategic approach to investment and performance tracking, NOCs can maximize the value of their investments and position themselves for long-term success.

it is recommended that the company should focus on developing its upstream assets in order to avoid stagnation. The company should also take steps to rebuild its upstream program by hiring an experienced upstream professional in a permanent role to lead the program. Additionally, the company's executive leadership and board should be encouraged to prioritize the upstream and commit to a long-term strategic vision and best practice operational processes. By doing so, the company can leverage its stakes in licenses and geological data to make discoveries and generate revenue.

The study has identified several strengths among these national oil companies. The National Oil Corporation of Kenya's strong geoscientific services and facilities can be instrumental in their exploration and production efforts. National Petroleum Corporation of Namibia's

(NAMCOR) effective upstream stakes and data management can enable them to make informed decisions and better manage their resources. The Ghana National Petroleum Corporation's (GNPC) experienced upstream technical staff and understanding of Ghana's geological potential can position them well to exploit the country's oil and gas resources. Finally, Sonatrach's financial and technical strength, along with its dynamic new strategy, can help them navigate the changing energy landscape and stay competitive. It is essential for these companies to leverage their strengths to overcome their weaknesses and stay ahead of the game.

In addition, they will need to develop clear and achievable strategic goals, backed by committed leadership, to guide their operations and investments. Finally, they will need to address the cultural barriers that hinder innovation, agility, and collaboration within the organization. By addressing these weaknesses, NOCs can increase their competitiveness, create more value for their respective countries, and contribute to sustainable economic development.

Following are key recommendations for the enhancement of NOC performance:

- Establish a baseline for the current conditions before the project starts. This will serve as a point of comparison to measure the project's impact. Baseline data could include metrics like revenue, customer satisfaction, or employee turnover.
- Disclosing financial and operational data can be helpful in shedding light on performance and allowing for more effective benchmarking against peers. This can lead to more effective decision-making and better business outcomes in the long term.
- Evaluating and improving internal processes is an essential part of achieving operational excellence. Through this an organization can achieve operational excellence, increase efficiency, reduce costs, and improve customer satisfaction. This approach requires ongoing commitment and investment, but it can lead to significant long-term benefits for your business.
- Formalizing roles, accountabilities, responsibilities, and committing resources is essential to implement the best operational practice in any organization. This will ensure that organization is well-equipped to

implement best operational practices. This approach will help to establish a culture of continuous improvement, increase efficiency, and achieve your business objectives.

- Championing best practice processes at the leadership level is essential to achieving operational excellence in any organization. Through this organization can create a culture of continuous improvement and achieve operational excellence in your organization. This approach requires ongoing commitment and investment, but it can lead to significant long-term benefits for your business.

References

Anderson, E., & Oliver, R. L. (1987). Perspectives on behavior-based versus outcome-based salesforce control systems. *Journal of Marketing, 51*, 76–88.

Ansari, S. (2015). *Researching Sindhi and Urdu students' reading habits and reading performance in a Pakistani university context*. Ph.D. Thesis, University of Bedfordshire, UK.

Atuahene-Gima, K., Li, H., & De Luca, L. M. (2006). The contingent value of marketing strategy innovativeness for product development performance in Chinese new technology ventures. *Industrial Marketing Management, 35*(3), 359–372.

Bailey, P., Farmer, D., Jessop, D., & Jones, D. (2005). *Purchasing principles and management* (9th ed.). Financial Times-Pitman Publishing.

Baraldi, A. N., & Enders, C. K. (2010). An introduction to modern missing data analyses. *Journal of School Psychology, 48*(1), 5–37.

Barnett, V., & Lewis, T. (1994). *Outliers in statistical data*. John Wiley and Sons.

Bryman, A., & Bell, E. (2011). *Business research methods* (3rd ed.). Oxford University Press.

Campbell, D., & Campbell, S. (2008). *Introduction to regression and data analysis*. Retrieved from: http://statlab.stat.yale.edu/workshops/IntroRegression/StatLab-IntroRegressionFa08.pdf.

Child, D. (2006). *The essentials of factor analysis* (3rd ed.). Library of congress Cateloging-in-Publication Data.

Daoud, J. I. (2017). Multicollinearity and regression analysis. *Journal of Physics: Conference Series, 949*(1), 012009.

DeCoster, J. (1998). *Overview of factor analysis*. Retrieved March 27, 2019, from http://www.stat-help

Deming, W. E. (1986). *Out of the crisis.* MIT press.

Dietz, J. (2006). *Enterprise ontology – Theory and methodology.* Springer.

Ellram, L. M. (1991). A managerial guideline for the development and implementation of purchasing partnerships. *International Journal of Purchasing and Materials Management, 27*(3), 2–8.

Ellram, L. M., & Edis, O. R. (1996). A case study of successful partnering implementation. *International Journal of Purchasing and Materials Management, 32*(3), 20–28.

Field, A. (2009). *Discovering statistics using SPSS: Introducing statistical method.* Sage.

Gorsuch, R. (1983). *Factor analysis* (2nd ed.). Lawrence Erlbaum Associates.

Hahn, C. K., Kim, K. H., & Kim, J. S. (1986). Costs of competition: Implications for purchasing strategy. *Journal of Purchasing and Materials Management, 22*(3), 2–7.

Haque, A. U. (2020). Varying occupational stress and organisational commitment within the university staff of contrasting economies (Cross-sectional comparative study of middle range public universities in Pakistan and the UK), Published DBA Thesis, UWTSD Repository. Retrieved from: https://repository.uwtsd.ac.uk/id/eprint/1570/.

Haque, A. U., Sher, A., & Urbański, M. (2020). Is the role of authentic leadership effective in managing occupational stress and psychological capital? *Forum Scientiae Oeconomia, 8*(2), 59–77.

Healy, M., & Perry, C. (2000). Comprehensive criteria to judge validity and reliability of qualitative research within the realism paradigm. *Qualitative Market Research, 3*(3), 118–126.

Homans, G. C. (1958). Social behavior as exchange. *The American Journal of Sociology, 63*, 597–606. https://doi.org/10.1086/222355

Jaggi, C. K., Verma, M., & Jain, R. (2018). Quantitative Analysis For Measuring and Suppressing Bullwhip Effect. *Yugoslav Journal of Operations Research, 28*(3), 415–433. https://doi.org/10.2298/YJOR161211019J

Johnson, R. A., & Wichern, D. W. (2002). Applied multivariate statistical analysis 5, 8). Prentice Hall.

Lamming, R. (1993). *Beyond partnership.* Prentice-Hall.

Luzon, B., & El-Sayegh, S. M. (2016). Evaluating supplier selection criteria for oil and gas projects in the UAE using AHP and Delphi. *International Journal of Construction Management, 16*(2), 175–183. https://doi.org/10.1080/15623599.2016.1146112

Lysons, K., & Farrington, B. (2006). *Purchasing and supply chain management.* Pearson Education.

Macbeth, D. K., & Ferguson, N. (1994). *Partnership sourcing: An integrated supply chain approach*. Financial Times Management/Pitman.
Monczka, R. M., Trent, R. J., & Handfield, R. B. (1998). *Purchasing and supply chain management*. International Thomson Publishing.
Newman, R. G. (1989). Single sourcing: Short-term savings versus long-term problems. *Journal of Purchasing & Materials Management, 25*(2), 20–26.
OECD. (2018). Considerations for assessing the risks of combined exposure to multiple chemicals. *OECD Series on Testing and Assessment*. https://doi.org/10.1787/ceca15a9-en.
Okoth, O. A. (2011). *Supply chain management practices in cement industry in Kenya*. Unpublished MBA project, University of Nairobi, Kenya.
Okoth, A. O., Atambo, W., & Muturi, W. (2017). Effects of procurement practices on the performance of public hospitals in Kenya: A comparative study of hospitals in Homabay and Kisii counties. *International Journal of Social Sciences and Information Technology, III*(II), 1899–1916.
Porter, M. E. (1985). *Competitive advantage: Creating and sustaining superior performance*. Free Press.
Shih, R. A., Belmonte, P. L., & Zandi, P. P. (2004). A review of the evidence from family, twin and adoption studies for a genetic contribution to adult psychiatric disorders. *International Review of Psychiatry, 16*(4), 260–283.
Slack, N., Chambers, S., & Johnston, R. (2010). *Operations management*. Pearson Education.
SMMT and DTI. (1994). *A review of the relationships between vehicle makers and suppliers*.
Treleven, M., & Schweikhart, S. B. (1988). A risk/benefit analysis of sourcing strategies: Single vs. multiple sourcing. *Journal of Operations Management, 7*(3–4), 93–114.
Tucker, L. R., & MacCallum, R. C. (1997). *Exploratory factor analysis. Ohio State University*. Ohio State University.
Waters, D. (2004). *Introduction to supply chain management* (2nd ed.). Palgrave Macmillan.
Yong, A. G., & Pearce, S. (2013). A beginner's guide to factor analysis: Focusing on exploratory factor analysis. *Tutorials in Quantitative Methods for Psychology, 9*(2), 79–94.
Zaid, M. A. (2015). Correlation and regression analysis. Ankara – Turkey: The statistical, Economic and Social Research and Training Centre for Islamic Countries (SESRIC).

Examining the Effect of Minimum Wage on Employment in the Malaysian Manufacturing Sector

Sheikh Ahmad Faiz Sheikh Ahmad Tajuddin, Suriyani Muhamad, Jumadil Saputra, Fauziah Abu Hasan, and Nor Fatimah Che Sulaiman

1 Introduction

Manufacturing is one of the dominant sectors that contribute to Malaysia's economy. In the fourth quarter of 2018, 22.8 per cent of the national gross domestic product (GDP) has been contributed by manufacturing (Department of Statistics Malaysia, 2018b). In the labour market, manufacturing has created numerous jobs for people. According to the Labour Force Survey 2018 (Department of Statistics Malaysia, 2018a), manufacturing was the second largest sector after services in terms of employment

S. A. F. S. A. Tajuddin
Faculty of Business and Management, Universiti Sultan Zainal Abidin, Kuala Terengganu, Malaysia

S. Muhamad • J. Saputra (✉) • F. A. Hasan • N. F. C. Sulaiman
Faculty of Business, Economics and Social Development, Universiti Malaysia Terengganu, Kuala Terengganu, Malaysia
e-mail: jumadil.saputra@umt.edu.my

F. A. Yamoah, A. ul Haque (eds.), *Corporate Management Ecosystem in Emerging Economies*, https://doi.org/10.1007/978-3-031-41578-4_4

in 2018. About 2.5 million people, including locals and foreigners, have been employed to work in the sector.

Since heavy industries were introduced in the early 1980s, Malaysia has been highly dependent on foreign workers. From 400,000 foreign workers employed in 1990, the number has tremendously increased to 1.57 million people in 2012 (Ministry of Home Affairs Malaysia, 2017). The main reason for the high inflow of foreign workers into the Malaysian labour market was due to the cheap labour that can be provided by those workers, especially the low-skilled foreign workers. Nevertheless, high dependency on foreign workers has triggered several economic and social problems in the country (Wei et al., 2018). High employment of low-skilled foreign workers would reduce productivity enhancement and compress the overall pay among the other workers. A reduction in the employment of locals would also be expected.

To address the issue, the government introduced the minimum wage policy in 2012. The implementation of a minimum wage policy would promote better living standards for poorly paid employees and reduce the dependency on low-skilled foreign workers (Senasi & Khalil, 2015). However, with the minimum wage policy in place and expectations to achieve these objectives, implementing the minimum wage policy would affect overall employment in Malaysia. Higher labour costs that the firms will incur due to the minimum wage would cause the employers to reduce their labour demand.

There were different views among the firms regarding policy implementation. The SMEs who were expected to be highly affected by the minimum wage was argued with the minimum wage implementation. Even though they have been given an extension until December 2013 to implement the policy; the SMEs viewed that the minimum wage will cause them higher labour costs. The firms are expected to reduce their unskilled workers to survive and cope with the increasing labour cost.

Previous researchers have had different views on the minimum wages' impact on employment. The minimum wage implementation would cause employers higher labour costs, which would result in employment reduction. Whilst Brecher and Gross (2019) suggested that a minimum wage would reduce the number of people getting employed, Karamanis et al. (2018) found that a minimum wage does not affect employment.

The study that has been conducted on the Greek labour market has found that labour demand is not affected by the minimum wage.

There were mixed findings from the previous studies on the effect of the minimum wage on employment. Hence, the objective of this chapter is to analyse the effect of the minimum wage on employment in the manufacturing sector of Malaysia.

2 Literature Review

As of today, most countries including developing and industrialized have implemented the minimum wage policy. All European countries that are registered with the International Labour Organization (ILO) have a minimum wage which at least covers part of the private sector. In Asia, 90 per cent of the Asian countries have the minimum wage legislation except for Singapore, Brunei, Bahrain and Macau. Meanwhile, Sweden, Denmark and Switzerland are among the developed nations that do not implement the minimum wage. These countries have high salaries and low unemployment levels (International Labour Organization, 2016). Additionally, Sweden and Denmark have a social contract in place that enables workers to receive a reasonable wage from their employers. These are among the factors that affect the government's decision not to implement the minimum wage policy in those countries.

In Asia, the implementation of the minimum wage in Asian countries was mostly introduced after the Second World War, which was from 1939 to 1945 (Starr, 1981). However, the definition of minimum wage differs among the countries. Asian countries apply multiple minimum wage rates while there are a few countries that use a single minimum wage rate such as Thailand and Korea. Van Klaveren et al. (2015) suggest that the countries will face difficulties in minimum wage fixing procedures and criteria if they decide to use multiple minimum wage rates. The multiple minimum wage rates that can be varied by industry, occupation or region require several considerations from the higher authorities to determine the actual minimum wage rate for every sector or region.

In Malaysia, enforcement has been introduced in the country in 2012 under the Malaysian Minimum Wage Order (MWO) 2012. The law requires a minimum wage of MYR900 per month throughout Peninsular Malaysia and MYR800 per month in East Malaysia. Under the minimum wage policy, all workers consisting of locals and foreigners are entitled to receive the minimum wage. The only parties that are not covered by the minimum wage are the domestic servants and apprentices who undergo training for more than two years. The minimum wage was fully implemented by all corporations in 2013, except for small and medium enterprises (SMEs) (Yuen, 2013). The SMEs have been given an extension to defer payment until December 2013 since they are expected to be more affected by the policy. Collectively, the minimum wage has been fully enforced in all stages since 1 January 2014.

In the early years of minimum wage implementation, Malaysia used to have multiple minimum wage rates, the same as most other Asian countries. According to ILO 2016, India has more than 1200 minimum wage rates, and the rates have been different across states, occupations and industries. Malaysia used to have two minimum wage rates and the rates are different between Peninsular Malaysia and East Malaysia. Starting in 2013, these states and federal territories in Peninsular Malaysia are required to follow the minimum wage of MYR900 per month. Meanwhile, Sabah, Sarawak and the Federal Territory of Labuan which is in East Malaysia are required to follow the minimum wage of MYR800 per month.

Moving forward, Malaysia aims to be a developed nation shortly (Khan et al., 2014). In order to realize the vision, Malaysia needs to transform from its current middle-income country to a high-income country as this is one of the criteria to be recognized as a developed nation. Hence, the government has announced a new minimum wage policy commencing January 2016. Based on the revised policy under the Minimum Wage Order (MWO) 2016, the minimum wage in Peninsular Malaysia has been increased to MYR1,000 and MYR920 in East Malaysia. This means that the workers in Peninsular Malaysia and East Malaysia will earn a minimum hourly wage of MYR4.81 and MYR4.42.

In 2018, the government announced a new minimum wage policy through the MWO (Amendment) 2018. In the amendment, the minimum wage rate would be standardized for both Peninsular Malaysia and East Malaysia. The second revision of the minimum wage rate will cause all the country workers, including Sabah and Sarawak, to receive the standardized minimum wage rate of MYR1,100. In the hourly rate, all the workers will be entitled to receive at least MYR5.29 per hour.

In October 2019, the government announced a new minimum wage rate for workers in major urban cities (International Labour Organization, 2019). Under the MWO 2020, the entitled workers would receive a minimum wage of MYR1,200 commencing February 2020. In 2022, the government has set a new minimum wage rate of MYR1,500 under MWO 2022. The revised rates are necessary to reflect the increase in the cost of living. The minimum wage policy aims to develop the Malaysian economy into a high-income country (Ghee et al., 2015). The system can alleviate poverty and promote better living standards for the poorly paid employees who are mostly involved in the unskilled job sector.

The government determines the minimum wage rate in Malaysia upon the recommendation of the National Wages Consultative Council (NWCC). NWCC is a council consisting of representatives from employers and employees, government and independent experts. Established in 2011, the council's primary function is to conduct research on the minimum wage and make recommendations to the government regarding the minimum wage. The Malaysian minimum wage rate is determined based on five factors, namely, poverty line income, employer's ability to pay salaries, consumer price index, real unemployment rate and productivity growth. According to the International Labour Organization (2012), NWCC has set an equation formula to determine the minimum wage rate. The equation formula is as follows:

$$\mathrm{MWi} = \mathrm{AVG}\left(\frac{\mathrm{PLI}}{\mathrm{Avg}\ \mathit{workers}\ \mathrm{per}\ \mathit{household}} + \mathit{Median\ wage}\right) X\left[1+\left(\frac{Pi}{100}\right)+\left(\frac{\mathrm{CPI}i}{100}\right)+\left(\frac{\mathrm{UE}i}{100}\right)\right] \tag{1}$$

Where,

MW = minimum wage (MYR).

PLI = poverty line income (MYR).

P = productivity growth (%).

CPI = consumer price index (% change).

UE = unemployment rate (%): actual unemployment rate minus natural unemployment rate (4%).

i = region.

The implementation of minimum wage policy remains controversial today, even though there have been a lot of countries that had implemented such policies. There are different views about the relationship between minimum wage and employment.

In a perfectly competitive market, unemployment happens when the binding minimum wage is set above the equilibrium wages (Lee & Saez, 2012). Since there is an increase in wages, the supply of labour will increase as people are more willing to work. Meanwhile, demand for labour will decrease as the firm incurs higher costs. As the supply is greater than the demand in the labour market, minimum wages will create unemployment. Figure 1 represents the employment effect of the minimum wage in a perfectly competitive market. Unemployment is bad because some skilled workers may not be hired due to the limited jobs

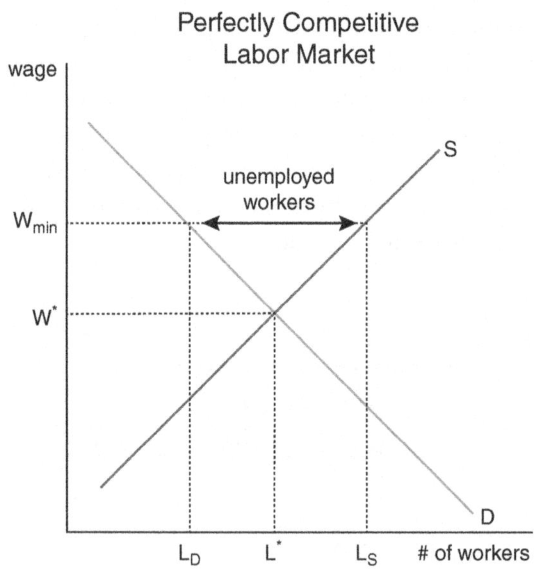

Fig. 1 Employment effect of the minimum wage in a perfectly competitive market

available. Unemployment can distort the productivity and the output of the economy. Based on Okun's law, a high unemployment rate is associated with a low gross domestic output and GDP (Okun, 1963; Plosser & Schwert, 1979).

Many studies have analysed the minimum wage's effect on employment dynamics. Studies done by Christl et al. (2018) in European countries have suggested that an increase in the minimum wage results in a higher number of jobless people among young employees. A minimum wage which has caused higher labour costs for employers would further affect the performance of the companies. The employers responded to the minimum wage by employing more senior and experienced employees as compared to young employees. Hiring experienced and productive employees would be able to offset the increase in labour cost due to the minimum wage. Hence, the authors have suggested that an increase in the minimum wage would reduce the employment of young employees.

In Asia, Fang and Lin (2015) studied the minimum wage and employment in China. Using the county-level panel dataset combined with urban household survey microdata conducted by the National Bureau of Statistics of China, they analysed the impact of minimum wage changes on employment in China from 2004 to 2009. The study found that minimum wage in China has a different impact on unemployment categorized on the different counties, schooling backgrounds and age groups. Their findings suggested that minimum wage changes have a significant negative effect on employment, particularly in the eastern and central regions. The study also found that females, young adults, and low-skilled workers are the most affected groups when there are minimum wage changes. In South Korea, Baek and Park (2016) focused on the minimum wage's impact on employment in manufacturing industries. The authors observed the impact in two periods: before introducing a minimum wage in 1987 and after 1987. The findings revealed that setting a minimum wage for plant-level employment would increase the labour cost, cost per employee, and total annual wage. Although the minimum wage caused higher labour costs, the impact of the minimum wage on employment, however, is unable to be proven.

Broecke et al. (2017) analysed the impact of the minimum wage on employment in emerging countries using a meta-analysis of literature reviews from 14 emerging countries, including China, South American countries, and South Africa. The study, which includes 56 empirical literature and 74 qualitative reviews, found that the minimum wage has various employment effects. The researchers added that the negative impact tended toward low-skilled workers and younger labour. However, such evidence is small. The findings implied that the effect of the minimum wage on employment differed between developed and emerging countries due to different regulations, employers' power and compliance with the minimum wage regulations.

In another setting, studies by Okey et al. (2020) in African countries found that implementation of the minimum wage would reduce employment. The authors observed 25 years to study the effect of the minimum wage from the year 1990 to 2015. A negative relationship was found between minimum wage and employment as it confirms the perspective of neoclassical economic theory, whereas the price of labour increases, the demand for labour decreases. The authors implied in their findings that companies in Africa mostly have low profitability and competitiveness, thus having a minimum wage would only increase their costs and reduce their profits.

The minimum wage policy has caused firms to review their employment decisions more precisely as they must incur high labour costs after the policy implementation. As Meer and West (2016) mentioned, higher labour cost triggered by the minimum wage has caused a decrease in the US's labour demand. The study used employment and wage data from the Bureau of Labor Statistics. In the short run, low-educated workers or low-skilled workers were estimated to be the most affected group by executing the minimum wage in terms of job losses. Higher labour costs incurred by the firms caused them to cut the size of their low-skilled workers. The study also found a negative relationship between minimum wage and employment growth in the long run. The higher labour cost induced by the minimum wage reduced job opportunities in the labour market.

However, some views suggest that a minimum wage can increase employment. In a monopsony market, the minimum wage set above the

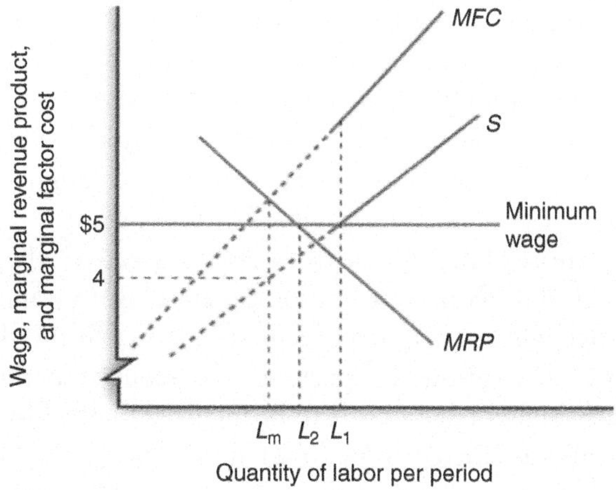

Fig. 2 Employment and wages: effect of minimum wage in a monopsony market

equilibrium wage can increase employment (Robinson, 1969). Figure 2 describes the employment effect of the minimum wage in a monopsony market. Before the minimum wage implementation, the employers maximize their profit (at the intersection of marginal revenue product—MRP curve—and marginal factor cost—MFC curve) by employing L_m units of labour with wages of $4 per hour. However, the government's minimum wage imposition of $5 per hour will invalidate the dashed section of the supply, S and MFC curves. The new MFC curve will be the horizontal line of the minimum wage, and the new intersection point will be between MRP and the new MFC (horizontal line of minimum wage). At this new equilibrium point, the employment increases from L_m to L_2 and the wages increase from $4 per hour to $5 per hour. Hence, the monopsony labour market shows that a minimum wage can increase employment and wages.

The theory was supported by Sabia (2009) who mentioned in his study that a minimum wage can result in employment in a non-competitive market. If a minimum wage is lower than the marginal cost of employing an extra worker, the firm can employ more employees at lower costs.

With the attainment of higher profit, the firm can boost employment. The theory is supported by the studies conducted by Wang and Gunderson (2012) and Lemos (2009). The results showed that the impact of minimum wages on unemployment is statistically insignificant and invalid.

Gavrel et al. (2010) analysed the short-term and long-term effects of the minimum wage on unemployment. The result showed that the minimum wage increase affects the firms to be less selective. The workers are quickly employed to reduce the cost of maintaining a vacancy. Thus, the minimum wage will cause employment to increase in the short run. In the long run, job creation is expected to be reduced as the minimum wage will cause higher labour costs to be incurred by the firms. However, unemployment is predicted to be lowered as soon as the differentiation between workers and jobs is sufficient. Nevertheless, after reaching a limit, the minimum wage increase will increase unemployment, regardless of the degree of differentiation.

Also, Mastracci and Persky (2008) indicated that the minimum wage increase would not contribute to the extensive job losses. The study was done to analyse the effects of the minimum wage's increases on employment in Illinois. Illinois is a state located in the Midwestern region of the US. The study applied the labour market data collected from the National Bureau of Economic Research and developed the time-series model to estimate the effect. Using the ordinary least squares method, the findings revealed that the increase in minimum wage per hour from $5.15 to $6.50 in 2015 would only increase the total labour costs by less than 1 per cent. Indeed, the minimum wage increases would raise the employment of low-wage workers in Illinois. This effect happened as Illinois is a labour-based services industry that is highly dependent on minimum wage workers.

Past studies have shown different views on the relationship between minimum wage and employment. Whilst some views suggested minimum wage would reduce employment, some studies have found a positive relationship between minimum wage and employment. This study would examine the effect of minimum wage on employment in the Malaysian manufacturing sector.

3 Materials and Methods

The study aims to estimate the effect of the minimum wage on employment. Apart from the minimum wage and employment, the study has selected the size, profit, age and location of the firm as the controlled variables. The size is the firm's size and is measured by the sales turnover of the firm. The study only considered medium and large firms. Based on the SME Corporation Classification, a medium manufacturing firm has a sales turnover between MYR15 million to MYR50 million while a large manufacturing firm has a sales turnover of more than MYR50 million. The profit is the profit that the firm generates in a particular year. The age is the number of years the firm has operated, and the location is the firm's location which is divided into zones, namely, Klang Valley zone (Kuala Lumpur and Selangor), southern zone (Negeri Sembilan, Melaka and Johor), northern zone (Kedah and Perlis) and eastern zone (Pahang, Terengganu, and Kelantan).

The model of the study is as follows:

$$\mathrm{EMP}_{\mathrm{it}} = \beta_0 + \beta_1 \mathrm{MW}_{\mathrm{it}} + \beta_2 \mathit{SIZE}_{\mathrm{it}} + \beta_3 \mathit{PROFIT}_{\mathrm{it}} + \beta_4 \mathrm{AGE}_{\mathrm{it}} + \beta_5 \mathrm{LOC}_{\mathrm{it}} + \varepsilon_{\mathrm{it}}$$

Where

EMP	is the total number of workers,
MW	is the minimum wage,
SIZE	is the firm's size,
PROFIT	is the firm's profit,
AGE	is the number of years the firm has to operate,
LOC	is the firm's location.

A panel data analysis covering the periods of 2008 to 2017 has been conducted in this research. The study used a questionnaire and focused on the manufacturing industry. In the study 297 manufacturing firms that are registered with the Federation of Malaysian Manufacturers (FMM) were randomly selected to examine the effect of minimum wage on employment.

4 Results

The results of the study were divided into two parts, namely, before the minimum wage period (2008–2012) and during the minimum wage period (2013–2017). The panel data for 2008–2012 and 2013–2017 were regressed separately to examine the effect of minimum wage on employment. The analysis continued with the diagnostic tests after the linearity and normality checks. The diagnostic tests involved multicollinearity, heteroscedasticity and serial correlation checks. Further analyses were conducted on the pooled ordinary least square (OLS) model, random effects model and fixed effects model. The STATA application was used to run the panel data.

Descriptive Statistics Analysis

Descriptive statistics summarized the statistics of the variables employed in the model which consist of employment, minimum wage, firm's size, profit, age and location. The descriptions of the variables include the number of observations, mean, median, standard deviation and minimum and maximum values of each variable data. Tables 1 and 2 reported the descriptive statistics for the data periods 2008–2012 and 2013–2017.

Table 1 displays all the variables in the period of 2008–2012 have 1485 observations. The mean for employment and minimum wage are 879.19 and 692.20. The profit has the highest mean and standard deviation of 6,326,612 and 4.32e+07, respectively. The size has the lowest mean and standard deviation that is 1.42 and 0.49. The age and zones

Table 1 Descriptive statistics of determinants and employment for the period of 2008–2012

Variable	Obs.	Mean	Standard deviation	Min	Max
EMP	1485	879.19	5358.58	23	110,645
MW	1485	692.20	78.43	500	880
SIZE	1485	1.42	0.49	1	2
PROFIT	1485	6,326,612	4.32e+07	28,880	1.17e+09
AGE	1485	27.21	11.12	2	81
ZONES	1485	2.36	1.29	1	4

Table 2 Descriptive statistics of determinants and employment for the period of 2013–2017

Variable	Obs	Mean	Standard deviation	Min	Max
EMP	1485	941.41	5911.73	44	130,000
MW	1485	940	49.01	900	1000
SIZE	1485	1.42	0.49	1	2
PROFIT	1485	8,232,106	4.92e+07	2286	1.09e+09
AGE	1485	32.21	11.12	7	86
ZONES	1485	2.36	1.29	1	4

have the standard deviation of 11.12 and 1.29. In terms of maximum and minimum values, profit has the highest maximum value of 1.17e+09 and the highest minimum value of 28,880. The size has the lowest maximum and minimum values of 2 and 1, respectively. The maximum value for employment and minimum wage are 110,645 and 880 while their minimum value is 23 and 500.

Based on Table 2, there are also 1485 observations for all the variables in the period of 2013–2017. The mean for employment and minimum wage are 941.41 and 940. The profit has the highest mean and standard deviation of 8,232,106 and 4.92e+07 respectively. The profit also has the highest maximum value of 1.09e+09 and the highest minimum value of 2286. The mean, standard deviation, the maximum and minimum values for the size and zones in this period are the same as from 2008 to 2012. The age has maximum and minimum values of 86 and 7. The maximum value for employment and minimum wage are 130,000 and 1000 while their minimum value is 44 and 900.

Regression Analysis

Diagnostic checks were conducted to test the problems of multicollinearity, heteroscedasticity and serial correlation. The study also has made further analyses of the pooled OLS model, random effect model and fixed effects model. Breusch–Pagan LM test and Hausman test were conducted to decide whether the pooled OLS, random effect or fixed effect is the appropriate model in the study. As the result of the Breusch–Pagan LM test is significant (p-value < 0.05) and the Hausman test's result is not significant (p-value > 0.05) for the periods of 2008–2012 and 2013–2017, the random effect model is the appropriate model in the study for both periods. The output of the regression results for the periods of 2008–2012 and 2013–2017 are based on the random effect model as shown in Tables 3 and 4.

The multicollinearity problem is detected by using the variance inflation factor (VIF). As the VIF is 1.24 which is less than 10, there is no

Table 3 Random effect results with dependent variable: EMP from 2008 to 2012

Variable	Coefficients	*t*-Stats
MW	0.1745	0.0622***
SIZE	-309.8803	36.1026***
PROFIT	0.0012	0.0000***
AGE	0.6998	1.5708
ZONES	25.3137	13.7512
Constant	539.0088	80.7104
R^2	0.3388	
N	1355	
Breusch–Pagan LM test	2085.05	0.0000
Hausman test	46.89	0.8592
Multicollinearity (VIF)	1.24	
Heteroscedasticity (x^2 – stat)	1.3e+07	0.0000
Serial correlation (F – stat)	129.27	0.0000

Note: ** and *** indicate 5% and 1% significant levels, respectively

Table 4 Random effect results with dependent variable: EMP from 2013 to 2017

Variable	Coefficients	*t*-Stats
MW	-0.0013	0.0.0266***
SIZE	-188.1760	19.4875***
PROFIT	0.0024	0.0000***
AGE	0.8582	1.0527
ZONES	7.7521	7.4148
Constant	262.0875	19.6533
R^2	0.4857	
N	1310	
Breusch–Pagan LM test	2537.76	0.0000
Hausman test	3.67	0.0553
Multicollinearity (VIF)	1.09	
Heteroscedasticity (x^2 – stat)	7.5e+07	0.0000
Serial correlation (F – stat)	44.93	0.0000

Note: ** and *** indicate the 5% and 1% significant levels, respectively multicollinearity problem. For the heteroscedasticity check, modified Wald statistic is used to detect the problem. Based on the table above, the significant *p*-value of the x^2 stat indicates that there is a heteroscedasticity problem which means the variances are not constant. The serial correlation problem is detected by using the Wooldridge test. The significant *p*-value of the F-stat indicates that there is a serial correlation problem. As the diagnostic checks detected heteroscedasticity and serial correlation problems from 2008 to 2012, the standard errors in the model were estimated by Rogers (1993) clustered at the firm level. Clustering at the firm level results in a robust estimator of cross-sectional heteroscedasticity and within-panel correlation.

Based on the random effect model in the table above, the findings suggested that the minimum wage and employment have a significant positive relationship before the minimum wage policy was implemented. An increase in minimum wage by MYR100 would increase the number of workers by 17 people. More people would be willing to work to entitle the higher wages offered by employers. With no minimum wage policy being implemented before 2013, the firms were able to hire more workers without having to pay a regulated amount of minimum wage.

There are four controlled variables in the study and the findings suggested that only the size and profit are significant. The negative relationship between size and employment indicates that large firms would have a higher number of workers as compared to small firms. Meanwhile, profit has a positive relationship with employment. High-profit and large firms would require more workers as the firms require more manpower to operate the machines.

The diagnostic checks for the period of 2013–2017 also indicate the presence of heteroscedasticity and serial correlation problems. Hence, the standard errors in the model are clustered at the firm level to rectify the problems. On the basis of the random effect model in the table above, the findings reveal that the effect of minimum wage on employment is significant at *p*-value < 0.01 with a negative relationship. After the minimum wage policy has been implemented, an increase in the minimum wage by MYR1000 would reduce the number of workers by 1 person. The increase in labour costs has caused firms to reduce their employment.

In terms of the controlled variables, the findings suggested that only the size and profit are significant. The negative relationship between size and employment indicates that large firms would have a higher number of workers as compared to small firms. Meanwhile, profit has a positive relationship with employment. High profit and large firms would require more workers as the firms require more manpower to operate the machines.

5 Findings and Discussions

The empirical results based on the random effect model show a significant relationship between minimum wage and employment for both periods before minimum wage and during minimum wage. Before the minimum wage period, the findings revealed that the increase in wages would increase employment. Since there is no minimum wage policy to be adhered to by the employers during the period, the employers can employ more workers with low wages, especially low-skilled workers. However, the findings for the period of minimum wage have reported a significant negative relationship between the minimum wage and employment. After the minimum wage policy was introduced in 2012, employers needed to incur higher labour costs, which then cost them employment losses.

The findings reveal that the increase in the minimum wage would result in unemployment. This result supports the arguments by Brecher and Gross (2019) and Nguyen (2017) that the minimum wage has cost employers higher labour costs, which would result in a reduction in employment. Consistent with the classical economic theory of labour market, the implementation of minimum wage in the labour market would cause unemployment or a reduction in the employment.

The increasing standards and requirements by the Ministry of Human Resources to employ the workers together with the higher labour cost due to the minimum wage policy have caused employers to reduce the non-performing workers and focus on the productive workers in low-skilled jobs.

Nevertheless, the firms must come up with initiatives to make sure all the workers are productive and can contribute to the firm's performance. Forging ahead with the fourth industrial revolution, having productive workers through good training and business plans are the key instruments for firms to remain competitive in the industry.

6 Conclusion

This study concludes that the minimum wage affects the employment of manufacturing firms in Peninsular Malaysia. Before the minimum wage was introduced, low-skilled foreign workers were highly employed. Low participation rate from the local people in low-skilled jobs due to the cheap salary has forced employers to hire foreign workers to fill the labour shortage. Hence, the high dependency of employers towards foreign workers and the low salary received by the low-skilled workers caused the government to introduce the minimum wage policy in 2012. The implementation of the minimum wage policy has had an impact on the number of local and foreign workers. The policy has managed to reduce the dependency of manufacturing firms on low-skilled foreign workers. With higher labour costs that need to be incurred, employers have replaced their low-skilled foreign workers with more productive workers. The higher minimum wage would also attract more local workers to join the low-skilled jobs. However, the implementation of the minimum wage policy has affected overall employment negatively. Employers must incur higher labour costs due to the minimum wage. To reduce their costs and remain competitive in the industry, employers have responded by laying off some of their workers. Hence, this study suggested that a minimum wage would reduce employment.

References

Baek, J., & Park, W. (2016). Minimum wage introduction and employment: Evidence from South Korea. *Economics Letters, 139*, 18–21.

Brecher, R. A., & Gross, T. (2019). A minimum-wage model of unemployment and growth: The case of a backward-bending demand curve for labor. *International Journal of Economic Theory, 15*(3), 297–309.

Broecke, S., Forti, A., & Vandeweyer, M. (2017). The effect of minimum wages on employment in emerging economies: A survey and meta-analysis. *Oxford Development Studies, 45*(3), 366–391.

Christl, M., Köppl-Turyna, M., & Kucsera, D. (2018). Revisiting the employment effects of minimum wages in Europe. *German Economic Review, 19*(4), 426–465.

Department of Statistics Malaysia. (2018a). *Labour force survey time series statistics.* https://www.dosm.gov.my/v1/uploads/files/%0A3_TimeSeries/LFS_1982–2018/12.TABLE_12.pdf.%0A.

Department of Statistics Malaysia. (2018b). *Malaysia economic performance fourth quarter 2018.* https://www.dosm.gov.my/v1/index.%0Aphp?r=column/pdfPrev&id=aHRydmZMSmtNL0lTbW43SjVOSlZkQT09%0A

Fang, T., & Lin, C. (2015). Minimum wages and employment in China. *IZA Journal of Labor Policy, 4*, 1–30.

Gavrel, F., Lebon, I., & Rebière, T. (2010). Wages, selectivity, and vacancies: Evaluating the short-term and long-term impact of the minimum wage on unemployment. *Economic Modelling, 27*(5), 1274–1281.

Ghee, T. C., Mooi, S. K., & Sang, M. L. M. (2015). An initial review of the implementation of the Malaysian minimum wage order: A case for a win-win intention, implementation and enforcement. *The Journal of Developing Areas, 49*(4), 313–324.

International Labour Organization. (2012). *National Wages Consultative Council Act 2011.* https://www.ilo.org/dyn/natlex/natlex4.detail?p_isn=89540&p_lang=en

International Labour Organization. (2016). *Minimum wage policy guide.* https://www.ilo.org/global/topics/wages/minimum-wages/lang%2D%2Den/index.htm

International Labour Organization. (2019). *Minimum Wages Order 2020.* https://www.ilo.org/dyn/natlex/natlex4.detail?p_isn=109409&p_lang=en

Karamanis, K., Ch, B., & Ioakimidis, M. (2018). Greek labour market: The evaluation of minimum wage and unemployment during the period 2000-2017. *Journal of International Studies, 11*(4), 93–105.

Khan, R. A., Liew, M. S., & Ghazali, Z. B. (2014). Malaysian construction sector and Malaysia vision 2020: Developed nation status. *Procedia-Social and Behavioral Sciences, 109*, 507–513.

Lee, D., & Saez, E. (2012). Optimal minimum wage policy in competitive labor markets. *Journal of Public Economics, 96*(9–10), 739–749.

Lemos, S. (2009). Minimum wage effects in a developing country. *Labour Economics, 16*(2), 224–237.

Mastracci, S. H., & Persky, J. J. (2008). Effects of state minimum wage increases on employment, hours, and earnings of low-wage workers in Illinois. *Journal of Regional Analysis and Policy, 38*(8), 268–278.

Meer, J., & West, J. (2016). Effects of the minimum wage on employment dynamics. *Journal of Human Resources, 51*(2), 500–522.

Ministry of Home Affairs Malaysia. (2017). *Official documents, national publication 2016*. https://www.data.gov.my/data/ms_MY/dataset/%0Ajumlah-pekerja-asing-plks-aktif-mengikut-sektor%0A.

Nguyen, C. V. (2017). Do minimum wages affect firms' labor and capital? Evidence from Vietnam. *Journal of the Asia Pacific Economy, 22*(2), 291–308.

Okey, M. K. N., Adjor, M. D., & Ketor, Y. E. (2020). How does minimum wage affect employment? Evidence from selected African countries. *International Journal of Economics and Accounting, 9*(2), 132–154.

Okun, A. M. (1963). *Potential GNP: Its measurement and significance*. Cowles Foundation for Research in Economics at Yale University.

Plosser, C. I., & Schwert, G. W. (1979). Potential GNP: Its measurement and significance: A dissenting opinion. *Carnegie-Rochester Conference Series on Public Policy, 10*, 179–186.

Robinson, J. (1969). *The economics of imperfect competition*. Springer.

Rogers, W. (1993). Regression standard errors in clustered samples. *Stata Technical Bulletin, 13*, 19–23.

Sabia, J. J. (2009). Identifying minimum wage effects: New evidence from monthly CPS data. *Industrial Relations: A Journal of Economy and Society, 48*(2), 311–328.

Senasi, V., & Khalil, S. (2015). Implementation of minimum wage policy in Malaysia: Manufacturing employers' perceptions of training provision and fringe benefits. *International Journal of Humanities and Social Science, 5*(12), 87–94.

Starr, G. (1981). Minimum wage fixing: International experience with alternative roles. *International Labour Review, 120*, 545.

Van Klaveren, M., Gregory, D., & Schulten, T. (2015). *Minimum wages, collective bargaining and economic development in Asia and Europe: A labour perspective*. Springer.

Wang, J., & Gunderson, M. (2012). Minimum wage effects on employment and wages: Dif-in-dif estimates from eastern China. *International Journal of Manpower, 33*(8), 860–876.

Wei, A. J., Murugasu, A., & Wei, C. Y. (2018). Low-skilled foreign workers' distortions to the economy. In *Central Bank of Malaysia*.

Yuen, J. L. F. (2013). Minimum wage policy in Malaysia: Its impact and the readiness of firms. *World Applied Sciences Journal (Economic, Finance, and Management Outlooks), 28*, 19–26.

Leveraging International Student Mobility to Enhance the Competitiveness of Developing Countries in the Global Market

Negar Sohaee

1 Introduction

The international student movement trend has increased in recent years as more students seek international educational experiences to improve their skills and broaden their horizons. In today's rapidly changing global economy, it is critical that countries remain competitive and have a workforce with the latest skills and knowledge (Waters, 2006, 2009). This is especially true when the gap between human capital in developing countries and that in developed countries is large (Wei, 2013; Zainab et al., 2019). To close this gap, developing countries need to find innovative solutions to improve the skills of their workforces and their competitiveness in global markets. A proven solution is the transfer of international students.

By leveraging the expertise and knowledge of students from all over the world, developing countries can strengthen their human capital and become more competitive in global markets (King, 2003: 163–166).

N. Sohaee (✉)
Faculty of Business, Yorkville University, Toronto, ON, Canada
e-mail: nsohaee@yorkvilleu.ca

F. A. Yamoah, A. ul Haque (eds.), *Corporate Management Ecosystem in Emerging Economies*, https://doi.org/10.1007/978-3-031-41578-4_5

This article examines the role international student mobility plays in bridging the skills gap in developing countries and explores the benefits it brings to both students and host countries.

2 Definition of International Student Mobility

International student migration refers to the movement of students from one country to another in pursuit of educational opportunities (OECD, 2019; Dewey, 2021). This trend has increased in recent years as students seek international experiences to improve their skills, broaden their horizons, and gain valuable experience of different cultures and educational systems (Dewey, 2021). International student mobility enables students to gain new insights and knowledge from a variety of educators, institutions, and cultures. By studying in different countries, students gain new perspectives, improve their cross-cultural skills, and gain a competitive advantage in the global marketplace. In addition, international student mobility also serves as a tool to fill skills gaps in developing countries, as it attracts talented students who bring new ideas, skills, and knowledge that help improve the human capital of the host country (Wei, 2013; Zainab et al., 2019).

3 Overview of the Benefits of International Student Mobility

International student mobility offers many advantages for both the student and the host country. For students, it offers opportunities to immerse themselves in new cultures, learn from different educators, and gain valuable experience of different educational systems (Lu et al., 2009; Tremblay, 2005). It will also help you improve your intercultural and linguistic skills and increase your global awareness. Studying in another country offers students the opportunity to build an international network that is invaluable to their future careers. For the host country, International

Student Mobility brings together talented students from around the world who bring new ideas, skills, and knowledge that will help improve the human capital of the host country. This increase in human capital can lead to greater competitiveness in the global market and the development of local economies. International student mobility can also foster innovation and entrepreneurship as international students bring new perspectives and ideas to their host countries. In addition, it can also promote cultural exchanges and improve international relations between countries.

The thesis of this article is:

> International student mobility enhances the competitiveness of developing countries in global markets by providing access to new ideas, skills and knowledge and helping to bridge the skills gap that exists between developed and developing countries. Can play an important role in improving (Waters, 2006, 2009). The movement of talented students from around the world allows developing countries to benefit not only from the exchange of ideas and knowledge, but also from the cross-cultural experiences that students bring. This will lead to improved human capital and a more competitive workforce in the global market, contributing to the development of the local economy and the promotion of cultural exchanges.

4 Importance of Closing the Skills Gap in Developing Countries

Bridging the skills gap in developing countries is essential to becoming more competitive in global markets and promoting economic growth and stability. The skills gap refers to the difference between the skills and knowledge of a country's workforce and the skills and knowledge that country needs to remain competitive in the global marketplace. In many developing countries, this gap is large and hinders their ability to compete with developed countries in terms of economic growth, innovation, and entrepreneurship. It can also limit the ability of people in these countries to secure good jobs and improve their living standards (Lo, 2019). The impact of the skills gap is not limited to individuals; it affects entire nations. An inadequately skilled and knowledgeable workforce can lead to a lack of economic growth, high unemployment, and a reduced ability to attract foreign investment. These issues can lead to a vicious cycle where underinvestment leads to underinvestment in employment opportunities, leading to underdevelopment of skills. Bridging the skills gap is essential to promoting development and economic growth and stability in developing countries. By improving the skills and knowledge of their workforce, developing countries can become more competitive in global markets, attract investment, and create new employment opportunities. This will help break the cycle of poverty and lack of economic growth facing many developing countries. Moreover, a more skilled and knowledgeable workforce could lead to more innovation and entrepreneurship, further driving economic growth and development. Addressing the skills gap in developing countries is therefore critical not only to individual success but also to the success of the country.

5 Explanation of the Skills Gap

Skills gap is a term that describes the difference between the skills and knowledge of a country's workforce and the skills and knowledge that a country needs to remain competitive in the global marketplace. This gap is caused by a variety of factors, including lack of access to education and training, lack of investment in education and training programs, and a mismatch between the skills provided by education and training programs and the skills required in the workforce. Skills gaps are often large in developing countries, hampering their ability to compete with developed countries in terms of economic growth, innovation, and entrepreneurship (Lo, 2019). This gap can also limit the ability of people in these countries to secure good jobs and improve their living standards. Workers may be in short supply, hindering the development of these industries and limiting the ability of these countries to attract investment and create new job opportunities. The impact of the skills gap is not limited to individuals, it affects entire nations. An inadequately skilled and knowledgeable workforce can lead to a lack of economic growth, high unemployment, and a reduced ability to attract foreign investment. These issues can lead to a vicious cycle where underinvestment leads to underinvestment in employment opportunities, leading to underdevelopment of skills. Addressing the skills gap in developing countries is therefore critical to boosting economic growth, creating employment opportunities, and improving the living standards of individuals.

6 The Impact of the Skills Gap on the Competitiveness of Developing Countries

The skills gap is the mismatch between the skills workers have and the skills employers need in their workforce. In developing countries, this gap can have a significant impact on their competitiveness in the global market. International student mobility, or the movement of students from country to country for educational purposes, helps bridge the skills gap by providing access to quality education and skills. This creates a better-prepared workforce that can compete effectively in global markets and ultimately boost economic growth and development (Waters, 2006, 2009).

Skills gaps have a significant impact on the competitiveness of developing countries in global markets. Here's why:

- Firms lose productivity because it can be difficult to find workers with the skills needed to meet market demand.
- Skills shortages can force businesses to operate below capacity, slowing economic growth (Fakunle, 2021; Levent, 2016).
- Opportunities for employment and promotion are limited, as workers without the necessary qualifications cannot get higher paying jobs.

Bridging skills gaps through international student mobility is important because it can equip workers with the skills they need to compete in global markets, increase business productivity, drive economic growth, and create new job opportunities.

7 The Need for a Solution to Close the Skills Gap

Santandreu Calonge and Aman Shah (2016) used a qualitative lineage of existing literature to examine the impact of massive open online courses (MOOCs) on the skills gap between graduates and employers. The skills gap is the gap between the skills graduates possess and the skills employers need in their workforce. The results of this research show that MOOCs can fill this gap and help graduates develop the skills needed for employability.

Developing countries face significant challenges in improving their competitiveness in global markets, and bridging the skills gap is essential to meet these challenges. Traditional solutions such as in-country training programs and vocational training are often limited in access, quality, and scalability. In this context, the authors highlighted international student mobility as a promising solution for bridging the skills gap in developing countries. Access to quality education and training opportunities abroad equips students with the skills and knowledge they need to succeed in the global marketplace. This not only benefits individual students but also contributes to the development of the country's workforce, promoting economic growth and competitiveness in the global market. MOOCs and international student mobility offer promising solutions to the skills gap in developing countries. While MOOCs help graduates acquire the skills they need for employability, international student mobility is critical to developing a nation-wide workforce and advancing economic growth and competitiveness in global markets, providing access to quality education and training opportunities abroad that serve.

8 The Role of International Student Mobility in Closing the Skills Gap

By granting access to high-quality educational and training opportunities that can aid in the development of the skills and knowledge required to compete in the global market, international student mobility plays a significant role in bridging the skills gap. The following are just a few ways that international student mobility can close the skills gap:

1. Access to high-quality education and training: Students who study abroad have the chance to acquire education and training from some of the top colleges and institutes in the world (Banks & Bhandari, 2012).
2. Exposure to new ideas and cultures: Students who study abroad are exposed to different ideas and cultures, which can widen their perspectives and strengthen their ability to think critically and solve problems (Salleh & Sulaiman, 2013; Gregersen-Hermans, 2015).
3. Development of soft skills: Students who participate in international student exchange programs can enhance their social and communication abilities, which are highly desired by employers in the global market (Lo, 2019; Tran, 2016).
4. Enhanced language skills: Students have the chance to enhance their language skills while studying overseas, which can boost their employability and competitiveness in the global market (Roy et al., 2019).

Overall, by giving access to high-quality education and training, expanding horizons, and developing abilities that are in great demand on the international market, international student mobility plays a significant role in closing the skills gap.

9 Evidence of the Effectiveness of International Student Mobility in Closing the Skills Gap

The usefulness of international student mobility in bridging the skills gap is backed by a wealth of evidence. Among the crucial proofs are:

- Greater employability: According to studies, those who have studied abroad are more likely to get employment and make greater earnings than those who have not (Beaven & Borghetti, 2015).
- Enhanced language skills: It has been discovered that students who have studied abroad have improved language skills, which can increase their competitiveness in the international market (Roy et al., 2019).

- Development of transferable skills: International student mobility has been shown to promote the development of transferable skills such as critical thinking, problem solving, and adaptability, which are highly valued by employers (Rizvi, 2011).
- Positive impact on economic growth: Studies have shown that countries with higher international student mobility tend to have higher levels of economic growth and competitiveness in the global market (Levent, 2016).
- Better intercultural awareness: Studying abroad has been found to improve intercultural awareness and understanding, which can lead to better relations and greater cooperation between countries (Roy et al., 2019).

Overall, the evidence supports the conclusion that international student mobility can play an important role in reducing the skills gap and improving the competitiveness of developing countries in the global market (Waters, 2006, 2009).

10 The Benefits of International Student Mobility for the Students and the Host Country

International student mobility benefits both students and the host country. Some of the main advantages are:

For students:

- Access to quality education and training: Studying abroad offers students the opportunity to receive education and training from some of the world's leaders' universities and institutions (Weckstein, 2003).
- Communication with new people, ideas, and cultures: Studying abroad also exposes students to new things, ideas, and cultures that can broaden and strengthen their perspective, critical thinking, and problem-solving skills (Salleh & Sulaiman, 2013).

- Creation soft skills: International student mobility helps students develop important soft skills such as communication, teamwork, and adaptability which are very highly valued by employers in the global market (Roy et al., 2019).
- Improved language skills: Studying abroad also gives students an opportunity to improve their language skills, which can improve their skills, employment, and competitiveness in the global market (Roy et al., 2019).

For host country:

- Economic benefits: International students boost spending on tuition, housing, and other costs, which benefits the host nation's economy (Haussen & Uebelmesser, 2016).
- Cultural exchange: Encouraging international student mobility fosters cultural understanding and interchange, which can improve relations between nations (Fabricius et al., 2017).
- Greater diversity within the educational system: The educational system is enriched by the diversity that international students bring to it, which benefits all students.
- Better international reputation: Having overseas students can help the host nation's standing as an attractive location for study and research.

Globally speaking, access to high-quality education and training, cultural exchange, and economic advantages are all provided by the movement of foreign students.

11 The Benefits of International Student Mobility for Developing Countries

To increase their competitiveness in the global market, developing nations might use the potent tool of international student mobility. International student mobility offers developing nations a variety of advantages that can significantly advance their social and economic progress. The ability to access high-quality education and training is one of the main advantages of international student mobility. Students from poor nations can acquire education and training from some of the top colleges and institutions in the world by studying abroad, which can contribute to the development of the human capital required for economic growth and competitiveness (Levent, 2016). Additionally, international student mobility can encourage the exchange of knowledge and skills between nations. Studying abroad gives students the opportunity to gain information and skills that they can then use to advance their home nations' workforces and spur economic development (Knight, 2012). This may also result in a "brain gain" effect, whereby students who study abroad come home with priceless abilities and information that may promote competitiveness and economic growth (Gérard & Sanna, 2017).

Another advantage of international student mobility for developing nations is improved linguistic skills. Students who study abroad can develop their language skills, which will make them more employable and competitive on the international market. In a world where English is increasingly used for communication and international business, this can be very significant (Roy et al., 2019). Another significant advantage of the mobility of overseas students is their increased cultural understanding. International student mobility can result in improved ties and increased international cooperation through fostering cultural interchange and understanding (Bohman & Borglin, 2014; Roy et al., 2019). Building bridges and promoting more mutual understanding and collaboration among nations can do wonders for the expansion and development of the world economy.

Mobility among international students can also encourage entrepreneurship and creativity. Students can broaden their perspectives and boost their creativity by studying overseas, where they will be exposed to new concepts and technological advancements. Students may be motivated to become entrepreneurs and launch their own firms as they are exposed to new ideas and ways of thinking, which could result in the creation of jobs and economic growth in their home nations (Formica, 2002; García-Agustín et al., 2015). Additionally, students who study abroad could develop networks and relationships with people from other nations, which can be important for future business ventures. These connections may give students access to new markets, funding, and resources, which may support the expansion and prosperity of their businesses. Overall, international student mobility can be a significant factor in fostering entrepreneurship and innovation as well as helping to develop the human capital required for economic development and competitiveness in developing nations (Hou & Du, 2022).

In conclusion, increasing the mobility of international students can significantly improve developing nations' competitiveness in the global market (Wei, 2013). International student mobility can have a long-lasting effect on the economic and social development of developing nations by facilitating access to high-quality education and training, encouraging the transfer of skills and knowledge, enhancing language proficiency, and raising cultural awareness (Bohman & Borglin, 2014).

12 Challenges and Opportunities in Implementing International Student Mobility

(A). Challenges in implementing international student mobility:

- Cost: Because studying abroad can be costly, many students from developing nations may not have the financial means to take part in programs that promote international student mobility (Choudaha & De Wit, 2014).
- Lack of knowledge: It is possible that many students in developing nations are unaware of the opportunities for international study and may not have access to the knowledge and materials required to take part in these programs (Pagania et al., 2019).
- Visa restrictions: In addition to posing obstacles to international student mobility, visa regulations and other immigration laws can also prevent students from developing nations from taking part in these initiatives (Gallup-Black, 2004).
- Language barriers: Language barriers can significantly hinder students' academic success and their ability to fully engage in the cultural and social aspects of life in the host country while they are studying abroad (Souto-Otero et al., 2013).

(B). Opportunities for collaboration and cooperation between countries:

- Bilateral agreements: Nations can cooperate to create bilateral agreements that promote international student mobility, making it simpler for students to study abroad and for universities to work together on joint research and education projects (Ann, 2019).
- Joint programs and initiatives: Countries can also work together on joint programs and initiatives that support the growth of human capital and promote international student mobility, such as joint research projects and student exchange programs (Chi Hou et al., 2017).

(C). The role of universities and governments in promoting international student mobility:

- Universities: By providing degree programs and research opportunities that draw students from all over the world, universities play a crucial role in fostering international student mobility (Cheng, 2021). They can also offer guidance and tools to support students in adjusting to life abroad and achieving academic success.
- Governments: Governments can contribute to international student mobility by supporting programs for student exchange and by establishing laws that make it easier for students and researchers to move between nations. They can also work to loosen immigration laws and regulations that may restrict the mobility of international students.

13 Conclusion

Concluding their quest to increase competitiveness in the global market, developing nations can benefit from international student mobility in a variety of ways. Students from developing nations can access educational and training opportunities, build their human capital, and connect with new ideas, technologies, and networks by taking part in international student mobility programs. Globally speaking, developing countries face opportunities and challenges because of international student mobility. It is possible to overcome these obstacles and take advantage of the opportunities provided by international student mobility to increase the competitiveness of developing nations in the global market by collaborating and utilizing the assets and knowledge of universities and governments.

In their quest to increase competitiveness in the global market, developing nations can benefit from international student mobility in a variety of ways. Students from developing nations can access educational and training opportunities, build their human capital, and connect with new ideas, technologies, and networks by taking part in international student mobility programs.

The advantages of international student mobility for developing nations are as follows:

- Increased opportunities for education and training.
- Development of human capital.
- Promotion of entrepreneurship and innovation.
- Establishment of new linguistic and cultural ties.

Lastly, consider the significance of international student mobility in raising competitiveness. For developing nations looking to increase their competitiveness, international student mobility is a useful tool. The development of human capital as well as economic growth and innovation can be supported by international student mobility by giving students access to cutting-edge concepts, tools, and networks.

To promote international student mobility as a means of bridging the skills gap It is crucial for universities, governments, and other stakeholders to collaborate in promoting and supporting these programs in order to fully capitalize on the advantages of international student mobility. This might entail supporting student exchange initiatives with money and other resources, relaxing immigration laws and visa requirements, and promoting student study abroad opportunities. It is possible to support the development of human capital and increase the competitiveness of developing nations in the global market by taking steps to promote international student mobility.

References

Ann, H. (2019). Explaining international student mobility to Canada: A review. In *Outward and upward mobilities: International students in Canada, their families, and structuring institutions* (pp. 56–75). University of Toronto Press.

Banks, M., & Bhandari, R. (2012). *Global student mobility. The SAGE handbook of international higher education* (pp. 379–397). Palgrave Macmillan US.

Beaven, A., & Borghetti, C. (2015). Intercultural education for student mobility. *Intercultural Education, 26*(1), 7.

Bohman, D. M., & Borglin, G. (2014). Student exchange for nursing students: Does it raise cultural awareness'? A descriptive, qualitative study. *Nurse Education in Practice, 14*(3), 259–264.

Cheng, M. (2021). Shifting trends in international student mobility: Embracing diversity and responding to change. *Trends & Insights*, 1–6.

Chi Hou, A. Y., Hill, C., Chen, K. H. J., Tsai, S., & Chen, V. (2017). A comparative study of student mobility programs in SEAMEO-RIHED, UMAP, and campus Asia: Regulation, challenges, and impacts on higher education regionalization. *Higher Education Evaluation and Development, 11*(1), 12–24.

Choudaha, R., & De Wit, H. (2014). Challenges and opportunities for global student mobility in the future: A comparative and critical analysis. In *Internationalisation of higher education and global mobility* (p. 23). Symposium Books Ltd.

Dewey, J. (2021). *International student mobility*. Salem Press Encyclopedia.

Fabricius, A. H., Mortensen, J., & Haberland, H. (2017). The lure of internationalization: Paradoxical discourses of transnational student mobility, linguistic diversity and cross-cultural exchange. *Higher Education, 73*(4), 577–595.

Fakunle, O. (2021). Developing a framework for international students' rationales for studying abroad, beyond economic factors. *Policy Futures in Education, 19*(6), 671–690.

Formica, P. (2002). Entrepreneurial universities: The value of education in encouraging entrepreneurship. *Industry and Higher Education, 16*(3), 167–175.

Gallup-Black, A. (2004). *International student mobility: Project atlas* (Vol. 37, pp. 10–11). International Higher Education.

García-Agustín, P., Beas-Collado, M. I., & Ripollés-Meliá, M. (2015). UJI EMPREN: How to enhance entrepreneurship from the university side? In *INTED2015 Proceedings* (pp. 7070–7078). IATED.

Gérard, M., & Sanna, A. (2017). Students' mobility at a glance: Efficiency and fairness when brain drain, and brain gain are at stake. *Journal of international Mobility, 4*, 43–74.

Gregersen-Hermans, J. (2015). The impact of exposure to diversity in the international university environment and the development of intercultural competence in students. In *The European higher education area: Between critical reflections and future policies* (pp. 73–92). Springer.

Haussen, T., & Uebelmesser, S. (2016). Student and graduate migration and its effect on the financing of higher education. *Education Economics, 24*(6), 573–591.

Hou, C., & Du, D. (2022). The changing patterns of international student mobility: A network perspective. *Journal of Ethnic and Migration Studies, 48*(1), 248–272.

King, R. (2003). International student migration in Europe and the institutionalisation of identity as 'Young Europeans'. In *Migration and immigrants: Between policy and reality. Essays in honour of Hans Van Amersfoort* (pp. 155–179). Aksant Academic Publishers.

Knight, J. (2012). Student mobility and internationalization: Trends and tribulations. *Research in Comparative and International Education, 7*(1), 20–33.

Levent, F. (2016). The economic impacts of international student mobility in the globalization process. *Journal of Human Sciences, 13*(3), 3853–3870.

Lo, W. Y. W. (2019). Beyond competition: A comparative review of conceptual approaches to international student mobility. *Globalisation, Societies and Education, 17*(3), 261–273.

Lu, Y., Zong, L., & Schissel, B. (2009). To stay or return: Migration intentions of students from People's Republic of China in Saskatchewan, Canada. *Journal of International Migration and Integration/Revue de l'integration et de la migration internationale, 10*, 283–310.

OECD. (2019). *Education at a glance 2019*. OECD.

Pagania, R. N., et al. (2019). Key factors in university-to-university knowledge and technology transfer on international student mobility. *Knowledge Management Research & Practice, 18*(4), 405–423.

Rizvi, F. (2011). Theorizing student mobility in an era of globalization. *Teachers and Teaching, 17*(6), 693–701.

Roy, A., Newman, A., Ellenberger, T., & Pyman, A. (2019). Outcomes of international student mobility programs: A systematic review and agenda for future research. *Studies in Higher Education, 44*(9), 1630–1644.

Salleh, K. M., & Sulaiman, N. L. (2013). Malaysia leadership competencies: A model for effective performance. *International Journal of Human Resource Management and Research, 3*(2), 63–70.
Santandreu Calonge, D., & Aman Shah, M. (2016). MOOCs, graduate skills gaps, and employability: A qualitative systematic review of the literature. *The International Review of Research in Open and Distance Learning, 17*(5), 67–90.
Souto-Otero, M., Huisman, J., Beerkens, M., De Wit, H., & Vujić, S. (2013). Barriers to international student mobility: Evidence from the Erasmus program. *Educational Researcher, 42*(2), 70–77.
Tran, L. T. (2016). Mobility as 'becoming': A Bourdieuian analysis of the factors shaping international student mobility. *British Journal of Sociology of Education, 37*(8), 1268–1289.
Tremblay, K. (2005). Academic mobility and immigration. *Journal of Studies in International Education, 9*(3), 196–228.
Waters, J. L. (2006). Geographies of cultural capital: Education, international migration and family strategies between Hong Kong and Canada. *Transactions of the Institute of British Geographers, 31*(2), 179–192.
Waters, J. (2009). In pursuit of scarcity: Transnational students, 'employability', and the MBA. *Environment and Planning A, 41*(8), 1865–1883.
Weckstein, P. (2003). Accountability and student mobility under title I of the no child left behind act. *Journal of Negro Education, 72*, 117–125.
Wei, H. (2013). An empirical study on the determinants of international student mobility: A global perspective. *Higher Education, 66*, 105–122.
Zainab, B., Javed, B., Zakai, S. N., & Malik, S. (2019). Perceptions of international student mobility: A qualitative case study. *Journal of Education and Educational Development, 6*(2), 269–287.

Corporate Governance as a Catalyst to Performance of Banks in Ghana: The Moderating Role of Firm Controls and Strategy

Clement Dodoo, Fred A. Yamoah, and Adnan ul Haque

1 Introduction

Lately, corporate governance has become an inevitably significant phenomenon fundamentally due to the corporate outrage's quantity, which has led to a decline in investor esteem, a decline in speculator certainty and occasionally huge bank disappointments (Klapper & Love, 2004). For investors, an incentive can be guaranteed through practical corporate

C. Dodoo
Integration & Remedial Management, Equity Group Holdings PLC, Nairobi, Kenya

F. A. Yamoah (✉)
Department of Management, School of Business, Economics and Informatics, Birkbeck, University of London, London, UK
e-mail: f.yamoah@bbk.ac.uk

A. ul Haque
Faculty of Business, Yorkville University, Toronto, ON, Canada

F. A. Yamoah, A. ul Haque (eds.), *Corporate Management Ecosystem in Emerging Economies*, https://doi.org/10.1007/978-3-031-41578-4_6

governance, guaranteeing the proper utilization of firms' assets, improving speculator certainty and empowering access to capital (Denis & McConnell, 2003). With respect to the governance procedures of money and related framework, concerns have been raised, and this is predominantly due to the expanding government weight and universal organizations such as IMF, IFC and the World Bank. These improvements are depended upon the suggestions for the owners, boards and the management of banks.

In the late 1980s and mid-2000s, Ghana experienced comprehensive monetary and budgetary changes. The significant budgetary division change was an attempt to improve how banks are administered. The local actions at transforming Ghana's corporate governance corresponded with the Bank of Ghana endeavours at improving the effectiveness of the bank governance structures. For instance, the Bank of Ghana tried to modify corporate governance practices in states to ensure the money keeps qualified and capable sheets of chiefs, the mixing of official and non-official executives, and interior control and bookkeeping strategy manuals (Asiedu-Mante, 1998).

The aim of this article is to evaluate corporate governance as a catalyst to performance of banks in Ghana, specifically considering the moderating role of firm controls and strategy.

The research is significant in contributing to the knowledge of corporate governance in two ways. As the focus of the field of corporate governance has been primarily on board size, foreign ownership, board composition, and their impact on firm performance, with limited theoretical and empirical research on how firm strategies and control policies could impact these relationships. This research begins to address this imbalance. Secondly, the acceptance of the notion that firm strategies and control policies lead to bank's financial gains. Therefore, the use of control policies and corporate strategies as a moderator in the association between board characteristics and financial performance will deliver empirical evidence of the influence of firm strategies and control policies to financial performance in corporate governance. Moreover, the study presents a clear idea of how applied as a management tool to attain success.

2 Literature Review

Originated from a Greek word "kyberman" and derived from Latin, it is identified as "gubernare" and in French was known "governor". In furthermost of the contexts, it correlated to the act of governing. Governance is identical with the "direction and control" and "exercise of authority" (Zingales, 1998, p. 2). The term "governance" indeed evolved over time. Various definitions can be termed as a narrow view and a broad view of corporate governance. The narrow view defines corporate governance from the perspective of the relationship amid the organization and the shareholders and the means of satisfying the shareholders' interests, whereas broad perspective defines it as more encompassing, connecting not only the organisations' association with shareholders but all other stakeholders such as employees, customers, suppliers, bondholders and others. The complex and dynamic nature of the banking industry, with its constantly evolving regulatory and market environments, creates unique challenges for boards and governance structures. In this context, there is a widely held view that the unique nature of banking institutions presents challenges for effective corporate governance, regardless of whether they are in developed or developing economies. This view is supported by research conducted by Macey and O'Hara (2016).

In a broader context, financial performance is defined as the degree to which financial objectives are or have been achieved. In this light, the return on value is a degree that demonstrates to speculators the benefit that is being produced from the capital contributed by the investors (Epps & Cereola, 2008). This study uses agency theory and the resource-based view theory to describe the association between performance moderated by firm controls, strategy and corporate governance.

The current study's theoretical framework is founded on agency theory. Agency theory emerged from the Berle and Means work (Berle & Means, 1932). In this study, the clear inference for corporate governance from an agency theory perspective is that satisfactory monitoring or control mechanisms are required to be developed to protect shareholders from management's conflicts of interest; the so-called agency costs of modern capitalism (Kiel & Nicholson, 2003; Fama & Jensen, 1983).

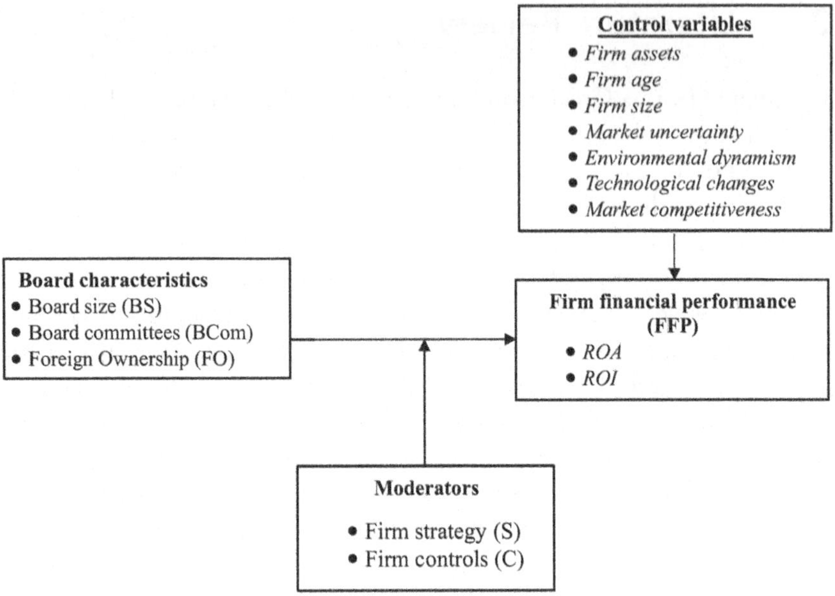

Fig. 1 Conceptual model

According to resource-based view theory, a firm's ability to achieve sustained competitive advantage depends on its ability to develop and leverage these resources effectively.

The study demonstrated the influence on firm performance of board characteristics considering the control systems and strategies put in place. Consequently, this study proposes the conceptual model indicated as below (Fig. 1):

3 Hypotheses Development

There are deviating perspectives regarding the relationship between the firm's performance and board's size. According to the agency theory model, the board is accountable for controlling and managerial monitoring, addressing the agency problems related with the managers opportunistic inclinations. Whereas the agency perspective is that a larger board is well equipped to conduct the monitoring function due to the higher number of directors in such regard, there have been statements for consideration of context related ideal board size (Fama & Jensen, 1983). Therefore, the study hypothesises that:

H_1: There is a positive relationship between board size and financial performance.

To deal with technical matters, the board committees consist of directors whereas the full board may not have enough time to give in-depth consideration (Puni, 2015). These committees are audit, remuneration and nomination. The audit committee assists board and shareholder in audit, internal control functions and financial reporting (Cadbury, 1992).

To ensure the firm has relevant board composition and membership characteristics to match the firm's environment, the nomination committee takes that responsibility. On the other hand, compensation or remuneration helps the board of directors in founding and monitoring remunerations in various forms as recompense and incentives for directors and all board members (Cadbury, 1992; OECD, 2015).

As per the agency theory framework, executive compensation can have a significant impact on executive behaviour and performance. Incentive-driven compensation systems, such as performance-based pay or equity-based compensation, can motivate executives (Bosse & Phillips, 2016; Van Puyvelde et al., 2012; Walsh & Seward, 1990). There have been varied results from studies on remuneration committees' effect on firm performance. The study hypothesises that:

H_2: There is a positive and significant effect of board committee effectiveness on bank performance.

Agency theory proposes that since the stakes of foreign corporate ownership are greater and less fragmented compared to the stakes held by shareholders of foreign institutions, the rewards of these higher shareholders are more aligned to achieve an effective monitoring role. As per Chhibber and Majumdar (1999), the degree of a foreign firm's control over a domestic firm is certainly associated with the degree of resource commitment to technology transfer. Moreover, Dhar and Ganguly

(1988) study revealed that foreign-controlled companies have business relations beyond mere equity participation. Therefore, the study hypothesises that:

H_3: There is a positive relationship between foreign ownership and financial performance.

As utilized in the study, the moderating role of firm strategy relates to the diverse objectives and interests of top management and key shareholders. An effective firm strategy defines a correct balance amid stakeholder and management interests to minimize the dysfunctional conflicts in teams collaborating. Thus, the study hypothesises that:

H_4: The positive relationship between board size and firm financial performance will be high when there are effective firm strategies than in cases where there are ineffective firm strategies in the firm.

The role of the firm's strategy in establishing a positive association amid its financial performance and board committees puts significant consideration on two main strategies that enable the firm to be distinctive. That is, committee members with diverse experiences assist in forming strategies that provide firms with innovative ways to develop new products (Duru et al., 2016). Effective firm strategies assist board members to come up with novel ideas to reach greater market and enhance the firm's image. Therefore, the study hypothesises that:

H_5: The positive relationship between board committees and firm financial performance will be high when there are effective firm strategies than in cases where there are ineffective firm strategies in the firm.

The firm's strategy plays a vital role in the dependency of the ownership structures that are at play in firms. In addition, the foreign ownership characteristics of boards encourage the greater cost leadership inspiring the use of cost reduction measures by executives that have always been in place in firm's operations without compromising on the goods and services quality produced by firms (Bhatt & Bhatt, 2017). Thus, the study hypothesises that:

H_6: The positive relationship between foreign ownership and firm financial performance will be high when there are effective firm strategies than in cases where there are ineffective firm strategies in the firm.

The impactful roles of firm controls on the association amid firm's financial performance and board characteristics narrate to external and internal controls introduced within such firms. Firms with appropriate internal controls in place are more likely to enhance the operational efficiency required to attain greater levels of financial gains in contrast to the firms that do not undertake correct internal and external controls (Hoskisson et al., 2017). From this argument, the researcher suggests that:

H_7: The positive relationship between board size and firm financial performance will be high when there are effective firm controls than in cases where there are ineffective firm controls in the firm.

The firm's undertaking of preventive and protective activity is always a central view in the evaluation of the moderating role of the positive relatioinship between board committes and firm control and its financial performance. The firms with control structures often make greater returns on investment in contrast to those who do not uphold some of these structures (Fernández-Gago et al., 2016). Amid board members and other management, the correct separation of duties and responsibilities can ensure that no single individual is permitted all powers to record, undertake authorization, and undertake entire financial transactions in firm without others' involvement (Fuzi et al., 2016). There, the study hypothesises that:

H_8: The positive relationship between board committees and firm financial performance will be high when there are good and strong firm controls than in cases where there are weak firm controls in the firm.

Despite the board members ownership of the firm, there is a necessity for firms to ensure the measures are in place to prevent the collusion of internal control when needed (Hoskisson et al., 2018). Moreover, there is a positive impact when there is an efficient separation of duties amid foreign-owned firms instituting internal control measures, leading to the positive impact on the firm's financial performance (Volonté & Gantenbein, 2016). The researcher hypothesizes that:

H_9: The positive relationship between foreign ownership and firm financial performance will be high when there are effective firm controls than in cases where there are ineffective firm controls in the firm.

4 Research Methodology

Study has a realism ontological stance by exploring the reality as an independent subject with clear objectivity. The epistemological stance is to know the truth about existing variables from the literature. Thus, this research falls into the positivist paradigm. The study employed causal relationship assessment to discover the corporate governance practices that impact the bank's performance in Ghana. Hence, explanatory research design has been considered. Board members and management position holders of Ghana's commercial bank are the population of the study. We employed purposive sampling as it helps in the selection of a specific audience (Haque et al., 2018). Moreover, random sampling was used to select the directors, board members and managers of the chosen commercial banks. From a list of all board of directors and management members from the Bank of Ghana, a sample of 400 respondents were randomly selected. As per the BOG sampling frame, the estimated number of board members and management members is 800. The study used Cochran's formula to calculate an ideal sample size, given a desired level of precision, desired confidence level and the estimated proportion of the attribute present in the population.

The Cochran formula is:

$$n = \frac{Z^2 pq}{e^2}$$

Where:

e is the desired level of precision (i.e., the margin of error),
p is the (estimated) proportion of the population which has the attribute in question,
q is $1 - p$.

The confidence level corresponds to a *Z*-score. This is a constant value needed for this equation. Here are the *z*-scores for the most common confidence levels:

- 90% – *Z* Score = 1.645
- 95% – *Z* Score = 1.96
- 99% – *Z* Score = 2.326

The study employed a 95% confidence level with its corresponding *Z* score and used an error of margin of 0.05. Thus, sample approximation derived is mathematically presented as follows:

$$n = \frac{(1.96)^2 (0.5)(0.5)}{(0.05)^2} = 384$$

A total of 400 questionnaires were sent out to respondents which was considered an adequate representation of the population.

At the respondent's respective bank in Accra, the questionnaires were administered. The data was collected over eight-week period. At the end, two hundred and seventy-four (274) questionnaires were retrieved, yielding a response rate of 68.5%. At the end of the checks, three (3) questionnaires were found to be incomplete and were discarded concluding that the study documented approximately, 67.8% net response rate.

Five-point Likert scale developed from the literature at hand was used, also reflecting content validity through pre-existing literature work (Creswell, 2014). The common method variance was confirmed through the obtained data by the exploratory factor analysis (Varimax rotation). Face-to-face survey was considered for data collection method. IBM SPSS version 25 software was used to conduct analysis, followed by the confirmatory factor analysis using AMOS 25. The confidentiality and anonymity of the respondents were ensured during and after the research.

5 Results, Findings and Discussion

Descriptive Statistics (Table 1)

The study's main target population for primary data was the heads of department and board members of commercial banks in Ghana. The study measured 271 respondents in the final analysis, including managers (21.4%), heads of unit (26.2%), executive committee members (7.7%), directors (2.6%), executive directors (1.5%), CEO/MD (1.5%), board chairmen (0.7%) and other positions of influence (38.4%) (Table 2).

The variables of corporate governance comprised foreign ownership, firm controls, financial performance, assets and liability committee, risk management committee, board size, audit committee, board composition and firm strategy, whereas the control variables were market, environmental dynamism, competitiveness and uncertainty and technology uncertainty.

Hierarchical regression analysis was used to test the study hypotheses. The relationship between financial performance of banks in Ghana and corporate governance variables, moderated by firm controls and strategy, was measured. The variables of the corporate governance considered were board composition, board size and foreign ownership (Tables 3 and 4).

A significant positive relationship between board size and financial performance was observed. Moreover, a significant positive association was observed between financial performance and board composition. In addition, a positive relationship between foreign ownership and financial performance was detected, though it was not significant. These findings lend support to the first two hypotheses of this study. Thus, two of the corporate governance variables, board size and board composition, had significant positive impact on the financial performance of banks in Ghana. The third hypothesis, however, was not supported in this case.

The relationship between firm strategy and financial performance as well as firm controls and financial performance was primarily explored. Firm controls were positively and significantly related to financial performance; however, firm strategy was negatively and trivially related to financial performance. Additionally, the study discovered that firm

Table 1 Background information

Variable	Characteristics	Frequency	Percent
Gender	Male	163	60.1
	Female	108	39.9
Age	20–30 years	43	15.9
	31–40 years	163	60.1
	41–50 years	56	20.7
	51–60 years	9	3.3
Education	PhD/DBA	12	4.4
	Masters	99	36.5
	Bachelors	151	55.7
	HND	6	2.2
	Others	1	0.4
	No response	2	0.7
Position	Board chairman	2	0.7
	Director	7	2.6
	Executive director	4	1.5
	CEO/MD	4	1.5
	Executive committee member	21	7.7
	Head of unit	71	26.2
	Manager	58	21.4
	Others	104	38.4
Years of operations	Below 3 years	5	1.8
	4–6 years	37	13.7
	7–9 years	23	8.5
	10–12 years	20	7.4
	13–15 years	37	13.7
	16 years and above	149	55.0
Total assets	Less than GHc500 million	7	2.6
	GHc501-1billion	66	24.4
	GHc1-2billion	105	38.7
	Above GHc 2billion	93	34.3

Source: Author's Fieldwork

strategy does not moderate the positive relationship amid board size and financial performance. Though, firm strategy meaningfully moderates the positive relationship amid board composition and firm financial performance. Moreover, firm strategy did not meaningfully moderate the association between foreign ownership and financial performance. The fifth study hypothesis was supported, whereas hypotheses four (4) and six (6) were not supported in this case. Furthermore, the study revealed that firm controls meaningfully moderate the association between board size

Table 2 Corporate governance variables

Variable	Characteristics	*f*	%
Board size	10 or less	82	30.3
	11 to 20	71	26.2
	21 to 30	40	14.8
	31 to 40	28	10.3
	41 and above	50	18.5
Board composition	IDs to RDs (%25–%100)	53	19.6
	IDs to RDs (%50–%100)	121	44.6
	IDs to RDs (%75–%100)	77	28.4
	No IDs	20	7.4
Audit	The percentage of independent directors on the audit committee (%25–%100)	67	24.7
	The percentage of independent directors on the audit committee (%50–%100)	104	38.4
	The percentage of independent directors on the audit committee (%75–%100)	80	29.5
	No percentage of independent directors on the audit committee	20	7.4
Governance, nomination and remuneration	The percentage of independent directors on the committee (%25–%100)	71	26.2
	The percentage of independent directors on the committee (%50–%100)	113	41.7
	The percentage of independent directors on the committee (%75%–%100)	65	24.0
	No percentage of independent directors on the committee	22	8.1
Assets and liability	The percentage of independent directors on the committee (%25–%100)	90	33.2
	The percentage of independent directors on the committee (%50–%100)	99	36.5
	The percentage of independent directors on the committee (%75–%100)	60	22.1
	No percentage of independent directors on the committee	22	8.1
Risk management	The percentage of independent directors on the committee (%25–%100)	95	35.1
	The percentage of independent directors on the committee (%50–%100)	97	35.8
	The percentage of independent directors on the committee (%75–%100)	61	22.5
	No percentage of independent directors on the committee.	18	6.6
Foreign ownership	FWFO (%25–%100)	21	7.7
	FWFO (%50–%100)	100	36.9
	FWFO (%75–%100)	72	26.6
	Firm without foreign ownership	78	28.8

Source: Author's Fieldwork

Table 3 Regression results of the effect of corporate governance and financial performance moderated by firm controls and strategies

	Financial performance		
	Model 1	Model 2	Model 3
Variables	*b* (*t*-values)	*b* (*t*-values)	*b* (*t*-values)
Control variables			
Constant	-0.207 (-0.957)	-0.309 (-1.641)	-0.322 (-1.711)$^{+}$
Total assets (dummy)	0.381 (5.463)***	0.042 (0.611)	0.042 (0.605)
Firm age (dummy)	0.001 (0.058)	0.004 (0.236)	0.012 (0.620)
Employee size (log)	0.025 (0.837)	0.055 (2.068)*	0.054 (2.008)*
Market competitiveness and uncertainty	0.020 (0.355)	0.057 (1.167)	0.088 (1.800)$^{+}$
Environmental dynamism	-0.053 (-0.915)	-0.114 (-2.332)*	-0.124 (-2.506)*
Technology uncertainty	0.095 (2.855)**	0.105 (3.625)***	0.112 (3.953)***
Independent variable			
Board size		0.167 (3.950)***	0.187 (4.426)***
Board composition		0.184 (3.448)***	0.182 (3.385)***
Foreign ownership		0.102 (1.842)$^{+}$	0.077 (1.411)
Firm strategy		-0.025 (-0.543)	-0.023 (-0.472)
Firm controls		0.453 (7.371)***	0.434 (6.974)***
Interaction effect			
Firm strategy × board size			-0.057 (-0.876)
× Board composition			0.107 (2.188)*
× Foreign ownership			-0.032 (-0.418)
Firm controls × board size			0.296 (3.941)***
× Board composition			0.164 (1.914)$^{+}$
× Foreign ownership			0.159 (1.902)$^{+}$
R^2	0.167	0.443	0.492
F value	7.205***	15.228***	11.678***
ΔR^2		0.276	0.049
Partial *F* value		20.877***	3.325***
Degrees of freedom	6/216	11/211	17/205
Durbin Waston test	1.820		

Note: Unstandardized regression coefficients were reported with *t*-values for each effect in parentheses. $^{+}p<0.10$, $^{*}p<0.05$, $^{**}p<0.01$, $^{***}p<0.001$ (two-tailed test)

and financial performance, board composition and financial performance, as well as the association amid foreign ownership and financial performance. These findings are in support of the study hypotheses seven (7) and eight (8), considered in the study. The study discovered that firm controls significantly moderate the relationship between foreign ownership and financial performance, supporting hypothesis nine (9). These

Table 4 Summary of hypotheses

Hypothesis	Expected outcome	Empirical conclusions	Outcome
There is a positive relationship between board size and financial performance	+	Supported	Significant
There is a positive and significant effect of board committee effectiveness on bank performance	+	Supported	Significant
There is a positive relationship between foreign ownership and financial performance	+	Not supported	Not significant
The positive relationship between board size and firm financial performance will be high when there are effective firm strategies than in cases where there are ineffective firm strategies in the firm	+	Not supported	Not significant
The positive relationship between board committees and firm financial performance will be high when there are effective firm strategies than in cases where there are ineffective firm strategies in the firm	+	Supported	Significant
The positive relationship between foreign ownership and firm financial performance will be high when there are effective firm strategies than in cases where there are ineffective firm strategies in the firm	+	Not supported	Not significant
The positive relationship between board size and firm financial performance will be high when there are effective firm controls than in cases where there are ineffective firm controls in the firm	+	Supported	Significant
The positive relationship between board committees and firm financial performance will be high when there are good and strong firm controls than in cases where there are weak firm controls in the firm	+	Supported	Significant

(*continued*)

Table 4 (continued)

Hypothesis	Expected outcome	Empirical conclusions	Outcome
The positive relationship between foreign ownership and firm financial performance will be high when there are effective firm controls than in cases where there are ineffective firm controls in the firm	+	Supported	Significant

results suggest that situations where there is larger board size with independent directors as well as the involvement foreign owners, the bank tend to be financially sound especially when there is effective control mechanism with risk management procedures and policies laid down to follow, operations policy, a treasury and market risk policy, credit policy in anti-money laundering policy in place and it is effectively applied.

6 Conclusion and Recommendations

The findings of the study suggest that the characteristics of the board of directors can positively influence a company's financial performance. This supports the agency theory's focus on the board as a key monitoring mechanism, as well as the resource dependency theory's emphasis on effective resource management. By selecting board members with the right skills and experience, companies can help ensure that they are able to effectively manage their resources and maximize financial performance. The study found a positive relationship between certain corporate governance characteristics (board size, board committee, and foreign ownership) and financial performance. This supports the idea that the composition and structure of a company's board of directors can have an impact on its financial outcomes. Moreover, these results suggest that having a larger board and specialized committees can positively impact a company's financial performance. On the other hand, the study did not find a significant relationship between foreign ownership and financial performance. This suggests that the influence of foreign ownership on financial performance may be more nuanced and context-dependent and cannot be generalized across all companies or industries.

The study also found support for the resource-based theory, which emphasizes the role of a firm's resources and capabilities in shaping its performance. Specifically, the relationship between corporate governance characteristics and financial performance was moderated by the different strategies and control systems in place within the firm. Furthermore, in situations where a company had a large board with independent board committees and foreign ownership, and had effective control mechanisms with risk management procedures and policies in place, the company tended to be financially sound. Additionally, in conjunction with the independence of the board and diverse committee, the company was able to engage in strategic revisions such as opening foreign markets, outsourcing, diversification or developing know-how, and instituting efficient internal operational systems. The study's findings contribute to the existing literature on corporate governance and financial performance in several ways.

The study supports the use of both agency theory and resource-based theory in assessing the relationship between corporate governance and financial performance. This suggests that both theories have merit in explaining how corporate governance affects a company's financial outcomes, and that a comprehensive understanding of this relationship requires consideration of both agency and resource-based factors. Secondly, the study highlights the importance of firm strategies and control systems in moderating the relationship between corporate governance and financial performance.

Based on the analysis and conclusion, we recommend the following:

Establish Good Relationship Between Board of Directors and Management

The study's findings suggest that there is a strong relationship between good corporate governance and increased financial performance in banks. This implies that companies that prioritize corporate governance practices are more likely to achieve better financial outcomes. Given these findings, it is important for both boards and senior managers to be aware of the inter-relationships between corporate governance and financial performance in their institutions. They should make efforts to ensure that their corporate governance practices are effective and aligned with the company's goals and strategies, and that they have appropriate control systems and risk management procedures in place.

Promote Good Corporate Governance

The findings of the study have important implications for the corporate governance practices of commercial banks in Ghana. The study recommends that commercial banks focus on their board size and composition to signal to potential investors and depositors that they prioritize good corporate governance practices. The study suggests that most non-executive directors should be included on the board to bring independence of mind and judgement on issues of strategy and governance.

Develop New Strategies and Have Firm Controls over Management

The study's findings suggest that the effectiveness of corporate governance practices in promoting financial performance is contingent upon the presence of appropriate firm controls and risk management procedures. The study recommends that firms with large board sizes should implement controls to ensure compliance with laws and regulations and to promote accurate financial reporting and timely delivery of financial documents. This can help companies identify areas where they are not achieving success and revise their strategies accordingly, which can ultimately improve their financial performance.

References

Asiedu-Mante, E. (1998). Financial markets in Ghana. In *Issues in central banking and bank distress*. WAIFEM.

Berle, A., & Means, G. (1932). *The modern corporation and private property*. Commerce Clearing House.

Bhatt, P. R., & Bhatt, R. R. (2017). Corporate governance and firm performance in Malaysia. *Corporate Governance, 17*(5), 896–912. https://doi.org/10.1108/CG-03-2016-0054

Bosse, D. A., & Phillips, R. A. (2016). Agency theory and bounded self-interest. *The Academy of Management Review, 41*(2), 276–297. http://www.jstor.org/stable/24906232

Cadbury, A. (1992). *Report of the committee on the financial aspects of corporate governance*. Gee & Co. Ltd.

Chhibber, P. K., & Majumdar, S. K. (1999). Foreign ownership and profitability: Property rights, control, and the performance of firms in Indian industry. *The Journal of Law and Economics, 42*(1), 209–238. https://doi.org/10.1086/467423

Creswell, J. W. (2014). *Research design: Qualitative, quantitative and mixed methods approaches* (4th ed.). Sage.

Denis, D. K., & McConnell, J. J. (2003). International corporate governance. *Journal of Financial and Quantitative Analysis, 38*(1), 1–36.

Dhar, A., & Ganguly, P. (1988). Altered expression of platelet surface glycoproteins during storage. *British Journal of Haematology, 70*(1), 71–75. https://doi.org/10.1111/j.1365-2141.1988.tb02436.x

Duru, A., Iyengar, R. J., & Zampelli, E. M. (2016). The dynamic relationship between CEO duality and firm performance: The moderating role of board independence. *Journal of Business Research, 69*(10), 4269–4277. Elsevier.

Epps, R. W., & Cereola, S. J. (2008). Do institutional shareholder services (ISS) corporate governance ratings reflect a company's operating performance? *Critical Perspectives on Accounting, Elsevier, 19*(8), 1135–1148.

Fama, E. F., & Jensen, M. C. (1983). Separation of ownership and control. *The Journal of Law & Economics, 26*(2), 301–325. http://www.jstor.org/stable/725104

Fernández-Gago, R., Cabeza-García, L., & Nieto, M. (2016). Corporate social responsibility, board of directors, and firm performance: An analysis of their relationships. *Review of Managerial Science, 10*(1), 85–104. Springer.

Fuzi, S. F., Halim, S. A., & Julizaerma, M. K. (2016). Board independence and firm performance. *Procedia Economics and Finance, 37*, 460–465. https://doi.org/10.1016/s2212-5671(16)30152-6

Haque, A. U., Aston, J., & Kozlovski, E. (2018). The impact of stressors on organizational commitment of managerial and non-managerial personnel in contrasting economies: Evidences from Canada and Pakistan. *International Journal of Business, 23*(2), 166.

Hoskisson, R. E., Chirico, F., Zyung, J., & (Daniel), & Gambeta, E. (2017). Managerial risk taking: A multitheoretical review and future research agenda. *Journal of Management, 43*(1), 137–169. https://doi.org/10.1177/0149206316671583

Hoskisson, R. E., Gambeta, E., Green, C. D., & Li, T. X. (2018). Is my firm-specific investment protected? Overcoming the stakeholder investment dilemma in the resource-based view. *Academy of Management Review, 43*(2), 284–306.

Kiel, G. C., & Nicholson, G. J. (2003). Board composition and corporate performance: How the Australian experience informs contrasting theories of corporate governance. *Corporate Governance: An International Review, 11*(3), 189–205.

Klapper, L. F., & Love, I. (2004). Corporate governance, investor protection, and performance in emerging markets. *Journal of Corporate Finance, 10*(5), 703–728.

Macey, J. R., & O'Hara, M. (2016). Bank corporate governance: A proposal for the post-crisis world. *Economic Policy Review, 22*, 85–105.

OECD. (2015). *G20/OECD principles of corporate governance*. OECD Publishing. https://doi.org/10.1787/9789264236882-en

Puni, A. (2015). Do board committees affect corporate financial performance? Evidence from listed companies in Ghana. *International Journal of Business and Management Review, 3*(5), 14–25.

Van Puyvelde, S., Caers, R., Du Bois, C., & Jegers, M. (2012). The governance of nonprofit organizations: Integrating agency theory with stakeholder and stewardship theories. *Nonprofit and Voluntary Sector Quarterly, 41*(3), 431–451. https://doi.org/10.1177/0899764011409757

Volonté, C., & Gantenbein, P. (2016). Directors' human capital, firm strategy, and firm performance, Journal of Management & Governance, Springer. *Accademia Italiana di Economia Aziendale (AIDEA), 20*(1), 115–145.

Walsh, J. P., & Seward, J. K. (1990). On the efficiency of internal and external corporate control mechanisms. *The Academy of Management Review, 15*(3), 421–458. https://doi.org/10.2307/258017

Zingales, L. (1998). Corporate governance. The New Palgrave Dictionary of Economics and the Law, 1998, https://doi.org/10.2139/ssrn.46906.

A Framework for Understanding Agribusiness Stakeholders Decision-Making Dynamics in the Pesticide Industry of Pakistan

Muhammad Imran, Ayesha Nida, and Fred A. Yamoah

1 Introduction

The overall population of the world is estimated to rise to 9 billion by 2050 (Gerland et al., 2014). To oblige this expansion in world population, food production will essentially have to rise too. In any case, new cultivate-able land is restricted, so sustainable production and increasing productivity of existing cultivated land is a significant angle to address

M. Imran
School of Business Management, Kedah, Malaysia

A. Nida
Institute of Business Management and Administrative Sciences,
The Islamic University of Bahawalpur, Bahawalpur, Pakistan

F. A. Yamoah (✉)
Department of Management, School of Business, Economics and Informatics,
Birkbeck, University of London, London, UK
e-mail: f.yamoah@bbk.ac.uk

F. A. Yamoah, A. ul Haque (eds.), *Corporate Management Ecosystem in Emerging Economies*, https://doi.org/10.1007/978-3-031-41578-4_7

global food security (Popp et al., 2013). Most agricultural products depend on the utilization of chemicals to keep up high crop yields. The utilization of these chemicals in current agrarian practices is seen as a fundamental part of the rise of the agricultural industry. Be that as it may, a large portion of the pesticides applied to cultivated lands may affect non-target organisms and taint soil and water resources (Damalas & Eleftherohorinos, 2011). Lately, there has been an expanding worry that pesticides comprise a risk to the general public through deposits in the food supply. There is a need to decide the degree of the genuine issue concerning the utilization of pesticides. Pesticides are chemical substances used to terminate animals, herbs, insects, and pests in agricultural, household, and industrial setting. The primary groups of ordinarily used pesticides comprise herbicides (used to terminate herbs/plants), insecticides (used to kill insects), fungicides (used to kill fungus), fumigants, and rodenticides (Xu et al., 2018). In particular, the use of protective measures for pesticides (PPBs), enforced by WPS—including long-sleeved shirts, long trousers closed footwear, tidy work clothing, and soap cleaning—could reduce exposure to agricultural pesticides and potentially minimize adverse health outcomes (Curwin et al., 2003; Ekqvist et al., 2019). Unsafe pesticide usage relates to increased hazards to human health, whereas pesticide safety and adequate hygiene procedures are desirable safety behaviors that can lower these risks (Hashemi et al., 2012; Fan et al., 2015). Several studies, however, have demonstrated that, despite clear awareness of the negative effects of pesticides (Abdollahzadeh et al., 2016), farmers fail to use precautionary measures to reduce the occurrence of poisoning (Hashemi et al., 2012). Organochlorine, organophosphate, and carbamate insecticides are of leading interest because of their toxicity and persistence in the ecosystem. Organochlorine insecticides are banned for agricultural and domestic use in most of the developed countries, but they are still used in some non-western developing countries. Most of the pesticides are broad-spectrum and kill both target and non-target objects (Ekqvist et al., 2019).

This research will answer the following questions:

(i) Does the knowledge of pesticide use influence the protective behavior concerning pesticide use?
(ii) Does the intention to reduce pesticide use influence the protective behavior concerning pesticide use?
(iii) Does the past health experience with pesticide influence the protective behavior concerning pesticide use?
(iv) Does the attitude toward pesticides use mediates the relationship between knowledge of pesticide use and protective behavior concerning pesticide use?
(v) Does the attitude toward pesticides use mediates the relationship between intention to reduce pesticide use and protective behavior concerning pesticide use?
(vi) Does the attitude toward pesticides use mediates the relationship between past health experience with pesticide and protective behavior concerning pesticide use?

2 Literature Review and Hypotheses Development

Theory of Planned Behavior

To better understand why people do what they do, it has always been a matter of importance to identify the variables that influence behavior. Theory of reasoned action (TRA) attempts to understand and explain how various influences, such as motivation, work together to bring about a particular action behavior. Theory of reasoned action (TRA) was first proposed by Jacob and Fishbein in 1975 and lately upgraded by Jacob in 1985 to the theory of planned behavior (TPB). The theory of planned behavior (TPB), as depicted in Fig. 1, is an augmentation of the TRA model that includes a new construct called "perceived behavioural control," which measures how much an individual believes their behavior is within their volitional control (Ajzen, 1991). Due to the inclusion of perceived behavior control (PBC), TPB is regarded one of the most predictive models of consumer behavior (Maichum et al., 2016)

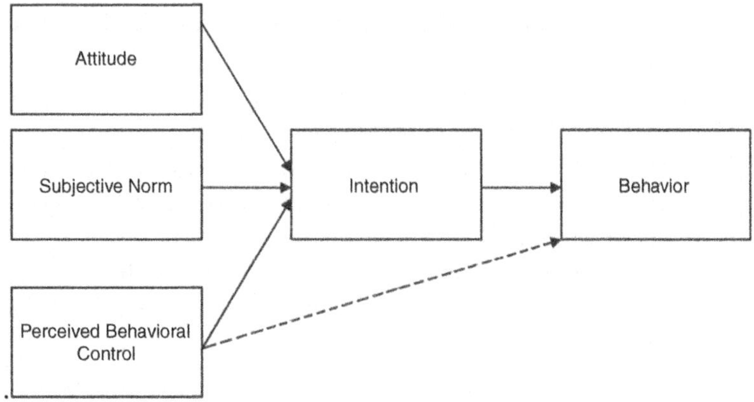

According to the TBP model, an individual's behavior is governed by his or her intention to engage in that behavior, and three key conceptually independent factors, attitudes, subjective norms, and perceived behavioral control (PBC), can predict a person's behavioral intention (BI) (Ajzen, 2006a). Behavioral belief influences attitude toward behavior, whereas normative beliefs impact perceived subjective standards, according to the idea. The PBC is influenced by control beliefs (Ajzen, 2006b; Davis et al., 2002).

Pesticides

Pesticides are the things that have been categorized for their tremendous assistance in pest management. They are useful tools for agricultural creation, so they have been incorporated into the growing process to prevent infestations create crop issues, as well as shield crops from losses, both in terms of food and decreased yield (Damalas, 2009). They play a critical role in the demand for food caused by vector-borne diseases, alongside assorted other options (Cooper & Dobson, 2007).

Farmers Attitude Toward Pesticide Use

Research has shown that agricultural farmers in developing nations often fail to meet best practices when it comes to handling pesticides (Ntow et al., 2006; Wumbei et al., 2019). Acute as well as chronic health effects can be caused by pesticide exposure.

One of the various factors which contribute to enormous growth in agricultural production is the use of pesticides. Pesticides are important inputs of modern agricultural production and because they are highly capable of protecting crops from pesticides and guarantee high crop yields (Ahmed et al., 2011; Cooper & Dobson, 2007). About 25 million farmers and farm workers suffer from poisoning, and three million farmers and farm workers suffer from severe pesticide poisoning every year, resulting in approximately 180,000 deaths among rural workers in developing countries every year (Hashemi et al., 2014).

Protective Behavior Concerning Pesticide Use

Human behavior reflects either the action or reaction of an individual to external or internal sources of stimulation. Behavior can be traced to innate characteristics and imposed influences and learned patterns. Survival behavior is inborn and reflected in the nervous systems. By the way, this kind of behavior is linked to various species. Contrarily, learned behavior is molded by the exposure to and practice and alterations in the individual (Zinn & Skorupa, 2015).

Knowledge of Pesticide Use

Knowledge can influence performance, but it is not the only variable. The reason for this is that people differ in their levels of knowledge. It is determined by their understanding. To be able to adopt new technology, system behavior, or practices, consumers must have a working knowledge of the current market.

Attitude Toward Pesticide Use

There are various attitudes placed on different aspects of the concept of importance. According to Eagly and Chaiken (1993), attitudes are expressions of the psychological tendency to evaluate something either positively or negatively. Consider this description: "This example emphasizes all three aspects of attitudes being the same, as a tendency, is about an entity, and can also be described as how an attitude is focused" (Eagly & Chaiken, 2007). Attitudinal objects can be objects, moods, people, or feelings. Attitudes are not to be considered feelings, as well (Albarracin & Shavitt, 2018). Personal protective equipment reduces exposure to dermally, by wearing gloves, long sleeves, and eye wear by using goggles. That makes it less likely you can inhale or swallow pesticide residues, which can cause serious poisoning. (Dobbs & Pretty, 2004).

Past Health Experience with Pesticides

One learns more from his own experience than from getting all the correct answers, the way different types of information about the same piece of information can impart (Nisbett & Ross, 1980). Even if the factual content is constant, people's experiences may alter new facts, systems, procedures, or practices. Psychological research suggests that individuals act by how they experienced their emotional discomfort (Gilbert et al., 1998). Each individual's behavior about something is affected by reference to their past personal experience.

Intention on Pesticide Use

Researchers have indicated that behavioral intentions are the immediate determinant of behavior, and many have used intentions as a proxy for actual behaviors (Ajzen, 1985). Erickson and Johansson (1985) stated that behavioral intention refers to the motivational components that determine a specific behavior. The stronger the intention to adopt the behavior, the more likely the behavior would be adopted.

Knowledge of Pesticides Use Toward Protective Behavior Concerning Pesticides Use

Knowledge has in particular concentrated on pro-environmental and health behavior concepts and environment-mindedness (Arcury, 1990). Studies on the effect of information on health behavior (Jensen, 2002) and its connection to health have instead looked at the influence of health knowledge on students' food and nutrition beliefs (Bettinghaus, 1986). Behavioral intentionality, as a result of these attitudes, influences (Ajzen & Fishbein, 1975). Knowledge of pesticide use significantly influences the farmer's protective behavior (Akter et al., 2018). Motivating from it, the scholar proposed the following hypothesis:

H1: There is a significant impact of knowledge about pesticides on farmers' protective behavior concerning pesticides use.

Intention to Reduce Pesticides Use Toward Protective Behavior Concerning Pesticides Use

Designed according to the TPB (Ajzen, 1985), intention is the major influencing factor in physical activity and behavior. It is believed that attitude, an objective norm, and PBC affect physical activity by influencing intentions. Perceived behavioral control is a significant factor in an increase or decrease in behavior. Knowledge about an object or a fact that either came from past personal perception or experience or the experience from anyone else can be a contributor to an intention toward behavior (Ajzen, 1991). Motivating from this, the following hypotheses is developed.

H2: There is a significant impact of intention to reduce pesticide use on farmers' protective behavior concerning pesticides use.

Past Health Experience with Pesticides Toward Protective Behavior Concerning Pesticides Use

People value their personal experiences greatly. An increasing body of evidence suggests that an individual's own experience is essential, but facts often get lost in the process of finding out more (Fox & Hadar, 2006; Newell & Rakow, 2007). Studies (Skogan, 1987; Small & Simonsohn, 2008) have found that the personal experience includes affective information as well as information about how one was accosted, but not whether it was accurate or not. Experience with pesticides regarding their health influences them to adopt protective behavior (Akter et al., 2018). Based on these arguments, the following hypothesis is developed.

H3: There is a significant impact of past health experience with pesticides on farmers' protective behavior concerning pesticides use.

Mediating Effect of Attitude Toward Pesticides Use on the Relationship Between Knowledge of Pesticides and Farmers' Protective Behavior Concerning Pesticides Use

Attitudes can be categorized as effects, thoughts, and actions. Cognitive, affective, and behavioral views of attitudes as being causal (Haddock & Zanna, 1993), for example, perceived messages or advertisements can lead to behavioral changes (i.e., values, beliefs, perceptions, emotions, actions, opinions, characteristics, abilities, interests, purposes, etc.) and that they ascribe to that entity or trait have been revealed in many analyses, it has nonetheless received many accolades. These three concepts are inseparable (Eagly & Chaiken, 1993). Attitudes do not always need to be formed or expressed through cognitive, affective, and behavior processes. Attitudes focus on how a consumer feels about the products, rather than on how they think or know. According to Akter et al. (2018), attitude toward pesticide use has a significant and positive impact on farmers' protective behavior to use pesticides. Based on prior literature, the researcher proposed the following hypothesis.

H4: Attitude toward pesticide use significantly mediates the relationship between knowledge of pesticides and farmers' protective behavior concerning pesticides use.

Mediating Effect Attitude Toward Pesticides Use on the Relationship between Intention to Reduce Pesticides Use and Farmers' Protective Behavior Concerning Pesticides Use

The TPB is a famous news behavioral model that attempts to explain variation in regardless had some success (Ajzen, 1991; Rosenfeld et al., 2006). According to TPB, an individual's attitude toward a specific object determines their behavior, so the intention is seen as the outcome of the attitude that is the most distal predictor of behavior (Arvola et al., 2008). TPB has been used in the sense of pro-environmental practices widely and effectively (Yazdanpanah & Forouzani, 2015; Yazdanpanah et al., 2014). So, there can be an argument that the theory supports the linkage of attitude toward pesticides to use pesticides.

H5: Attitude toward pesticides significantly mediates the relationship between intention to reduce pesticide use and farmers' behavior protective behavior concerning pesticides use.

Mediating Role of the Attitude Toward Pesticides on the Relationship Between Past Health Experience with Pesticide and Farmers' Protective Behavior Concerning Pesticide Use

The theory of reasoned action (TRA) was extended to create TPB (Jafarabadi et al., 2017). TRA is a social psychological model that argues that an individual's actual conduct in performing a specific action is directly influenced by his or her behavioral purpose, which is in turn influenced by experience, subjective norms, and attitude toward the behavior (Ajzen & Fishbein, 1975). Experience with a series of practices may affect potential actions with those procedures. The theory of reasoned action (TRA) was extended to create TPB (Jafarabadi et al., 2017). Experience with a series of practices may affect potential actions with those procedures.

H6: Attitude toward pesticide use significantly mediates the relationship between personal experience with pesticide and farmers' protective behavior concerning pesticides use.

Research Framework

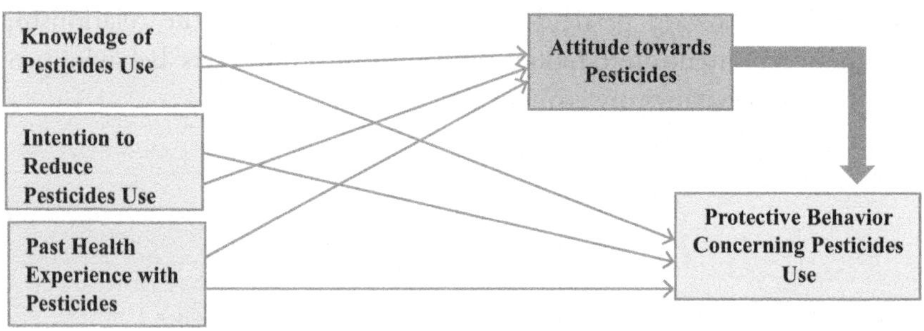

Fig. 1 Research model of knowledge of pesticides use, intention to reduce pesticides use, past health experience with pesticides and protective behavior concerning pesticides use with a mediating role of the top attitude toward pesticides use

3 Research Methodology

A research methodology is a systematic process that is adopted to find the answer to specific research questions which are developed to conduct research. According to Collis and Hussey (2009), there are different stages in research methodology that are employed to analyze the viability of the research problem in a specific study. In some cases, there are various ways to answer the specific question or achieve the specific research objectives. The present study looks into the impact of knowledge of pesticide use, attitude toward pesticides, and personal experience with pesticide on the protective behavior of farmers through the mediating effect of intention to use pesticides. The researcher makes deliberate choices in research methodology, to differentiate the study from similar researches that are conducted on relevant topics. The present chapter aims to attain the research objective by using the different scientific methods and approaches that are deliberately chosen for this study. Moreover, a brief explanation is given in this chapter. The current research is grounded in the theory of planned behavior, responses are based on the farmers' perception and are likely to be collected and measured objectively rather than subjectively.

To collect the data on all the identified variables, the researcher designed a structured questionnaire which comprises three different sections. The first section of the questionnaire is dedicated to inquiring about the personal information (demographics) of the respondents (e.g., gender, age, cultivation type, experience, etc.). The second section is dedicated to measuring all the independent variables (e.g., knowledge of pesticide use, attitude toward pesticides, and personal experience with pesticide) and mediating variable (intention to use pesticides). The third section of the questionnaire inquiries about the protective behavior of the farmers concerning pesticide use. The present research uses the snowball sampling technique to collect the data from respondents. Snowball sampling is a type of non-probability sampling in which data is collected on a referral basis. The target population of the study is fruit and vegetable farmers in South Punjab, Pakistan. According to Saunders et al. (2007), data collected through the quantitative survey is easy to handle, compare, and analyze. The structured adapted questionnaire helps the researchers to record the right and valuable responses of employees, closer to the context of the research topic. The deductive approach and quantitative measures for data are helpful for data handling, analyzing, and concluding. This study research uses the quantitative approach as the responses are collected through the structured close-ended questionnaire (i.e., 5-point Likert scale ranging from "strongly disagree" to "strongly agree").

4 Data Analysis

The main objective of the present research study is to understand and empirically examine the impact of knowledge of pesticide use, attitude toward pesticides, and past health experience with pesticides on protective behavior concerning pesticides use among the vegetables and fruit farmers of South Punjab, Pakistan. Data was collected and analyzed with a statistical package of social sciences (SPSS 20.0) to calculate Cronbach alpha. It can provide information about the model and the relative contribution of each of the independent variables that make up the model. KMO and Bartlett's test, correlations (bivariate correlation measures the association between two continuous variables without establishing directional causality), regression analysis (it describes the relationship between one or more predictor variable and response variable), and describe statistic (it describes a set of data with a measure of central tendency and measure of dispersion).

Reliability Analysis

Reliability of the construct of all the variables is ensured by the Cronbach's alpha test. In the present study, internal reliability is assessed by Cronbach's alpha. Composite Cronbach's alpha of the construct knowledge of pesticide use is 0.803, attitude toward pesticides is 0.623, past health experience is 0.662, intention to use pesticides is 0.792, and for protective behavior concerning pesticides, it is 0.681. Cronbach's alpha value for all the constructs is better than the recommended value of 0.50 by Mohajan (2017). Thus, the values of Cronbach's alpha test indicate that all the items of this construct are reliable, and further tests can be run with confidence. Table 1 shows this:

Table 1 Reliability of measurement scales

Variable	No. of items	Cronbach's alpha
Knowledge of pesticide use	10	0.803
Attitude toward pesticides	5	0.623
Past health experience	4	0.662
Intention to use pesticides	4	0.792
Protective behavior concerning pesticides	3	0.681

Table 2 KMO and Bartlett's test

Kaiser–Meyer–Olkin measure of sampling adequacy		0.727
Bartlett's test of sphericity	Approx. Chi-square	4.882E3
	Df	406
	Sig.	0.000

Kaiser–Meyer–Olkin (KMO) and Bartlett's Test

Kaiser–Meyer–Olkin test or KMO test ensures the adequacy of the research sample. The value of KMO test should be 0.5 or above in a valid sample. Bartlett's test shows the strength of association between the variables, and it also shows satisfaction with the results. Mohajan (2017) suggested that the value of the KMO test should be above 0.5. The data collected in this study shows the KMO value of 0.727, which is good enough for an adequate and spherical sample (Table 2).

Response Rate

The researcher floated the 400 questionnaires to the vegetable and fruit farmers of South Punjab, Pakistan, using snowball sampling (a type of non-probability sampling). Out of 400 questionnaires, 385 were collected back in the full form of responses. Thus, the response rate was 96% (Table 3).

Table 3 Response rate

Questionnaire delivered	Questionnaire received	Questionnaire received in complete form	Response rate
400	388	385	96%

Table 4 Crop type

Valid	Frequency	Percentage	Valid percentage	Cumulative percentage
Vegetables	234	60.8	60.8	60.8
Fruits	151	39.2	39.2	100.0
Total	385	100.0	100.0	

Respondent Demographics

Crop Type

The total sample size of the study is 385 and there are no missing values in the collected data. So, all 385 samples are considered in the study. Table 4 shows the crop type where the farmers are working. The table shows that the majority of respondents are vegetable farmers, and their total number in the sample is 234 that is 60.8% of the total sample. Rest of the 151 respondents are fruits farmers, which is 39.2% of the total sample size. This indicates that vegetable farming is more common in South Punjab, Pakistan (Fig. 2).

Experience of Respondents

The table below indicates the experience demographics of the respondents. Of the total sample size, 144 respondents have farming experience of between 1 and 5 years, which is 37.4% of the total sample. Of the total respondents, 162 (which are 42.1%) have experience of between 6 and 10 years. Total 59 respondents are in the experience bracket of 11 to 15 years, which is 15.3%. Only 15 respondents are in the experience bracket of 16 to 20 years which is 3.9%. Only 5 employees have experience of over 25 years which is 1.3% of the total respondents (Table 5 and Fig. 3).

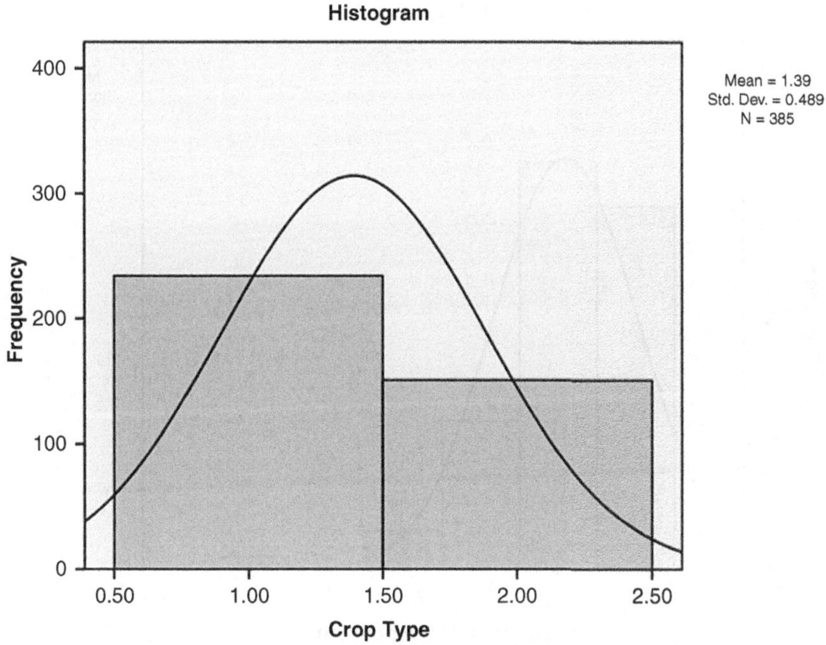

Fig. 2 Crop type

Table 5 Experience

		Frequency	Percentage	Valid percentage	Cumulative percentage
Valid	1 to 5 years	144	37.4	37.4	37.4
	6 to 10 years	162	42.1	42.1	79.5
	11 to 15 years	59	15.3	15.3	94.8
	16 to 20 years	15	3.9	3.9	98.7
	Above 25 years	5	1.3	1.3	100.0
	Total	385	100.0	100.0	
	1 to 5 years	144	37.4	37.4	

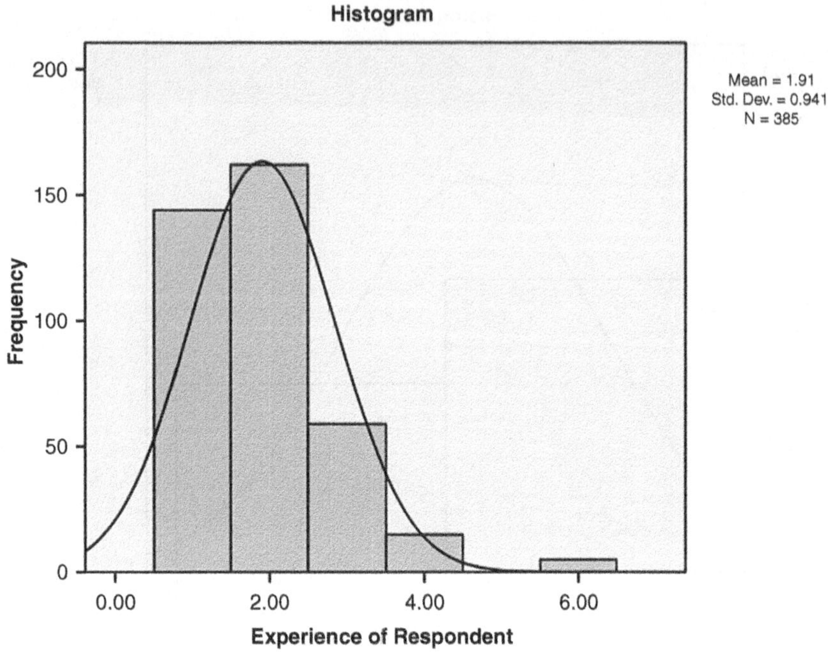

Fig. 3 Experience

Table 6 Age of respondents

		Frequency	Percentage	Valid percentage	Cumulative percentage
Valid	20 to 25 years	24	6.2	6.2	6.2
	26 to 30 years	78	20.3	20.3	26.5
	31 to 35 years	192	49.9	49.9	76.4
	36 to 40 years	61	15.8	15.8	92.2
	41 to 45 years	12	3.1	3.1	95.3
	Above 45	18	4.7	4.7	100.0
	Total	385	100.0	100.0	

Age of the Respondent

Table 6 represents the age of the respondent. According to the table, 24 of the total respondents are in the age bracket of 20 to 25 years, which is 6.2%, 78 (20.3%) are in the age bracket of 26 to 30 years, 192 (49.9%)

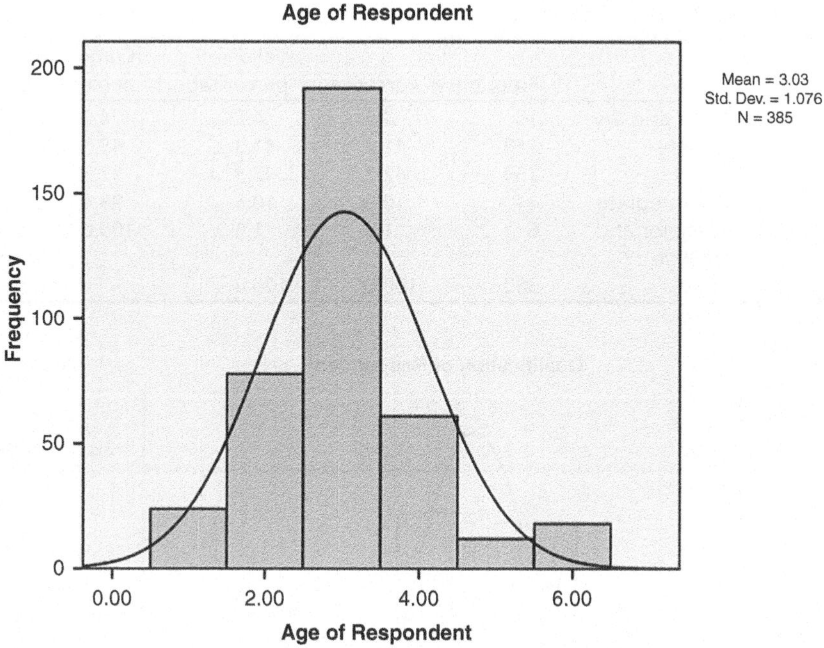

Fig. 4 Age of respondents

are in the age bracket of 31 to 35 years, 61 (15.8%) are in the age bracket of 36 to 40 years, 12 (3.1%) are in the age bracket of 41 to 45 years, and 18 (3.9%) are above 45 years of age (Fig. 4).

Qualification of Respondents

Table 7 indicates the educational demographics of the respondents. The education level of 16 farmers (4.2% of the total respondents) is up to the primary level. The education level of 159 farmers (41.3% of the total respondents) is middle. 163 (42.3%) of total respondents are Matric qualified. 41 farmers have an education level of intermediate and remaining 6 farmers have the bachelor's degree or above that are 10.6% and 1.6% of the total respondents, respectively (Fig. 5).

Table 7 Qualification of the respondents

		Frequency	Percentage	Valid percentage	Cumulative percentage
Valid	Upto primary	16	4.2	4.2	4.2
	Middle	159	41.3	41.3	45.5
	Matric	163	42.3	42.3	87.8
	Intermediate	41	10.6	10.6	98.4
	Bachelor and above	6	1.6	1.6	100.0
	Total	385	100.0	100.0	

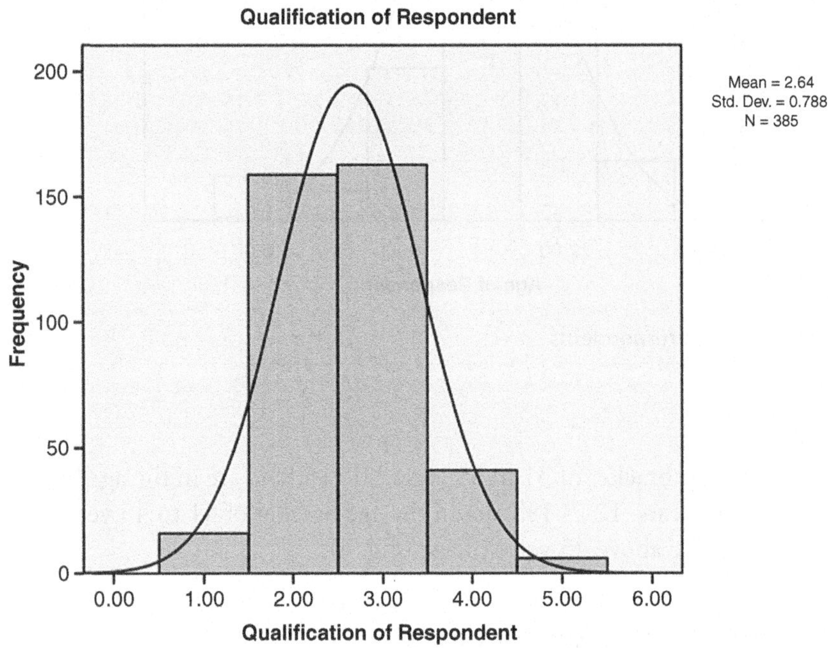

Fig. 5 Qualification of the respondents

Discriminant Validity

Fornell and Larcker criterion and HTMT are applied to measure the discriminant validity of the collected data. According to Fornell and Larcker, if the average variance explained (showed in diagonal matrix) surpasses the squared correlation of latent variables, then the assumption

Table 8 HTMT

	ATT	INT	KNO	PHE	PB
ATT					
INT	0.061				
KNO	0.382	0.058			
PHE	0.259	0.051	0.434		
PB	0.433	0.093	0.389	0.508	

of discriminant validity is supported. In the table of Fornell and Larcker criterion, all the diagonal values (square roots of AVEs) are greater than the other values in the same row/column (correlation). Therefore, the assumption of discriminant validity is supported by Fornell and Larcker criterion. To achieve discriminant validity, the HTMT values must be less than 0.90. This demonstrates the construct's discriminant nature. All correlation coefficients were less than 0.90 in the HTMT study (Gold et al., 2001). The discriminant validity of the concept was determined using the heterotrait–monotrait (HTMT) ratio (Table 8).

Correlation

According to Fielding & Schreier (2001), correlation is a statistical tool, which represents the nature and strength of the relationship between two or more quantitative variables. Bivariate correlation is used in the present section to evaluate the relationship of protective behavior concerning pesticide use with knowledge of pesticide use, attitude toward pesticides, past health experience with pesticides, and intention to use pesticides. According to Collis and Hussey (2013), bivariate correlation measures the association between two continuous variables without establishing directional causality. While, as per the analysis, knowledge of pesticide use and attitude toward pesticides are positively correlated with protective behavior concerning pesticides, and correlation is significant at the *P*-value below 0.05 level. On the other hand, past health experience and intention to use pesticides are not significantly correlated with protective behavior concerning pesticides (Table 9).

Table 9 Correlation

	Knowledge of pesticide use	Attitude toward pesticide use	Past health experience with pesticides	Intention to use pesticides	Protective behavior concerning pesticide use
Knowledge of pesticide use	1	0.300[a]	-0.175[a]	-0.007	0.379[a]
		0.000	0.001	0.894	0.000
	385	385	385	385	385
Attitude toward pesticide use	0.300[a]	1	-0.015	0.008	0.336[a]
	0.000		0.767	0.874	0.000
	385	385	385	385	385
Past health experience with pesticides	-0.175[a]	-0.015	1	-0.018	0.017
	0.001	0.767		0.720	0.745
	385	385	385	385	385
Intention to use pesticides	-0.007	0.008	-0.018	1	-0.004
	0.894	0.874	0.720		0.940
	385	385	385	385	385
Protective behavior concerning pesticide use	0.379[a]	0.336[a]	0.017	-0.004	1
	0.000	0.000	0.745	0.940	
	385	385	385	385	385

[a]Correlation is significant at the 0.01 level (two-tailed)

Structural Equation Modeling

Structural equation modeling (SEM) is implied to test the hypotheses. SEM is based on regression tools. According to Fielding (2018), regression analysis is a statistical valuation to analyze or estimate the relationship between independent and dependent variable(s). An analysis is as under (Fig. 6):

Table 10 shows the direct effects of knowledge of pesticides use, intention to reduce pesticides use and past health experience on attitude toward pesticides use and farmers' protective behavior concerning pesticides. It also states the direct effect of attitude toward pesticides use on farmers' protective behavior concerning pesticides use.

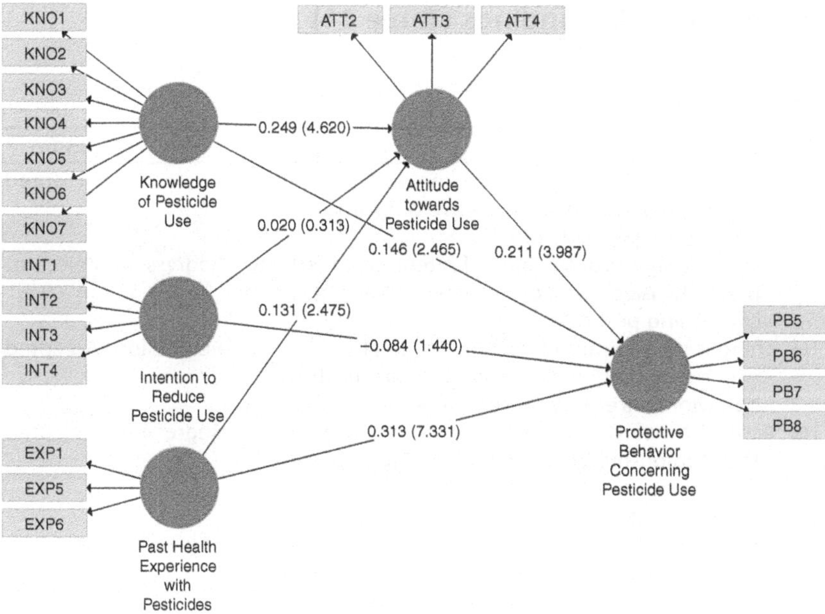

Fig. 6 Structural equation modeling

Table10 Direct effects

	Beta	M	S.D	*T*	*P* values
Attitude toward pesticide use → Protective behavior concerning pesticide use	0.211	0.215	0.053	3.987	0
Intention to reduce pesticide use → Attitude toward pesticide use	0.02	0.025	0.065	0.313	0.754
Intention to reduce pesticide use → Protective behavior concerning pesticide use	-0.08	-0.078	0.061	1.299	0.195
Knowledge of pesticide use → Attitude toward pesticide use	0.249	0.26	0.054	4.62	0
Knowledge of pesticide use → Protective behavior concerning pesticide use	0.199	0.209	0.056	3.578	0
Past health experience with pesticides → Attitude toward pesticide use	0.131	0.13	0.053	2.475	0.014
Past health experience with pesticides → Protective behavior concerning pesticide use	0.341	0.338	0.044	7.826	0

Summary of the Findings (Table 11)

Table 11 Summary of Findings

#	Statements	Method	Result
H1	There is a significant impact of knowledge about pesticides on farmers' protective behavior concerning pesticide use.	Regression	Accepted
H2	There is a significant impact of intention to reduce pesticide use on farmers' protective behavior concerning pesticide use.	Regression	Rejected
H3	There is a significant impact of past health experience with pesticides on farmers' protective behavior concerning pesticide use.	Regression	Accepted
H4	Attitude toward pesticide use significantly mediates the relationship between knowledge of pesticides and farmers' protective behavior concerning pesticide use.	Regression	Accepted
H5	Attitude toward pesticides significantly mediates the relationship between intention to reduce pesticide use and farmers' behavior protective behavior concerning pesticide use.	Regression	Rejected
H6	Attitude toward pesticide use significantly mediates the relationship between experience with pesticide and farmers' protective behavior concerning pesticide use.	Regression	Accepted

5 Conclusion

The main objective of the present study is to define the use and importance of pesticides in Pakistan and explain the determinants of farmers' protective behavior concerning pesticide use. The first research question of this study is: does the knowledge of pesticide use affect the protective behavior concerning pesticides use? Findings from the analysis indicate a significant positive effect of knowledge of pesticides use has a significant and positive effect on the farmers' protective behavior concerning pesticide use. The result from this analysis agrees with the findings from the past studies (Bagheri et al., 2019; Nasab et al., 2009) that pointed out that level of knowledge among farmers to use pesticides develops the protective behavior among them regarding the application of the pesticide. According to the statistical analysis generated in this study, attitude toward pesticides use does not mediate the relationship between intention to reduce pesticides use and protective behavior concerning pesticides use. Sixth and final question of the present study is about the mediating effect of attitude toward pesticides use on the relationship between past health experience with pesticides and protective behavior concerning pesticides use.

6 Suggestions

The present study suggests developing a pool of knowledge among farmers and other farmworkers about the pesticides use and their potential benefits and drawbacks to develop protective behavior in their farm practices and pesticide application. The present study also implies raising awareness about the use of protective equipment and introduces the law and regulations about peptide application to promote safe pesticide use and reduce exposure risks.

7 Limitation and Recommendation

Like all the other investigations, present study also addresses some limitations. Firstly, the present study is based on the data collected from the vegetable and fruit farmers of South Punjab, Pakistan. Therefore, the results may not apply to any other geographical location or other farmers growing different crop types. So, a future study may come up with different respondents to make more generalizable results. Secondly, the present study collects quantitative data, which may give a general focus. Therefore, a future study may come up with qualitative data for more in-depth insights into farmer's perceptions. A future study may come with a more mediating or moderating variable for a more comprehensive framework to add to the literature of the theory of planned behavior (TPB).

References

Abdollahzadeh, G., Sharifzadeh, M. S., & Damalas, C. A. (2016). Motivations for adopting biological control among Iranian rice farmers. *Crop Protection, 80*, 42–50.

Ahmed, I., Zia, M. A., Iftikhar, T., & Iqbal, H. M. (2011). Characterization and detergent compatibility of purified protease produced from aspergillus Niger by utilizing agro wastes. *BioResources, 6*(4), 4505–4522.

Ajzen, I. (1985). From intentions to actions: A theory of planned behavior. In *Action control* (pp. 11–39). Springer.

Ajzen, I. (1991). The theory of planned behavior. *Organizational Behavior and Human Decision Processes, 50*(2), 179–211.

Ajzen, I. (2006a). *Constructing a theory of planned behavior questionnaire.* Retrieved from http://people.umass.edu/aizen/pdf/tpb.measurement.pdf

Ajzen, I. (2006b). *Behavioral Interventions Based on the Theory of Planned Behavior*. Technical Report. Retrieved from: https://www.researchgate.net/publication/245582784_Behavioral_Interventions_Based_on_the_Theory_of_Planned_Behavior

Ajzen, I., & Fishbein, M. (1975). A Bayesian analysis of attribution processes. *Psychological Bulletin, 82*(2), 261.

Akter, M., Fan, L., Rahman, M. M., Geissen, V., & Ritsema, C. J. (2018). Vegetable farmers' behaviour and knowledge related to pesticide use and related health problems: A case study from Bangladesh. *Journal of Cleaner Production, 200*, 122–133.

Albarracin, D., & Shavitt, S. (2018). Attitudes and attitude change. *Annual Review of Psychology, 69*, 299–327.

Arcury, T. A. (1990). Environmental attitude and environmental knowledge. *Human Organization, 49*, 300–304.

Arvola, A., Vassallo, M., Dean, M., Lampila, P., Saba, A., Lähteenmäki, L., & Shepherd, R. (2008). Predicting intentions to purchase organic food: The role of affective and moral attitudes in the theory of planned behaviour. *Appetite, 50*(2–3), 443–454.

Bagheri, A., Bondori, A., Allahyari, M. S., & Damalas, C. A. (2019). Modeling farmers' intention to use pesticides: An expanded version of the theory of planned behavior. *Journal of Environmental Management, 248*, 109291.

Bettinghaus, E. P. (1986). Health promotion and the knowledge-attitude-behavior continuum. *Preventive Medicine, 15*(5), 475–491.

Collis, J., & Hussey, R. (2009). *Business Research: A Practical Guide for Undergraduate and Postgraduate Students* (3rd Edn.). Basingstoke: Palgrave Macmillan.

Collis, J., & Hussey, R. (2013). *Business Research: A Practical Guide for Undergraduate and Postgraduate Students*. London: Palgrave Macmillan.

Cooper, J., & Dobson, H. (2007). The benefits of pesticides to mankind and the environment. *Crop Protection, 26*(9), 1337–1348.

Curwin, B. D., Hein, M. J., Sanderson, W. T., Nishioka, M., & Buhler, W. (2003). Acephate exposure and decontamination on tobacco harvesters' hands. *Journal of Exposure Science & Environmental Epidemiology, 13*(3), 203–210.

Damalas, C. A. (2009). Understanding benefits and risks of pesticide use. *Scientific Research and Essays, 4*(10), 945–949.

Damalas, C. A., & Eleftherohorinos, I. G. (2011). Pesticide exposure, safety issues, and risk assessment indicators. *International Journal of Environmental Research and Public Health, 8*(5), 1402–1419.

Davis, R. A., Flett, G. L., & Besser, A. (2002). Online Cognition Scale (OCS) [Database record]. APA PsycTests. https://doi.org/10.1037/t44755-000

Dobbs, T. L., & Pretty, J. N. (2004). Agri-environmental stewardship schemes and "multifunctionality". *Review of Agricultural Economics, 26*(2), 220–237.

Eagly, A. H., & Chaiken, S. (1993). *The psychology of attitudes*. Harcourt Brace Jovanovich College Publishers.

Eagly, A. H., & Chaiken, S. (2007). The advantages of an inclusive definition of attitude. *Social Cognition, 25*(5), 582–602.

Ekqvist, I., Röös, E., & Tidåker, P. (2019). Grain legumes on the Swedish market: Origin and pesticide use in the production.

Erickson, G. M., & Johansson, J. K. (1985). The role of price in multi-attribute product evaluations. *Journal of Consumer Research, 12*(2), 195–199.

Fan, S. P., Liberman, Z., Keysar, B., & Kinzler, K. D. (2015). The Exposure Advantage: Early Exposure to a Multilingual Environment Promotes Effective Communication. *Psychological Science, 26*(7), 1090–1097. https://doi.org/10.1177/0956797615574699

Fielding, N., & Schreier, M. (2001). Introduction: On the compatibility between qualitative and quantitative research methods. Paper presented at the Forum Qualitative Sozialforschung/Forum: Qualitative Social Research.

Fox, C. R., & Hadar, L. (2006). "Decisions from experience"= sampling error+ prospect theory: Reconsidering Hertwig, Barron, Weber & Erev (2004). *Judgment and Decision making, 1*(2), 159.

Gerland, P., Raftery, A. E., Ševčíková, H., Li, N., Gu, D., Spoorenberg, T., et al. (2014). World population stabilization unlikely this century. *Science, 346*(6206), 234–237.

Gilbert, J. K., Boulter, C., & Rutherford, M. (1998). Models in explanations, part 1: Horses for courses? *International Journal of Science Education, 20*(1), 83–97.

Gold, A., Malhotra, A., & Segars, A. (2001). Knowledge Management: An Organizational Capabilities Perspective. *Journal of Management Information Systems, 18*, 185-214.

Haddock, G., & Zanna, M. P. (1993). *Predicting prejudicial attitudes: The importance of affect, cognition, and the feeling-belief dimension*. ACR North American Advances.

Hashemi, S. M., Hosseini, S. M., & Hashemi, M. K. (2012). Farmers' perceptions of safe use of pesticides: Determinants and training needs. *International Archives of Occupational and Environmental Health, 85*(1), 57–66.

Hashemi, S. M., Peshin, R., & Feola, G. (2014). From the farmers' perspective: Pesticide use and pest control. In *Integrated pest management* (pp. 409–432). Springer.

Jafarabadi, A. R., Bakhtiyari, A. R., Toosi, A. S., & Jadot, C. (2017). Spatial distribution, ecological and health risk assessment of heavy metals in marine surface sediments and coastal seawaters of fringing coral reefs of the Persian Gulf, Iran. *Chemosphere, 185*, 1090–1111.

Jensen, B. B. (2002). Knowledge, action and pro-environmental behaviour. *Environmental Education Research, 8*(3), 325–334.

Maichum, K., Parichatnon, S., & Peng, K.-C. (2016). Application of the Extended Theory of Planned Behavior Model to Investigate Purchase Intention of Green Products among Thai Consumers. *Sustainability, 8*, 1077. https://doi.org/10.3390/su8101077

Mohajan, H. K. (2017). Two criteria for good measurements in research: Validity and reliability. *Annals of Spiru Haret University. Economic Series, 17*(4), 59–82.

Nasab, H. S., Tavakoli, R., Ghofranipour, F., Kazemnejad, A., & Khavanin, A. (2009). Evaluation of knowledge, attitude and behavior of workers towards occupational health and safety. *Iranian Journal of Public Health, 38*(2), 125–129.

Newell, B. R., & Rakow, T. (2007). The role of experience in decisions from description. *Psychonomic Bulletin & Review, 14*(6), 1133–1139.

Nisbett, R. E., & Ross, L. (1980). *Human inference: Strategies and shortcomings of social judgment*. Prentice-Hall.

Ntow, W. J., Gijzen, H. J., Kelderman, P., & Drechsel, P. (2006). Farmer perceptions and pesticide use practices in vegetable production in Ghana. *Pest Management Science: formerly Pesticide Science, 62*(4), 356–365.

Popp, J., Pető, K., & Nagy, J. (2013). Pesticide productivity and food security. A review. *Agronomy for Sustainable Development, 33*(1), 243–255.

Rosenfeld, P. J., Brown, D. M., Heier, J. S., Boyer, D. S., Kaiser, P. K., Chung, C. Y., & Kim, R. Y. (2006). Ranibizumab for neovascular age-related macular degeneration. *New England Journal of Medicine, 355*(14), 1419–1431.

Saunders, M., Lewis, P., & Thornhill, A. (2007). *Research methods. Business students* (4th ed.). Pearson Education Limited.

Skogan, W. G. (1987). The impact of victimization on fear. *Crime & Delinquency, 33*(1), 135–154.

Small, D. A., & Simonsohn, U. (2008). Friends of victims: Personal experience and prosocial behavior. *Journal of Consumer Research, 35*(3), 532–542.

Wumbei, A., Houbraken, M., & Spanoghe, P. (2019). Pesticides use and exposure among yam farmers in the Nanumba traditional area of Ghana. *Environmental Monitoring and Assessment, 191*(5), 1–16.

Xu, N., Zhang, Q., Hou, B., Cheng, Q., & Zhang, G. (2018). A novel magnesium metal–organic framework as a multiresponsive luminescent sensor for Fe (III) ions, pesticides, and antibiotics with high selectivity and sensitivity. *Inorganic Chemistry, 57*(21), 13330–13340.

Yazdanpanah, M., & Forouzani, M. (2015). Application of the theory of planned behaviour to predict Iranian students' intention to purchase organic food. *Journal of Cleaner Production, 107*, 342–352.

Yazdanpanah, M., Hayati, D., Hochrainer-Stigler, S., & Zamani, G. H. (2014). Understanding farmers' intention and behavior regarding water conservation in the middle-east and North Africa: A case study in Iran. *Journal of Environmental Management, 135*, 63–72.

Zinn, Y., & Skorupa, A. (2015). A new approach to education on ground source materials. *CC&T, Cadernos de Ciência & Tecnologia, 32*(1/2), 229–244.

Innovation Management in the Public Sector: How Leaders Oversee Employees' Innovative Work Behaviour?

Wan Noor Azreen Wan Mohamad Nordin
and Nurul Liyana Mohd Kamil

1 Introduction

Innovation has been widely discussed by prominent scholars for two decades ago. Innovation is a crucial element in sustaining the competitiveness and sustainable growth of emerging economies. Therefore, the public sector is crucial to every economy and needs innovation management to provide the greatest products, procedures, ideas and services for

W. N. A. W. M. Nordin
Faculty of Business and Economics, Universiti Malaya,
Kuala Lumpur, Malaysia

N. L. M. Kamil (✉)
Faculty of Business and Economics, Universiti Malaya,
Kuala Lumpur, Malaysia

Department of Management, London School of Economics and Political Science, London, UK
e-mail: nurulliyana@um.edu.my

F. A. Yamoah, A. ul Haque (eds.), *Corporate Management Ecosystem in Emerging Economies*, https://doi.org/10.1007/978-3-031-41578-4_8

social and economic development. However, the proliferation of the COVID-19 pandemic has had a significant economic impact, prompting the public sector to place a greater emphasis on innovation management out of concern for both economic growth and human welfare.

The competitive public sector is pursuing numerous strategies to improve innovation management, including accelerating digitalization, maintaining concentration on core markets and increasing focus on "outside the box" concepts (Kanesarajah & White, 2020). The challenges experienced during the pandemic encouraged the public sector to become interested in creating an innovative culture as a means of improving operational effectiveness. In addition, leadership should be practised in the public sector as it is a significant source of innovation management. Therefore, the ability, skills, opportunities and willingness of employees to innovate are significantly influenced by the public sector. We, therefore, sought to investigate the contribution of leadership to fostering employee innovation performance.

The innovation performance of employees can be seen from their innovative work behaviour. Innovative work behaviour is characterised by an exploration of the degree to which employees embrace and are able to put new ideas into practice when introducing, launching and promoting new approaches for procedures, products and services (Janssen, 2000). Employees have been able to innovate in roles, groups and work organisations due to their involvement in organisations. In this context, employees are able to deal with Covid-19 by introducing new ideas and problem-solving strategies to be able to improve procedures, products, or services by being able to recognise and take advantage of possibilities in accomplishing organisational goals. However, we enquired how the public sector would encourage their employees to engage in innovative work behaviour during the proliferation of Covid-19. Leaders have a significant influence on employees' innovative work behaviour.

Previous research has demonstrated that leadership style has a significant influence on innovative work behaviour (Breevaart et al., 2014; Kang et al., 2015). The public sector should determine whether its leadership style encourages employees to participate in creative problem-solving. Although there is consensus regarding the significance of leaders in inspiring innovative work behaviour, literature on multilevel studies that integrate leadership and innovative research is scarce. We think that at the organisational level, transformational leadership and transactional leadership can have an impact on the individual level, which encourages employees to exhibit more innovative work behaviour.

The purpose of both transformational leadership and transactional leadership is to inspire individuals to participate in the implementation of new products, services, or procedures and to foster their ability to innovate. Transformational leadership and transactional leadership are leadership that motivate employees to accomplish desired outcomes. To better understand the effect of this leadership theory on innovative work behaviour, this study examined both transformational leadership and transactional leadership towards employees' innovative work behaviour in the public sector. We believe that the interaction between transformational leadership and transactional leadership might affect employees' innovative work behaviour and that one of the many unresolved problems will be addressed by the job autonomy mechanism, which involves the relationship indicated.

Previous studies have limitedly studied the impact of the process of influencing the mechanism of employee freedom in performing their duties on transformational leadership and transactional leadership. Job autonomy, a state of employees characterised by greater intrinsic motivation and self-determination in executing work behaviour (Ryan & Deci, 2000), is a mechanism that can mediate the interaction between transformational leadership, transactional leadership and innovative work behaviour. Job autonomy is a motivational factor in obtaining employees' job outcomes, and transformational leaders inspire and encourage. Even transactional leadership rewards employees who demonstrate innovative work behaviour.

This study makes two theoretical contributions to the prior literature. First, our study suggests that both transformational leadership and transactional leadership encourage employees to engage in innovative work behaviour in the public sector. Second, our research contributes to the expanding body of knowledge on innovation management; a factor that both transformational leadership and transactional leadership depend on the degree of employee perceptions of job autonomy. Practically, our finding provides practitioners with more guidelines regarding what leaders can do and how job autonomy affects different levels of employees' innovative work behaviours. Accordingly, this study seeks to fulfil two objectives: (1) to investigate how transformational leadership and transactional leadership affect employees' innovative work behaviours and (2) to promote the ongoing development of the transformational leadership and transactional leadership paradigms, particularly by investigating a novel and significant mediator, i.e., job autonomy.

2 Theory and Hypotheses Development

Leadership and Innovative Work Behaviour

Leadership (such as transformational leadership and transactional leadership) plays a critical role in encouraging employees to engage in innovative work behaviour on daily tasks. A leader that practises transformational leadership empowers employees to come up with innovative solutions and take on challenging tasks that have the potential to transform their careers. Contrarily, transactional leadership places a greater emphasis on motivating employees to focus on their roles than on offering new activities (Bass, 1999).

Employees will create better job performance goals, recognise and analyse their workplace, and be inspired to change their behaviour to be more innovative if their leaders provide them with solid direction and examples of how to do their jobs effectively. Consequently, it is believed that transformational leadership is the primary kind of leadership in various stages of idea development or problem-solving, gaining support for new ideas and putting new ideas into practice. Transformational leadership can inspire employees to adopt innovative work behaviour if they articulate their goals for their jobs, challenge the status quo and make changes to their work environment. This is because employees have faith and confidence in transformational leadership, which motivates them to express their opinions and generate novel ideas.

Transformational leadership is considered a constructive addition to transactional leadership, which is an exchange relationship where expectations are stated and the immediate self-interests of leaders and followers are addressed (Bass, 1999). Transactional leadership is a crucial high-level construct that can influence employees' innovative work behaviour by implementing component contingent rewards and management by exception (Bass, 1999).

Although transactional leaders are claimed to set goals and monitor employee performance, they reward employees who are able to fulfil the required standards by achieving performance targets. Employees will be encouraged to use more innovative work behaviour in an effort to meet the transactional leader's expectations and display excellent performance to get the leader's appreciation. Next, when transactional leaders reward or recognise employees for good performance, it will encourage employees to be more motivated by their jobs and foster more innovative working conditions.

According to the self-determination theory, transformational leadership and transactional leadership are able to increase the innovative work behaviour of employees if these leaders are successful in motivating employees to change and develop innovation in their tasks to improve the function of social conditions in the workplace (Ryan & Deci, 2000). Based on the above understanding, we discussed the empirical evidence to support the relationship between both transformational leadership and transactional leadership and innovative work behaviour. A previous study conducted by Kang et al. (2015) on 39 CEOs and 105 managers from young firms in the United States revealed that both transformational leadership and transactional leadership styles had a substantial impact on the innovative work behaviour of their subordinates.

Therefore, hypothesize that:

H1: Transformational leadership positively relates to employees' innovative work behaviour.

H2: Transactional leadership positively relates to employees' innovative work behaviour.

Leadership and Job Autonomy

Leadership has the ability to influence how independently employees perform their tasks. Employees will have freedom in their decision-making under transformational leadership that inspires them to develop their skills and improve their performance. Employees would feel more confident if they are given the freedom to handle current duties and problems under transformational leadership that focuses towards achieving employee goals. Giving employees job autonomy would make them feel trusted to offer new suggestions and ideas for their organisation (Bass, 1999).

Even though leaders who practise transformational leadership are better at encouraging employees' job autonomy; however, transactional leadership also gives employees more freedom to choose how to carry out their jobs. Transactional leadership encourages employees who use their job autonomy to work effectively to accomplish goals by rewarding them when they succeed.

The theory of self-determination states that supportive conditions, such as allowing employees freedom in their jobs, are necessary for the maintenance and improvement of existing tendencies (Ryan & Deci, 2000). If the leaders give inspiration, motivation, (transformational leadership) and rewards (transactional leadership) for acknowledged performance, employees with high levels of job autonomy are able to complete tasks and solve problems. Prior studies by Breevaart et al. (2014) on Norwegian naval cadets demonstrated how transformational leadership and transactional leadership had a favourable influence on job autonomy.

Based on the above arguments, we assume that:

H3: Transformational leadership positively relates to employees' job autonomy.
H4: Transactional leadership positively relates to employees' job autonomy.

Job Autonomy and Innovative Work Behaviour

A considerable relationship exists between the degree of job autonomy and innovative work behaviour. Employees who have autonomy over how they do their tasks will have more opportunities to make decisions and contribute novel ideas. Employees can organise, plan and complete their tasks by creating job autonomy. Therefore, leaders should provide their employees with the opportunity to adopt innovative work behaviour and disassociate from their traditional employment habits.

Empirical evidence proved that Flemish employees' job autonomy is positively associated with exhibiting innovative work behaviour. According to the self-determination theory, individuals' intrinsic motivation to engage in innovative work behaviour is greatly influenced by their need for autonomy (Ryan & Deci, 2000). Employees who are intrinsically motivated are considered to play a vital role in the development of innovative work behaviour. Therefore, we propose that job autonomy has the potential to influence innovative work behaviour:

H5: Employees' job autonomy positively relates to innovative work behaviour.

Leadership, Job Autonomy and Innovative Work Behaviour

Leadership that gives employees a degree of autonomy over their jobs has a significant impact on their ability to enhance innovative work behaviour. Transformational leadership that promotes information sharing and learning activities, and is intellectually stimulated in generating current problem solutions, is able to generate intrinsic motivation in individuals to provide creative solutions.

Consistent with the self-determination theory, employees with high intrinsic motivation would demonstrate that transformational leadership allows them freedom in carrying out their jobs, which encourages them to engage in innovative work behaviour (Ryan & Deci, 2000). Those who are working under transformational leadership would have the freedom to assume responsibility for offering new ideas, making decisions and putting those ideas into practice, allowing them to exhibit innovative work behaviour.

In contrast to transformational leadership, transactional leadership is said to be able to support innovative work behaviour by granting employees the freedom to perform their duties. Transactional leadership clearly communicates expectations to employees and provides them with the freedom to meet those goals. Employees will receive rewards if they exercise job autonomy to meet requirements and are appreciated by transactional leaders. These benefits boost their motivation and promote innovative work behaviour.

Therefore, we propose the following hypotheses:

H6: Employees' job autonomy mediates the relationship between transformational leadership and innovative work behaviour.
H7: Employees' job autonomy mediates the relationship between transactional leadership and innovative work behaviour.

3 Research Methodology

Design and Participants

After receiving ethical approval from the university's ethics committee, data were collected between January 2021 and April 2021 using an online questionnaire, as Malaysia was still under a movement control order (MCO) at the time of data collection. The final sample consisted of 269 respondents from 27 different organisations, including state governments, public agencies and ministries in Malaysia. The culture of Malaysian research is typically characterised by a relatively low response rates with the use of random sampling methods; therefore, we used the snowball approach, which requested organisations to nominate managerial officers who can participate in this study after gaining approval from the Director or Secretary of Division.

The majority of respondents were female (57.6%), with various educational backgrounds (bachelor's degree, 51.7%; master's degree, 36.4%; doctoral degree, 8.9%; and diploma, 3.0%). Most of the respondents have working experience ranging from fewer than 10 years to 20 years (84.7%). Each organisational team in the matched sample had between 8 and 15 participants.

Measures

All study measurements were administered in Malay and back translation was used to translate the questionnaire, unless otherwise stated. Both English and Malay translators are experts in the field of management, and they are proficient in both English and Malay languages.

Transformational leadership: The 12-item transformational leadership scale was used (Rafferty & Griffin, 2004). This scale's reported alpha value is 0.92. Responses are rated on a scale of 1 (strongly disagree) to 7 (strongly agree). Following is an example of questions: *"My leader behaves in a manner which is thoughtful of my personal needs"* and *"My leader sees that the interests of employees are given due consideration."* The participants were asked the question, "My leader," using organisational references in the scale. The scale recorded a reliability of 0.94.

Transactional leadership: Transactional leadership was assessed using five items from Podsakoff et al. (1990). The scale in the previous study had good reliability and validity (i.e., 0.90). The following example items are: *"My leader always gives me positive feedback when I perform well,"* and *"My leader gives me special recognition when my work is very good,"* on a seven-point scale (1 = strongly disagree to 7 = strongly agree; for this study, $\alpha = 0.96$). Using organisational reference in this scale, participants are posed with the question, "My leader."

Job autonomy: Four items from the Occupational Diagnostic Survey by Hackman and Oldham (1980) were used to evaluate job autonomy. Example items are as follows: *"I have fully complete responsibility for deciding how and when the work is to be done,"* and *"I have full freedom in deciding how the work is to be done."* Responses were rated on a five-point scale ranging from 1 (*strongly disagree*) to 5 (*strongly agree*; for this study, $\alpha = 0.80$).

Innovative work behaviour: Nine items from Janssen's (2000) survey were used to gauge innovative work behaviour. Hood psychometric properties are those with a high internal consistency of $\alpha = 0.95$. Innovative work behaviour was rated on a seven-point scale ranging from 1 *(strongly agree)* to 7 (*strongly disagree*). Examples of items include: *"I am introducing innovative ideas into the work environment in a systematic way,"* and *"I am evaluating the utility of innovative ideas"* (for this study, $\alpha = 0.95$).

Analysis Strategy

Given that our study used multilevel data, we tested each hypothesis using hierarchical linear modelling (HLM). Two samples must be used in HLM, one aggregated at the organisational level and the other at the individual level. Therefore, we conducted several tests to determine if transformational leadership and transactional leadership possess group-level properties. We measure organisational agreement using the mean $r_{(wg)}$. The result supports the organisational team's high level of agreement, which is attributed to transformational leadership's mean [$r_{(wg)} = 0.89$ (SD = 0.29)] and transactional leadership's mean [$r_{(wg)} = 0.88$ (SD = 0.48)] (George & Bettenhausen, 1990). The inter-organisational variance for both transformational leadership and transactional leadership was assessed using ICC (1), and the results gave a value of 0.07 and 0.04, respectively. This means that organisational factors were responsible for 7% of the variance in transformational leadership and 4% of the variance in transactional leadership. Values of >0 and as small as 1.00 are acceptable for the aggregation procedures, as suggested by Kahn (2011). There is good evidence that both transformational leadership and transactional leadership are group (organisational)-level phenomena due to the sufficient between-group variance and consistency of perceptions within groups.

Hypothesis Testing

We first tested the null model (Model 1) to validate the level of between-group variance in the measure. Innovative work behaviour regressed on transformational leadership (H1) and transactional leadership (H2) to test the cross-level direct effect hypotheses (Model 2 and Model 3). We regressed job autonomy in relation to transformational leadership (H3) and transactional leadership (H4). We regressed for innovative work behaviour on job autonomy (for H5).

In our study, several steps were taken to test the meso-mediated relationship to examine cross-level mediation by using low-level mediation analysis [i.e., X (Level 2) ➔ M (Level 1) ➔ Y (Level 1)]. This measure was performed to test the mediation hypothesis (H6 and H7). The first step examined if there is a significant association between the antecedent and outcome variables (X ➔ Y). Step 2, *path a*, involved testing whether there is a substantial relationship between the antecedent and mediating variable (X ➔ M). A mediation test on the outcome variable (M ➔ Y) was required for step 3. Step 4, *path b*, tested the relationship between the mediator and the outcome variable (M ➔ Y), controlling for the antecedent variable (X). The findings of the mediation path were then reported together with the lower- and upper-level values of the 95% confidence interval (CI) for indirect effects.

4 Results

The results of the descriptive analysis and the correlation of the variables at the individual level are displayed in Table 1.

Hypothesis (H1) proposes that Level 2 transformational leadership and innovative work behaviour have a positive relationship. The influence of transformational leadership on innovative work behaviour was

Table 1 Means, standard deviation, reliabilities and Pearson bivariate correlations

	Variables	*M*	SD	α	1	2	3	4
1	Transformational leadership	5.49	0.94	0.94	1			
2	Transactional leadership	5.40	1.09	0.96	0.79**	1		
3	Job autonomy	3.97	0.65	0.80	0.31**	0.25**	1	
4	Innovative work behaviour	5.83	0.80	0.95	0.41**	0.36**	0.35**	1

Note: Bivariate correlations only between lower-level variables, $n = 269$
*$p<0.01$

significantly positive ($\gamma = 0.31$; SE = 0.12; $p < 0.05$; Table 2, Model 2). Transformational leadership was also found to largely explain the between-group change in variance in innovative work behaviour, which supports the hypothesis. The predictions of hypothesis (H2) that transactional leadership is favourably associated with innovative work

Table 2 HLM random intercept and slope models for innovative work behaviour

	Innovative work behaviour			
Effect	Null	Model 1 Random intercept and fixed slope	Model 2 Random intercept and random slope	Model 3 Random intercept and random slope
Lower-level effects	5.83	4.10 (0.28)	2.48 (0.71)	2.75 (0.68)
Intercepts (γ_{00})	(0.05)	0.44 (0.07)***	0.42 (0.07)***	0.43 (0.07)***
Job autonomy (γ_{10})				
Cross-level effects			0.31 (0.12)*	0.26 (0.12)*
Transformational leadership (γ_{01})				
Transactional leadership (γ_{01})				
Variance components	0.64	0.55	0.55	0.63
Within-team (L1) variance (σ^2)	0.01	0.01	0.001	0.002
Intercept (L2) variance (τ_{00})				
Slope (L2) variance (τ_{11})				
Additional	0.02	0.02	0.002	0.004
information	642.51	606.31	600.74	601.98
ICC	3	4	5	5
-2 log likelihood (FML)	0	0.14	0.14	0.14
Number of estimated parameters				
Pseudo R^2				

Note: individuals, $n = 269$; organisations = 27. FML= full information likelihood estimation; L1 = Level 1; L2 = Level 2. For the cross-level effects, the first value is the parameter estimate (γ); for the lower-level effects, the first value is the parameter estimate (β), and the value in parenthesis is the standard error

*$p < 0.05$; **$p < 0.01$; ***$p < 0.001$

behaviour have been confirmed. Transactional leadership was found to positively influence innovative work behaviour ($\gamma = 0.26$; SE = 0.12; $p < 0.05$;Table 2, Model 3).

Hypotheses H3 and H4 suggest that transformational leadership and transactional leadership, respectively, will predict job autonomy. In this study, neither hypothesis is supported. We discovered that there is no discernible relationship between transformational leadership ($\gamma = 0.12$; SE = 0.11, p = not significant [ns]), transactional leadership ($\gamma = 0.10$; SE = 0.10, p = not significant [ns]) and job autonomy. Hypothesis H5 suggests that job autonomy is predicted to positively influence innovative work behaviour, and this relationship is confirmed by the findings. Job autonomy and innovative work behaviour were revealed to be significantly positively associated ($\beta = 0.44$; SE = 0.07; $p < 0.001$; Table 2, Model 1). With regards to the mediation hypothesis (H6), we anticipated that job autonomy would be a key factor in relating transformational leadership and innovative work behaviour. For the relationship between transformational leadership and job autonomy, mediation effects were estimated using parameter estimates for the *path a* ($\gamma = 0.12$; SE = 0.11; p = not significant [ns]; Table 3, Model 1), whereas, for the relationship between job autonomy and innovative work behaviour with transformational leadership, mediation effects were estimates using parameter estimates using the *path b* ($\beta = 0.42$; SE = 0.07; $p < 0.001$;Table 2, Model 2). With a 95% confidence interval (CI) of [-0.042, 0.155], transformational leadership does not significantly influence innovative work behaviour through job autonomy. It should be emphasised that the relationship is significant if the CI does not contain 0. Therefore, the hypothesis (H6) is rejected.

To test hypothesis (H7), we proposed that transactional leadership and innovative work behaviour are mediated by job autonomy. For Model 2 (Table 2), the parameter estimates for *path a* for the relationship between transactional leadership and job autonomy are as follows: $\gamma = 0.10$; SE = 0.10, p = not significant [ns]. The parameter estimates for *path b* for the relationship between job autonomy and innovative work behaviour with

Table 3 HLM random intercept and slope models for job autonomy

	Job autonomy		
Effects	Null	Model 1 Random intercept and fixed slope	Model 2 Random intercept and fixed slope
Lower-level effects	3.97	3.29 (0.59)	3.45 (0.55)
Intercepts (γ_{00})	(0.04)		
Cross-level effects		0.12 (0.11)ns	0.10 (0.10)ns
Transformational leadership (γ_{01})			
Transactional leadership (γ_{01})			
Variance components	0.43	0.42	0.42
Within-team (L1) variance (σ^2)	0.0003	0.001	0.001
Intercept (L2) variance (τ_{00})			
Slope (L2) variance (τ_{11})			
Additional information	0	0.002	0.002
ICC	531.70	530.34	530.80
-2 log likelihood (FML)	3	4	4
Number of estimated parameters	0	0.02	0.02
Pseudo R^2			

Note: individuals, $n = 269$; organisations = 27. FML= full information likelihood estimation; L1 = Level 1; L2 = Level 2. For the cross-level effects, the first value is the parameter estimate (γ); for the lower-level effects, the first value is the parameter estimate (β) and value in parenthesis is the standard error

$*p < 0.05$; $**p < 0.01$; $***p < 0.001$

transactional leadership are $\beta = 0.43$ (SE = 0.07, $p < 0.001$; Table 2, Model 3). Transactional leadership does not significantly influence innovative work behaviour through job autonomy, as indicated by the 95% confidence interval (CI; -0.041, 0.133). This hypothesis is rejected.

As shown in Fig. 1, the final model represents both the direct and mediated paths.

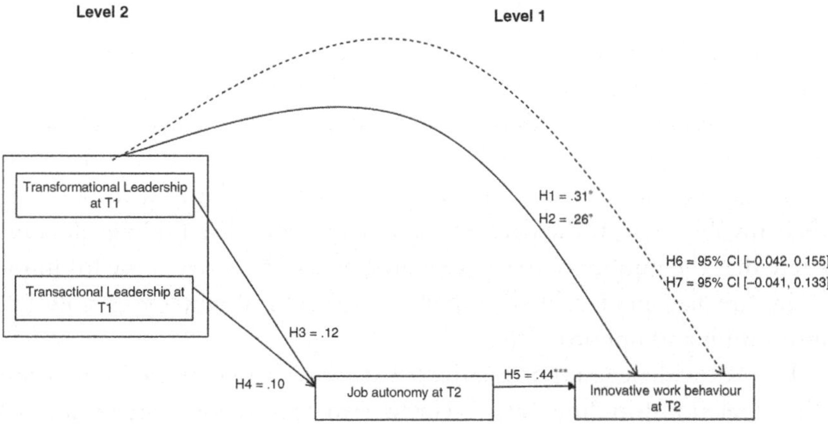

Fig. 1 Final model. *$p<0.05$, ***$p<0.001$. Note: *CI* confidence interval

5 Findings and Discussions

Theoretical Implications

This study seeks to examine the impact of both transformational leadership and transactional leadership on employees' innovative work behaviour in the context of the public sector. In addition, we also examined how job autonomy affects the relationship between different leadership styles and innovative work behaviour. Data was collected from managerial officers working in the public sector to achieve the research objectives. Seven hypotheses were proposed in conjunction with the literature review. Three hypotheses investigated the direct effects of different leadership styles and levels of job autonomy on innovative work behaviour. The three hypotheses that demonstrated the positive effects of transformational leadership, transactional leadership and job autonomy on innovative work behaviour have all been confirmed. This is in line with the research of Kang et al. (2015), who found that these leadership styles have a significant impact on how innovatively employees perform.

Therefore, transformational leadership emphasises employees who work hard to support the introduction and development of new ideas, while transactional leadership recognises and rewards the need to have a clear vision. This demonstrates how leaders urge employees to think "outside the box" and find solutions to numerous problems to maintain customer service and emerging economies during COVID-19. In fact, a strong demand for autonomy affects an individual's intrinsic motivation to engage in innovative work behaviours (Deci & Ryan, 2000). In addition, leaders offer chances for giving employees a platform in boosting their involvement in the decision-making process. The findings demonstrate that the public sector can execute leadership to give space for innovation management, which supports the growth of employees' abilities, motivation and opportunities.

Further evidence supporting the self-determination theory comes from direct relationship findings. According to this theory, organizational innovation management should be used in situations where good leadership (for example, transformational and transactional) is required to boost employees' potential for innovation and engagement in their work. The theory of self-determination states that the motivation provided by these two leaders can change and develop innovative ideas in how they carry out their duties more successfully (Ryan & Deci, 2000), which aids public sector employees in enhancing innovative work behaviours.

Besides, the findings indicate that four hypotheses need more explanation. Neither transformational leadership nor transactional leadership demonstrated a positive effect on job autonomy. This contrasts with Breevaart et al.'s (2014) argument that transformational leadership and transactional leadership promote encouraging job autonomy. We believe that the conflicting results can be attributed to a large correlation. Furthermore, our research has demonstrated that there is no mediation role for job autonomy between different leadership styles and innovative work behaviour. This demonstrates that transformational leadership and transactional leadership, which provide freedom, are unable to affect civil servants' innovative work behaviour. Likely, the pattern of these findings is frequently observed when there is a weak relationship between the independent variable and the mediator but a statistically significant relationship between the independent variable and the outcome and between the mediator and the outcome when reported with values of the 95% confidence interval (CI).

Practical Implications

This study highlights the importance of encouraging employees' innovative work behaviours through leader involvement and enhanced employee autonomy. Respectively, effective transformational leadership and transactional leadership, as well as a high degree of job autonomy in the decision-making process, are more efficient in improving employees' innovative work behaviour. This indicates that in order to motivate employees to develop their skills and abilities in carrying out the assigned duties, the organization should select an effective leadership style. Both transformational and transactional leaders have the ability to develop initiatives or strategies that encourage their employees to contribute to the objectives of the organization by coming up with innovative ideas and suggestions. These leadership styles have encouraged employees to enhance innovative work behaviour, particularly in the public sector where the proliferation of Covid-19 necessitates more effective innovation management in organizations. In addition, organizations tend to provide employees' job autonomy in order to maximise output.

The findings indicate a relationship between employees' job autonomy and their innovative work behaviour. This signifies that the public sector is likely to encourage their employees' innovative work behaviour if it can boost their freedom towards the jobs assigned. Organizations must not only focus on effective leadership, but they need to make sure that their employees have sufficient freedom over their decisions in order to encourage employees to demonstrate their innovativeness. Organizations should be conscious of the importance of job autonomy and the ways in which it may be used to develop innovative work behaviour in the public sector. Therefore, the public sector should determine the appropriate level of autonomy offered to their employees in order to encourage their innovative work behaviour. For instance, organizations should provide employees with the freedom they need to succeed in their tasks without the interference of their leaders. Employees are more likely to use innovative solutions to complete tasks when given the freedom to choose how they work. If organizations give enough freedom to their employees, they will be better equipped to tackle a variety of job problems in the future and will be able to do so with innovative solutions.

Therefore, the public sector should concentrate on using transformational leadership and transactional leadership to motivate employees by giving them opportunities, including them in generating and developing innovative ideas and putting job assignments into practice. In essence, the public sector also needs to give its employees a sense of meaning in their job by allowing them the freedom to design their own job, change the way they perform and finish the job until they are satisfied. As a result, the public sector is able to encourage employees to engage in innovative work behaviour.

Limitations and Future Recommendations

Certainly, our current research has several limitations. Our study relies on data from a single source, which introduces common method bias. Thus, the measuring method may be partially responsible for the observed relationship. Future studies may conduct longitudinal research to determine the direction of the relationship in order to overcome this constraint. However, this study measured between-group effects using organisational-level data aggregated, which may decrease the possibility of cross-level effects brought on by individual subjective biases.

Second, we solely used information gathered from the public sector in Malaysia. Some cultural influences may probably impact the findings of our study and restrict generalisability. Therefore, it is recommended that future studies explore different sample frames to generalise our findings. In addition, this study explores the different leadership styles and innovative work behaviour of Malaysian public sector employees, expressing concerns about the implications in other situations, particularly in developing countries. Future studies may be able to learn more about how other countries use transformational leadership and transactional leadership to encourage innovative work behaviour among their employees by replicating and testing this model in different countries.

6 Conclusion

Innovation is crucial to achieving organizational objectives, particularly in the public sector. The current study indicates that transformational leadership, transactional leadership and job autonomy have a direct impact on employees' innovative work behaviour. However, neither transformational nor transactional leadership has an impact on employee job autonomy, and even job autonomy does not mediate the relationship between these two leadership styles and innovative work behaviour in the public sector. However, it can be concluded that the public sector should concentrate on innovation management in the workplace through the encouragement of leaders to their employees and the freedom of employees to determine their own work decisions, which provides empirical support for the self-determination theory. As a result of these findings, the public sector can use these dimensions to foster innovative thinking among public servants by putting them into practice through transformational leadership, transactional leadership and job autonomy. Therefore, it is believed that the finding of this study will benefit organizational behaviour practitioners and stimulate further research to gain new knowledge about this topic.

References

Bass, B. M. (1999). Two decades of research and development in transformational leadership. *European Journal of Work and Organizational Psychology, 8*(1), 9–32. https://doi.org/10.1080/135943299398410

Breevaart, K., Bakker, A., Hetland, J., Demerouti, E., Olsen, O. K., & Espevik, R. (2014). Daily transactional and transformational leadership and daily employee engagement. *Journal of Occupational and Organizational Psychology, 87*(1), 138–157. https://doi.org/10.1111/joop.12041

Chen, G., Farh, J. L., Campbell-Bush, E. M., Wu, Z., & Wu, X. (2013). Teams as innovative systems: Multilevel motivational antecedents of innovation in R&D teams. *Journal of Applied Psychology, 98*(6), 1018. https://doi.org/10.1037/a0032663

Deci, E. L., & Ryan, R. M. (2000). The" what" and" why" of goal pursuits: Human needs and the self-determination of behavior. *Psychological Inquiry, 11*(4), 227–268. https://doi.org/10.1207/S15327965PLI1104_01

George, J. M., & Bettenhausen, K. (1990). Understanding prosocial behavior, sales performance, and turnover: A group-level analysis in a service context. *Journal of Applied Psychology, 75*(6), 698–709. https://doi.org/10.1037/0021-9010.75.6.698

Hackman, J.R. & Oldham, G.R. (1980). *Work redesign* Mass, Addison-Wesley.

Janssen, O. (2000). Job demands, perceptions of effort-reward fairness and innovative work behaviour. *Journal of Occupational and Organizational Psychology, 73*(3), 287–302. https://doi.org/10.1348/096317900167038

Kahn, J. H. (2011). Multilevel modeling: Overview and applications to research in counseling psychology. *Journal of Counseling Psychology, 58*(2), 257–271. https://doi.org/10.1037/a0022680

Kanesarajah, V., & White, E. (2020). Chasing change: Innovation and patent activity during COVID-19. A report on the pandemic's impact on the global R&D community and innovation lifecycle. Clarivate. Retrieved from: https://clarivate.com/derwent/wp-content/uploads/sites/3/dlm_uploads/2020/06/DW507408683-COVID-19-Report_FINAL.pdf?utm_campaign=EM1_Report_Derwent_COVID_19_Survey_Apr_IPS_Global_2020_ClientsProspects.

Kang, J. H., Solomon, G. T., & Choi, D. Y. (2015). CEOs' leadership styles and managers' innovative behaviour: Investigation of intervening effects in an entrepreneurial context. *Journal of Management Studies, 52*(4), 531–554. https://doi.org/10.1111/joms.12125

Podsakoff, P. M., MacKenzie, S. B., Moorman, R. H., & Fetter, R. (1990). Transformational leader behaviors and their effects on followers' trust in leader, satisfaction, and organizational citizenship behaviors. *The Leadership Quarterly, 1*(2), 107–142. https://doi.org/10.1016/1048-9843(90)90009-7

Rafferty, A. E., & Griffin, M. A. (2004). Dimensions of transformational leadership: Conceptual and empirical extensions. *The Leadership Quarterly, 15*(3), 329–354. https://doi.org/10.1016/j.leaqua.2004.02.009

Ryan, R. M., & Deci, E. L. (2000). Intrinsic and extrinsic motivations: Classic definitions and new directions. *Contemporary Educational Psychology, 25*(1), 54–67. https://doi.org/10.1006/ceps.1999.1020

Challenges and Implications of Cryptocurrencies, Central Bank Digital Currencies, and Electronic Money

Henri Kouam

1 Introduction

New cryptocurrencies are emerging daily, providing alternatives to traditional payments and enabling new mediums of exchange such as cash. These currencies span Bitcoin,[1] Litecoin, and Ethereum designed to provide some characteristics of money as well as asset classes that enable the transfer and/or store of value across societies. In less than a decade, Bitcoin has gone from being an obscure curiosity to a household name. In recent times, Bitcoin has risen—with ups and downs—from a few cents per coin to over $4000. In the meantime, hundreds of other

[1] Bitcoin is an example of a non-central bank digital currency. It was invented by an unknown programmer who used the pseudonym Satoshi Nakamoto and was released as open-source software in 2009 along with a white paper describing the technical aspects of its design (see Box A for further details).

H. Kouam (✉)
Prima Finance, and Investment, Yaounde, Cameroon

F. A. Yamoah, A. ul Haque (eds.), *Corporate Management Ecosystem in Emerging Economies*, https://doi.org/10.1007/978-3-031-41578-4_9

cryptocurrencies—equaling Bitcoin in market value—have emerged (Graph 1, left-hand panel).

While it seems unlikely that Bitcoin or its sisters will displace sovereign currencies, they have demonstrated the viability of the underlying blockchain or distributed ledger technology (DLT) and its credible use and application across other sectors such as manufacturing, health care, investment, cyber security, and big data. Venture capitalists and financial institutions are investing heavily in DLT projects that seek to provide new financial services as well as deliver old ones more efficiently. Bloggers, central bankers, and academics are predicting transformative or disruptive implications for payments, banks, and the financial system at large.

Findings from Andolfatto (2015), Andolfatto et al. (2016), Broadbent (2016), Raskin and Yermack (2016), and Skingsley (2016) attest to this sea-change in mediums of exchange as consumers and transformative implications for economies, financial systems, and consumer investment behavior is already changing reflecting a macroeconomic backdrop characterized by ultra-accommodative interest rates, low economic growth, and a shortage of investment opportunities, with over 20% of global debt yielding negative returns.

The transformative changes likely embedded in the increased use and adoption of cryptocurrencies across economies suggest a need to better understand the nature of cryptocurrencies. Similarly, it is imperative to understand the implications of these novel sources of investment on macroeconomic outcomes, monetary policy, and consumer behavior. This chapter outlines the nature of crypto currencies, outlines the inherent differences to cash, and how best to leverage their investment characteristics without compromising financial stability (Fig. 1).

2 Can Bitcoin Serve as a Medium of Exchange?

It is not clear that Bitcoin can ever replace cash, as it operates via democratic consensus, is supported by distributed ledger technology, and has a limited number of users.

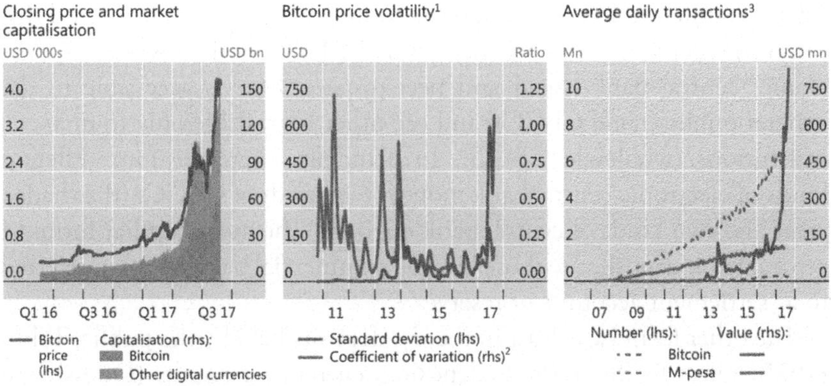

Fig. 1 Bitcoin appears to be a volatile investment but not a credible store of value. Sources: Central Bank of Kenya; CoinDance; CoinDesk; www.blockchain.info

This chapter defines cryptocurrencies as an electronic form of central bank money that can be exchanged in a decentralized manner known as peer-to-peer, meaning that transactions occur directly between the payer and the payee without the need for a central intermediary.[2]

Unlike cash issued by the central bank, Bitcoin is supported by distributed ledger technology that serves as a medium of exchange between its users. Furthermore, it does not have the characteristics inherent in "cash" issued by a central authority, as it is not recognized by governments as a legitimate store of value, and the democratic consensus which underpins the cryptocurrency is limited to its users. Secondly, cryptocurrencies are not accessible to individuals who do not participate in the purchase or sale of Bitcoin, Litecoin, Ethereum, etc.

In this spirit, Bjerg (2017) includes the universality of accessible currencies as central to the legitimacy of central-bank-issued currencies. It is important to note that central banks across the world are issuing digital currencies to leverage the technological advances latent in distributed ledger technology; it is, therefore, imperative to make a distinction between cryptocurrencies and central bank digital currencies (CBDCs).

[2] The purest form of peer-to-peer transaction is a cash exchange. On a computer network, the peer-to-peer concept means that transactions can be processed without the need for a central server.

This taxonomy reflects what appears to be emerging in practice and distinguishes between two potential types of CBCC, both of which are electronic: central bank-issued and peer-to-peer. One is accessible to the general public (retail CBCC), and the other is available only to financial institutions (wholesale CBCC). In principle, there are four different kinds of electronic central bank money: two kinds of CBCCs (the shaded area) and two kinds of central bank deposits. The most familiar forms of central bank deposits are those held by commercial banks—often referred to as settlement accounts or reserves.

The other form is, at least in theory, deposits held by the public. Tobin (1987) refers to this form as deposited currency accounts (DCAs).[3] So far, central banks have generally chosen not to provide DCAs (Fig. 2).

This distinguishes CBCCs from other existing forms of electronic central bank money, such as reserves, which are exchanged in a centralized fashion across accounts at the central bank. Moreover, the taxonomy distinguishes between two possible forms of CBCC: a widely available, consumer-facing payment instrument targeted at retail transactions, and

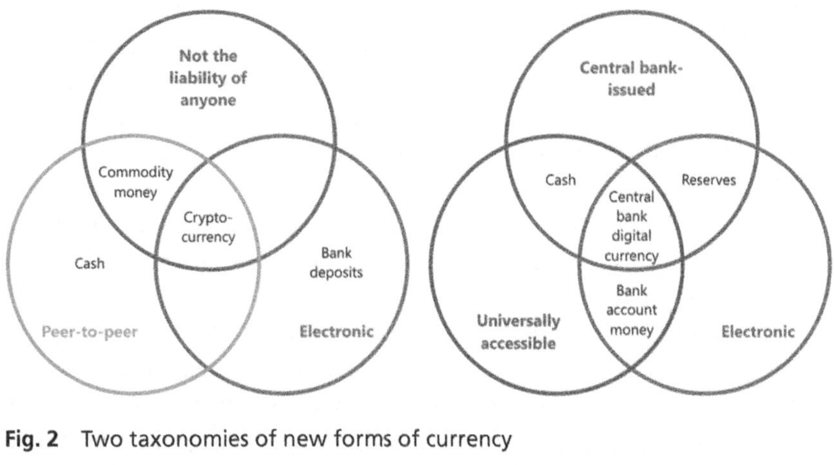

Fig. 2 Two taxonomies of new forms of currency

[3] In a 1987 speech, Nobel laureate James Tobin argued that, in order to avoid relying too heavily on deposit insurance to protect the payment system, central banks should "make available to the public a medium with the convenience of deposits and the safety of currency, essentially currency on deposit, transferable in any amount by check or other order" (Tobin (1987, p. 6); see also Tobin (1985)). That is, people should be able to store value without being subject to the risk of bank failure.

a restricted-access, digital settlement token for wholesale payment applications. As illustrated in the chart above, cryptocurrencies are not backed by a central issuer; as such, they are not the liability of any one party and operate based on distributed ledger technology (see chart below).

Distributed ledger technology (DLT) refers to the protocols and supporting infrastructure that allow computers in different locations to propose and validate transactions and update records in a synchronized way across a network. The idea of a distributed ledger—a typical record of activity shared across computers in different locations—is not new. Such ledgers are used by organizations (e.g., supermarket chains) with branches or offices across the country. However, in a traditional distributed database, a system administrator typically performs the key functions necessary to maintain consistency across the multiple copies of the ledger. The simplest way to do this is for the system administrator to maintain a master copy of the ledger, which is periodically updated and shared with all network participants (Bech & Garrat, 2017).

By contrast, the new systems based on DLT, most notably Bitcoin and Ethereum, are designed to function without a trusted authority. Bitcoin maintains a distributed database in a decentralized way by using a consensus-based validation procedure and cryptographic signatures. In such systems, transactions are conducted in a peer-to-peer fashion and broadcast to the entire set of participants who work to validate them in batches known as "blocks."

Since the ledger of activity is organized into separate but connected blocks, this type of DLT is often referred to as "blockchain technology." The blockchain version of DLT has successfully powered Bitcoin for several years. However, the system is not without drawbacks: it is costly to operate (preventing double-spending without the use of a trusted authority requires transaction validators (miners) to employ large amounts of computing power to complete "proof-of-work" computations); there is only probabilistic finality of settlement, and all transactions are public. These features are not suitable for many financial market applications. Current wholesale DLT payment applications have abandoned the standard blockchain technology in favor of protocols that modify the consensus process to allow enhanced confidentiality and scalability. Examples of protocols currently being tested by central banks include Corda and

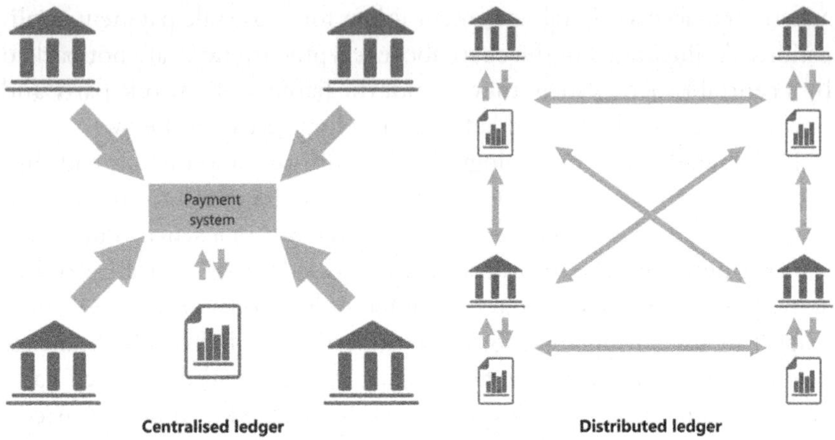

Fig. 3 Distributed ledger system. Source: Santander InnoVentures (2015) (See also Chapman et al. (2017), CPMI (2015), and Benos et al. (2017). The amount of energy currently being used by Bitcoin miners is equal to the energy consumption of Lebanon and Cuba (see http://digiconomist.net/bitcoin-energy-consumption). For a detailed description of proof-of-work, see https://en.bitcoin.it/wiki/Proof_of_work)

Hyperledger Fabric. Corda replaces blockchain with a "notary" architecture. The notary design utilizes a trusted authority and allows consensus to be reached on an individual transaction basis rather than in blocks, with limited information sharing (Fig. 3).

Admittedly, this prompted caution from the G20 and Kouam (2019), who illustrate the implications of financial stability and disintermediation in the financial system. It is important to note that cryptocurrencies do have characteristics inconsistent with financial stability in the absence of intentional and targeted regulation. Bitcoin is an example of a non-central bank digital currency. It was invented by an unknown programmer who used the pseudonym Satoshi Nakamoto and was released as open-source software in 2009, along with a white paper describing the technical aspects of its design (see Box A for further details).

3 What Are the Risks Associated with Cryptocurrencies?

Legal Certainty and Sound Governance

One of the drawbacks of cryptocurrencies is the uncertainty surrounding claims among participants. The likes of Bitcoin and Litecoin are not based on any assets or reserves at a central bank, which prevents the creators from incurring any losses and significantly exposes the users of said currencies.

The absence of legal certainty over the convertibility of cryptocurrencies for cash or any other asset is symptomatic of a lack of governance that could prove futile over the long run for developing economies that are already prone to capital outflows, courtesy of political uncertainty.

Money Laundering: Terrorist Activities and Illicit Activities

Cryptocurrencies operate via democratic consensus, but distributed ledger technologies prevent regulators from performing a vital function. This is particularly salient for law enforcement and counterterrorism activity that is salient for both advanced and developing market economies. Furthermore, cryptocurrencies could enhance sanctions busting, which has outsized implications for the global world order. It can be seen as a credible tool for money laundering across the globe. This holds grave implications for tax shifting, more so for developing economies that currently see over 2 billion in tax evasion.

Safety, integrity, and efficiency of payment systems: Payment systems are a way for consumers and institutions to execute transactions across borders and within economies. The emergence of new cryptocurrencies will create new forms of clearing that can compromise the legitimacy, not least efficiency, of such systems. The integrity of payment systems is central to the democratic underpinnings of cash and the functioning of financial systems. New currencies that are disconnected from the financial system can create systemic risk and impose significant pressure on payment systems in the event of a run or a sudden loss of monetary value.

4 Cyber Security and Operational Resilience

Admittedly, distributed ledger technology can be termed "highly secure," but by no means does this mean the technology underpinning cryptocurrencies is unassailable. However, its mode of operation is decentralized, reducing the probability of targeted attacks against a centralized server or location at any given time.

Meanwhile, it should be noted that such operational risks are symptomatic of any digitized systems that rely on a complex network of electronic systems. However, credit card fraud can be mitigated by a range of novel tools such as multi-factor authentication, biometric log-in processes, and geo-location instant messaging tools confirming the user's identity and passwords. This has been increasingly employed by banks across the globe in a bid to lessen cyber security risks and bolster resilience. The cyber security risks of a cryptocurrency that relies on democratic consensus and a decentralized *modus Operandi* are evident, but these are much less prominent than traditional electronic transactions. However, hackers targeted Bitcoin on September 26, as confirmed by KuCoin Global CEO Johnny Lyu (Kucoin, 2020). The breach affected Kukoin's Bitcoin (BTC), Ether (ETH), and ERC20 hot wallets after private keys were leaked. Reports estimate the breach to have affected $150 million in user funds. This suggests the fallibility inherent in digital systems and exposure, as well as the transfer of risk to consumers, cannot be understated.

Similarly, sub-Saharan African countries such as Nigeria and Kenya have equally been prone to bank fraud, including but not limited to identity theft, beneficial owners, financial inclusion, discrimination, blacklisted consumers, etc. Esoimeme (2020) finds that a bank verification number (BVN) could bolster cyber resilience if properly implemented. While this does not eradicate the propensity for fraud, it bolsters cyber resilience across the system. Meanwhile, there are other issues that accrue to centralized information systems, the majority of which will form the basis of electronic currencies and central bank-issued digital currencies.

In Kenya, consumers challenged the legitimacy of its National Integrated Information Management System (NIIMS) as amended by the Statute Law Miscellaneous (Amendment Act) 2018. One of the petitioners' grounds of contention, which will form a central part of this discussion, was that there are no adequate and/or proper safeguards for the protection of the data and/or personal information intended for collection under the NIIMS system; hence, there is a violation and/or threat of violation of the right to privacy guaranteed under Article 31 of the Constitution (Kimani, 2019). If distributed ledger technology fails to implicitly protect consumer data, such concerns will likely emerge much more strongly for cryptocurrencies such as Bitcoin, Ethereum, and Litecoin. There is an ample space for regulators to begin designing legislation designed to protect consumers' interests if cryptocurrencies are to become operational in developing market economies.

5 Market Integrity and Bitcoin

Concerns regarding the integrity of cryptocurrency markets are a hurdle to mainstream and institutional adoption of digital assets, in addition to being a key concern for regulators. To improve market integrity and provide consumers with the confidence they deserve, policymakers may need to enact legislation to support the orderly and secure functioning of crypto markets. Such legislation will comprise banking authorities such as COBAC for CEMAC member countries as well as domestic regulatory bodies that are designed to support market functioning and lessen the spillovers from cryptocurrencies into the real economy. The amount of Bitcoin that can be issued at any given time is limited, and there are no regulators or market makers to ensure the smooth functioning of peer-to-peer exchanges.

Data Privacy and Portability

Privacy concerns are little associated with blockchain technology as unique identification numbers and a foolproof system protect consumer data and users of its peer-to-peer lending. As outlined above, the distributed ledger technology is not unassailable, as Bitcoin has been subject to hacks. One of the features of peer-to-peer exchange facilitated by distributed ledger technology is anonymity. Unlike traditional modes of exchange such as cash or other electronic payments, cryptocurrencies promise anonymity, enabling their users to exercise their right to purchase without any legislative impediments from governments; the anonymity is symptomatic of cash, but the risks inherent with digital forms of payment are consumers' data that are stored online.

The information risks associated with cash are muted, but regulators must ensure that consumer data is protected in a rigorous manner.

Consumer and Investor Protection

There are no clear definitions for investor and consumer protection as the distributed ledger technology does not provide any way to trade the founders of cryptocurrencies. Furthermore, cryptocurrencies operate via democratic consensus, which absolves any one party of counterparty risks. This does not make it immune to such risks but rather reduces the chances to near-zero that a user account may be hacked from a distance. It provides a safety net for consumers, institutions, and regulators. One could argue that this differs for the latter, who may struggle to regulate unfair and illegal behavior. Meanwhile, there are several other concerns about consumers that should be outlined. For example, an event-triggered sell-off could have adverse implications for financial stability, but unlike the financial crisis, where blame was attributed to banks, the value of the currency is contingent on demand and scarcity. It is, therefore, challenging to design legislation protecting investors over the long run, but it is indispensable that regulators explicitly prohibit banks and financial institutions from using consumer deposits to invest in cryptocurrencies.

Tax Compliance

Tax evasion and avoidance are endemic in developing market economies due to an inability to coordinate global surveillance and the ability of multinationals to shift profits to tax havens. From the standpoint of cryptocurrencies, they will provide a credible vehicle for global companies to evade taxes as retained earnings can be otherwise termed investments that are subject to different tax regimes across different jurisdictions. According to the IMF, developing economies lose over 2 trillion on average, which constrains government spending and exacerbates the impact of weaker external balances. With cryptocurrencies, governments will not have to design and implement legislation but equally identify and verify how to enforce such laws.

This will ensure that over time, the tax burden of countries is evenly spread between investors and other workers across society whilst enabling them to broaden their tax base and facilitate broad-based inclusive development. This is especially the case for emerging market economies and developing market economies like India and South Korea, which will be increasingly exposed to a high level of mining. It is, therefore, imperative for policymakers to ensure that such cryptocurrencies are not used as a means to evade taxation that has grave socio-economic costs to nations, not least developing economies with structural economic imbalances facilitated by free trade policies that have not sufficiently accounted for tax loopholes. Whilst such unfortunate economic effects are endemic to cryptocurrencies, it is important to consider the tax implications of cryptocurrencies prior to legislating their operation in developing market economies. The economic fallout can be seen from two standpoints:

1. The cost of hedging against macroeconomic risks such as inflation or risk-adjusted returns in developing economies can exacerbate liquidity and banking crises. For example, if consumers seek to insulate their portfolios and investments from inflation, they can increasingly rotate their assets into cryptocurrencies, which can further reduce the value of the exchange rate and precipitate a currency crisis. This imposes costs on the fiscal balances of developing economies, as their governments have to spend more to attenuate the costs of banking or cur-

rency crises. Meanwhile, the cost of borrowing for banks and governments equally rises following periods of macroeconomic stress, more so as one in three countries is at risk of debt distress.
2. The second costs that accrue from non-compliance or tax evasion are lower government revenues. This is particularly endemic in developing market economies, which are prone to tax evasion as domestic regulation is not sufficiently harmonized with global standards to prevent tax shifting across jurisdictions. This constrains spending on vital infrastructures such as roads, schools, and energy that are necessary for economic development.

More worrying is the fact that developing economies are commodity exporters whose revenues are exposed to the global business cycle as well as economic activity prone to different tax countries. Tax avoidance and hedging impose grave costs on policymakers' ability to spend, thereby slowing economic development. The issue of tax compliance, therefore, cannot be overstated.

Monetary and Financial: Hedging and Monetary Policy Transmission

Cryptocurrencies are a credible vehicle of investment for some, as they are a store of value in some regards and can be converted to cash based on the given amount of sellers at any one time. However, they impose grave costs on the financial system, not least financial stability, as individuals can use cryptocurrencies to hedge against inflation or other macroeconomic outcomes such as low growth or weaker returns on investments.

The disintermediation caused by cryptocurrencies can enable investors to store their assets in cryptocurrencies and cause the currency to depreciate. A weaker currency not only causes prices to rise but also equally depresses economic growth. As such, the economy is prone to hedging and inflation overshoots if individuals park their assets in cryptocurrencies. This obviously has implications for monetary policy, whereby central banks will have to raise policy rates to keep a lid on inflation even as the economy slows. As a result, such pro-cyclical monetary policy outcomes could amplify the shock from uncontrolled investments in cryptocurrencies. Over time, the inverse relationship between the performance of cryptocurrencies and the exchange rate will induce pressures for monetary policy that will have to contend with episodes of financial instability and lower economic growth.

More worrying are the transmission mechanisms from monetary policy that could be assuaged by renewed investments in cryptocurrencies as the purchasing power of cash remains impeded by the uncertainty created by the linkage between cryptocurrencies and traditional exchange rates.

Admittedly, limits could be set on the number of deposits that can be credibly invested in cryptocurrencies, and enhanced convertibility can result in greater financial stability over the long run. This is especially the case in countries such as the Central African Republic (CAR) where Bitcoin has been deemed legal tender and will be used to clear and exchange a range of goods and services across the country. However, such an outcome is only likely if crypto companies own deposits at the central bank to ensure convertibility.

The International Trading System

Capital flows form the backbone of the modern-day economy, with liquidity and foreign direct investment necessary for its functioning of the modern-day economy. Cryptocurrencies will discourage investment in traditional assets that have a positive impact on the real economy via employment, the employment channel, and network effects that eventually spill over into the informal sector in developing market economies. Should cryptocurrencies become ubiquitous, it is not unlikely that huge swathes of capital will be transferred from traditional asset classes like stock, bonds, real estate, and commodities to crypto money. This is even more likely as over 20% of global debt is negative yielding and investors will be looking for other means to generate higher returns. Not only are the development implications of cryptocurrencies dire, but they can also equally serve as an anchor for a new type of investment, which does not particularly relate to the modern-day economy.

6 Fair Competition: Cross-border Effectiveness

The last decade has exposed the frailties and vulnerabilities of an increasingly interconnected and interlinked global economy, with centralized clearing and free-flowing capital across borders. It is important for cryptocurrencies to regulate sufficiently in advance, imposing restrictions on the amounts of deposits that can be used to invest in these assets, ensuring smooth market functioning, and creating the right incentive for market participants and platform owners to effectively transact. The rationale for forward-looking regulation and legislation is imminent, but this should champion fairness for a rudderless currency with significant domestic ramifications.

7 Recommendations

- Policymakers should ensure that a group of public sector staff are aware of and knowledgeable about blockchain technologies. They should ensure that the security concerns that could arise as well as the financing issues and hedging that are implicit in Bitcoin can be spotted. Admittedly, this can enable the formation of tech units that seek to better understand distributed ledger technology and can implement this across other sectors such as manufacturing, retail, and health care. A complete and up-to-date understanding of blockchain is indispensable to assuaging security concerns should they arise whilst ensuring that consumer data and interactions are shielded from tech bandits or other forms of assailants.
- Secondly, policymakers should discourage hedging by ensuring that any electronic currencies hold large liquid deposits at a central bank to ensure convertibility. This will reduce sudden spikes in the value of the currency as investors or citizens seek to flee episodes of risk, such as a sudden plunge in the value of the currency caused by an exogenous or endogenous shock such as COVID-19. This will equally lessen financial stability risks as commercial banks will be sufficiently liquid to

improve the transmission mechanism from monetary policy. Liquid deposits will improve financial stability, not least guarantee it over the long run.

- An effective tax mechanism should be set up to ensure that cryptocurrencies are contributing to the societies where each trade occurs. For example, policymakers could design a tax based on each trade and a certain sum to reflect the creation of economic activity on the financial side of the economy; the proceeds from such taxes can be used, explicitly, to upskill and digitize the workforce. An example includes the creation of job transitions.

8 Conclusion

Cryptocurrencies are an electronic form of central bank money that can be exchanged in a decentralized manner known as peer-to-peer, meaning that transactions occur directly between the payer and the payee without the need for a central intermediary.[4] Unlike cash issued by the central bank, Bitcoin is supported by distributed ledger technology that serves as a medium of exchange between its users. The currency is driven by technological advances and has come to firm a credible mode of exchange for market participants across advanced, emerging, and developing market economies.

This chapter finds that Bitcoin does not possess unique characteristics that enable it to function as money. While it operates via democratic consensus, supported by distributed ledger technology (DLT), its ability to replace cash is very unlikely. However, it can credibly serve as a medium of exchange and enable consumption and non-monitored economic activity that are inherently absent from traditional forms of payment such as notes and coins. Even though cash can be used in the absence of a digital trail, Bitcoin serves as an anchor for the digital age, characterized by online payments and electronic forms of engagement.

[4] The purest form of peer-to-peer transaction is a cash exchange. On a computer network, the peer-to-peer concept means that transactions can be processed without the need for a central server.

This finds that Bitcoin is a salient form of investment, albeit speculative and prone to wild Swings. There are several issues spanning governance, money laundering, tax evasion, and data privacy that suggest a more cautious approach to adopting it across countries. This is particularly the case for developing market economies that do not have sufficiently advanced data regulation. It is imperative that countries identify the types and forms of regulation that will be ideal for their circumstances, as this will lead to better regulation and effective data protection, which has been a concern for some policymakers.

Of course, this does not come without some caveat; the General Data Protection Regulation (GDPR) is a step in the right direction as it enables individuals to have greater control of their data. The paper advocates cautious optimism and mechanisms to prevent speculative behavior on the part of banks and private investors from preventing the proliferation of financial stability risks. They should equally place limits on the amount of savings and deposits invested in Bitcoin, if at all. Finally, credible monitoring mechanisms should be designed by lawmakers to understand blockchain technology and reduce the probability of data breaches. These recommendations, amongst others, should equally be accompanied by effective tax legislation that reflects the twenty-first-century needs of domestic economies; this is particularly salient for developing economies that are prone to tax evasion and global tax hemorrhaging.

This article posits the challenges associated with crypto currencies in the context of developing, emerging, and advanced economies. While it does not explicitly advocate the ban of cryptocurrencies, their functioning in the economy should be accompanied by a set of measures that address data, privacy, security, and economic and financial issues.

References

Andolfatto, D. (2015, 3 February). Fedcoin: On the desirability of a government cryptocurrency. MacroMania, blogpost.

Andolfatto, D., Berentsen, A. & Waller, C. J. (2016). Monetary Policy with Asset-Backed Money, Waller. *Journal of Economic Theory, 164*, pp. 166-186.

Bech, M., & Garrat, R. (2017). *Central bank cryptocurrencies*. BIS Quarterly Review.
Benos, E, R Garratt and P Gurrola-Perez (2017): "The economics of distributed ledger technology for securities settlement", Bank of England, Staff Working Papers, no 670, August.
Bjerg, O. (2017). Designing new money – the policy trilemma of central bank digital currency. Copenhagen Business School (CBS) Working Paper, June.
Broadbent, B. (2016, 2 March). *Central banks and digital currencies*. Speech at the London School of Economics.
Chapman, J, R Garratt, S Hendry, A McCormack and W McMahon (2017). "Project Jasper: are distributed wholesale payment systems feasible yet?", Bank of Canada, Financial System Review, June, pp 1–11.
Committee on the Global Financial System (2015). "Central bank operating frameworks and collateral markets", CGFS Papers, no 53, March.
Esoimeme, E. (2020). A critical analysis of the Bank verification number project introduced by the central Bank of Nigeria. *SSRN Electronic Journal*. https://doi.org/10.2139/ssrn.2544934
Kimani, D. (2019). Are we ready for a data Bank? An analysis of the sufficiency of Kenya's legal and institutional framework on data protection and identity. *SSRN Electronic Journal*. https://doi.org/10.2139/ssrn.3424673
Kouam, H. (2019). Facebook's Libra and financial stability risks for Emerging Markets. LinkedIn. https://www.linkedin.com/pulse/facebooks-libra-financial-stability-risks-emerging-markets-kouam/
Kucoin. (2020). *KuCoin CEO livestream recap - latest updates about security incident*. Press Release.
Raskin, M., & Yermack, D. (2016). Digital currencies, decentralized ledgers and the future of central banking. NBER Working Papers, no 22238, May.
Skingsley, C. (2016). Should the riksbank issue e-krona? speech at FinTech Stockholm, 16.

On the Prospects of Sustainable Tourism in Bangladesh

Tahmina Akhter and Adnan ul Haque

1 Introduction

A country with six wonderful seasons located in the north-eastern region of South Asia with a low-lying plain span of 1,47,570 square kilometers is Bangladesh (mofa, 2023). The Padma (Ganges), Brahmaputra (Jamuna), Meghna, and Karna-Fuli rivers are the most notable rivers in this nation (worldatlas, 2023). The third-longest sandy beach in the world, the Gulf of Bengal, stretches for 120 kilometers down the southernmost tip of this lovely nation (Statista, 2023). The majority of India borders the country's other three sides: West Bengal on the western side, Assam on the northern side, and Tripura and Mizoram on the eastern side (Britannica, 2023a, 2023b, 2023c, 2023d).

The term "sustainable tourism" describes travel practices that consider the negative effects of tourism on the environment, society, and economy while making the necessary adjustments to lessen such effects. Along with

T. Akhter • A. ul Haque (✉)
Faculty of Business, Yorkville University, Toronto, ON, Canada
e-mail: ahaque@yorkvilleu.ca

F. A. Yamoah, A. ul Haque (eds.), *Corporate Management Ecosystem in Emerging Economies*, https://doi.org/10.1007/978-3-031-41578-4_10

considering traveler demands, it also considers the needs of the host communities, small companies, and the environment (Revfine, 2023). The concept of sustainable tourism is becoming more and more popular in Bangladesh since it places a strong emphasis on the preservation of the country's rich cultural heritage, environmental protection, and regional economic development. A mutually beneficial relationship between tourists, their local communities, and the environment is the aim of sustainable tourism, which aims to benefit all parties (Mihalic, 2016). There are many chances for ecotourism and adventure tourism in Bangladesh thanks to its natural attractions, which include beaches, mangrove forests, and wildlife reserves. The promotion of the country's rich cultural heritage, which includes mosques, temples, ancient ruins, and traditional crafts, can benefit from cultural tourism (Jahan, 2016).

However, there are obstacles to the growth of sustainable tourism in Bangladesh as well, such as a lack of official assistance and a limited infrastructure. Despite these obstacles, sustainable tourism has the potential to support both the economic growth and the preservation of Bangladesh's distinctive natural and cultural resources. The aim of this research is to briefly analyze the potential of the tourism industry, specifically the opportunities and challenges interlinked with promoting sustainable tourism in Bangladesh.

2 Literature Review

The Concept of Sustainable Tourism

Sustainable tourism refers to a way of traveling that aims to have a positive impact on the environment, local communities, and the economy. As the negative effects of the current tourism industries can be seen through issues such as air traffic pollution and environmental degradation, it is now more important than ever for people to travel sustainably. Promoting sustainable ways of tourism can potentially help a country attain their long-term sustainability goals (Nowreen & Mohiuddin, 2021). Tourism can also benefit several factors in society. As shown in the graph below,

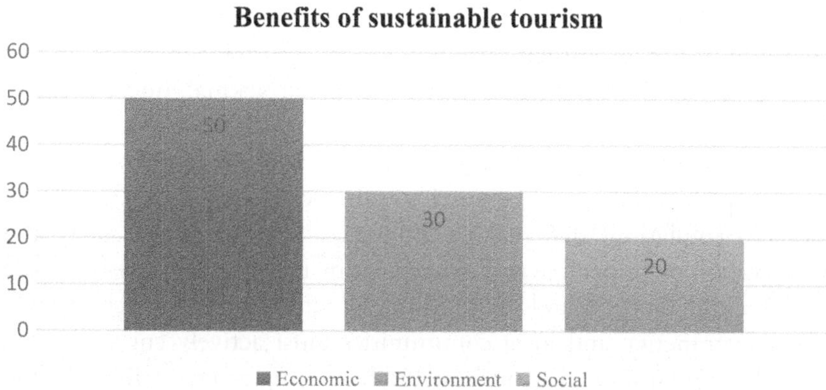

Fig. 1 Benefits of sustainable tourism. Source: adopted from the work of (Islam, 2015)

the economy tends to gain the most from sustainable tourism practices. Having visitors practice sustainable ways of touring will also ensure future environmental protection. It is also beneficial for the society to have sustainable practices for touring to ensure safety for local communities (Fig. 1).

Environmental protection is a key component of sustainable tourism, reducing the negative effects of tourism on the environment by implementing measures such as waste reduction, water and energy conservation, wildlife protection, etc. For example, eco-friendly lodgings may use waste management techniques and renewable energy sources to lessen their carbon footprint (Nekmahmud & Fekete-Farkas, 2021). The preservation of local economies is another crucial component of sustainable tourism, making sure that neighborhood communities may gain from tourism while preserving their cultural identity and traditional practices. Promoting the employment of local workers, assisting neighborhood businesses, and taking part in cultural exchange initiatives. For example, a sustainable tour company might conduct cultural excursions that provide tourists with an immersive and real experience while simultaneously helping local communities. Alternatively, taking actions such as supporting regional businesses, making investments in community facilities, and making sure that the advantages of tourism are distributed fairly and equally can also help with local community preservation. To help the community and lower their carbon footprint, a sustainable hotel can buy their groceries and supplies from local vendors (Nekmahmud & Fekete-Farkas, 2021).

To maintain long-term success, sustainable tourism requires organizations to plan and execute their actions effectively, including having policies and regulations that make a difference. Prioritizing the safety and preservation of vulnerable regions, regulating the number of visitors, and utilizing different methods of tourism. All affected parties such as tourists, governments, and local communities must actively engage in and contribute to sustainable tourism. Implementing a responsible method for tourism that increases awareness and highlights the significance of sustainable tourism is crucial. For example, encouraging tourists in the country to choose eco-friendly lodgings support local restaurants and businesses and take part in sustainable activities (Nowreen & Mohiuddin, 2021).

Sustainable tourism is a travel strategy that seeks to support long-term sustainability for the environment, local communities, and economy. It calls for careful balancing of economic, social, and environmental factors, efficient planning and management, and active involvement from all parties. In the end, there is only one planet we all call home. There will be no tourism in the future if we don't act now to preserve our home. Beautiful destinations from all around the world must be preserved, and we must tour these destinations with sustainability in mind. It is essential that we take immediate action to protect and preserve our planet, ensuring that tourism can remain a positive source of economic growth while safeguarding the environment and the local culture (Nekmahmud & Fekete-Farkas, 2021).

3 Bangladesh in Terms of Sustainable Tourism

Bangladesh is a nation with a rich cultural history, varied topography, and an abundance of natural resources, all of which offer tremendous potential for the development of a sustainable tourist industry. However,

Bangladesh's tourist sector has had to contend with several issues, such as poor infrastructure, little investment, and a lack of knowledge regarding sustainable tourism practices (Jahan, 2014).

There are a few threats that Bangladesh faces for sustainable tourism as shown in the graph below. The topmost threat is seasonal pressure from visitors and encouraging sustainable practices among them. The popular tourist destinations in the country are not well equipped to accommodate large numbers of visitors in a sustainable manner. This also impacts natural resources which is another threat. Alongside being a tropical country, Bangladesh faces many different natural disasters as well within a year which can affect sustainable tourism. There is also a threat to air and water quality as high amounts of pollution in air and water can also create obstacles to sustainable tourism (Fig. 2).

Despite these obstacles, significant initiatives to encourage sustainable tourism in Bangladesh have been taken. The creation of eco-tourism hotspots, such as the Sundarbans mangrove forest, which is home to the Royal Bengal tiger and many other wildlife species, is one such initiative. By designating the Sundarbans as a UNESCO World Heritage site and creating the Sundarbans Biosphere Reserve, the Bangladeshi government has taken action to conserve the area (UNESCO, 1997).

The creation of community-based tourism initiatives is an additional effort to support sustainable tourism in Bangladesh. By incorporating local communities in the tourism sector and giving them opportunities to make money from tourism-related activities, these projects seek to

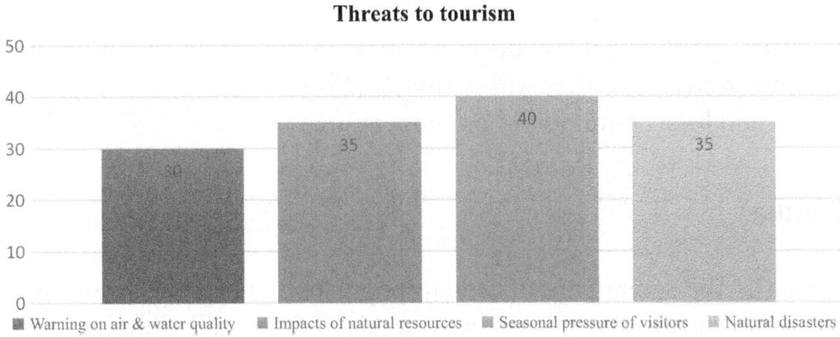

Fig. 2 Threats to tourism. Source: adopted from the work of (Islam, 2015)

support regional economic growth. For instance, local groups in the Chittagong Hill Tracts region have set up homestays and cultural tours that let visitors get a taste of the area's distinctive culture and traditions (Chowdhury et al., 2021).

Tour Operators Association of Bangladesh (TOAB) has been promoting sustainable tourism practices in the nation in addition to these activities. For the benefit of its members, TOAB has created a code of ethics that outlines expectations for ethical tourism behavior, such as reducing waste, using less resources, and assisting local communities.

However, Bangladesh has not yet fully adopted sustainable tourism practices, and more work is required to address the issues the sector is now facing. This entails raising investment in the sector as well as enhancing the standard of tourism infrastructure, such as roads, lodgings, and transit. Additionally, there is a need to increase awareness of the significance of sustainable tourism practices and the favorable effects that these practices may have on local communities and the environment among both the tourism sector and travelers (Chowdhury et al., 2021).

4 Tourist Destinations in some Major Cities of Bangladesh

Touring these beautiful destinations all around Bangladesh responsibly has the potential to advance Bangladesh's economic and social progress. The creation of eco-tourist locations, community-based tourism programs, and increasing investment in the tourism sector are all necessary to encourage sustainable tourism practices in the nation. Adopting sustainable tourism practices will positively affect the government, tourism sector, and local communities by cooperating (Table 1).

Dhaka

Dhaka is the seventh most densely populated city in the world, well known for its diverse culinary heritage, rickshaws, and cultural festivals. As the capital city of Bangladesh, it is the largest city in the country as

Table 1 Comparing three major cities of Bangladesh based on land, population, and GDP

Dhaka	Chittagong	Sylhet
Dhaka is the capital city of Bangladesh, situated in the bank of the Buriganga River, which is a channel of the Dhaleswari River. Dhaka is Bangladesh's most populous city and is one of the largest metropolises in South Asia (Britannica, 2023a, 2023b, 2023c, 2023d). Presently, Dhaka is a home to 23,210,00 people (macrotrends, 2023a, 2023b, 2023c), with a nominal GDP contribution of $160 billion (wikiwand, 2023a, 2023b). Dhaka offers lots of historic, modern, and ecofriendly tourists' destinations.	The second-largest city in Bangladesh and the busiest seaport on the Bay of Bengal is Chittagong. Between the Chittagong Hill Tracts and the Gulf of Bengal, the city is situated on the banks of the Karnaphuli River (Britannica, 2023a, 2023b, 2023c, 2023d). **There are currently 5,380,000 people** (macrotrends, 2023a, 2023b, 2023c) **living in Chittagong, and the city's nominal GDP is about $43 billion** (wikiwand, 2023a, 2023b). Visitors can find many natural and commercial tourism spots in Chittagong.	Sylhet is the northeastern city of Bangladesh and is located along the north bank of the Surma River (Britannica, 2023a, 2023b, 2023c, 2023d). Sylhet is the fourth largest city of Bangladesh and a home of 964,000 *people* (macrotrends, 2023a, 2023b, 2023c) *with the nominal GDP contribution of $16 billion* (dbpedia, 2023). *The city is well-known for its natural tea gardens and Sufi shrines, in addition to a variety of other beautiful natural settings that attract many tourists.*

well as the economic hub. Many people from many different religions and backgrounds travel to be part of the festivals such as Pohela Boishak (Bengali New Year's Day), Ekushe February (International Mother's Language Day), Pohela Falgun (First Day of Spring), etc. Dhaka offers a range of tourist attractions for visitors to explore. A popular tourist destination is Lalbagh Fort. This seventeenth-century fort is a major tourist attraction in Dhaka, known for its architectural beauty and historical significance, which was built by Shahzada Muhammed Azam, son of Emperor Azam. It is a testament to the Mughal era in Bangladesh and offers visitors a glimpse into the country's rich cultural heritage.

Ahsan Manzil is another important tourist attraction. This nineteenth-century palace is one of the most significant historical landmarks in Dhaka and was the residence of the Nawab Khwaja Abdul Ghani. The palace is now a museum and offers visitors a glimpse into the luxurious lifestyle of the Bengal aristocracy.

Dhaka is known for its cultural heritage, and the Baitul Mukarram Mosque is an area that many locals and tourists travel to see in Dhaka. This mosque is the largest in Bangladesh and is an important religious and cultural site in Dhaka. The mosque is an impressive example of modern Islamic architecture and is a popular tourist destination for those interested in learning more about the religious heritage of the country. More evidence of cultural and historic remarks can be found at the National Museum in Dhaka, another tourist attraction. This museum is the largest in Bangladesh and offers a rich collection of artifacts and exhibits that showcase the country's past and traditional heritage. The museum is a great place to learn about the country's past and present through historical artifacts and is a popular tourist destination for those interested in cultural tourism.

Another display of history can be found here at Shaheed Minar. This memorial tower is dedicated to the language movement of 1952 and is a symbol of national unity and cultural pride. In 1952, Bangladesh was part of Pakistan as East Pakistan. West Pakistan (present-day Pakistan) wanted to make Urdu the national language instead of Bengali. This decision was not accepted by the people of Bangladesh who have spoken primarily Bengali in this region and riots broke out across the country costing innocent lives. The tower is in the center of Dhaka and is a popular destination among tourists and locals all over the country. Aside from architectural and historical attractions, there are also large open green spaces in the city. Ramna Park is a very large park in the center of the busy city, and it is a popular gathering place for locals and tourists alike. The park is known for its lush greenery, beautiful gardens, and peaceful atmosphere, making it a great place to relax and enjoy the city's green spaces. There is also a large zoo located in the city, which is quite a popular attraction among children and families in Dhaka. It is home to a wide range of animals, including tigers, elephants, and monkeys. The zoo is a great place to explore for families and is a popular destination for animal lovers (Banglapedia, 2021).

Chittagong

Chittagong is the second largest city in Bangladesh, located between Chittagong Hill Tracts and the Bay of Bengal, on the bank of the famous river Karnaphuli. The city has been well known since the tenth century to Arab sailors for its fine natural harbor. This is one of the active port cities in South Asia. Numerous ancient mosques and Sufi shrines can be found in the city's older area. The Mughals constructed the Anderkilla Imperial Jame Mosque after capturing Chittagong in 1666. It was formerly a component of a huge hilltop fort. The Roman Catholic Diocese of Chittagong is one of the several churches in the region. The Bengali Buddhist priesthood is headquartered in Chittagong. One of the most popular tourist attractions in Chittagong and a real-payment destination among foreigners around the world is Cox's Bazar. It is a long, sandy beach town that is known for its natural beauty and sun-kissed beaches. It also holds the record for the second longest beach in the world. Black sandy beaches, a rich collection of seafood, and beautiful ocean scenery are just a few of the beauties that make this beach such an attractive getaway destination.

Aside from the ocean, there is a whole other side of colorful scenery in Chittagong called Rangamati. The colors in this location are from the rich soil that resembles a reddish-brown color. This is a famous district known for its scenic beauty with waterfalls, hills, indigenous cultures, and trekking. Related to Rangamati, there is Chittagong Hill Tracts, a group of hill districts that offer stunning views of rolling hills, waterfalls, and traditional communities. Bandarban is another mountainous district in Chittagong known for its waterfalls, hot springs, and trekking trails. In addition to its natural beauty, Chittagong also offers a wide range of museums for tourists to discover. Ethnological Museum is a museum showcasing the diverse culture and heritage of Bangladesh, specifically in this region of the country. Fatehpur Sikri is a Mughal city and UNESCO World Heritage Site, known for its grand architecture and historical significance. Zia Memorial Museum is another museum dedicated to the late President Ziaur Rahman, showcasing his life and achievements related to the independence war of Bangladesh in 1971 (Banglapedia, 2021).

Sylhet

Sylhet is the fourth largest city in Bangladesh, and it is in the northeastern part of the country on the north bank of the river Surma. The climate, rainfall, and high lands make this city a desirable place to grow tea trees. This has since become a major tea production region of the country and this region also attracts a lot of tourists as well every year. A popular location is called Jaflong, which is known for its natural scenic beauty of tea gardens and rolling hills. Another destination is Srimangal, which is a beautiful town known for its tea plantations and natural beauty. In addition to tea gardens and green scenarios, Sylhet is also known for a lake called Madhabpur Lake which is a serene lake surrounded by tea gardens and hills, popular for boating and picnicking. The surreal and picturesque landscape of these tea gardens is simply not available anywhere else in the world. The colors of rolling hills, the lush greenery, the soothing sound of natural falls, the biodiversity, and the delicate scent of tea leaves. Lawachara National Park is a protected area that is home to diverse species of wildlife, including the Bengal tiger, elephant, and hoolock gibbon. There are also islands around this area that have similar natural beauty to the mainland. Ratnodweep is a small island on the Surma River, that is known for its scenic beauty and historical significance.

However, aside from the natural beauty, visitors can also learn about Sylhet's history and culture. There are two renowned Sufi destinations in the city: Shahjalal (R.) Mazar and Shahporan (R.) Mazar. The Shrine of Hazrat Shah Jalal is a revered shrine dedicated to the famous Sufi saint Hazrat Shah Jalal. Lalbagh Fort is an ancient fort built by the Mughal emperor Aurangzeb, located in the heart of Sylhet city. Mahasthan Garh is an archaeological site and a former city of ancient Bengal, known for its historic ruins and archaeological significance (Banglapedia, 2021).

5 Sundarbans

The name Sundarbans means "beautiful forest" in English. The largest mangrove delta in the world is in the Khulna division of Bangladesh. Sundarbans is a sprawling tract of protected natural areas in the Gulf of

Bengal that straddles the Padma, Brahmaputra, and Meghna Rivers between India and Bangladesh (Unesco, 2021). There are 260 different species of birds, Bengal tigers, Indian pythons, crocodiles, and river sharks among the famous animals who call this place home (Naturewanderers, 2023). Tourism is especially popular here as the royal Bengal tigers' sightings are more prominent between the time frame of March and September. Tigers are prone to heat exhaustion during this time, and they go to the edge of the river to get a drink of water (Naturewanderers, 2023). There are cruises, jungle hikes, botanical explorations, and some of the best honey in the world available for tourists visiting the area (Naturewanderers, 2023). However, it is an endangered area as it faces threats from deforestation and climate change. It is one of the extremely important natural features. India and Bangladesh must work together to improve the sustainable tourism to protect the forest.

6 Marketing and Developmental Strategies

For sustainable tourism to work in Bangladesh, a significant marketing campaign needs to happen for changes to be implemented. Collaborating with local and international organizations to develop sustainable tourism initiatives and tap into new markets (Uddin et al., 2022).

Strategies in Sylhet

Preservation, education, and protection are vital pillars that Bangladesh should center its marketing strategies around. Environmental and cultural protection has been at the forefront of sustainability in Bangladesh. The nation can implement measures to protect its natural resources, such as reducing waste and conserving water, to ensure the long-term sustainability of its tourist destinations. Bangladesh can promote and protect its cultural heritage through the development of cultural tourism programs and the preservation of historic sites. Sylhet, known for its gorgeous and fruitful tea fields, is a historic site that many come and visit in Bangladesh. Through education and training, Bangladesh can provide local communities and stakeholders that take part in sustainable tourism practices a way to elevate their knowledge for long-term sustainability (Chowdhury et al., 2021).

Strategies in Chittagong

E-Marketing and destination branding are important strategies that Bangladesh should focus on, as Bangladesh can develop a strong brand image through marketing campaigns that highlight its unique natural, cultural, and heritage attractions (Biplab Roy, 2015). Chittagong is a prime example of Bangladesh showcasing its pristine beauty. Utilizing digital platforms such as Instagram, Tik Tok, and Facebook to reach out to potential tourists and promote its destinations is a vital tool to make cities like Chittagong world-renowned (Md. Afjal Hossain, 2020).

Strategies in Dhaka

Community involvement and infrastructure development are critical aspects in the successful marketing of Bangladesh. Encouraging local communities such as the populous community in the capital, Dhaka to participate in the development and management of tourism destinations can create a sense of ownership and reduce the negative impact of tourism (Md. Abdul HALIM, 2022). Investing in developing the necessary infrastructure, such as roads, airports, and accommodations, will make its destinations more accessible and appealing to tourists (Afrin & Hasan, 2021). Overall, implementing sustainable tourism practices can not only help preserve the natural and cultural heritage of Bangladesh but also promote economic growth and provide new job opportunities.

7 Challenges Related to Sustainable Tourism in Bangladesh

The idea of sustainable tourism is a holistic approach which touches the main three sectors of local lives: economy, culture, and environment. To exist and develop the country in a sustainable way, Bangladesh is facing several challenges. The graph below shows the top factors that are challenging sustainable tourism in Bangladesh. From the graph, the topmost factor is a lack of awareness among the population. A sustainable way of living and touring is not an everyday practice among the general population. Due to this factor, there is also a lack of policies mandating sustainable practices which is another challenge shown in the graph. This—along with disturbances of natural regeneration, natural disasters, and construction—affects tourism and creates obstacles in implementing a sustainable tourism environment (Fig. 3).

Lack of infrastructure is a well-known story within Bangladesh. This populous nation faces a shortage of modern tourist facilities and infrastructure, which limits the growth and development of its tourist destinations. Poor planning and management negatively impact the local communities and environment to reach out to the destination of beneficiary tourism. Limited investment in the tourism industry is also hurting the growth of this industry in Bangladesh. Environmental degradation is a challenge that is facing many nature-rich nations across the world. Bangladesh is unfortunately no exception to this onset challenge, as the rapid growth of tourism in Bangladesh has led to an increase in pollution, deforestation, and the destruction of wildlife habitats. Many

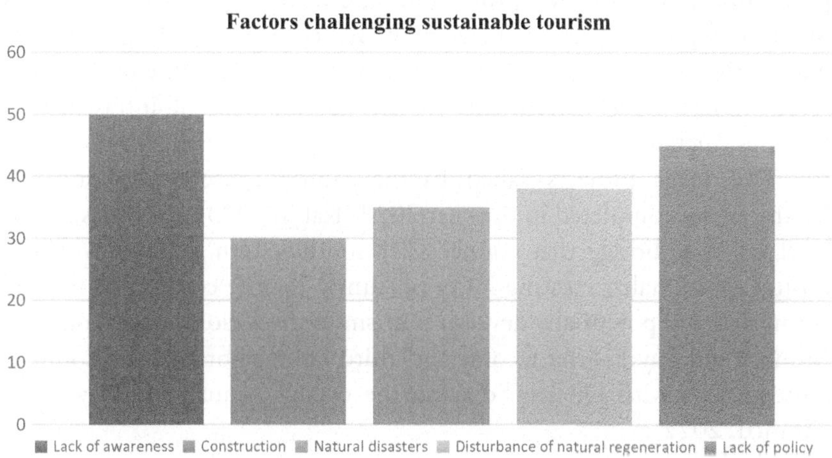

Fig. 3 Factors challenging sustainable tourism. Source: adopted from the work of Islam (2015)

communities in Bangladesh do not have a proper understanding of the importance of sustainable tourism practices, which can lead to the neglect of the environment and cultural heritage.

On the other hand, a challenge that is not quite known but is a large deterrent is the competition from similar nations that have more to offer for tourism. Bangladesh faces competition from neighboring nations such as India, Thailand, and Nepal. Nations that have heavily invested in tourism pose a threat to tourism within Bangladesh. Coincidentally, political instability runs parallel to this issue that Bangladesh faces. Tourists look for stability within the government so that they feel safe and protected when they travel to a country. Overcoming the challenge of political instability and rising to the level of experience that competing nations offer can allow Bangladesh to build a trustworthy, tourist-friendly destination for foreigners as well as local tourists.

8 Recent Progress (in Terms of Sustainable Tourism)

To overcome these challenges, Bangladesh needs to implement sustainable tourism practices, such as investing in infrastructure development, promoting environmental protection, and engaging local communities in tourism planning and management. In recent years, Bangladesh has made progress in key sectors: infrastructure and environment. The government has made investments in the development of infrastructure facilities, such as hotels and resorts, to attract more visitors to the country. Two mega projects called Padma multipurpose bridge and the Metrorail are completed in the year 2022 (Kabir, 2023). Padma is a two-level rail-road-bridge that connects 21 southwestern districts with the capital city, Dhaka, creating an opportunity for the country to be well connected and potentially develop tourism in the region. It also connects Mongla and Payra—the second and third largest ports of the country, respectively—with Dhaka, boosting the overall annual GDP by 1.2% (Ahmed, 2022).

Dhaka Metro Rail is also a massive and ongoing project to connect the populated areas of Dhaka. This is operated by Dhaka Mass Transit Company Limited (DMRC). The MRT Line 6, from Uttara to Agargaon, started operating in December 2022 and the whole metro rail project is expected to be completed by 2025. This improvement of infrastructure has the potential to unite the different regions of the country, allowing tourists to explore more parts of Bangladesh with convenience (Adhikary & Habib, 2022). Bangladesh is also promoting eco-tourism and responsible travel practices, with a focus on preserving its natural and cultural heritage. The government and NGOs are working with local communities to help them benefit from the growth of tourism and promote sustainable tourism practices. There are many world-class hotels, restaurants, and leisure sites that are currently developing in Dhaka as well as throughout the other major cities of Bangladesh. The country has implemented measures to reduce waste and conserve water to protect its natural resources for future generations. The government is also making efforts to preserve its cultural heritage by promoting cultural tourism and restoring historic sites with cultural heritages. The residents of Jurachhari Upazilla in Rangamati in Chittagong endured a severe water crisis that caused a food crisis and significantly disrupted the daily lives of locals. Locally, they established a Climate Resilience Committee (CRC), with UNDP's assistance, where they carried out a safe water supply project using solar panels for households at a cost of $15,000. They set up a tube well that serves five neighborhoods and is powered by 12 solar panels. The committee members support each other to protect and preserve the project. This is an example of a small but wonderful initiative taken by a community to improve community-based tourism (CBT).

Another example is that, since 2018, the Manipuri community in Bangladesh from the Kamalganj sub-district of Sylhet division has been formally running community-based tourism. The community offers the visitors an immersive local and cultural experience at their exceptionally well-run homestays by sharing their local cuisine, organic farming, traditional music, rituals, handmade crafts, textiles, etc. The CBT is also dedicated to defending and maintaining local biodiversity and the environment, including endangered bird species. Bangladesh is taking steps towards sustainable tourism development, but more needs to be done to successfully overcome the challenges and achieve long-term sustainability (Uddin et al., 2022).

9 Recommendations

Sustainable tourism is a long-term commitment which helps preserve the natural and cultural resources, while at the same time supports local communities and economies. Bangladesh is already in the process of practicing sustainable tourism, but there are still several ways to promote sustainable tourism:

- Promoting eco-friendly accommodations, choosing hotels, guesthouses, or homestays. Eco-friendly accommodations can be any residence that has adopted sustainable practices, such as recycling programs, energy-efficient appliances, and utilizing locally grown and organic foods.
- Educating the masses to respect the environment and be mindful of the impact of pollution. Continuing to disregard nature will lead to damaging natural habitats and weaken the nation against natural disasters.
- Respond to the ongoing energy crisis in Bangladesh. The use of solar farms, hydroelectric dams, and biofuel technologies can propel Bangladesh to lift many people out of the energy crisis. Working on solving this issue will stimulate the local economy and will aid in the redevelopment of its internal infrastructure.
- Protecting the Bengali wildlife ecosystem. Building and upholding nature reserves to ensure species thrive will aid in the preservation of habitats lost to climate change. Educating and investing in wildlife tourism will bring local communities together for the betterment of Bangladesh.
- Showcasing the rich history and culture of the regions within Bangladesh. Many regions have different cultural experiences that many can partake in and build their knowledge to share with the rest of the world.

10 Conclusion

In Bangladesh, sustainable tourism is a new idea that has just gained popularity. It has the potential to play a significant role in promoting economic growth, preserving cultural heritage, and protecting the environment in Bangladesh. Tourists looking for real experiences will find the country to be a tempting destination in South Asia for its natural beauty and diverse cultural heritage. Nonetheless, it is crucial to use sustainable tourism methods to make sure that the industry helps both the environment and the residents. The key priorities for sustainable tourism in Bangladesh should include safeguarding the nation's natural resources, promoting regional culture and customs, and strengthening local populations. This can be accomplished through the creation of ecotourism initiatives, the encouragement of community-based tourism, and support for local businesses. Also, it's important to educate visitors about sustainable tourism methods and motivate them to act responsibly while visiting Bangladesh. Campaigns, education, and training can all help with this. Ultimately, Bangladesh's economy, society, and environment may benefit from sustainable tourism. Bangladesh can draw more visitors and encourage them to follow ethical practices to protect its natural and cultural resources by implementing sustainable tourism principles. Despite infrastructural, political, social, and economic drawbacks, both the private and government sectors in Bangladesh are trying to achieve a competitive, attractive, and welcoming environment to deliver tourism in a way which can benefit both the local residents and the people who are choosing Bangladesh as their next travel destination.

References

Adhikary, T. S., & Habib, W. (2022, December 28). MRT Line-6: Twist and turns. *The daily Star*. Retrieved from https://www.thedailystar.net/special-events/dhaka-metro-rail-opening/news/mrt-line-6-twist-and-turns-3206966

Afrin, A., & Hasan, A. (2021). Development and Investment in the Tourism Industry of Bangladesh: Scenario and Prospect analysis. In A. Hassan (Ed.), *Tourism in Bangladesh: Investment and development perspectives* (pp. 49–62). Springer.

Ahmed, M. (2022, August 11). Economic impact of Padma Bridge. The Daily Star. Retrieved from https://www.thedailystar.net/business/economy/news/economic-impact-padma-bridge-3092311.

Banglapedia. (2021, June 18). Retrieved from BANGLAPEDIA: https://www.banglapedia.org/english/index.htm

Biplab Roy, R. (2015). Building a strong brand image of Cox's bazar as. *American Journal of Tourism Management, 4*(2), 27–34. https://doi.org/10.5923/j.tourism.20150402.01

Britannica. (2023a, March 5). Retrieved from www.britannica.com: https://www.britannica.com/place/Bangladesh

Britannica. (2023b, March 5). Retrieved from www.britannica.com: https://www.britannica.com/place/Dhaka

Britannica. (2023c, March 5). Retrieved from www.britannica.com: https://www.britannica.com/place/Chittagong

Britannica. (2023d, March 5). Retrieved from www.britannica.com: https://www.britannica.com/place/Sylhet

Chowdhury, M. I., Alauddin, M., & Uddin, M. (2021). Sustainable tourism in Bangladesh: The demand for investment and development. In A. Hassan (Ed.), *Tourism in Bangladesh: Investment and development perspectives* (pp. 368–381). Springer. https://doi.org/10.1007/978-981-16-1858-1_4

dbpedia. (2023, March 5). Retrieved from dbpedia.org: https://dbpedia.org/page/Economy_of_Sylhet

Islam, M. (2015). Study on factors influencing tourism: Way forward for sustainable tourism in Bangladesh. *Journal of Tourism, Hospitality and Sports*, 2312–5187. Retrieved from https://www.researchgate.net/publication/293263713_Study_on_Factors_Influencing_Tourism_Way_Forward_for_Sustainable_Tourism_in_Bangladesh.

Jahan, & Amin. (2014). Sustainable tourism development in Bangladesh: An empirical study on Sylhet. *Journal of Business Studies*, 239–260. Retrieved from https://www.researchgate.net/publication/328031010_Sustainable_Tourism_Development_in_Bangladesh_An_Empirical_Study_on_Sylhet

Jahan, R. (2016). Identifying the key factors influencing sustainable tourism in Bangladesh: A quantitative analysis. In *Atlantis Press* (pp. 468–473). Atlantis Press. Retrieved from https://www.atlantis-press.com/proceedings/atf-16

Kabir, F. H. (2023, January 1). *Mega projects in 2022: After two opened, sight set on more in 2023*. The Finacial Express. Retrieved from https://thefinancialexpress.com.bd/economy/mega-projects-in-2022-after-two-opened-sight-set-on-more-in-2023-1672541680 macrotrends. (2023a). Retrieved from www.macrotrends.net/cities/20119/dhaka/population: https://www.macrotrends.net/cities/20119/dhaka/population

macrotrends. (2023b). Retrieved from www.macrotrends.net: https://www.macrotrends.net/cities/20115/chittagong/population.

macrotrends. (2023c). Retrieved from www.macrotrends.net: https://www.macrotrends.net/cities/20136/sylhet/population.

Md. Abdul Halim, M. J. (2022). Local community perception about tourism impact and community support. *GeoJournal of Tourism and Geosites, 44*(4), 1260–1270. https://doi.org/10.30892/gtg.44410-942

Md. Afjal Hossain, J. J. (2020). Promoting Bangladesh tourism through the internet: Theoretical. *Canadian Journal of Business and Information Studies*, 87–95. Retrieved from http://www.universepg.com/journal/cjbis

Mihalic, T. (2016). Sustainable-responsible tourism discourse e Towards 'responsustable'. *Journal of Cleaner Production, 111*, 461–470. Retrieved from https://www.sciencedirect.com/journal/journal-of-cleaner-production

mofa. (2023). Retrieved from mofa.gov.bd: https://mofa.gov.bd/site/page/6dde350b-1ca6-4c69-becd-a3f12cf14ac1/Bangladesh%2D%2DAn-Introduction.

Naturewanderers. (2023, March). Retrieved from www.naturewanderers.com: https://www.naturewanderers.com/asia/india/sundarbans-national-park.php

Nekmahmud, M., & Fekete-Farkas, M. (2021). Green marketing, investment and sustainable development for green tourism. In A. Hassan (Ed.), *Tourism in Bangladesh: Investment and Development perspectives* (pp. 345–367). Springer.

Nowreen, S., & Mohiuddin, M. (2021). The principles and practices of sustainable tourism investments and development in Bangladesh. In A. Hassan (Ed.), *Tourism in Bangladesh: Investment and development perspectives* (pp. 387–403). Springer.

Revfine. (2023, March 5). Retrieved from www.revfine.com: https://www.revfine.com/sustainable-tourism/#what-is-sustainable-tourism

Statista. (2023). Retrieved from www.statista.com: https://www.statista.com/statistics/519674/longest-beaches-in-the-world/.

Uddin, R., Rungchavalnont, P., & Sima, S. (2022, December 31). *UNDP.org.* Retrieved from UNDP.org: https://www.undp.org/bangladesh/blog/community-based-tourism-connecting-thailands-experiences-and-reframing-sustainable-tourism-bangladesh

UNESCO. (1997, January 1). https://whc.unesco.org/en/list/798/. Retrieved from https://whc.unesco.org: https://whc.unesco.org/en/list/798/

Unesco. (2021). Retrieved from whc.unesco.org: https://whc.unesco.org/en/list/798/.

wikiwand. (2023a, March 5). Retrieved from www.wikiwand.com: https://www.wikiwand.com/en/Economy_of_Dhaka

wikiwand. (2023b, March 5). Retrieved from www.wikiwand.com: https://www.wikiwand.com/en/Economy_of_Chittagong

worldatlas. (2023, March). Retrieved from www.worldatlas.com: https://www.worldatlas.com/articles/major-rivers-of-bangladesh.html

Impact of Bank's Customer Relationship Management on Customer Satisfaction and Loyalty of SMEs: The Moderating Role of Advisory Services and Capacity Building

Genevieve Pearl Duncan Obuobi, Fred A. Yamoah, and Adnan ul Haque

1 Introduction

CRM has become a popular tool for organizations seeking to grow and maintain their customer base. It can be viewed as an organizational strategy, philosophy, or process designed to improve the quality of services and products offered to customers. A strong relationship between an

G. P. D. Obuobi
Tarragon Edge Ltd, Accra, Ghana

F. A. Yamoah
Department of Management, School of Business, Economics and Informatics, Birkbeck, University of London, London, UK

A. ul Haque (✉)
Faculty of Business, Yorkville University, Toronto, ON, Canada
e-mail: ahaque@yorkvilleu.ca

F. A. Yamoah, A. ul Haque (eds.), *Corporate Management Ecosystem in Emerging Economies*, https://doi.org/10.1007/978-3-031-41578-4_11

organization and its customers leads to increased levels of customer satisfaction and retention. Essentially, CRM is a strategy that enables ongoing engagement aimed at creating lasting partnerships between organizations and their customers over time. Managing these relationships has become a key aspect of every business (Susanta, Taher, and Nimran, 2013).

Over the years, CRM has been used by organizations to increase customer satisfaction and retention (Dyche, 2002). This is because CRM focuses on developing and maintaining personalized relationships with individual customers, with the goal of securing and managing these relationships for the long term (Zablah et al., 2004). Many organizations that implement CRM hope to acquire and retain customers, and research has shown that CRM can increase profits by ensuring customer satisfaction and loyalty (Mohammed & Rashid, 2012; Akroush et al., 2011; Reinartz et al., 2004). When customers have their specific needs met by a product or service, they tend to be satisfied and repurchase that product or service, even when competitors offer alternatives. This kind of satisfaction, and resulting loyalty, is what effective CRM can achieve. As Ndubisi (2007) explained, it is more cost-effective to maintain loyal customers than to attract and serve new ones.

The study seeks to measure the level of satisfaction and loyalty of SMEs to their banks because of the inclusion of these non-financial services in the CRM approach.

Additionally, this study also highlights the importance of incorporating non-financial services into the CRM approach of banks. By providing advisory and capacity-building services, banks can add value to their customers beyond just financial transactions. This can increase customer satisfaction and loyalty, leading to long-term profitable relationships. This is especially important for SMEs, as they often lack the resources and expertise to access such services from other sources (LaBarbera & Mazursky, 1983).

The findings of this study can also guide banks in the development of targeted marketing strategies for their SME customers. By understanding the needs and preferences of their customers, banks can tailor their marketing efforts to provide the most relevant and valuable services. This can lead to increased customer retention and loyalty, as well as new customer acquisition through positive word-of-mouth recommendations from satisfied SMEs.

Overall, the proposed CRM model and the insights derived from this study can provide a framework for banks to effectively manage their relationships with SMEs, leading to increased customer satisfaction, loyalty, and profitability. With relevant employees, organizations can improve collaboration and communication, resulting in better decision-making and faster response times (Ginsberg & Sinacore, 2013). In a nutshell, CRM can be a powerful tool for organizations looking to improve customer relationships, increase revenue, and achieve a range of other business benefits.

The purpose of this study is "to evaluate the impact of incorporating non-financial services, such as advisory and capacity building, into the customer relationship management (CRM) approach of banks on the satisfaction and loyalty of small and medium-sized enterprises (SMEs) that are customers of the banks."

2 Literature Review

CRM is a business strategy that focuses on building and maintaining strong relationships with customers using technology, data analysis, and personalized communication (Elkordy, 2014). The goal of CRM is to improve customer satisfaction and retention by understanding their needs and providing them with tailored products and services. CRM involves a combination of tools and techniques that help organizations manage interactions with customers, such as contact management, sales automation, marketing automation, and customer service (Rahimi & Kozak, 2017). These tools help organizations capture and analyze customer data, track customer interactions, and provide personalized recommendations and solutions (Karakostas et al., 2005).

One of the key benefits of CRM is that it can help organizations increase customer loyalty and retention (Rababah et al., 2007). By providing personalized experiences and anticipating customer needs, organizations can create a stronger emotional connection with their customers, leading to increased customer satisfaction and loyalty in the long run (Iriqat & Daqar, 2017; Anabila & Awunyo-Vitor, 2013). In addition, CRM can help organizations increase efficiency and productivity by automating repetitive tasks and streamlining processes by centralizing customer data and making it easily accessible to all (Zakaria & Mohammadhossein, 2012).

SMEs in Ghana

The roles of SMEs have been emphasized in the literature as being significant in many economies such as developed and developing economies across the globe. On this note, the literature has indicated that, based on the enormous role of SMEs in the development of national economies (Famiyeh et al., 2015). Some developed economies, including the USA, initiated certain strategic measures to finance their SMEs in the form of loans and also to provide financial and legal counseling as well as export. The recognition of SMEs in the Ghanaian economy is increasing due to their role in the development of the economy (Akroush et al., 2011; Eid, 2007; Hussain et al., 2009). Currently, the concept of SME is established in the manufacturing industry, health, education, agriculture, finance, and commerce (Akroush et al., 2011; Eid, 2007; Hussain et al., 2009).

Currently, it is stated that the SMEs in Ghana are mainly driven by dynamic enterprises that operate in varied forms of activities within urban areas and self-employment outlets. In this case, the definition of SMEs in Ghana is based on the number of employees they are able to employ. The literature indicates that the application of this definition has, however, created a lot of controversies and some level of uncertainty with respect to official records on the acceptable number of employees required to qualify an enterprise as an SME. However, Ghanaian SMEs are said to be without setbacks and challenges. This is common in many developing economies around the world and Ghana is no exception.

Product and Service Innovation Success

The notion that innovation develops over time and assumes new forms has become acceptable to researchers and practitioners. Several studies have indicated the importance of product innovation in the success of organizations as organizations that are market-drivers tend to generate products that change the market requirements (e.g., Narver & Slater, 1990; Jaworski & Kohli, 1993). Thus, an organization's ability to innovate suggests a competitive advantage in a dynamic environment. Even though in the traditional perspective there is a distinction between process and product innovation, in services, both process and product innovation are seen to be intertwined.

Knowledge Management on Customer Satisfaction

Knowledge management, defined as representing the process of knowledge sharing and collaboration among task forces, includes four models namely innovation, skill, responsiveness, and productivity (Mentzas et al., 2003). Norozian (2005) asserted that knowledge management is the capability of a corporation to use its rational principles, such that the facts and information of individuals' and groups' understanding are used to accomplish a purpose through the procedure of knowledge creation and knowledge distribution and by means of technology.

Functional Diversity

Some of the scholars have, in this sense, indicated that functional diversity has gained attention in most extant literature in explaining innovation performance, including success and failure of innovations (Van Beers & Zand, 2014). Therefore, literature suggests that organizations are more likely to adopt functional diversity if they seek to link innovation to functional capabilities of their partners through their cognitive function or knowledge (Van Beers & Zand, 2014).

Strategic Alignment

The literature indicates that strategic alignment is related to the process of planning in business. The literature suggests that strategic alignment is very important in enhancing firms' competitive advantage. Shedding light on this, strategic alignment has been matched with other pseudonyms in the literature such as fit, integration, bridge, harmony, fusion, and linkage for easy identification within other contexts by other scholars (Ciborra, 1997; Smaczny, 2001; Henderson and Venkatraman, 1999). However, all these suggest the incorporation of business strategies in the process of planning business.

Organizational Capabilities

The human capacity building is the "practice of providing people with the knowledge, expertise, and opportunity to access information, knowledge, and training that enables them to perform effectively" (UNDP, U 1992). Azikiwe (2006) defined capacity building as "the process by which individuals, irrespective of sex, are provided with the expertise and understanding they need to perform effectively and efficiently in their different callings." In all these instances, it is required that the firm must be able to be more efficient than its competitors with similar resources at their disposal. Another concern is related to the possibility of developing a comprehensive and mutually exclusive classification of organizational capabilities. In this case, it is revealed that achieving this is impossible because these organizational capabilities are infinite in variety.

Competitive Environment

In studying the characteristics of SMEs, Easterby-Smith et al. (2008) indicated that the important distinguishing factors between SMEs and larger companies include their environment (organizational environment and competitive environment) and management practices. In the literature, it is seen that it is commonly believed among many economists that organizations' strength and competitiveness are based on their ability to adopt operational strategies that are able to put them ahead of their competitors by occupying strategic market positions and being profitable (Rababah et al. 2007). Firms that are competitive are said to have sustainable profitability when compared to their competitors.

Product/Service Characteristics

While product innovation is said to be investment-driven and highly technological, it is said to have a characteristic that is prevalent in highly technological industries. In this industry, the rate of product innovation distinguishes industries into leaders and followers. These distinctions that are found to be determined by the performance, time, and quality of product launching are important factors of the industries (Bazini et al., 2012; Vasiliu, 2012; Aldaihani et al. 2018).

Role of Advisory Services in the Relationship Between Customer Focus and Customer Satisfaction

Customer focus is the process of understanding customer needs, focusing and directing organizational processes and activities in order to achieve the successful fulfillment of the identified customer need (Drummond & Ensor, 2005). Directing organizational processes and activities in order to achieve the successful fulfillment of customer needs ultimately leads to customer satisfaction (Armstrong, 2006). Offering technical advice to a business has an impact on the activities of that business in terms of its relationship with its bank (Kanagal, 2012). Khedkar (2015) showed a high positive correlation between focusing on key customer requirements and customer satisfaction and loyalty. Advisory services from banks ensured that the resources of the organization, especially the human component, were well utilized in such a way that enhanced its performance (Khedkar 2015). Banks that provide advisory services will be able to offer good services to their customers (in this case, SMEs) in terms of meeting their needs and specifications (Verma & Chaudhuri, 2009).

Empirical Review of Literature

The review of the literature shows that the study of product success is developmental from new product development to new product performance to new product success. However, the review shows there is a negative relationship between product success and failure. When a product fails to achieve success, it fails. Also, in the literature, the study of product success and failure is best suited within the context of new product studies. Over the years, a considerable number of studies have looked at new product development from different dimensions. Several studies have focused on some aspects of new product development such as new product development model, new product development innovation management, new product development process, new product development strategy, new product development game, new product development performance, new product development projects, new product development stages, and new product development teams. Table 2 shows a summary of the literature on previous studies on product/service success through phases from product development to product success (Fig. 1).

Hypothesis driven from the literature are as follows:

H1: *Customer focus will positively impact customer satisfaction.*
H2: *Knowledge management will have a significant positive relationship with customer satisfaction.*

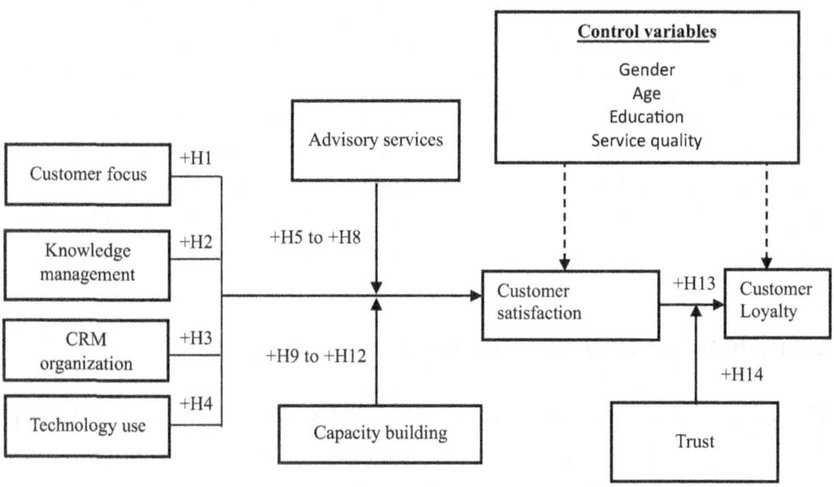

Fig. 1 Proposed conceptual model of CRM

H3: *Customer relationship management organization will have a significant positive relationship with customer satisfaction.*
H4: *CRM technology will have a significant positive relationship with customer satisfaction.*
H5: *The positive relationship between customer focus and customer satisfaction will be stronger when advisory services are good than when they are not good.*
H6: *The positive relationship between knowledge management and customer satisfaction will be stronger when advisory services are good than when they are not good (otherwise).*
H7: *The positive relationship between CRM organization and customer satisfaction will be stronger when advisory services are good than when they are not good.*
H8: *The positive relationship between technology use and customer satisfaction will be higher when advisory services are good than when they are not good.*
H9: *The positive relationship between customer focus and customer satisfaction will be stronger when capacity building is high than when it is low.*
H10: *The positive relationship between knowledge management and customer satisfaction will be higher when capacity building is high than when it is low.*
H11: *The positive relationship between CRM organization and customer satisfaction will be stronger when capacity building is high than when it is low.*
H12: *The positive relationship between CRM technology and customer satisfaction will be higher when capacity building is high than when it is not.*
H13: *There is a positive relationship between customer satisfaction and customer loyalty.*
H14: *The positive relationship between customer satisfaction and customer loyalty is stronger when there is trust than when there is none.*

3 Research Methodology

The epistemological stance of this study is pragmatic paradigm. The pragmatic approach to research design uses mixed methods and researchers focus their attention on what and how "to research based on the intended consequences" (Creswell, 2014, p. 39). The researcher adopts a pragmatic paradigm, which is the mixed-method approach of conducting research to understand both the subjective and objective sides of the research. First, the objective side of the research examined the factors affecting innovation success. Then followed by understanding the grounded knowledge of the phenomenon based on the subjective side. The methodology of the research is all about making decisions concerning your choice of a method, how your objectives will be fulfilled, ways of getting data for the research, and the method of data analysis. The survey has been used as the primary method for the quantitative analysis. A survey, or sample survey, is a method of collecting data from a sample that is representative of a study population (Haque, 2020). The research will obtain data for statistical and quantitative analysis through a sample survey to ascertain the robustness of its findings. This study uses a survey strategy followed by a qualitative case study.

The case study method is also utilized in the study aside from the survey as they appear to be the most appropriate and suitable research methods for the purposes of this research because the qualitative information required for inductive purposes will be sourced from SMEs involved in product and service innovation. The qualitative data were collected mainly to facilitate understanding of contextual issues during the study and explain the findings and results of the study. The sequential explanatory strategy also permitted explanation of the subject matter by testing elements of the study theories and generalizing the results and findings to the population (Terrell 2011, p. 264). Qualitative study is more about useful truth than factual truth (Faizan et al., 2019; Haque & Yamoah, 2021). Further, the researcher made use of a case study as the research for the study. According to Yin (2014), a case study is a study wherein the researcher "investigates a contemporary phenomenon (the 'case') in depth and within its real-world context."

For the purpose of this study, the study population included all SMEs in Ghana. The target population for the study comprised selected SMEs in Ghana, mainly situated in the industrial hub of the country. The main target of the study included individuals who were involved in the day-to-day decisions of the firm. The total number of items used in measuring the dependent, independent, and moderating variables in the questionnaire were 55, and therefore, the sample frame was between 275 and 550. The study employed a 95% confidence level with its corresponding Z score and used an error margin of 0.05. Thus, the sample approximation derived is mathematically presented as follows:

$$n = \frac{(1.96)^2 (0.5)(0.5)}{(0.05)^2} = 384$$

The researcher employed only primary data for the analysis. The researcher's primary data was derived in the form of administered questionnaires from respondents who had in-depth knowledge about the subject under study. Some research assistants were trained about the purpose of the study and were used for the enumeration, which took a period of four weeks. The end of the enumeration process showed a retrieval rate of 100%. The study only used participants who showed demonstrable understanding of the concepts of the study. The researcher used 10%, 5%, 1%, and 0.1% as the significant levels for testing the variables in the study. The data for the study was only used for academic purposes. All the data will be collected from respondents willingly.

4 Results, Findings and Discussions

Measurement of Validity and Reliability

The study equally ensured that the research instrument covered constructs and contents relevant to the theoretical underpinnings of factors affecting innovation's success. To establish reliability, the instruments were subjected to extensive review and scrutiny by research experts. The research experts' scrutiny determined the appropriateness of the instruments and the constructs under investigation. The main procedures used to assess reliability were Cronbach's alpha and composite reliability while average variance explained (AVE) and discriminant validity were used to assess the validity of the instrument.

Measurement of Scales

Data for the study was gathered using a structured questionnaire. The questionnaire comprised two sections: A, asking questions on independent variables and main dependent variables, and B, asking questions about the demographic characteristics of the respondents.

Common Method Variance

The data obtained was subjected to exploratory factor analysis with Varimax rotation.

Quantitative Data Analysis Procedure

This procedure was adopted as a first step in the development of a confirmatory factor analysis. These were done with the help of IBM SPSS version 25 software. Next, the researchers proceeded to perform confirmatory factor analysis using AMOS 25.

Demographic Description (Table 1)

Table 1 Demographic characteristics of respondents

Variable	Characteristics	Frequency	Percent
Gender	Male	228	52.4
	Female	198	45.5
Age	25–30 years	154	35.4
	31–40 years	208	47.8
	41–50 years	48	11.0
	51–60 years	25	5.7
Position	CEO	53	12.2
	Executive director	40	9.2
	Manager	99	22.8
	Head of business unit	81	18.6
	Chief finance officer	62	14.3
	Chief operating officer	53	12.2
	Others	26	6.0
Level of education	PhD/DBA	5	1.1
	Masters	103	23.7
	Bachelors	165	37.9
	HND	146	33.6
	Others	14	3.2
Years in operation	Below 3 years	98	22.5
	4–6 years	176	40.5
	7–9 years	62	14.3
	10–12 years	55	12.6
	13–15 years	30	6.9
	16 years and above	12	2.8
Estimated total asset	Less than GHc500 million	183	42.1
	GHc500 million–800 billion	190	43.7
	GHc801–1.5 billion	49	11.3
	GHc1.5–2 billion	7	1.6
	Above 2 billion	1	0.2

Note: The number of responses differ across variables due to missing responses

Test of Homogeneity (Table 2)

A Levene's test for the threat of unequal variance was run. The results showed that the variables had equal variances, indicating the presence of homoscedasticity for all variables.

Table 2 Levene's test of homogeneity

	Levene's Statistic	
Variables	*F*	*p*-value
1. Customer value	0.000	0.992
2. Customer focus	2.416	0.121
3. Knowledge management	0.046	0.829
4. CRM organization	0.362	0.547
5. Technology use	0.890	0.346
6. Advisory services	0.053	0.818
7. Capacity building	1.141	0.286
8. Trust	0.986	0.321
9. Customer satisfaction	0.132	0.716
10. Customer loyalty	1.912	0.167

Organizational Capabilities and Success of Product/Service Innovation

The current study therefore conceptualized that organizational capability positively relates to the success of product/service innovation rather than its failure. The study observed a significant positive relationship between organizational capability and product/service innovation success, lending support to the first hypothesis of the study. This is an indication that the ability of organizations to adapt their culture and structure to suit their product innovation strategy will increase the success of their products and services over what is provided by their competitors (Van Beers and Zand 2014). This assertion was confirmed in the case study, as experts mentioned that organization capabilities are paramount for firms' product and service innovation success (Tables 3 and 4).

Competitive Environment and Success of Product/Service Innovation

The findings of the study lent support to this hypothesis, an indication that situations where potential customers are very satisfied and loyal to competitors' products compared to the products of an existing firm lead to failure of product/service innovation. Competitive environment creates opportunities for competitors to copy products/services.

Table 3 Regression results of the relationship between CRM and customer satisfaction moderated by advisory services and capacity building

	Customer satisfaction		
	Model 1	Model 2	Model 3
Variables	β(t-values)	β(t-values)	β(t-values)
Control variables			
Years of operation	-0.055 (-1.085)	0.030 (0.828)	0.040 (1.105)
Total assets	0.020 (0.398)	-0.001 (-0.036)	-0.009 (-0.265)
Employee size	0.013 (0.259)	0.051 (1.486)	0.045 (1.321)
Customer value	0.115 (2.377)*	0.079 (2.265)*	0.062 (1.780)†
Main effects			
Customer focus		0.265 (4.353)***	0.278 (4.410)***
Knowledge management		0.188 (3.141)**	0.211 (3.388)***
CRM organization		0.229 (5.343)***	0.234 (4.662)***
Technology use		0.144 (3.526)***	0.156 (3.177)**
Advisory services		0.049 (1.223)	0.038 (0.847)
Capacity building		0.121 (2.276)*	0.165 (2.959)**
Interaction effects			
Customer focus × advisory services			0.034 (0.885)
Knowledge management ×			0.066 (1.688)†
CRM organization ×			0.052 (1.424)
Technology use ×			0.066 (1.789)†
Customer focus × capacity building			0.154 (4.303)***
Knowledge management ×			0.128 (3.303)***
CRM organization ×			0.112 (3.034)***
Technology use ×			0.088 (2.179)*
R^2	0.016	0.513	0.541
F value	1.696 ***	44.196***	26.933***
ΔR^2	0.016	0.497	0.028
Partial *F* value	1.696	71.407***	3.122**
Degrees of freedom	4/426	10/420	18/412
Durbin Waston test	1.982		

†$p < 0.10$, *$p < 0.05$, **$p < 0.01$, ***$p < 0.001$ (one-tailed test)
Note: Standardized regression coefficients were reported with t-values for each effect in parentheses

Product/Service Characteristics and Success of Product/Service Innovation

The findings of the study lent support to this hypothesis as a significant positive relationship was observed between product characteristics and the success of product/service innovation. This is an indication that a

Table 4 Summary of hypotheses

Hypothesis	Expected outcome	Empirical conclusions	Outcome
1. There is a positive relationship between customer focus and customer satisfaction	+	Supported	Significant
2. There is a positive relationship between knowledge management and customer satisfaction	+	Supported	Significant
3. There is a positive relationship between CRM organization and customer satisfaction	+	Supported	Significant
4. There is a positive relationship between technology use and customer satisfaction	+	Supported	Significant
5. The positive relationship between customer focus and customer satisfaction is stronger when advisory services are effective	+	Not supported	Not significant
6. The positive relationship between knowledge management and customer satisfaction is stronger when advisory services are effective	+	Supported	Significant
7. The positive relationship between CRM organization and customer satisfaction is stronger when advisory services are effective	+	Supported	Significant
8. The positive relationship between technology use and customer satisfaction is stronger when advisory services are effective	+	Not supported	Not significant
9. The positive relationship between customer focus and customer satisfaction is stronger when capacity building is high	+	Supported	Significant
10. The positive relationship between knowledge management and customer satisfaction is stronger when capacity building is high	+	Supported	Significant
11. The positive relationship between CRM organization and customer satisfaction is stronger when capacity building is high	+	Supported	Significant

(*continued*)

Table 4 (continued)

Hypothesis	Expected outcome	Empirical conclusions	Outcome
12. The positive relationship between technology use and customer satisfaction is stronger when capacity building is high	+	Supported	Significant
13. There is a positive relationship between customer satisfaction and loyalty	+	Supported	Significant
14. The positive relationship between customer satisfaction and customer loyalty is stronger when trust is high than low	+	Supported	Significant

firm's product/service superior that is new and improves customer's work efficiency compared to competitor's products/services, leads to product/service innovation success where growth is seen in the profitability of new products/services compared with business unit objectives. This outcome was also supported in the test case scenario.

Moderating Role of Functional Diversity

The current study assessed the moderating role of functional diversity (cognitive) in the relationship between innovation factors (organizational capability, competitive environment, and product/service characteristics) and the success of product/service innovation through developed hypotheses four (4), five (5), and six (6). The case discussion also confirmed that functional diversity played a moderating role in the relationship between organizational capabilities, competitive environment, product/service characteristics, and product/service innovation success.

Moderating Role of Functional Diversity in the Organizational Capability and the Success of Product/Service Innovation Relationship

The current study therefore hypothesized that the relationship between organizational capabilities and product/service innovation success would be enhanced when functional diversity is cognitive than when it is affective. The findings of the study showed that the interaction between functional diversity and organizational capability was negatively related to product/service innovation success. This implies that the positive relationship between organizational capability and product/service innovation success is weaker when functional diversity is high than when it is low.

Moderating Role of Functional Diversity in the Competitive Environment and the Success of Product/Service Innovation Relationship

The study again observed that the interaction between functional diversity and competitive environment was negatively related to product/service innovation success, which was in contrast to the study hypothesis.

Moderating Role of Strategic Alignment

Strategic alignment is related to the process of planning in business. The study conceptualized that strategic alignment moderates the relationship between innovation factors and the success of product/service innovation. Thus, three (3) hypotheses were developed and tested in this effect. These hypotheses were numbered seven (7) to nine (9) in the order in which they appeared in the study.

Moderating Role of Strategic Alignment in the Organizational Capability and the Success of Product/Service Innovation Relationship

Hypothesis seven (7) assessed the moderating role of strategic alignment in the relationship between organizational capability and the success of product/service innovation. The interaction between organizational capability and strategic alignment was observed to be positively related to product/service innovation success, an indication that the positive relationship between organizational capability and product/service innovation success is stronger when strategic alignment is high. Thus, the study hypothesis seven (7) was supported, lending support also to the view that firms that are able to align their culture and structure to conform to their strategies tend to have an increased competitive advantage to succeed as compared to their competitors who do not have these combinations (Grant, 1996).

Moderating Role of Strategic Alignment in the Competitive Environment and the Success of Product/Service Innovation Relationship

The study conceptualized that the positive relationship between competitive environment and product/service innovation success is enhanced when strategic alignment ensures that firms adopt competitively aggressive strategies that make them develop products to drive the market as a poor strategy would lead to failure. The findings of the current study showed that the interaction between strategic alignment and competitive environment was positively related to product/service innovation success, although not insignificant. This finding, which does not lend support to the study hypothesis eight (8), may suggest that strategic alignment may not necessarily play a major role in the marketing of an innovative product/service in the face of a competitive environment.

Moderating Role of Strategic Alignment in the Product Characteristics and the Success of Product/Service Innovation Relationship

The ninth hypothesis assessed the moderating role of strategic alignment in the relationship between product/service characteristics and the success of product/service innovation. The study hypothesized that the positive impact of product characteristics on product/service innovation success would be enhanced with the appropriate strategic alignment. In lending support to this hypothesis, the findings of the study showed that the interaction between strategic alignment and product/service characteristics was positively related to product/service innovation success. This implies that strategic alignment is important for the marketing of an innovative product/service.

5 Qualitative Case Study Data Analysis

This study adopted the resource-based view (RBV) to explain the effect of innovation factors on the success of product/service innovation among SMEs in Ghana. It can be inferred from the RBV that product development and performance are influenced by the resources at the disposal of the firm. The study, by exploring these innovative factors that influence the success of product/service innovation, concluded that organizational capability, competitive environment, and product/service characteristics are the main factors while considering the moderating roles of functional diversity and strategic alignment. Different interviews and focus groups confirmed that Ghana has a competitive environment that focuses on product innovation and organizational capabilities.

6 Conclusion and Recommendations

Innovation becomes inevitable the moment an organization realizes the need for improvement and expansion to beat the competition. But often, organizations embark on strategies to promote customer satisfaction and increase profit margins when, in fact, the attention needs to be directed at the success and failure of product/service innovation. The current study, with the aim to explore innovation factors that influence the success of product/service innovation in SMEs in Ghana, established a significant positive relationship between these observed innovation factors (organizational capability and product/service characteristics) and product/service innovation success. However, a negative relationship was observed between the competitive environment and the success of product/service innovation. Also, a moderation role for functional diversity and strategic alignment in this relationship was observed. These findings have significant implications for practitioners, investors, policymakers, and other stakeholders, considering the upspring of SMEs that produce similar goods and services in Ghana and the rate at which most are collapsing.

The positive relationship between organizational capability and product/service innovation success is an indication that dynamic improvement in the functions of organizations to adapt their culture and structure to suit their product innovation strategy will increase the success of their products and services over what is provided by their competitors. There is a need to identify a pattern of organizational culture that is in sync with the category of new product to be developed. Thus, an organization that has dynamic routine organizational capabilities will reflect this in its responsiveness to market trends, manufacturing flexibility, and developments that have taken place over a short period.

The negative relationship observed between competitive environment and the success of product/service innovation implies product/service innovation is challenged by competitors' products in the face of customer satisfaction and loyalty. This is seen as a major challenge to small firms, as large firms may be more capable of adapting to the dynamic challenges within the environment. Therefore, the failure or success of organizations is largely dependent on competition within the environment in which the organization operates, with regard to its complexity and volatility. It is commonly believed among many economists that organizations' strength and competitiveness are based on their ability to adopt operational strategies that are able to put them ahead of their competitors by occupying strategic market positions and being profitable.

Another major implication of this study is the positive relationship between product/service characteristics and the success of product/service innovation, which is an indication that the superiority of the product differentiates it from other products or competitive offerings in the market. The core product characteristics include product advantage, where a product meets the needs of customers.

In view of the above, SMEs or practitioners in the quest to achieve superiority in product/service innovation must consider the impact of organizational capability, product/service characteristics, and competitive environment. Another key implication of this study is the moderating role of functional diversity in the influence of organizational capability, product/service characteristics, and competitive environment on the success of product/service innovations. The findings of the study indicated that high functional diversity negatively influences the positive relationship between organizational capability and product/service innovation success, as well as the negative relationship between competitive environment and product/service innovation success is weaker when functional diversity is high than when it is low. As observed in this study, practitioners need to tread cautiously in the face of a highly competitive environment when it comes to their functional diversity. Furthermore, SMEs can ride on the positive moderating role of strategic alignment on the relationship between innovation factors and the success of product/service innovation to align all their strategies, which will give the firms a competitive advantage.

As a result of the findings of the study, the following were recommended:

Strengthen the capabilities of the organization: As hypothesized in the study, a significant positive relationship between organizational capability and product/service innovation success was observed, an indication that dynamic improvement in the functions of the organization is very essential to innovation. There is a need for SMEs to make a self-assessment of strengths and weaknesses in how they support their people to innovate (how might we enable our people to innovate?), if their organizational processes are supporting staff to innovate, and assess if they are utilizing the state-of-the-art tools and methods most suited to meet the needs of the workers in the innovation process.

Capitalize on product/service characteristics: As observed in this study, and is in line with the findings of Crawford and Benedetto (2003), the essence of product innovativeness is found in product characteristics as SMEs have their competitors coming into the market with new products that provide enhanced performance or an increased level of perceived value as compared to what is offered in the market in order to change the orientation of the competition. SMEs need to aim at meeting the needs of the customers having superiority in terms of specifications that differentiate the product from other products or competitive offerings in the market.

Customize the implementation of best innovation practices for your own organization: The findings of this study showed that the competitive environment has a negative relationship with product/service innovation success when it comes to small enterprises. It presents complex situations for SMEs to strive to innovate products/services to enhance their performance over their competitors (Pereira-Moliner et al., 2015). There is therefore a need for each enterprise to adopt an innovative practice to suit its own operating environment, specific to the industry in which it competes.

References

Akroush, M. N., Dahiyat, S. E., Gharaibeh, H. S., & Abu-Lail, B. N. (2011). Customer relationship management implementation: An investigation of a scale's generalizability and its relationship with business performance in a developing country context. *International Journal of Commerce and Management, 21*(2), 158–191.

Aldaihani, F. M. F., Ali, N., & A. Bin. (2018). The mediating role of customer empowerment in the effect of relationship marketing on customer retention:

An empirical demonstration from Islamic banks in Kuwait assessment view project quality governance in service sector. View project The Mediating Role. (99). Retrieved from http://www.europeanjournalofeconomicsfinance-andadministrativesciences.com

Anabila, P., & Awunyo-Vitor, D. (2013). Customer relationship management: A key to Organisational survival and customer loyalty in Ghana's banking industry. *International Journal of Marketing Studies, 5*(1), 107–117.

Armstrong, M. (2006). *A handbook of human resource management practice*. Kogan Page Publishers.

Azikiwe, U. (2006). Gender issues and education in Nigeria. Implications for growth & development. In *11th Annual International Management Conference Organized by Makerere* University Business School, Kampals, Uganda.

Bazini, E., Elmazi, L., & Sinanaj, S. (2012). Importance of relationship Marketing Management in the Insurance Business in Albania. *Procedia - Social and Behavioral Sciences, 44*(October 2011), 155–162.

Ciborra, C. U. (1997). De profundis? Deconstructing the concept of strategic alignment. *Scandinavian Journal of Information Systems, 9*(1), 67–82.

Crawford, C. M., & Benedetto. (2003). *New Products Management* (7th Edition). McGraw-Hill, USA.

Creswell, J. W. (2014). *A concise introduction to mixed methods research*. SAGE Publications.

Drummond, G., & Ensor, J. (2005). *Introduction to Marketing Concepts*. London: Routledge.

Dyche, J. (2002). *The CRM handbook: A business guide to customer relationship management*. Addison Wesley.

Easterby-Smith, M., Lyles, M. A., & Tsang, E. W. (2008). Inter-organizational knowledge transfer: Current themes and future prospects. *Journal of Management Studies, 45*(4), 677–690.

Eid, R. (2007). Towards a successful CRM implementation in banks: An integrated model. *The Service Industries Journal, 27*(8), 1021–1039.

Elkordy, M. (2014). Impact of CRM capability dimensions on organizational performance. *SMART Journal of Business Management Studies, 15*(2), 80.

Faizan, R., Haque, A. U., Cockrill, A., & Aston, J. (2019). Females at strategic level affecting logistics Firms' competitiveness: Qualitative comparative analysis. *Forum Scientiae Oeconomia, 7*(1), 57–71.

Famiyeh, S., Adaku, E., Kissi-Mensah, L., & Amoatey, C. T. (2015). Risk management for a tailings re-mining project in Ghana. *International Journal of Managing Projects in Business., 8*, 241.

Ginsberg, F., & Sinacore, A. L. (2013). Counseling Jewish women: A phenomenological study. *Journal of Counseling & Development, 91*(2), 131–139.

Grant, R. M. (1996). Prospering in dynamically competitive environments: Organizational capability as knowledge integration. *Organization Science, 7*(4), 375–387.

Haque, A. U. (2020). Varying occupational stress and Organisational commitment within the university staff of contrasting economies (cross-sectional comparative study of middle range public universities in Pakistan and the UK). Ph.D. Thesis, University of Wales Trinity Saint David, Lampeter, UK. Available online: https://repository.uwtsd.ac.uk/id/eprint/1570/

Haque, A. U., & Yamoah, F. A. (2021). The role of ethical leadership in managing occupational stress to promote innovative work behaviour: A cross-cultural management perspective. *Sustainability, 13*(17), 9608.

Henderson, J. C., & Venkatraman, H. (1999). Strategic alignment: Leveraging information Technology for Transforming Organizations. *IBM Journal of Research and Development, 38*, 472–484.

Hussain, I., Hussain, M., Hussain, S., & Sajid, M. A. (2009). Customer relationship management: Strategies and practices in selected banks of Pakistan. *International Review of Business Research Papers, 5*(6), 117–132.

Iriqat, R. A. M., & Daqar, M. A. M. A. (2017). The impact of customer relationship management on long-term customers' loyalty in the Palestinian banking industry. *International Business Research, 10*(11), 139.

Jaworski, B. J., & Kohli, A. K. (1993). Market orientation. *Journal of Marketing, 54*(3), 53.

Kanagal, N. B. (2012). Innovation and product innovation in marketing strategy. *Journal of Management and Marketing Research, 18*(2015), 1–25.

Karakostas, B., Kardaras, D., & Papathanassiou, E. (2005). The state of CRM adoption by the financial services in the UK: An empirical investigation. *Information and Management, 42*(6), 853–863.

Khedkar, D. E. (2015). Impact of service innovations in hospitality industry. *International Journal of Management Sciences and Business Research, 4*(11), 5.

LaBarbera, P. A., & Mazursky, D. (1983). A longitudinal assessment of consumer satisfaction/dissatisfaction: The dynamic aspect of the cognitive process. *Journal of Marketing Research, 20*(4), 393–404.

Mentzas, G., Apostolou, D., Abecker, A., & Young, R. (2003). *Knowledge assets management*. Springer-Verlag. Limited [Printed in Great Britain].

Mohammed, A. A., & Rashid, B. (2012). Customer relationship management (CRM) in hotel industry: A framework proposal on the relationship among

CRM dimensions, marketing capabilities, and hotel performance. *International Review of Management and Marketing, 2*(4), 220.
Narver, J. C., & Slater, S. F. (1990). The effect of a market orientation on business profitability. *Journal of Marketing, 54*(4), 20–35.
Ndubisi, N. O. (2007). Relationship marketing and customer loyalty. *Marketing Intelligence & Planning, 25, 98.*
Norozian, M. (2005). The use of knowledge management in governmental management. *Tadbir Quarterly, 156*, 24–29.
Pereira-Moliner, J., Font, X., Tarí, J. J., Molina-Azorín, J. F., Lopez-Gamero, M. D., & Pertusa-Ortega, E. M. (2015). The holy grail: Environmental management, competitive advantage and business performance in the Spanish hotel industry. *International Journal of Contemporary Hospitality Management, 27*(5), 714–738.
Rababah, K. A., Mohd, H., Ibrahim, H., & Din, A. M. (2007). Construction of extended adoption model of CRM systems at the healthcare organizational level in Malaysian private hospitals, pp. 726–733.
Rahimi, R., & Kozak, M. (2017). Impacts of customer relationship management implementation on customer satisfaction in hotels: Case of a budget hotel chain in the UK corresponding.
Reinartz, W., Krafft, M., & Hoyer, W. D. (2004). The CRM process: Its measurement and impact on performance by. *Journal of Marketing Research, 1*(January), 293–305.
Smaczny, T. (2001). Is an alignment between business and information technology the appropriate paradigm to manage IT in today's organisations? *Management Decision, 39*(10), 797–802.
Susanta, A. T., Idrus, M. S., & Nimran, U. (2013). The effect of relationship quality on customer advocacy: The mediating role of loyalty. *IOSR Journal of Business and Management, 10*(4), 41–52.
Terrell, S. R. (2011). Mixed-methods research methodologies. *Qualitative Report, 17*(1), 254–280.
UNDP, U. (1992). Human development report 1992: Global dimensions of human development.
Van Beers, C., & Zand, F. (2014). R&D cooperation, partner diversity, and innovation performance: An empirical analysis. *Journal of Product Innovation Management, 31*(2), 292–312.
Vasiliu, D. (2012). Approach to customer relationship management (CRM)-the new key sales success. *USV Annals of Economics & Public Administration, 12*(1), 144–153.

Verma, S., & Chaudhuri, R. (2009). Effect of CRM on customer satisfaction in service sector in India. *Journal of Marketing & Communication, 5*(2).

Yin, R. K. (2014). *Case study research: Design and methods*. Sage Publications. Kindle ed.

Zablah, A. R., Bellenger, D. N., & Johnston, W. J. (2004). An evaluation of divergent perspectives on customer relationship management: Towards a common understanding of an emerging phenomenon. *Industrial Marketing Management, 33*(6), 475–489.

Zakaria, N., & Mohammadhossein, N. (2012). CRM benefits for customers: Literature review (2005-2012). *International Journal of Engineering Research and Applications, 2*(6), 1578–1586.

Identifying the Global Demand for Cross-Border Higher Education of Malaysian Public Universities

Fadli Fizari Abu Hassan Asari, Suriyani Muhamad, Mahyudin Ahmad, Jumadil Saputra, and Azlina Zid

1 Introduction

Around 220 million students were enrolled in tertiary education globally in 2021. This number is double compared to 2000, and it is expected to increase to 380 million in 2030 (Murthi & Bassett, 2022). On the other hand, the value of the global higher education market, which has been estimated at USD17.91 billion in 2021, is expected to continue to rise to USD73.98 billion in 2029 (MMR, 2022). In terms of international

F. F. A. H. Asari • M. Ahmad
Faculty of Business and Management, Universiti Teknologi MARA Perlis Branch, Perlis, Malaysia

S. Muhamad • J. Saputra (✉)
Faculty of Business, Economics and Social Development, Universiti Malaysia Terengganu, Kuala Terengganu, Malaysia
e-mail: jumadil.saputra@umt.edu.my

A. Zid
Faculty of Sports Science and Recreation, Universiti Teknologi MARA Selangor Branch, Selangor, Malaysia

F. A. Yamoah, A. ul Haque (eds.), *Corporate Management Ecosystem in Emerging Economies*, https://doi.org/10.1007/978-3-031-41578-4_12

students, a survey concludes the excitement of students in five major higher education countries—the United States, the United Kingdom, Australia, Canada, and China—to study abroad, especially during the post-COVID-19 pandemic (Flywire, 2021). Statistically, the number of international students has increased to around 6.4 million, an increase of 24% compared to the last five years (UNESCO UIS, 2022). Approximately 52% of the international students come from the Asian continent.

The same statistics reported that the three sending countries are dominated by Asian countries. Specifically, China is in first place with 1.08 million students, India with half of that amount in second place, and Vietnam in third place with 132,559 students. At the same time, the presence of more students who are 'glocal' should be given more attention. They are tertiary students interested in education globally but want to study locally (Choudaha, 2017). Thus, they will choose countries that are close or even in the same region as their country of origin. In the case of China, tertiary students from South Korea, Thailand, and Pakistan monopolised the top three list of its international enrolments in two consecutive years (MoE China, 2018).

As underlined in Osawa (2016), there has been a threefold increase in tertiary education demand in the Asia-Pacific region since 2000. It led to a coordination meeting chaired by UNESCO and attended by high-ranking educational officials from ASEAN+6 countries. Brunei, Cambodia, Indonesia, Laos, Malaysia, Myanmar, Philippines, Singapore, Thailand, and Vietnam are the ASEAN countries. Meanwhile, +6 are Australia, China, India, Japan, New Zealand, and South Korea (Sharma, 2016). The meeting agreed to set a standard indicator, which is divided into three phases. Greater transparency among member countries, followed by a recognition system among institutions and countries, concluded with harmonisation among member countries, as implemented in Europe Bologna Process (Khalid et al., 2019).

For the Southeast Asia region, ASEAN International Mobility for Students (AIMS) is a collaboration initiated by Malaysia, Indonesia, and Thailand, which started in 2009 (Abdullah & Aziz, 2015). The regional tertiary student mobility programme continues to grow with the participation of other ASEAN countries such as Brunei, Philippines, and Vietnam and the involvement of other Asian countries such as Japan and South Korea (Chao, 2020). According to Karim et al. (2022), thousands have enjoyed the student mobility offered by AIMS, as well as various higher education collaborations among member countries that have been initiated under this agreement. As a result, collaborations among member countries and other countries in different regions and continents, such as ASEAN+6 and AIMS, are among the significant reasons why Asia dominates the demand for international education.

Although Malaysia receives thousands of international students, only 40% are registered with public universities, also known as Public Higher Education Institutions (PbHEIs) (MoHE, 2021). This ratio is very detrimental, as Malaysia has 20 public universities that belong to various fields and specialisations. In general, five are named research universities, 11 are known as comprehensive universities, and four are listed as specialised technical universities (Sheriff & Abdullah, 2017). In terms of similarity, each of these public universities needs to generate their income up to 30% by 2025 ("Menteri: Jana pendapatan sendiri (Minister: Generate your own income)", 2016). Thus, accepting more international students, who pay higher tuition fees than local students, is one of the major resources for income generation, as practised in the United States and the United Kingdom (Mitropoulos, 2020).

Due to its potential as the biggest sending continent for international students, Asia has been chosen as the focus for this study. The objective is to study and summarise the enrolment patterns for Asian tertiary students in Malaysian public universities, especially on the sub-continents and countries, levels of education, and types of gender. This timeline of 2008–2016 was chosen as it is the golden period for international tertiary enrolment in Malaysia. In detail, Malaysia was first ranked as the 11th most popular destination for worldwide higher education in 2008 (Mustapha, 2013). Eight years later, it was crowned the best country for openness to international higher education in 2016, on par with Germany (Morgan, 2016). Both excellent records and other achievements inspired Malaysia to set a target of 200,000 international enrolments in 2020. However, it did not work. Therefore, drastic action needs to be taken to put Malaysia back on the right track.

The data set of Asian tertiary enrolments in Malaysian public universities was provided by the Planning, Research & Policy Coordination Division, Ministry of Higher Education Malaysia, in Microsoft Excel format (MoHE, 2018). The data set shows tertiary enrolments from 147 countries in all 20 Malaysian public universities from 2008 to 2016. The data was divided into male, female, and total. Plus, apart from the total enrolment, eight levels of study, including Doctor of Philosophy, master's degree, postgraduate diploma, bachelor's degree, diploma, professional, matriculation, and others, have been listed. Nevertheless, three levels—Doctor of Philosophy (PhD), master's degree (Master), and bachelor's degree (Degree)—were selected. The reasons were (1) the enrolment size for these three levels of study was around 96.04% of total enrolment and (2) these three levels of study had non-zero enrolment compared to other levels of study. This study is further presented in three sections covering the enrolment patterns, summary of findings, and conclusion.

2 Enrolment Patterns

Geographically, Asia is the largest of the seven continents. In "Standard Country or Area Codes for Statistical Use (M49)" issued by the United Nations Statistical Commission, the Asian continent comprises 50 countries under five different sub-continents. The sub-continents are Central Asia, Eastern Asia, South-eastern Asia, Southern Asia, and Western Asia. Western Asia is the largest sub-continent of Asia with 18 countries while Central Asia is only five. The second biggest sub-continent is South-eastern Asia with 11 countries, followed by Southern Asia with nine countries and Eastern Asia with seven countries. The full list of these 50 Asian countries is shown in Table 1.

From 2008 to 2016, the highest number of Asian sending countries was 44 countries in 2013. Western Asia was the biggest sending sub-continent with 14 countries, followed by South-eastern Asia and Southern Asia, both with 10 countries, and Eastern Asia with 6 countries. Central Asia became the smallest sending sub-continent with only five countries. Geographically, this proportion is logical. Western Asia has the largest number of countries while Central Asia has the smallest number. The remaining three sub-continents, South-eastern Asia, Southern Asia, and Eastern Asia, are ranged between the two regions as shown in Fig. 1.

Conversely, the six non-sending countries were Malaysia as the host country and another five Asian countries. In detail, one country was from the Eastern Asian sub-continent, Macao, and four countries were from

Table 1 List of the Asian countries

Central Asia	Eastern Asia	South-eastern Asia	Southern Asia	Western Asia	
Kazakhstan	China	Brunei Darussalam	Afghanistan	Armenia	Oman
Kyrgyzstan	China, Hong Kong SAR	Cambodia	Bangladesh	Azerbaijan	Qatar
Tajikistan	China, Macao SAR	Indonesia	Bhutan	Bahrain	Saudi Arabia
Turkmenistan	DPR of Korea	Lao PDR	India	Cyprus	State of Palestine
Uzbekistan	Mongolia	Malaysia	Iran (IRI)	Georgia	Syrian Arab Republic
	Republic of Korea	Myanmar	Maldives	Iraq	Turkey
	Japan	Philippines	Nepal	Israel	United Arab Emirates
		Singapore	Pakistan	Jordan	Yemen
		Thailand	Sri Lanka	Kuwait	
		Timor-Leste		Lebanon	
		Viet Nam			

Source: Adapted from the Standard Country or Area Codes for Statistical Use (M49), United Nations Statistical Commission (UNSC, 2020)

the Western Asian sub-continent. Specifically, Armenia, Cyprus, Georgia, and Israel. These countries have never sent their tertiary students to Malaysia during the same period. Other than the year 2013, the number of home countries ranged from 42 to 43 per year. In detail, three sub-continents of Asia, South-eastern Asia with 10 sending countries, Southern Asia with 9 sending countries, and Western Asia with 14 sending countries have consistently sent their students from 2008 to 2016. Meanwhile, Central Asia and Eastern Asia had an ever-changing number of sending countries.

Figure 1 shows in Central Asia, four countries—Kazakhstan, Kyrgyzstan, Tajikistan, and Uzbekistan—enrolled their students in Malaysian public universities from 2008 to 2012. Only since 2013,

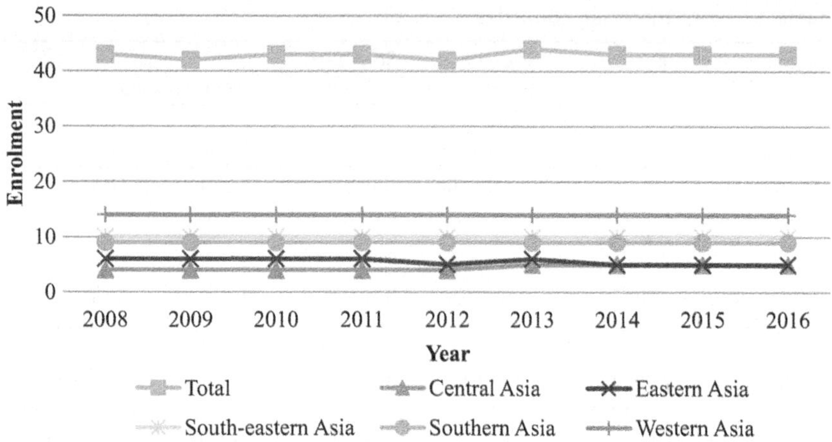

Fig. 1 Enrolments of Asian tertiary students in Malaysian public universities (by sub-continents—number of countries). Analysis made based on data released by the MoHE (2018)

Turkmenistan joined as the fifth sending country from the same region. For Eastern Asia, all six countries—China, Hong Kong, North Korea, Japan, Mongolia, and South Korea—registered their students at Malaysian public universities for 2008–2011 and 2013. However, the number decreased to only five when Mongolia withdrew its enrolments in four different years, 2012 and 2014–2016.

In terms of percentage, the overall sample per population is 90%. In detail, Central Asia, South-Eastern Asia, and Southern Asia recorded a 100% sample per population. Meanwhile, Eastern Asia has 86% and Western Asia has 78%. All the analyses made are based on the statistics issued by the Malaysian Ministry of Higher Education (MoHE, 2018). Table 2 shows the difference in population number and sample size for the sample (Asia) and five sub-samples within it (Central Asia, Eastern Asia, South-eastern Asia, Southern Asia, and Western Asia).

For Asian enrolled students, the highest number welcomed by Malaysia was 25,420 in 2013, as shown in Fig. 2. This factor may be contributed by the maximum number of 44 sending countries recorded in the same year, as presented earlier in Fig. 1. The four sub-continents, Eastern Asia, South-eastern Asia, Southern Asia, and Western Asia, registered a

Table 2 List of the Asian sending countries (population number versus sample size)

	Sample (Asia)	Sub-sample 1 (Central Asia)	Sub-sample 2 (Eastern Asia)	Sub-sample 3 (South-eastern Asia)	Sub-sample 4 (Southern Asia)	Sub-sample 5 (Western Asia)
Population	49	5	7	10	9	18
Sample	44	5	6	10	9	14
Percentage (sample/population)	90%	100%	86%	100%	100%	78%

Analysis made based on data released by the MoHE (2018)

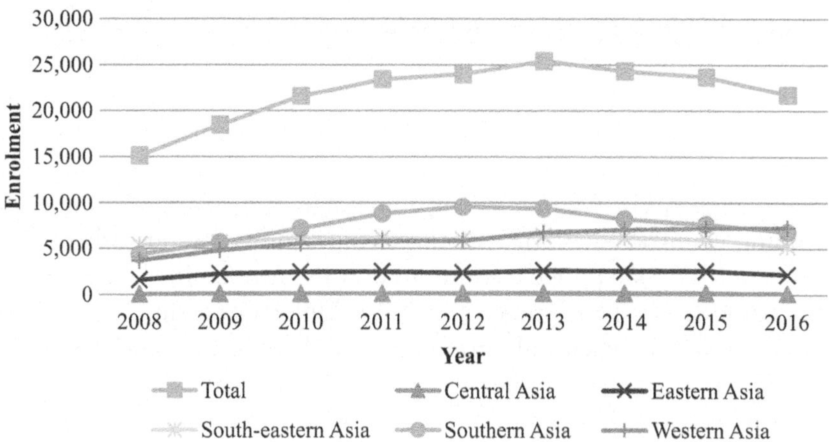

Fig. 2 Enrolments of Asian tertiary students in Malaysian public universities (by sub-continents – number of students). Analysis made based on data released by the MoHE (2018)

four-digit enrolment. Only Central Asia reported enrolment in the tens and hundreds of students for the same period. For the first two years, 2008 and 2009, neighbouring students from South-eastern Asia monopolised seats in Malaysian public universities at an average rate of 5500 enrolments per year.

The pattern changed when students from Southern Asia dominated the total enrolment for the next six consecutive years, starting from 2010 until 2011. This sub-continent took over the chart in 2010 with 7228 students and recorded the highest enrolment in 2012 with 9574 students, before experiencing a declining trend down to 7666 students in 2011. Following the enrolment of less than 7000 Southern Asia students in 2016, Western Asia headed the charts in the same year, with 7297 students. These changes indicate that the demand for Malaysian higher education is dynamic and not limited to the dominance of any single sub-continent or country.

In the same Fig. 2, there was a consistent increase in enrolment over the nine years for Western Asia. Started with 3708 students in 2008, it doubled up in 2016, with 7297 students. It was the highest enrolment among the sub-continents in that year. Meanwhile, in the sub-continent where Malaysia as the host country is located, South-eastern Asia reported enrolment at a consistent rate in the range of 5400–6400 students. The 1000-range fluctuated trend was marked by the highest enrolment amounting to up to 6404 students in 2013. For Eastern Asia and Central Asia, these two regions were ranked second last and last in the enrolment chart, respectively. Despite having a one-digit and changing number of sending countries, Eastern Asia successfully enrolled thousands of students in Malaysian public institutions over the period. The highest number reported was 2636 students in 2013. Different conditions occurred for Central Asia when only maximum numbers of 211 students could enrol in 2011, far behind the other four sub-continents. From the bright perspective, even though the number recorded for this sub-continent was too small compared to others, this proves that Malaysian higher education still has a demand throughout the Asian continent. The demand includes the smallest Asian sub-continent with only five regional countries, which is Central Asia.

In addressing types of enrolment in Malaysian public universities, three levels of study, namely, Doctor of Philosophy (*PhD*), master's degree (*Master*), and first degree (*Degree*), are the focus of discussion. The aggregate amount for these three levels of study is known as total. The total value is also displayed in the same figure. In the first three years of 2008, 2009, and 2010, Asian students were more interested in pursuing a *Master*, than a *PhD* and a *Degree*, as depicted in Fig. 3. However, this situation changed as more and more Asians were interested in completing

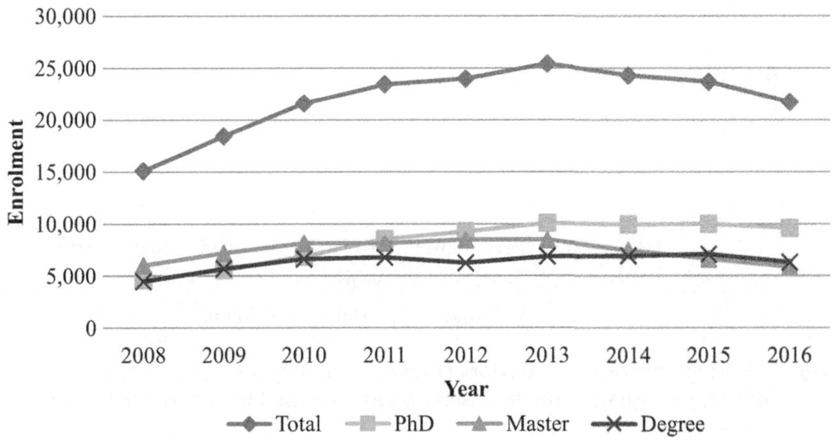

Fig. 3 Enrolments of Asian tertiary students in Malaysian public universities (by levels of study). Analysis made based on data released by the MoHE (2018)

their *PhD* in Malaysia during the 2011–2016 period. This period was also two-thirds of the sampling time. A three-digit difference of 401 students between the *PhD* and the *Master* level in 2011 was reported. The difference was later grown-up to as high as 3749 students in 2016.

For the *Degree*, it maintained its lowest enrolment for six out of nine years. Basically, in 2008 and from 2010 to 2014, compared to the *Master* and the *PhD*. In 2009, its enrolment was slightly higher than the *PhD* with a total difference of 150 students. Meanwhile, in 2015 and 2016, the *Degree* surpassed the *Master* by 459 and 462 students, respectively. It shows that enrolment patterns were inconsistent for all three levels of study. Only in the last six years, 2011–2016, it is crystal clear that the *PhD* got more attention than *Degree* and *Master*. The enrolment peak for both postgraduate levels was recorded in 2013. In detail, there are 10,083 students for the *PhD* and 8463 students for the *Master*. On the other hand, the *Degree* reported the highest enrolment in 2015, with 7079, just over 7000 students, once in the nine years.

More *male* students from the Asian continent were enrolled in Malaysian public education institutions than *female* for the entire period of 2008–2016. It is shown in Fig. 4. In a ratio, for every *female*, the number of *males* ranged from as low as 1.79 in 2011 to as high as 2.00 in

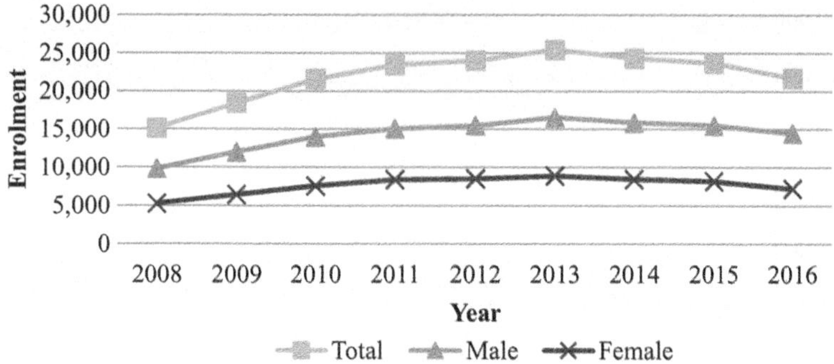

Fig. 4 Enrolments of Asian tertiary students in Malaysian public universities (by types of gender). Analysis made based on data released by the MoHE (2018)

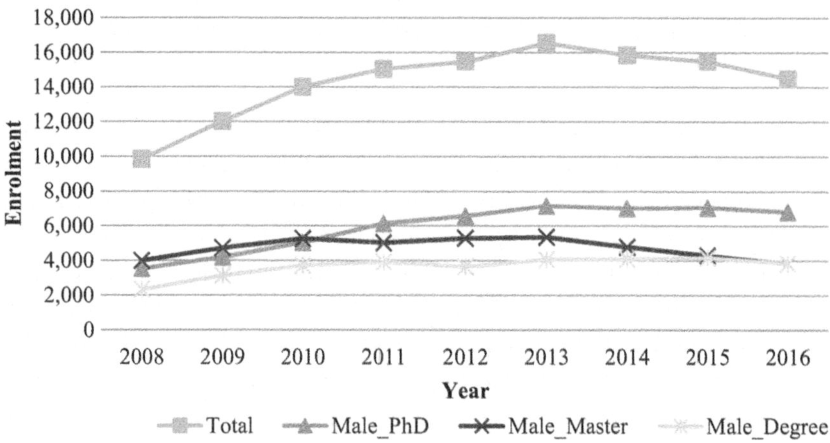

Fig. 5 Enrolments of Asian tertiary students in Malaysian public universities (by types of gender—*male* only). Analysis made based on data released by the MoHE (2018)

2016. The larger slice of the pie owned by *male*, up to two-thirds of the total enrolments, reflects a similar shape between both curves, *male* and total. The highest enrolment was recorded in 2013, with *male* at 16,543 students, exceeded the *female* at 8877 students. Both genders also exhibited a similar pattern of increases from 2008 to 2013 before declining consistently for the last three years. More detailed data can be seen in Fig. 5, which shows the enrolment pattern of *male* students. Meanwhile,

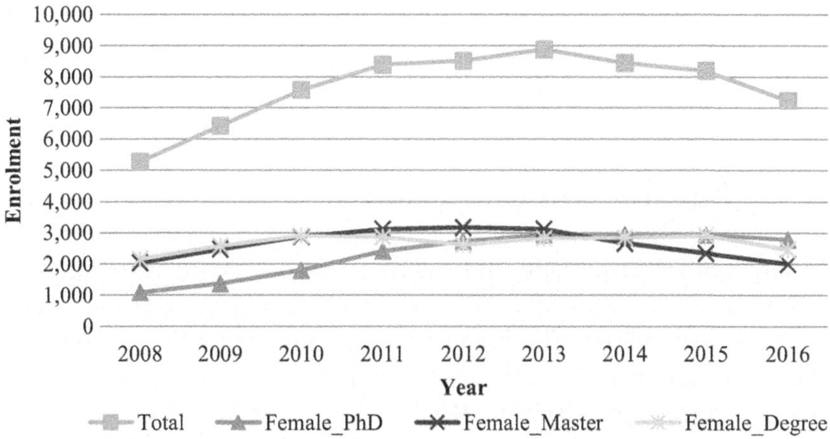

Fig. 6 Enrolments of Asian tertiary students in Malaysian public universities (by types of gender—*female* only). Analysis made based on data released by the MoHE (2018)

Fig. 6 exhibits the number of *female* students, for the same period of 2008–2016.

There was an identical pattern for *male* during the first three years. The three levels of study—*Degree*, *Master*, and *PhD*—saw the development of enrolment positively, at a double-digit growth rate. The immense amount of enrolment was dominated by the *Master* level, followed by *PhD* and *Degree*. Only starting in 2011, more students of this gender (*male*) chose to pursue a *PhD* instead of a *Master* or a *Degree*. The largest increase in enrolment for the *PhD* was 9% in 2013. Simultaneously, fluctuations appeared in *Master* and *Degree* enrolments. Both levels later approached a similar amount in 2016, differentiated by only five students.

For *female*, the mixed pattern occurred throughout the research period. In the first three years, the number of *Degree* students was approximately the same as the number of *Master* students and massively ahead of *PhD* students. However, the gap between Master and *Degree* decreased from 116 in 2008 to only 24 in 2010. It shows that the interest in *female* was almost the same for both *Degree* and *Master*. In the next three years, *Master* topped the chart. However, the *master's* growth was only one-digit and turned negative in 2013. On the other hand, there was a two-digit increase in growth for the *PhD*, especially in 2011 and 2012. The growth ensured the PhD's dominance in the last three years, though closely approached by the *Degree*.

3 Results and Discussions

In terms of sub-continents and countries, 44 out of 49 Asian countries sent their tertiary students to Malaysia at a time. Converted to a percentage, it is around 90%. This high percentage proves that Malaysian public higher education is in widespread demand in the Asian continent and five sub-continents within it. Regarding the number of sub-continent enrolments over total enrolments, Southern Asia was the largest with 34%. It was followed by Western Asia and South-Eastern Asia, both with 27%. Eastern Asia was next with 11%, while Central Asia with 1%. For intra-continent analysis, there were mixed patterns related to the dominant country in a sub-continent. Most sub-continents had a dominant country, such as Uzbekistan for Central Asia, China for Eastern Asia, Indonesia for South-eastern Asia, and Iran for Southern Asia. For Western Asia, though Iraq dominated this sub-continent by a difference of 1% over Yemen, these two countries always exchanged their rank as the biggest sending country. All the information is displayed in Fig. 7.

In other words, these dominant countries can be considered traditional sending countries for Malaysian public higher education, based on the whole period of 2008–2016. Therefore, relevant parties such as the Ministry of Higher Education and public universities need to sustain enrolment from these countries through continuous networking and promotion. At the same time, other home countries that are not market dominators should also be given proper attention. Even though the number is too small and limited to a single figure, this tiny enrolment is a massive proof that Malaysian public higher education is still in demand in those countries. It is to ensure that their enrolment increases and approaches the volume ever recorded by the dominant countries. On the other hand, there were Asian countries that never sent their students to Malaysian public universities for the entire period, such as Armenia, Cyprus, and Georgia in the Western Asia sub-continent and Macao in

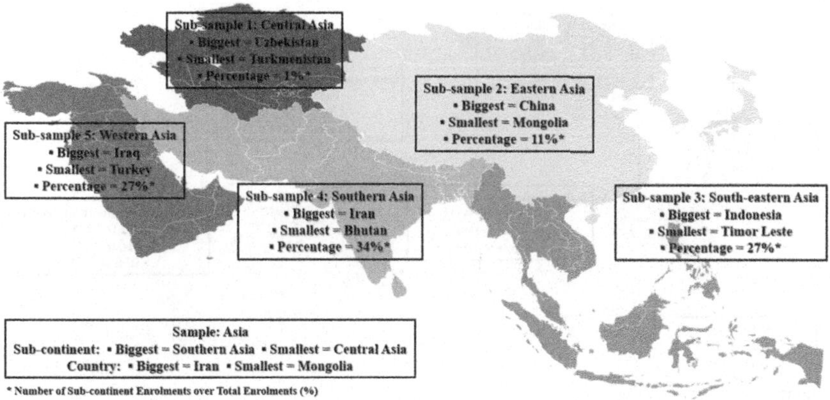

Fig. 7 Summarisation of types of sub-continents and countries in demand for Malaysian public universities by Asian tertiary students. Analysis made based on data released by the MoHE (2018)

the Eastern Asia sub-continent. Thus, securing existing markets and exploring new markets must be done simultaneously. These are to ensure sustainability in demand for Malaysian public tertiaries among Asian prospective students.

During the same period, these public universities exhibited mixed patterns in demand for their levels of study. Significantly, PhD was the top choice for two-thirds of the period, 2011–2016. Conversely, the Master was the earlier preferred choice from 2008 until 2010. Simultaneously, the programme at the undergraduate level also successfully attracted students from the Asian continent. On average, PhD generated the biggest demand with 38%, followed by Master with 33%, and Degree with 29%. In other words, the international demand for Malaysian public higher education occurred at both levels—undergraduate and postgraduate. In general, each sub-continent pattern was different, despite the demand that existed at both undergraduate and postgraduate levels. For sub-continents such as Central Asia, Eastern Asia, and South-eastern Asia, the *Degree* level was the top choice. On the other hand, for two other sub-continents—Southern Asia and Western Asia—most of their students were more interested in pursuing studies at the *PhD* level. The sub-continents preference for the levels of study is presented in Fig. 8.

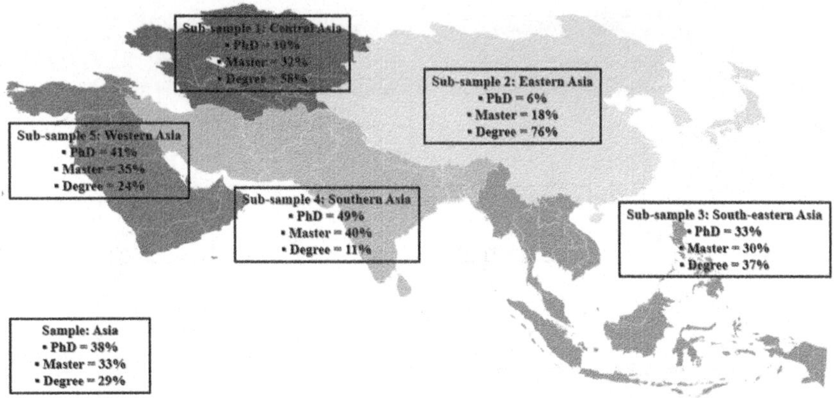

Fig. 8 Summarisation of levels of study in demand for Malaysian public universities by Asian tertiary students. Analysis made based on data released by the MoHE (2018)

For gender-based comparison, total demand for Malaysian public higher education from the Asian continent, at the *PhD*, *Master*, and *Degree* levels, were entirely monopolised by *male* students. However, there were two exceptional cases at the sub-continent level. In detail, *female* students exceeded the *male* students, namely *Master* level in Eastern Asia and *Degree* level in South-eastern Asia. These unique statistics prove that Malaysia can still attract *female* students to ensure a balanced gender ratio in the future. The need to study at the tertiary level is far more critical, beyond the boundaries of gender. This matter should be taken seriously, especially by those responsible for promoting Malaysian higher education globally. It includes Education Malaysia Global Services (EMGS) and international affairs office in the 20 Malaysian public universities. For total enrolment, consistency in the range of 20,000–25,000 students in the last seven years, despite the fluctuating process, proves that this demand is in a consistent state. Similarly, its ability to achieve as high as 25,420 students in 2013, despite starting as low as 15,113 students in 2008. The increase was supported by the growth of up to 68% within five years.

For types of gender, on average, *female* students accounted for 35% of the total enrolment from 2008 to 2016. In detail, the highest percentage recorded was only 36% in 2011, and the lowest value in 2016 with 33%. At the sub-continent level, the lowest difference between genders was recorded in Eastern Asia with 4%. On the other hand, a vast difference of 60% was recorded in Western Asia. All are presented in Fig. 9. In other words, the enrolment of Asian *female* students in Malaysian public universities lags far behind *male* students. This issue is also similar to what has been concluded earlier in part 1.2.2. The statement, however, contradicts Selingo (2019), Carotenuto (2015), and Redden (2008). They concluded that female students, especially from the US, are more likely to study abroad than males. The female ratio even increased to two-thirds of total outbound students in 2019 (Selingo, 2019). The economic advancement and openness to gender equality in the sending country may contribute to the differences between Western countries and Eastern countries. Thus, it is a golden opportunity, as Malaysia is a progressive country and is fair to all genders.

For Sitarz (2021), more quotas need to be opened to welcome more international female students, especially in the science, technology, engineering, and mathematics (STEM) field. One of the reasons is that some Asian countries do not encourage their local females to take up this field, causing them to go abroad to fulfil their interest (Henry & Andrews,

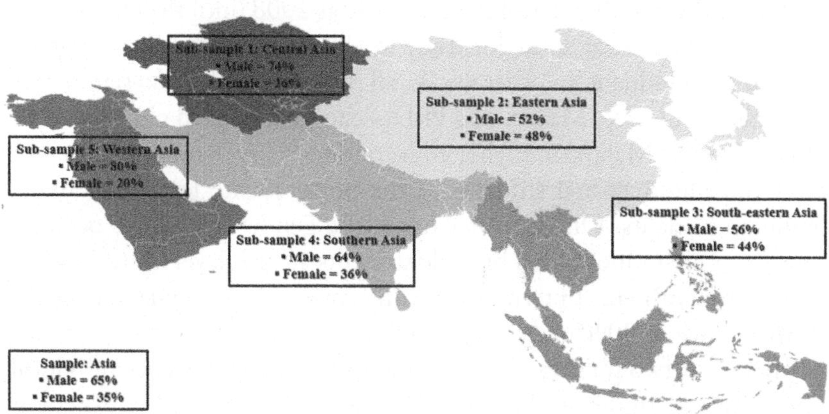

Fig. 9 Summarisation of types of gender in demand for Malaysian public universities by Asian tertiary students. Analysis made based on data released by the MoHE (2018)

2017). From another perspective, reaching full potential regardless of gender is essential in developing a country, primarily Asian countries. If safety and security are the issues, Malaysia is the country that should be at the top of the list. It has just been named the 16th most peaceful country in the world, according to the latest Global Peace Index (GPI) 2019 ("Malaysia ranked world's 16th", 2020). At the same time, Malaysia is also the most popular Muslim-friendly country for 2019, in front of big names like Turkey and the United Arab Emirates (UAE), as reported in the Crescent Rating Muslim Women in Travel 2019 (Agency, 2020). These rankings are significant proof that Malaysia can be promoted as a suitable global learning destination for women. At the same time, Malaysia's efforts must also consider the macro factors in both countries (home and host), which are empirically explained in detail in the next sub-chapter.

4 Conclusion and Policy Implications

In conclusion, this study has successfully identified enrolment patterns throughout the study period. In general, Malaysia is the preferred choice of sending countries from the same continent. This statement is also supported by the five-digit enrolment, as early as 2008 until the end of 2016. The demands exist at all major study levels, including both undergraduate and postgraduate. In other words, all these levels of Malaysian tertiary education—Degree, Master, and PhD—can be marketed globally. At the same time, the Malaysian higher education industry is more successful in attracting international students at the postgraduate level than undergraduate students. On the other hand, the gender imbalance occurs as most seats are monopolised by male students at each level of study and in every sub-continent. In terms of sending countries, Malaysia managed to be the choice of 90% of Asian countries.

Therefore, two policies are proposed. First, on the existence of "glocal" phenomenon. In detail, the tertiary students are interested in experiencing a global experience but want to study in the countries closest to the socioeconomics of their origin country. This phenomenon needs to be taken seriously. Without neglecting traditional sending countries, more new countries with smaller student numbers need to be explored. It also includes the remaining four countries—Macao, Armenia, Cyprus, and Georgia—that did not send their students to Malaysian public universities during the study period. The post of education attache should be introduced in these countries. This effort enables the promotional activities to be done continuously in order to create the first enrolment for each non-sending country. If cost becomes an obstacle, the educational promotion can be placed under the Trade Attache. It is realistic given that tertiary education is also a trade commodity, but in the form of services.

For sub-continent that send students in small amount like Central Asia, alumni institutions need to be strengthened. The alumnus can be official spokespersons for their alma maters as well as Malaysia from time to time. Second, on the shortage of international female tertiary students in Malaysian public universities. It is another unique opportunity that can be discovered, given that Malaysia has a good record in gender equality and public safety. Malaysia's current best rankings, such as the Global Peace Index (GPI) 2019 and the Crescent Rating of Muslim Women in Travel 2019, need to be placed immediately on websites, especially on the Education Malaysia website and also on all websites of Malaysian public universities. The display allows prospective female students to compare Malaysia with other alternative countries of their choice.

The Ministry of Higher Education and the Ministry of Women, Family and Community Development can work together to produce procedures that enable international female students to feel safer in Malaysia. Perhaps the same operational unit and careline that deals with local women matters can extend its functions in serving these international females. The policies and practices of some Asian countries that limit the offering of STEM courses to women need to be addressed by public universities. More STEM quotas need to be opened to female international students as they can contribute back in terms of professional knowledge and technical skills to their origin country. At the same time, this action can reduce the local enrolment gap between the social sciences and science and technology fields that public universities are currently experiencing.

References

Abdullah, D., & Aziz, M. I. A. (2015). Locating Malaysia's place within the ASEAN higher education landscape: Current status, challenges and future prospects. In R. Bhandari & A. Lefébure (Eds.), *Asia: The next higher education superpower?* Institute of International Education. https://www.iie.org/Research-and-Insights/Publications/Asia-The-Next-Higher-Education-Superpower

Agency. (2020, December 9). *Malaysia is the top country for Muslim-friendly travel.* The Star. https://www.thestar.com.my/lifestyle/travel/2020/12/09/malaysia-is-the-top-country-for-muslim-friendly-travel.

Carotenuto, M. (2015, October 9). *Why do more U.S. women study abroad than men?* The Washington Post. https://www.washingtonpost.com/news/answer-sheet/wp/2015/10/09/why-do-more-u-s-women-study-abroad-than-men/

Chao, R. Y. (2020). Intra-ASEAN student mobility: Overview, challenges and opportunities. *Journal of Applied Research in Higher Education.* https://doi.org/10.1108/JARHE-07-2019-0178

Choudaha, R. (2017). Three waves of international student mobility (1999–2020). *Studies in Higher Education, 42*(5), 825–832. https://doi.org/10.1080/03075079.2017.1293872

Flywire. (2021, June 2022). *Flywire survey reveals students optimistic about international education.* Flywire Corporation (Nasdaq: FLYW). https://ir.flywire.com/node/6891/pdf.

Henry, E. R., & Andrews, C. (2017, October 11). Trending: Female international student mobility. *Instead Global & Local Academic Branding.* https://services.intead.com/blog/trending-female-international-student-mobility.

Karim, M. R. A., Din, W. A., & Eranza, D. R. D. (2022). Enriching the experience of international mobility students through joint strategies and efforts: Feedback from international students and the success of share coil course at Universiti Malaysia Sabah. In *Proceedings of the Seminar Pengantarabangsaan Pengajian Tinggi 2022* (pp. 191–207). Universiti Sains Islam Malaysia.

Khalid, J., Ali, A. J., Nordin, N. M., & Shah, S. F. H. (2019). Regional cooperation in higher education: Can it lead ASEAN toward harmonization? *Southeast Asian Studies, 8*(1), 81–98. https://doi.org/10.20495/seas.8.1_81

Malaysia ranked world's 16th most peaceful. (2020, Jan 15). *Bernama.* https://www.bernama.com/en/news.php?id=1806599

Menteri: Jana pendapatan sendiri, bukan naikkan yuran universiti. (Minister: Generate your own income, not raise university fees). (2016, October 23).

ProjekMM News. https://www.projekmm.com/news/berita/2016/10/23/menteri-jana-pendapatan-sendiri-bukan-naikkan-yuran-universiti/1234033

Mitropoulos, A. (2020, July 14). *Loss of international students could damage US economy, experts say*. ABC News. https://abcnews.go.com/Business/loss-international-students-damage-us-economy-experts/story?id=71754388

MMR (Maximize Market Research). (2022, August). *Higher education market: Global industry analysis and forecast (2022–2029)*. https://www.maximizemarketresearch.com/market-report/global-higher-education-market/7167/#.

MoE China (Ministry of Education of the People's Republic of China). (2018). *Growing number of foreign students choosing to study in China for a degree across multiple disciplines*. en.moe.gov.cn/News/Top_News/201804/t20180403_332258.html#:~:text=Top News-, Growing number of foreign students choosing to study in, a degree.

MoHE (Malaysia, Ministry of Higher Education). (2018). Bilangan pelajar antarabangsa di universiti awam tahun 2008-2016 (Number of international students in public universities 2008–2016). [Spreadsheet file]. MoHE.

MoHE (Malaysia, Ministry of Higher Education). (2021). *Bab 1 - Makro institusi pendidikan tinggi. Statistik Pendidikan Tinggi 2019 (Chapter 1 - Macros of higher education institutions. Higher Education Statistics 2019)*. MoHE. https://www.mohe.gov.my/en/downloads/statistics/2021-1/849-statistik-pendidikan-tinggi-2021-03-bab-1-makro-institusi-pendidikan-tinggi/file

Morgan, J. (2016, May 4). Germany and Malaysia 'top performers' for internationalisation. *Times Higher Education*. https://www.timeshighereducation.com/news/germany-and-malaysia-top-performers-for-internationalisation

Murthi, M., & Bassett, R.M. (2022, November 15). Higher education: Understanding demand and redefining values. *World Bank Blogs*. https://blogs.worldbank.org/education/higher-education-understanding-demand-and-redefining-values

Mustapha, W. N. W. (2013, December 3). *Malaysia ranks high as regional education hub*. New Straits Time. https://www.asiaone.com/malaysia/malaysia-ranks-high-regional-education-hub.

Osawa, A. (2016). *Higher education data collection in Asia and the Pacific. Perspective from the UNESCO Institute for Statistics. Internationalization of Higher Education in ASEAN+6*. UNESCO. http://www.unescobkk.org/fileadmin/user_upload/apeid/HigherEdu/Indicators-Nov2016/UIS_AIMS-Aki.pdf

Redden, E. (2008, December 4). *Women abroad and men at home.* Inside Higher Ed. https://www.insidehighered.com/news/2008/12/04/women-abroad-and-men- home.

Selingo, J. (2019, March 1). *Why are so few male students studying abroad?* The Atlantic. https://www.theatlantic.com/education/archive/2019/02/male-students-studying-abroad/583828/

Sharma, Y. (2016, November 25). *The push for Asian HE internationalisation indicators.* University World News. http://www.universityworldnews.com/article.php?story=20161123124836365.

Sheriff, N. M., & Abdullah, N. (2017). Research Universities in Malaysia: What Beholds? *Asian Journal of University Education, 13*(2), 35–50. https://files.eric.ed.gov/fulltext/EJ1207763.pdf

Sitarz, K. (2021, March 19). International student mobility trends: A closer look at international female student opportunities. *Shorelight.* https://shorelight.com/student-stories/international-student-mobility-trends-a-closer-look-at-international-female/.

UNESCO UIS (United Nations Educational, Scientific and Cultural Organization Institute for Statistics). (2022). National Monitoring: Inbound internationally mobile students by continent of origin and National Monitoring: Outbound internationally mobile.

UNSC (United Nations Statistical Commission). (2020). *Methodology-Standard country or area codes for statistical use (M49).* UNSC. https://unstats.un.org/unsd/methodology/m49/

Business Schools and Their Connections with the Labour Market: An Exploratory Analysis of Pakistani Public Universities

Arif Toor, Ali Sher, and Adnan ul Haque

1 Introduction

Pakistan, a country in Southeast Asia, has a population of over 231 million where the literacy rate is 58% (O'Neill, 2023). Only about 35% of university graduates can find jobs each year (Academia Magazine, n.d.). These statistics question how well Pakistani universities are preparing their graduates to support their employment efforts. There is also a push by the government to create university courses in entrepreneurship and business management to increase graduate employability. This chapter examines the websites of business schools at public universities in the Federal Capital and four provinces of Pakistan to explore what kind of labour market connections have been placed there. We used the objectives of Bachelor of Business Administration (BBA) and Master of Business Administration (MBA) programmes to assess whether they relate to the terminology that can help the curricula connect with the

A. Toor • A. Sher • A. ul Haque (✉)
Faculty of Business, Yorkville University, Toronto, ON, Canada
e-mail: ahaque@yorkvilleu.ca

F. A. Yamoah, A. ul Haque (eds.), *Corporate Management Ecosystem in Emerging Economies*, https://doi.org/10.1007/978-3-031-41578-4_13

labour market requirements. We use transition and higher participation systems as theoretical frameworks for this exploration.

Transition systems consist of various features of a country's institutional arrangement, which promotes and supports young people's education-work transitions (Raffe, 2008). The links between various institutions within the education sector and those in the labour market are key dimensions of transition systems (Hannan et al., 1996). Iannelli and Raffe (2007) argued that systems in countries where education is strongly linked with the intended occupation or vocation are said to follow 'employment logic,' and the systems with weaker education-work linkage follow an 'education logic.' Furthermore, in countries with transition systems based on 'employment logic,' the industry has more substantial involvement in course development, delivery, and quality assurance.

Transition systems in most coordinated market economies, such as Germany, follow an 'employment logic.' In comparison, liberal market economies like Canada tend to fall into the 'education logic' category. Little information is available about Pakistan's economic structure; however, most indicators will place it somewhere closer to a market economy. This means that there is a weak link between education and the labour market in Pakistan. Research has also shown that for the recruitment of unregulated professionals in most liberal market economies, employers use qualifications to screen potential candidates and not as a signal of validation of specific skills (Wheelahan & Moodie, 2017). Research has also shown that the desire to earn higher qualifications might further crowd the market (Caroleo & Pastore, 2015) and hinder a successful transition to the labour market. In Pakistan, most business schools do not report any programme objectives on their website, which creates ambiguity about the nature of connections between programmes offered by these schools and the labour market. However, enrolment in these programmes has significantly increased in the last 20 years. Yet, the overall graduate employment rates in Pakistan remain low. Nonetheless, this does not seem to impact the higher enrolment trends. More and more students continue to be admitted to these programmes regardless of the percentage of graduates' employability. This warrants further investigation into the overall education system in Pakistan business schools, the programmes they offer, and their connections with the labour market.

2 Literature Review

The term 'transition systems' refers to a country's institutional arrangements that facilitate the transition of young people from school to work (Raffe, 2008). An analysis of the transition systems includes discussion of two, often overlapping segments of young people's lives: 1) when they are involved in making decisions that shape links between their education and labour market and 2) when they leave school and start jobs that mark the course of their future careers (Neumark, 2007). The studies of transition systems are generally considered a recent phenomenon, starting after the industrial revolution at the end of the nineteenth century and driven by social trends of mass schooling that focus on academic education and reduced the role of apprenticeship as an institution for acquiring work-related skills (Caroleo & Pastore, 2015; Charner et al., 1995; Neumark, 2007; UNESCO, 2012). According to Neumark (2007), evolving technology also challenged apprenticeships to provide the number of skilled workers needed, thus leading governments to invest more in vocational education at the college level; however, the explicit policy focus only began in the later part of the twentieth century when governments realized "unnecessary periods of joblessness and excessive job instability" (Neumark, 2007, p. 3) experienced by youth after graduating from school.

Research has also shown that despite the higher attainment levels of education and experienced workers, young people struggle to find jobs (Buchholz et al., 2009; Raffe, 2014). Charner et al. (1995) also reported similar challenges in the United States. There was no clear policy to guide youth in their school-to-work transition until the 1990s, and only a mosaic of programmes was established for this purpose. To respond to these challenges, governments shifted towards integrating academic and vocational skills with a clear focus on labour-market outcomes (Neumark, 2007), which led to a broader research focus on transition systems, including local, national, and cross-national analyses (Raffe, 2014). Today, the debate about transition systems, the education level of workers, and the expertise required in the labour market are critical dimensions of research on skill mismatch in an economy (Caroleo & Pastore, 2015).

Research has shown that the study of transition systems matters. There is merit in explaining the key differences in the transition systems of various countries (Raffe, 2014), which are based on the varying degrees of capitalism in these societies. Iannaelli and Raffe (2008) adapted the concept of societal logic coined by Maurice et al. (1986). They summarized various countries as dominating "education logic" or "employment logic" based on the institutional arrangements leading their young adults from school to work. Countries with strong links between education institutions and labour market actors such as employers, unions, and industry regulators exemplify employment logic.

In contrast, societies with weak associations between these institutions and actors are referred to as having education logic (Iannelli & Raffe, 2007). The study of transition systems cross-links with the literature on varieties of capitalism described by Hall and Soskice (2001). In Pakistan, education logic dominates in a liberal market economy where most sectors have a weak connection between education and the labour market.

Increasing enrolment in higher education might be explained through Marginson's (2016) concept of high participation systems (HPS). Although Marginson's (2016) study involved high school graduates and concluded that their parents' desire for higher education contributed to their choice of further education, he also argued that the trend of higher participation in education is not limited to a specific region or country. Other researchers also argue that most societies consider the level of education attained by their members as a means of modernization and social differentiation (Baker, 2011). This study attempts, in part, to analyse the higher enrolment levels at universities in Pakistan to see if the contributing factors are similar to the worldwide trends of higher participation as reported by Marginson (2016) or how they contribute to the mix.

3 Research Methodology

This section examines the websites of twenty-two business schools of public universities in the Federal Capital and four provinces of Pakistan to explore the presence of labour market connections. A Google search was conducted to find the websites of the business schools in Pakistan. We used the objectives of Bachelor of Business Administration (BBA) and Master of Business Administration (MBA) programmes to assess whether they relate to the terminology that can help the curricula connect with the labour market requirements. We utilized transition and higher participation systems as theoretical frameworks for this exploration.

The authors visited twenty-two business school websites of public universities in Pakistan. After visiting the business school websites, we were interested in finding out the BBA and MBA programmes' objectives and outcomes. Most of the business schools provided information on vision, mission, and objectives in a broader sense at the school or department level. However, most did not provide information on the programme objectives and outcomes at the BBA and MBA levels. Three business schools, two in KPK and one in Sindh, listed their BBA and MBA programmes' objectives and outcomes on their websites. In contrast, such information was not available on the websites of nineteen business schools. Table 1 provides a summary of the twenty-two business schools of public universities in Pakistan:

Table 1 Business schools of the selected public universities in Pakistan

Province	No. of business schools visited	BBA programme objectives and outcomes available	MBA programme objectives and outcomes available	Department/school level—vision, mission, and objectives available
Balochistan	2	0	0	2
KPK	7	2	2	6
Punjab	7	0	0	7
Sindh	4	1	1	4
Federal Capital (Islamabad)	2	0	0	2
Total	22	3	3	21

Since the data was extracted through the official websites, there is content validity (based on the information on the official websites). Moreover, face validity is considered by visiting and discussing it with the authorities. The overt observation was carried out, which means that authorities were informed before the observation was made. We used the funnel approach to draw major themes for categorization, which is an effective strategy for attaining useful truth (Haque & Yamoah, 2021; Yamoah & Haque, 2022). The information was gathered from the open public source's domain. The concerned authorities were assured that the shared details would only be used for academic purposes.

4 Findings and Discussions

The graphical representation is given below to explain the current scenario about the business schools in different provinces of Pakistan.
It is imperative to note from Table 1 and Fig. 1 that most business schools in Pakistan do not report their programme objectives on their website. This suggests that there are weak links between the programme curricula of these schools and the labour market they prepare graduates for. It is also important to note that university enrolment in Pakistan has increased from 3% in 2005 to 12% in 2019 (World Bank, 2022). This trend clearly

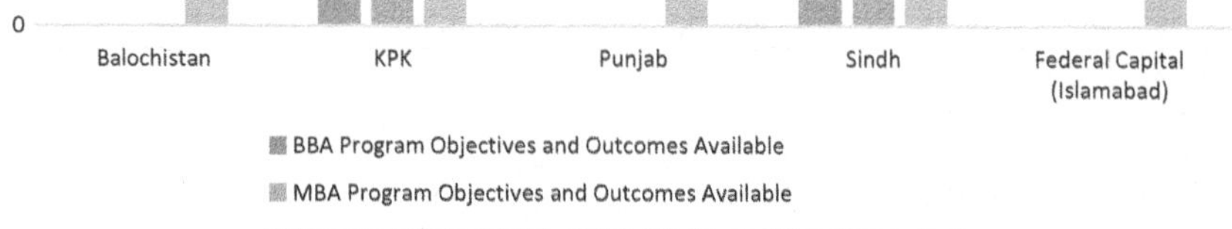

Fig. 1 Business schools in the public universities of Pakistan (own illustration based on primary data)

shows that people in Pakistan seem convinced that education is a prime source of better economic wellbeing. However, the faith in education to provide better employment outcomes in countries like Pakistan is less than promising. Most graduates are not able to find jobs in their field of study, if they are successful at all.

There seems to be a stronger argument in support of education's role in improving the lives of the people of Pakistan, but the fact that most business schools don't even mention the programme objectives on their website gives us a glimpse of the ambiguity that persists in the education system. The idea of having stronger links with employers is a popular marketing tool, but not routed in the data available on the websites.

5 Conclusion and Recommendations

Based on the findings, it is concluded that the programme objectives are not reported by the business schools in Pakistan on their official websites, irrespective of the province of operation. It is a strong indication of weak linkage between the labour market and the programme curricula of the considered business schools. In other words, one of the major reasons fresh graduates struggle to find placement and develop the required skills is the missing objectives of the programme. It is unfortunate that graduates are preparing and training for the desired labour market while not knowing exactly what the objective of the programme is and how it can assist them in the long run. According to the report of the World Bank (2022), Pakistan has significantly improved in terms of university enrolments in the last one-and-a-half decade by 9%, reflecting that it is a common trend in Pakistan to convince people about the importance of university education. In other words, the common trend and thought among individuals is that university education provides a better platform for improved economic conditions and wellbeing. Nonetheless, still the education providing better employment is very low. Though education appears to be promising, it is not rewarding. The tale of struggle among the majority of graduates for finding a field-relevant job is long. A stronger argument is posed in favour of the constructive role of the educational institutions in improving the prospects of life among individuals in Pakistan; however, the reality is that most of these educational institutions are not even mentioning the objectives of the programme on their websites. It is like one is expected to go through the programme without even knowing what an individual learns from the programme (learning objectives). Hence, it is concluded that within the education sector of Pakistan, there persists ambiguity. Moreover, from the analysis of the data sources, it is evident that one key factor for graduates' success is to view the stronger linkage between his/her institution and different companies providing job opportunities (employers); however, it is not properly incorporated. The popular marketing tool is not based on the data available on the institution's official websites.

Pakistani business schools must collaborate with employers to better understand the requirements of the jobs they offer to train students accordingly. In addition, the considerations must be considered when designing programme curricula. We suggest that these links between the employers and programmes should be made available on the programme websites. In terms of programme objectives, we suggest that they must be mapped with course outcomes and include a view of the labour market. Lastly, we recommend that programmes have an advisory committee with memberships from the labour market. The proposed advisory committee will share the industry insights with the programme directors and thus will provide timely and periodic feedback on the business curricula.

References

Academia Magazine (n.d.). *Only 35 percent of graduates acquire jobs yearly.* Retrieved from:https://academiamag.com/only-35-percent-graduates-acquire-jobsyearly/#:~:text=Annually%2C%20on%20average%2C%204%2C,with%20the%20issues%20of%20unemployment

Baker, D. P. (2011). Forward and backward, horizontal and vertical: Transformation of occupational credentialing in the schooled society. *Research in Social Stratification and Mobility, 29*(1), 5–29. https://doi.org/10.1016/j.rssm.2011.01.001

Buchholz, S., Hafacker, D., Mills, M., Blossfeld, H.-P., Kurz, K., & Hofmeister, H. (2009). Life course in the globalization process. *European Sociological Review, 25*, 53–71.

Caroleo, F. E., & Pastore, F. (2015). *Overeducation: A disease of the school-to-work transition system.* Accessed from https://papers.ssrn.com/sol3/papers.cfm?abstract_id=2606902

Charner, I., Fraser, B. S., Hubbard, S., Rogers, A., & Horne, R. (1995). Reforms of the school-to-work transition: Findings, implications, and challenges. *The Phi Delta Kappan, 77*(1), 40–60.

Hall, P.A., & Soskice, D. (2001). *Varieties of Capitalism: The Institutional Foundations of Comparative Advantage.* Oxford University Press.

Hannan, D., Raffe, D., & Smyth, E. (1996). Cross-national research on school to work transitions: An analytic framework. In P. Werquin, R. Breen, & J. Planas (Eds.), *Youth transitions in Europe: Theories and evidence* (pp. 409–442). CEREQ.

Haque, A. U., & Yamoah, F. A. (2021). The role of ethical leadership in managing occupational stress to promote innovative work behaviour: A cross-cultural management perspective. *Sustainability, 13*, 9608. https://doi.org/10.3390/su13179608

Iannelli, C., & Raffe, D. (2007). Vocational upper-secondary education and the transition from school. *European Sociological Review, 23*(1), 49–63. https://doi.org/10.1093/esr/jcl019

Marginson. (2016). The worldwide trend to high participation higher education: Dynamics of social stratification in inclusive systems. *Higher Education, 72*(4), 413–434. https://doi.org/10.1007/s10734-016-0016-x

Maurice, M., Sellier, F., & Silvestre, J.-J. (1986). *The social foundations of industrial power: A comparison of France and Germany.* MIT Press.

Neumark, D. (2007). Improving school-to-work transitions: Introduction. In *Improving school-to-work transitions* (pp. 1–23). Sage.

O'Neill, A. (2023). *Literacy rate in Pakistan 2019.* Retrieved from: https://www.statista.com/statistics/572781/literacy-rate-in-pakistan/

Raffe, D. (2008). The concept of transition system. *Journal of Education and Work, 21*(4), 277–296. https://doi.org/10.1080/13639080802360952

Raffe, D. (2014). Explaining national differences in education-work transitions: Twenty years of research on transition systems. *European Societies, 16*(2), 175–193. https://doi.org/10.1080/14616696.2013.821619

UNESCO. (2012). *School-to-work transition information bases.* UNESCO Asia and Pacific Regional Bureau for Education.

Wheelahan, L., & Moodie, G. (2017). Vocational education qualifications' roles in pathways to work in liberal market economies. *Journal of Vocational Education & Training, 69*(1), 10–27. https://doi.org/10.1080/13636820.2016.1275031

World Bank. (2022). *Literacy rate, adult total (% of people ages 15 and above) - Pakistan.* Accessed from https://data.worldbank.org/indicator/SE.ADT.LITR.ZS?locations=PK

Yamoah, F. A., & Haque, A. U. (2022). Strategic management through digital platforms for remote working in the higher education industry during and after the COVID-19 pandemic. *Forum Scientiae Oeconomia, 10*(2), 111–128. https://doi.org/10.23762/FSO_VOL10_NO2_6

Accountability Systems of Non-governmental Organisations (NGOs): Case Study from Ghana

Kwasi Awuah-Werekoh, Fred A. Yamoah, and Riffat Faizan

1 Introduction

Hayfron-Benjamin (2013) argues that the reliance of NGOs on external resources has led to concerns about their accountability as donors and other stakeholders demand greater transparency and effectiveness in the use of resources. This highlights the importance of effective accountability systems in NGOs, which can help build trust and ensure that resources are used efficiently and effectively to achieve the desired outcomes for beneficiaries. The aim of the study is to evaluate the accountability

K. Awuah-Werekoh
Ghana Maritime Authority, Accra, Ghana

F. A. Yamoah (✉)
Department of Management, School of Business, Economics and Informatics, Birkbeck, University of London, London, UK
e-mail: f.yamoah@bbk.ac.uk

R. Faizan
Faculty of Business, Yorkville University, Toronto, ON, Canada

F. A. Yamoah, A. ul Haque (eds.), *Corporate Management Ecosystem in Emerging Economies*, https://doi.org/10.1007/978-3-031-41578-4_14

systems of NGOs in threefold: to investigate the nature of accountability systems in NGOs, to examine how NGO accountability systems are influenced by the institutional environments of NGOs, and to explore the various strategies that NGOs adopt to respond to the institutional pressures that confront them. The study's focus on the nature of accountability systems in NGOs is important because it enables a better understanding of the mechanisms that NGOs use to ensure transparency, compliance, and effective governance. By exploring how institutional environments influence NGO accountability systems, the study can shed light on the contextual factors that shape the nature and effectiveness of these systems. The reason for the significant increase in the number of NGOs in recent decades can be attributed to the increase in funding received by the sector. Hulme and Edwards (2013) argue that the rise of NGOs has been facilitated by the growing importance of the development sector in international aid and the increasing emphasis on civil society as a driver of social change (Fig. 1).

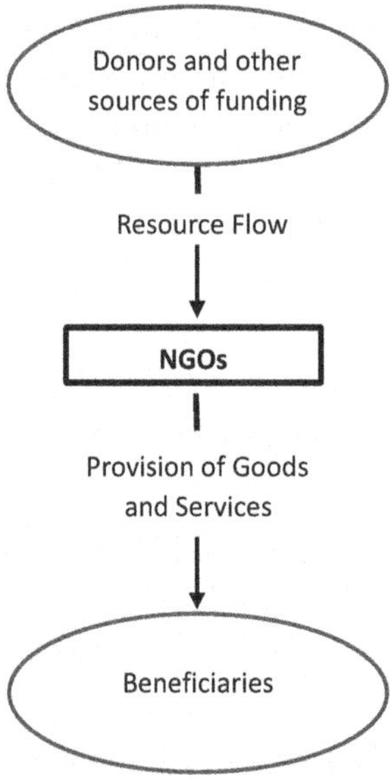

Fig. 1 NGO's scope of operation. Source: Research's own construct

2 Literature Review

In recent years, the issue of NGO accountability has become increasingly important, and NGOs that are deemed unaccountable may face sustainability risks, including challenges in securing funding from donors. Antlöv et al. (2006), Banks and Hulme (2012), Baur and Schmitz (2012), Gray et al. (2014), and O'Dwyer and Unerman (2008) have highlighted the importance of effective accountability mechanisms in NGOs and the potential consequences of failing to meet these expectations. In Ghana, the Ghana AIDS Commission (GAC), which was established by an act of Parliament to provide support nationally for HIV programmes, experienced problems with accountability between 2009 and 2010, which led to a reduction in donor support for the programme. This situation highlights the importance of effective accountability mechanisms in ensuring that NGOs are able to maintain public trust and secure the resources they need to carry out their work effectively. A review of the literature on NGO accountability reveals that there are two main types of accountability: upward accountability and downward accountability. Upward accountability refers to the accountability of NGOs to their donors, while downward accountability refers to their accountability to their beneficiaries and the broader public. The literature on NGO accountability has identified the importance of both upward and downward accountability mechanisms in ensuring that NGOs are transparent, effective, and accountable in their use of resources.

A plethora of research confirmed that NGO accountability is a vital aspect and has immense importance for both upward and downward accountability mechanisms (Ahmed et al., 2011; Goddard & Assad, 2006; Awio et al., 2011; Ebrahim, 2003a, b, 2005, 2009, Jordan, 2005; O'Dwyer & Unerman, 2008). The literature on NGO accountability emphasises the need for effective accountability mechanisms to ensure that NGOs are transparent and accountable in their use of resources and that they are able to achieve their intended social impact (Banks & Hulme, 2012; Brass, 2012; Fowler, 2013; Mercer & Green, 2013; Smillie et al., 2013). An extensive review of the literature led to the implementation of the theoretical framework, which is used to describe the findings of the study. The study argues that NGO accountability relations are influenced by the institutional forces within the environment. This highlights that the institutional pressures play an important role in inducing the principles and operations adopted by NGOs.

Institutional Theory

The main view of the new institutionalism is that society involves purposive, empowered, and bounded social actors, including states, individuals, and organisations that function therein, and that the social environment, to a larger extent, impacts the behaviour of social actors (Meyer, 2007).

The Theoretical Framework

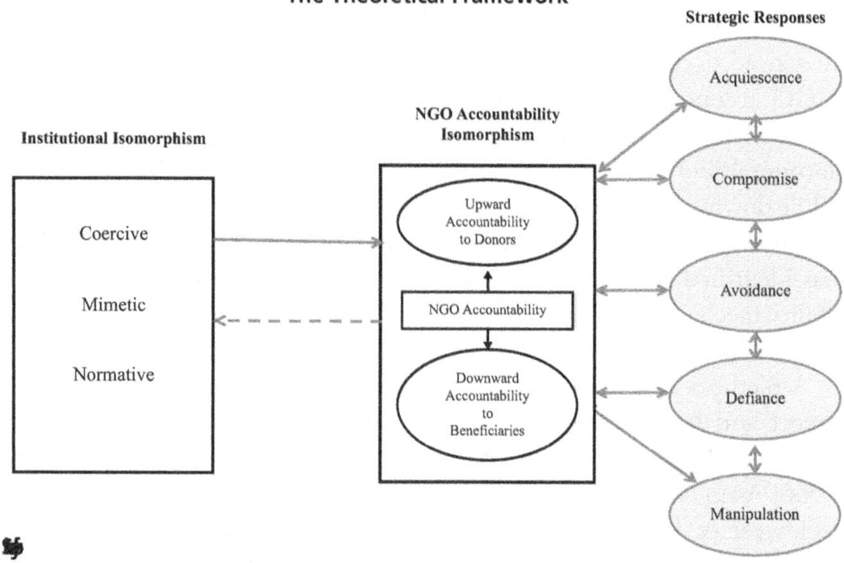

The study's framework provides a lens to examine the accountability systems of NGOs and their strategic responses to institutional pressures, which can inform policies and practices aimed at improving NGO accountability and effectiveness. It is highlighted that the NGO's relationship with the state at times has subsisted on conflict, which emerged from a basic lack of understanding of the relationships and dynamics (Hasmath & Hsu, 2013). Hasmath and Hsu (2013) suggest that absence of meaningful collaboration between the state and NGOs is not solely the outcome of the state seeking to limit the development of the sector, or fear of a possible opposing actor to the state, but contend that there is an absence of meaningful engagement between the state and NGOs, which is partially attributed to isomorphic pressures within state-NGO relations, and inadequate epistemic awareness of NGO activities on the part of the state (Hasmath & Hsu, 2013). The article argues that theory with a sociological dimension allows researchers to incorporate the views of social actors in illuminating the belongings institutional pressures have on observed relations.

3 Research Methodology

The interpretive approach in qualitative research aims to understand the social world of individuals by exploring their subjective experiences and perspectives. In this study, the interpretive approach is used to examine the accountability systems of an NGO operating in Ghana and investigate their strategic responses to institutional pressures. The interpretive approach to research is based on the belief that knowledge is socially constructed, meaning that individuals create meaning and understanding through their interactions with others and the world around them.

In the context of the study on NGOs' accountability systems in Ghana, the interpretive approach enables the researcher to gain a deep understanding of the perspectives and experiences of individuals within the NGO and the wider community. The interpretive philosophical stance was adopted for the study on the accountability systems of NGOs and their strategic responses to institutional pressures, as the researcher contends that the NGO accountability reality occurs in the minds of the active players within the sector, i.e., beneficiaries, donors, and NGO employees. Therefore, knowledge regarding NGO accountability systems could be socially constructed from the expectations and experiences of respondents in an interpretive manner. The researcher is of the view that without a positivist perspective, the NGO accountability systems cannot be unravelled. This allowed the researcher to understand the respondents' subjective viewpoints on empirical evidence analysis, attained through the interview process.

The interpretivist perspective approach enabled researcher to analyse, interpret, and report exactly the responses and experiences of respondents through their own perspectives. Therefore, the study is required to interpret the effect of the environment on NGO accountability mechanisms and the views of social performers in the NGO sector. The study adopted a qualitative research strategy to investigate the phenomenon at hand and be able to offer a unique descriptive understanding. Moreover, the qualitative research enabled the researcher to better comprehend and elaborate on the NGO accountability mechanisms and the consequences of environmental forces on these accountability systems with the opinion of developing/suggesting a supplementary all-inclusive accountability system that would sufficiently integrate and reflect the views of the affected social participants in the field.

The researcher adopted a case study technique for NGO accountability systems due to its superior contextual analysis (Fowler, 2013) and its ability to allow researchers to examine situations using various evidence together with interviews, documents, discussions, reviews, and observations, reflecting to focus on useful truth rather than factual truth (Faizan et al., 2019; Haque & Yamoah, 2021; Yamoah & Haque, 2022). As this is quantitative research, participants were not randomly selected. However, snowball sampling was also implemented during the interview process. In addition, identified contacts who were previously interviewed were requested to endorse other suitable participants who met the set standard/criteria to be interviewed as well. Data triangulation approach was adopted to gather data, expanding on a broader explanation, and to validate data (Yin, 2011).

The interviews were used as data collection instrument, enabling the researcher to have one-to-one verbal interactions with respondents, clarify questions for respondents if necessary to seek further explanation from respondents on vague responses (Rubin & Rubin, 2011). For an interview, 77 minutes was the average duration, whereas interviews took place in the natural settings/offices of the participants. The interviews were semi-structured, with open-ended questions, primarily guided by an interview guide, and in certain cases prejudiced by interesting responses within the foremost themes that led to further revelations and investigation to capture data (Haque & Yamoah, 2021; Yamoah & Haque, 2022).

Due to the greater volume of the data and its nature, the data collected from the focus group discussions and field interviews demanded the implementation and execution of a data reduction strategy to enhance data analysis. This strategy promoted the confirmation and identification of themes and emerging patterns. Procedural reliability and contextual validity mechanisms were used to evaluate the reliability (evidence independence) and validity (true reflection) of data (Creswell, 2012; Silverman, 2013). Moreover, the collection of data by the researcher himself along with the use of the qualitative research methods ensured data verification and accuracy. The use of the case study approach emanates from the researcher's philosophical stance that reality exists in the minds of social actors and knowledge can be attained by interrelating with the affected social actors. Therefore, an in-depth case study was considered for a community-based organisation using research methods such as interviews. The data analysis process was used for pre-coding and eventually coding the collected data, through the research questions and approaches along with the theoretical framework.

4 Findings and Discussions

Table 1 depicts the three research objectives and the most frequently used words/terms by respondents to describe them. The researcher used the identified frequently used words/terms as a basis to colour-highlight the paragraphs, sentences, and phrases that contain those words/terms and to examine the context within which they were used. Numbers were assigned to these highlighted phrases, and they were copied into separate files per research objective. In effect, the transcribed data were categorised according to the objective they sought to address.

For example, a scan through the 'blue colour' coded data relating to the first research objective (to investigate accountability relations both upward and downward in a particular NGO in Ghana), revealed the underlisted issues.

Table 1 Recurring words in relation to research objective

No.	Research objective	Distinctive colour	Most frequently used words/terms
1	To investigate accountability relations both upward and downward in a particular NGO in Ghana	Blue	Upward accountability Reports o types o content Review meetings External monitoring and auditing Financial and annual report Relationship with other NGOs Downward accountability Beneficiary involvement Community structures and registers Review meetings Reporting
2	To examine how accountability relations are shaped by the institutional environment within which the studied NGO operates	Green	Donors Diplomatic missions Professional firms Media Competition for funding Government and governmental agencies Financial and annual report The regulatory group of forces Department of Social Welfare Coalitions of NGOs Other groups Force, impose, influence, dump, sway, authorize, sanction, imitate, copy, emulate, mimic, duplicate, match
3	To investigate the various strategies adopted by the studied NGO to respond to the institutional pressures it faces	Red	Agree, comply, accept, consent, submit, concur, conform, obey, fulfil, follow, arrange, bargain, corporate, negotiate, confer, evade, dodge, circumvent, prevent, avert, elude, escape, get-out, sidestep, bypass, confront, resist, challenge, flout, disregard, disobey, oppose, contest, attack, manoeuvre, influence

Source: Researcher's own construct

Accountability relations are predominantly upward as reflected in Table 1 and via the decisions that are made regarding projects such as:

1. Overall project decisions
2. Project conceptualisation and location
3. Project objectives and activities
4. Selection of project implementing partners
5. Project closure

The field data analysis uncovered two main types of accountability systems: upward and downward, depicting the NGO's role in association to beneficiary group and compelling group of forces. The case study revealed that KKP plays a transitional role in obtaining funds and other resources from the compelling group (donors) to deliver public goods for the beneficiary group's benefit. Such existence of relationship automatically calls for accountability, a system that seeks to ensure the well-organised distribution of donor resources for the intended purpose.

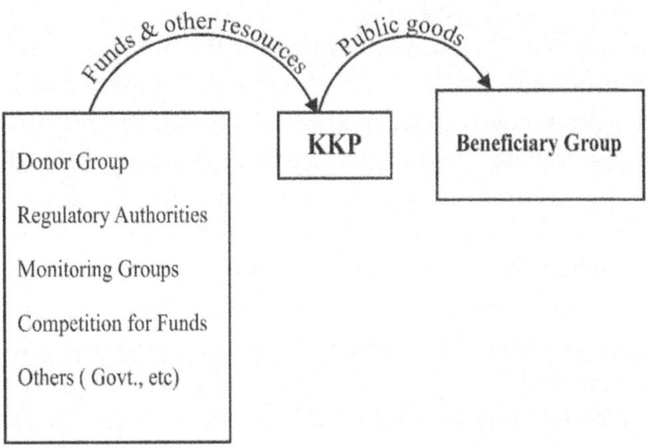

KKP and its donor's accountability relationship can be termed as upward accountability, where donors are the chief providers of most of the resources essential for NGOs like KKP to function. This supports the argument that the resource providers are well aware of their role in operational chain; therefore, they are able to mandate accountability from their subordinates (Chenhall et al., 2010; O'Dwyer & Unerman, 2008). As per the literature, NGO accountability is defined as highly contested, however, with one common defining point, the realisation of the existence of a superior body overseeing the activities of subordinates (Kendall & Knapp, 1995; Kaldor, 2013; Gray et al., 2014). Therefore, accountability is the right that arises from the association between the accountable organisations: the accountor and the accountee (Hulme & Edwards 2013; Fox & Brown, 1998). Moreover, the study witnessed that the scarcity of resources in association with the number of NGOs available has placed greater demand on available resources, increasing the power of resource providers over the resource users. Thus, concluding that resource providers are viewed as highly powerful stakeholders in their dealings.

Moreover, the study witnessed that apart from the provision of regular/periodic reports (narrative or financial), the NGO is obligated to submit any other 'as and when' or 'on demand' reports to donors upon request. Furthermore, collected data revealed that in contrast to upward accountability within the spheres of NGOs' operations, downward accountability was underdeveloped and did not attract much attention. In addition, various reasons accounted for the imbalance and weak state of downward accountability, one of the most significant was the realisation that stakeholders, particularly beneficiaries, have little to offer in terms of resource provision. The theoretical framework, in the research, explains the findings that three main institutional forces—coercive, mimetic, and normative—exist and affect accountability relations. Interviews within the NGO sector in Ghana revealed that all three institutional factors—coercive, normative, and mimetic—as suggested by DiMaggio and Powell (1991), were observed to some degree in the organisation's accountability association with its stakeholders as part of the organisation's legitimacy looking for behaviour, whereas coercive isomorphism emerged as the leading force that clarifies why certain decisions are made and also why such accountability relations are

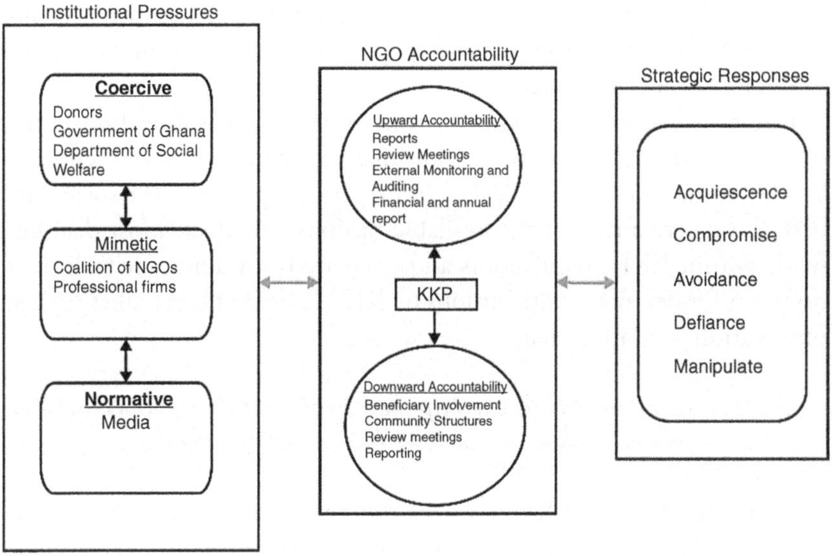

In addition, the study argues that with respect to donor-funded projects, the decision process originates as soon as the project is advertised, though the implementing organisations or beneficiaries have a limited role in these processes. Moreover, it was witnessed that project conceptualisation decisions are mostly done by the project funders, with little regard for the other stakeholders who may be related to the project in question. The study argues that in addition to solely being responsible for project conceptualisation decisions, to a greater extent, donors also controlled decisions on the project's objectives and, at times, activities to be undertaken to accomplish the set objectives. Furthermore, the study findings demonstrate that donors strategically select project-implementing partners through several means to ensure their set project objectives are attained. The study reveals that usually the basis for referral depends on the NGO's ability to submit reports and other needed documents on time. In addition, it is discovered that the selection has no impact on how well or gravely an expression of interest or calls for proposals from prospective NGOs have been responded to. The study revealed that, to a greater extent, there is a minimal impact of the forces of the 'other' on KKP's accountability relations, with the media as the foremost normative force. The study revealed that KKP actively responds distinctively to some institutional pressures as far as their accountability relations are concerned, and these responses range from active conformance to partial resistance.

Effective decision-making is very important for the successful running of every organisation. In the decision-making process, management must be able to have access to relevant information upon which to select the best alternative amongst the available options. In effect, most decisions made within KKP are offshoots and emanate from donors with little or no room for decision contributions by KKP. A field officer makes such an observation by stating that:

> *In my view, we are only here to help them implement their already decided projects… they make all the decisions, and we just follow. [FO3]*

The management of KKP has over the years undertaken a significant number of projects, including innovative HIV prevention (preventive strategies) among young people and the general population, wash up, tuberculosis advocacy and community involvement in early tuberculosis case detection, behaviour change support (BCS), nutrition and reproductive health centre, and child survival. At the time of data collection, KKP was implementing four major projects located in various parts of the country with several different donors, as outlined by the Executive Director (ED).

> *Currently, we are implementing four major projects running in the Greater Accra, Central, and the Brong Ahafo regions of Ghana. Normally as the year goes by other projects come by. We are hoping to start another one very soon on abortion care also in the Greater Accra region. Some of our donors are SIMAVI of the Netherlands, USAID, ADDR, The Global, Fund, FHI360, John Hopkins University (JHU), Ghana Aids Commission, Bristol-Myers Squibb and GAVI. [ED]*

When asked about the level of KKP management involvement in project decision-making, the Central Regional Programmes Coordinator (CRPC) noted:

> *You are there and a donor, or you see in the newspaper that there is a call for proposal; they want an NGO to do this or that in this and that region. We look at the requirements and if we realise that we qualify, we put in an application based on the project designed by whoever is calling for the proposal. In most cases we are not involved in project decisions at all.*

Even after the project has been awarded, the selected NGO still has no say in the decision to accommodate the conceptualised project to grassroots realities. For example, when asked whether donors generally involve KKP in project conceptualisation, selection, and location, Field Officer (FO1) answered that:

> *...of course donors will not involve you in such things. I don't think we matter that much. They only use us as a vessel to achieve their desired results.*

Further, Field Officer (FO3) noted that:

> *They [i.e. donors] just do it. They just do their things and put it out there and they want people to come and source it. They do not involve us in anything ... what we have to do is in the contract so we just get on with it... All they need is the results. They give us targets..., our aim is to try to exceed donor expectations and to do more than what is expected of us for the sake of future referrals.*

KKP did have a few successes in obtaining funding for KKP-led project interventions. However, in these experiences, the organisation has had to make fundamental changes to the initial proposal to suit prospective donors' desired project objectives, activities, outputs, and so forth before approval for support could be obtained.

> *We have been successful on a few of such initiatives and even then we had to make several changes for it to be accepted. If it does not meet their expectations, then forget about it. [Monitoring and Evaluation Officer (MEO)]*

The focus group discussion also revealed that any project that beneficiaries have suggested to KKP that they, i.e., the beneficiaries, felt could be very beneficial to them had never received any positive response on the part of KKP. But since KKP relies on donors to fund projects, the ultimate response to beneficiary-led projects rests with donors. This can be ascertained from the comment from a focus group participant:

In the past we have tried to suggest projects that we [felt] might help us better through KKP, but the response has always been, we do not provide the funds, we will talk to our donors and see how it goes but they mostly never come back to us on such issues again and even when they do, the response is always negative.

The argument is, because donors generally conceptualise projects and they define their objectives, it is normal that they define the activities to be undertaken to achieve these objectives. These are then transmitted to KKP and other stakeholder groups that may be associated with the project. When asked to comment on how project activities are set, the MEO noted that:

…donors normally provide a list of activities to be undertaken in a project for us to implement.

CRPC added:

To a very large extent, project objectives just like most other things, [are] an imposition and mostly come as part of the call for proposal documents. For instance as part of the call, they will tell you that the objectives of the project is ABC, so the only way KKP could apply is for KKP to assess itself as an organisation to determine which strategies will work best… So the strategies are sometimes flexible, but donors are firm on certain aspects that they don't compromise at all including objectives and activities. You need to do it exactly the way they want it.

In addition to donors defining project activities for KKP to only implement, they can alter (reduce) the number of activities at will. The PD particularly points out this issue:

Recently, there have been changes even to the budget lines of project activities. The budget lines have been drastically cut down. This means that we are restricted in terms of the number of activities we can implement under projects. Previously, there were a lot of activities that could be implemented under projects. Things like mobilisation, holding of seminars and durbars to sensitise beneficiaries and bring them together before and during the project implementation. But this time it is strictly on the implementation of the project, which does not help. Even if you want to do some creative activities, you need to seek approval from donors which is mostly not approved.

The PD added:

Once we [KKP] have responded to calls for proposals, we only wait upon donors to select us. Donors control the selection process. It is entirely outside our domain. All we do is basically to "hope and pray" that we will be selected. Donors have the choice and they exercise it accordingly.

In essence, donors have the option to terminate projects at will if KKP fails to abide by any of the conditions set out in the contract. Although respondents at KKP affirmed that the organisation has never experienced project termination from donors, an inspection of a donor service agreement revealed the possibility of project termination if KKP fails to meet any of the project conditions. A section of the service agreement document reads:

Without regard to the set term, [the donor] in its sole discretion, can terminate this Agreement at any time if it determines that the performance of [KKP] is unsatisfactory, [KKP] develops a conflict of interest with [the donor], [KKP] is in breach of this Agreement and does not cure that breach within ten (10) days' notice thereof from [the donor], or [KKP] files a petition in bankruptcy or there is an entering of judgment of bankruptcy by or against [KKP]. In all events, if this Agreement expires or is terminated by [the donor], [the donor] shall have no further obligations to [KKP], including the payment of any further funds to [KKP].

Project termination generally casts a permanent doubt on the image and credibility of the affected NGOs' ability to obtain funding from other donor sources. An interview with an official of a donor (D1) revealed a recent increase in the level of interaction and dialogue amongst donors. He comments:

Donors these days communicate among themselves a lot and therefore are able to know who is funding what organisation. Through these interactions, we are able to identify credible NGOs to partner with. Besides, calls for proposals are designed to fish out blacklisted NGOs. [D1]

In most cases, NGOs are asked to respond with reasons why the previous project was terminated, as evidenced by an extract (clause) from a service agreement that reads:

Has [KKP] ever been denied the right to work on a project, to bid on a project, or had a project suspended or terminated by any funder, for any reason? If yes, please attach an explanation.

Donor's quest to fish out NGOs that have experienced project termination in the past could be good, especially as it has the potential to help determine non-performing NGOs. However, it could also damage the reputation of NGOs unfairly.

The preferred way of project closure occurs when the project runs its course and comes to an expected end. In such a situation, the closure process will follow the contractual process enshrined in the contract, as specified by the donor. Project closures and processes vary depending on donor requirements.

The initial project closure process starts with the submission of both financial and narrative reports including end of project evaluation report to the donor and any unexpended funds have to be refunded to the donor. There is also end of project audit and the choice of auditor is at the discretion of the donor. [ED]

Various forms of external monitoring mechanisms are identified in the KKP-donor accountability relationship. In addition to the donor's unannounced visits to KKP project sites and offices for monitoring purposes, the donor also mandates other external bodies to monitor KKP. These external monitoring bodies, including embassies (Diplomatic Missions), the district, and other local assemblies, also monitor KKP periodically to ensure that the organisation adheres to agreed conditions. These mechanisms keep KKP on its toes to ensure that the organisation does what is expected from it. Donor (D2) who sponsored a health intervention project explained:

> *As part of the monitoring process, we involve the community health committee and the district health directorate to assist. Once KKP gives us their work plans and schedules, we forward them to these agencies and mandates them to occasionally and periodically visit project sites and report back to us.*

Furthermore, as mentioned above, KKP is also required to report to other external bodies such as the district assemblies and local authorities within KKP's operational jurisdiction and other governmental agencies.

> *In most cases, we are asked to send portions of our reports to the district assemblies and the Ghana Health Services and other professional bodies... On other occasions, donors could ask their own auditors to audit us. [MEO]*

KKP is subjected to external auditing in various ways. KKP is supposed to submit its work plans to donors who would occasionally do external auditing either at KKP offices or on project sites at unannounced intervals. This is to ensure that KKP is complying with all agreed-upon terms and conditions. The external auditing is in various forms and can take different dimensions. For example, it is revealed that one donor has contracted EY as their external auditors to constantly monitor KKP's work.

> *JHU for instance have contracted EY accountancy as their auditing firm. They audit the accounts and disburse funds to us. What they do is that at the end of every month; we prepare financial reports and send it to them for audit. Any queries or outstanding issues must be resolved with Ernst and Young before they release funds for subsequent phases of the project to us. [FM]*

On a number of occasions and as per the contract, KKP has had the opportunity to partner with other local and sometimes smaller NGOs to implement projects as implementing partners on their behalf. The PD explained:

> *KKP is a member of different NGO coalitions and depending on the type of project and the nature of the contract with donors, we sometimes use other*

smaller local NGOs as implementing partners. KKP have had the experience of sub-contracting to other NGOs. In a recent project, KKP partnered with thirty-nine [39] other local NGOs to implement the project.

It became apparent during interviews that the accountability relationship between KKP and these other smaller NGOs is also upward because it mirrors KKP-donors accountability relationship.

The evidence provided indicates that although KKP somehow accounts to beneficiaries, the level of accountability it accords to their beneficiaries is minimal compared to that accorded to their donors. When asked about the level of accountability of KKP to their beneficiaries, the PD remarked that:

As an organisation, we try as much as possible to account to beneficiaries but on different levels… not in the same category as donors. I hope you understand. It is obvious. Beneficiaries are at the receiving end just like KKP and on that basis, of course the level of accountability cannot be the same. In any case we try to be very open to them so they know some of our budget lines.

This comment suggests that beneficiaries are marginalised in the accountability process. The observed downward accountability relations within KKP include beneficiary involvement, community structures and registers, the application of review meetings, and reporting.

5 Conclusion and Recommendations

Research's main objective was to examine the accountability relations within an NGO and how such an organisation will reply to numerous institutional pressures. This study uses an NGO in Ghana as a case, supposedly called KKP. The case study approach was implemented due to its ability to meet the suitability tenets of qualitative research by defining, understanding, and explaining issues (Myers, 2013; Silverman, 2013). The methodology used in the research ensured completeness in observation and analysis by examining the perspectives of various actors within their natural settings. Moreover, it provided the researcher an opportunity to comprehend the accountability relations within KKP with the use of data collection methods such as interviews, observations, and documentary reviews in detail (Gray, 2013; Silverman, 2013; Yin, 1994). The researcher in this study was able to take advantage of the flexible nature of the case study approach by rescheduling interview appointments, incorporating emerging issues, and varying interview styles as necessary. The research implemented the new institutional sociology (NIS) to recognise the effects of institutional forces on KKP's response to these pressures and KKP's accountability relations (DiMaggio & Powell 1991). The study observed that the accountability relation between the main compelling stakeholder KKP is mainly upward in nature. It further observed that due to KKP's ability to often meet the donor-reporting requirements, they are able to draw other funding options via donor referrals and other benefits (Goddard & Assad, 2006). The study suggests that, in comparison with upward accountability, downward accountability from either KKP or donors to beneficiaries does not enjoy the same level of prominence within the NGO sector. The study argues and suggests that KKP does not follow accountability requirements as precisely as specified in their contractual obligations with third parties, mainly donors. The study further argues that KKP decisively duplicates some best-practised accountable organisations in response to institutional pressures to improve their contract/funding competitiveness and their responsibility relations. The study accomplishes and argues that KKP actively responds variedly to some institutional pressures as far as their accountability relations are concerned.

The following are the recommendations:

The sample size of the research on NGO accountability relations and their strategic responses focused on a single NGO in Ghana, and generalizing the findings may not be appropriate. In research, the sample size is an essential aspect of the study's validity, and a small sample size can limit the generalizability of the findings. While case studies provide valuable insights into a specific context or situation, they are not designed to be generalizable to other settings.

The findings of the study may be unique to the specific NGO and the Ghanaian context and may not be applicable to other NGOs or countries. While case studies provide valuable insights into a specific context or situation, they are not designed to be generalizable to other settings. The findings of the study may be unique to the specific NGO and the Ghanaian context and may not be applicable to other NGOs or countries.

The finding that coalitions of NGOs can play a significant role in shaping the accountability relations and strategic responses of NGOs is an important contribution to the literature on NGOs and accountability. The concept of NGO coalitions is a relatively new phenomenon in the sector, and there is a need for more research into their impact on accountability relations. A detailed study into the specific impact of NGO coalitions on NGO accountability relations can provide valuable insights into how these coalitions operate and how they influence accountability practices.

The influence of the media on NGO accountability relations is an area worth investigating. The media can play a crucial role in shaping public perceptions of NGOs and their accountability practices. As the media's role in all aspects of life continues to increase, understanding their influence on NGO accountability relations is becoming increasingly important.

There is a need to understand why donors and other stakeholders are reluctant to fully support downward accountability relations in the NGO sector. Downward accountability, which involves NGOs being accountable to the beneficiaries of their programmes, is critical for ensuring that aid and other services reach the intended recipients, particularly the poor and marginalised people in society.

References

Ahmed, Z., Hopper, T., & Wickramsinghe, D. (2011). *Counter hegemony and accountability in BRAC-a Bangladesh NGO* [online]. Accessed from http://hdl.handle.net/10292/5006

Antlöv, H., Ibrahim, R., & van Tuijl, P. (2006). NGO governance and accountability in Indonesia: Challenges in a newly democratizing country. In *NGO accountability: Politics, principles and innovations* (pp. 147–163). Earthscan.

Awio, G., Northcott, D., & Lawrence, S. (2011). Social capital and accountability in grass-roots NGOs: The case of the Ugandan community-led HIV/AIDS initiative. *Accounting, Auditing and Accountability Journal, 24*(1), 63–92.

Banks, N., & Hulme, D. (2012). The role of NGOs and civil society in development and poverty reduction. In *Brooks world poverty institute working paper 171*. University of Manchester.

Baur, D., & Schmitz, H. P. (2012). Corporations and NGOs: When accountability leads to co-optation. *Institute of Business Ethics, 9*(21), 9.

Brass, J. N. (2012). Why do NGOs go where they go? Evidence from Kenya. *World Development, 40*(2), 387–401.

Chenhall, R. H., Hall, M., & Smith, D. (2010). Social capital and management control system: A study of non-governmental organisation. *Accounting, Organisation and Society, 35*, 737–756.

Creswell, J. W. (2012). *Qualitative inquiry and research design: Choosing among five approaches*. Sage.

DiMaggio, P. J., & Powell, W. W. (1991). The iron cage revisited: Institutional isomorphism and collective rationality in organizational fields. In W. W. Powell & P. J. DiMaggio (Eds.), *The new institutionalism in organizational analysis* (pp. 63–82). University of Chicago Press.

Ebrahim, A. (2003a). Making sense of accountability: Conceptual perspectives for northern and southern nonprofits. *Nonprofit Management and Leadership, 14*(2), 191–212.

Ebrahim, A. (2003b). Accountability in practice: Mechanisms for NGOs. *World Development, 31*(5), 813–829.

Ebrahim, A. (2005). Accountability myopia: Losing sight of organizational learning. *Nonprofit and Voluntary Sector Quarterly, 34*(1), 56–87.

Ebrahim, A. (2009). Placing the normative logics of accountability in "thick" perspective. *American Behavioral Scientist, 52*(6), 885–904.

Faizan, R., Haque, A. U., Cockrill, A., & Aston, J. (2019). Females at strategic level affecting logistics firms' competitiveness: Qualitative comparative analysis. *Forum Scientiae Oeconomia, 7*(1), 57–71.

Fowler, A. (Ed.). (2013). *Striking a balance: A guide to enhancing the effectiveness of non-governmental organisations in international development*. Routledge.

Fox, J., & Brown, L. (1998). *The struggle for accountability: The World Bank, NGOs, and grassroots movements*. MIT Press.

Goddard, A., & Assad, M. J. (2006). Accounting and navigating legitimacy in Tanzanian NGOs. *Accounting, Auditing and Accountability Journal, 19*(3), 377–404.

Gray, R. (2013). Back to basics: What do we mean by environmental (and social) accounting and what is it for?—A reaction to Thornton. *Critical perspectives on Accounting, 24*(6), 459–468.

Gray, R., Brennan, A., & Malpas, J. (2014). New accounts: Towards a reframing of social accounting. *Accounting Forum, 38*(4), 258–273.

Haque, A. U., & Yamoah, F. A. (2021). The role of ethical leadership in managing occupational stress to promote innovative work behaviour: A cross-cultural management perspective. *Sustainability, 13*, 9608. https://doi.org/10.3390/su13179608

Hasmath, R., & Hsu, J. Y. J. (2013). Isomorphic pressures, epistemic communities and state-NGO collaboration in China. *The China Quarterly, 220*(December 2014), 936–954.

Hayfron-Benjamin, M. (2013). *An exploration of the roles of non-governmental organisations (NGOs) in the promotion of women's rights: The case of Abantu for development in Ghana.* PhD thesis, University of Education, Winneba.

Hulme, D., & Edwards, M. (Eds.). (2013). *Making a difference: NGO's and development in a changing world.* Routledge.

Jordan, L. (2005). *Mechanisms for NGO accountability.* GPPi Research Paper Series, 3.

Kaldor, M. (2013). *New and old wars: Organised violence in a global era* (3rd ed.). Wiley.

Kendall, J., & Knapp, M. (1995). *A loose and baggy monster: Boundaries, definitions and typologies: An introduction to the voluntary sector*. Routledge.

Mercer, C., & Green, M. (2013). Making civil society work: Contracting, cosmopolitanism and community development in Tanzania. *Geoforum, 45*, 106–115.

Meyer, J. W. (2007). Reflections on institutional theories of organizations. In R. Greenwood, C. Oliver, R. Suddaby, & K. Sahlin-Andersson (Eds.), *The handbook of organizational institutionalism*. Sage.

Myers, T. A. (2013). Accountability and Transparency in the Financial Services Sector: Advancing Sustainable Finance. *Journal of International Business Ethics, 6*(1/2), 72.

O'Dwyer, B., & Unerman, J. (2008). The paradox of greater NGO accountability: A case study of Amnesty Ireland. *Accounting, Organizations and Society, 33*(7–8), 801–824.

Rubin, H. J., & Rubin, I. S. (2011). *Qualitative interviewing: The art of hearing data*. Sage.

Silverman, D. (2013). *Doing qualitative research: A practical handbook* (4th ed.). Sage.
Smillie, I., Helmich, H., Randel, J., & German, T. (Eds.). (2013). *Stakeholders: Government-NGO partnerships for international development*. Routledge.
Yamoah, F. A., & Haque, A. U. (2022). Strategic management through digital platforms for remote working in the higher education industry during and after the COVID-19 pandemic. *Forum Scientiae Oeconomia, 10*(2), 111–128. https://doi.org/10.23762/FSO_VOL10_NO2_6
Yin R. K. (1994). *Case study research: Design and methods* (2nd ed.). Thousand Oakes, CA: Sage.
Yin, R. K. (2011). *Applications of case study research*. Sage.

Iran's Challenges in Maintaining Sustainable Development: From the Lens of Ecotourism

Adnan ul Haque, Irfan ul Haq, and Fred A. Yamoah

1 Introduction

Sustainable development has an inclusive, integrated, and human-oriented approach consisting of valuable in promoting, preserving, and improving ecological and health integrity in the long term for human needs (Makian & Hanifezadeh, 2021; Rezaeinejad & Khaniwadekar, 2021). The critical dimension is to accomplish economic dynamism, social equality, and a liveable environment without destroying the next generation's ability (Rezaeinejad & Khaniwadekar, 2021). The

A. ul Haque
Faculty of Business, Yorkville University, Toronto, ON, Canada
e-mail: ahaque@yorkvilleu.ca

I. ul Haq
SRIBP, Toronto, ON, Canada
e-mail: irfan@sribp.com

F. A. Yamoah (✉)
Department of Management, School of Business, Economics and Informatics, Birkbeck, University of London, London, UK
e-mail: f.yamoah@bbk.ac.uk

F. A. Yamoah, A. ul Haque (eds.), *Corporate Management Ecosystem in Emerging Economies*, https://doi.org/10.1007/978-3-031-41578-4_15

significance of conservation of natural resources in the urban environment is vital as a criterion for improving the quality of life along with areas of development of communities (Makian & Hanifezadeh, 2021). At present, the acceleration of culture and modern urban life has led to a decline in social interaction among citizens along with a neglect of the significance of public spaces for these social interactions (Harrison & Schipani, 2007). Therefore, the significance of urban green space in life and their sustainability, as well as their physical and social impacts on the urban system, are intolerable; therefore, the presence of green space in cities and its suitable dispersal areessential issues in urban planning (Carson & Taylor, 2008). Another significant issue, associated with the significance of green space use in cities, is multifunctional. The aesthetic, natural, and social aspects of this land use make it crucial to deal with the urban area issue. Moreover, the population increase has directly impacted the quality of the environment at the regional level directly (Malkina-Pykh, 2002). The vicious circle of low quality of life can indeed have a negative impact on sustainable development, particularly in third-world countries (Carson & Taylor, 2008). When people are struggling to meet their basic needs, such as food, shelter, and healthcare, they may not have the resources or energy to focus on improving their communities or the environment (Rezaeinejad & Khaniwadekar, 2021).

In recent years, greater focus has been on ecotourism due to its promising features, especially ecological and environmental potential to promote sustainability in the region (Kamyabi & Rajaee Rizi, 2018; Makian & Hanifezadeh, 2021). Moreover, it has been the fastest-growing segment of tourism (Carvache-Franco et al., 2019). There is no statistical data, but the trends suggest that ecotourism has increased in recent times as compared to mainstream tourism (Moghimehfar et al., 2014; Makian & Hanifezadeh, 2021). Nonetheless, the issues are evidently related to the ecotourism. It's also important to recognize that sustainable development is a complex and multifaceted issue that requires a holistic approach (Makian & Hanifezadeh, 2021; Rezaeinejad & Khaniwadekar, 2021). This means addressing social, economic, and environmental challenges simultaneously and recognizing the interconnectedness of these issues are pivotal to ensure sustainable ecotourism in the emerging economy. Moreover, the work of Rezaeinejad and Khaniwadekar (2021) argued that growth in the population along with the limited capacity to ensure sustainable consumption of natural resources (i.e., using it effectively and efficiently for present consumers while not sacrificing the use of natural resources for future generations). Note that the primary motivation of individuals is to visit those places for viewing natural attractions and indigenous culture without disrupting them in direct or indirect ways (Rezaeinejad & Khaniwadekar, 2021).

For emerging economies with unique natural resources and cultural environments, there are immense opportunities and prospects to gain higher benefits from ecotourism (Asadpourian et al., 2020). Iran is one such country that has rich natural resources, historical attractions, and diverse cultural attributes (Asadi, 2012; Ghorbani et al., 2015; Goharipour & Hajiluie, 2016; Makian & Hanifezadeh, 2021). Iran's tourism industry has often been viewed as competitively well placed because of its ecotourism (Asadi, 2012). The work of Goharipour and Hajiluie (2016) confirmed that Iran has availed several benefits from the development of ecotourism, especially in shape of natural resource conservation, economic growth, cultural values' preservation, employment, and community participation. Hadizadeh Zargar (2016) stated that ecotourism is the distinctive economic resource of Iran because of its ecological attraction. A plethora of research on Iran's development in various regions further indicates the potential of ecotourism (Ahmadi et al., 2018; Ganjali et al., 2014; Mobaraki et al., 2014; Rakhshan Nasab & Zarabi, 2010; Zarabi & Safarabadi, 2014; Makian & Hanifezadeh, 2021). Nonetheless, some of the literature at hand hinted towards the challenges interlinked with ecotourism. However, those are specific to the region rather than giving a holistic view of Iran's ecotourism. The significance of ecotourism has enhanced due to global interest in the subject matter (Nee & Beckmann, 2011), while the nature of Iran's ecotourism has immense potential (Ghorbani et al., 2015; Mansoori et al., 2014; Makian & Hanifezadeh, 2021). Iranian rural areas have been found to have a positive role in the development of ecotourism in the region (Khalili et al., 2020). However, the challenges related to ecotourism are understudied in the existing literature. The notion of sustainable tourism allows emerging economies to respond to the needs of tourists and generation and balance economic, environmental, social, and cultural dimensions to some extent (Makian & Hanifezadeh, 2021; Rezaeinejad & Khaniwadekar, 2021). This study highlights the challenges of Iran's ecotourism while examining the importance of ecotourism.

2 Literature Review

According to Das and Chatterjee (2015), poverty reduction and natural resource conservation in many parts of the world are the result of ecotourism. On the other hand, Teressa (2015) argued that the major role of ecotourism is the creation of job/employment opportunities, promotion and development of local businesses, and growth of domestic income. Tripathi and Jain (2017) found that the local culture and environment preservation and appreciation is the result of such type of tourism. This type of tourism helps us understand, appreciate, and preserve the environment and the local culture (Tripathi & Jain, 2017). Nonetheless, the challenges and threats to sustainable development are also the reality, despite all the opportunities created by ecotourism. Mgonja et al. (2015) expressed that the absence of access to investments and funds stops local people's involvement in the activities interlinked with ecotourism. For instance, the nonexistence of a proper design/framework for public policies is one of the main challenges for Mexico in the field of ecotourism, especially in social welfare and economic prosperity (González Fonseca, 2012). Moreover, in Ethiopia, the reduction of natural resources, limited awareness among the people, and environmental attraction's conservation are very little a point of concern among the local authorities (Otago, 2014). In Albania, ecotourism is facing challenges such as poaching, legal hunting, and uncontrolled grazing (Bego & Malltezi, 2011). Seasonal inaccessibility, inadequate infrastructure, poor financing, and poor facilities are key challenges to ecotourism in Nigeria (Ijeomah & Okoli, 2016). Moreover, Turkey is facing challenges in ecotourism development including skilled labour, inadequate services, nonexistence of responsible organization, and lack of proper operating plan (Cetinkaya, 2004). On the other hand, the work of Fernando and Shariff (2017) revealed Sri Lanka's ecotourism-related challenges, such as improper management, lack of a clear vision, absence of proper utilization of human and financial resources, and basic infrastructure related to ecotourism. Furthermore, the occurrence of mass tourists in natural destinations does not always favour ecotourism.

Moreover, the presence of diseases, political crises, and cultural and religious conflicts can impact the sustainability and development tourism both directly and indirectly (Rezaeinejad & Khaniwadekar, 2021). Study conducted by Rosselló et al. stated that the eradication of diseases such as yellow fever, Ebola, and malaria in affected countries had contributed to an increase of 10 million tourists worldwide. Few studies have simultaneously examined the economic, social, and environmental effects of sustainable development on ecotourism (Carson & Taylor, 2008; Asadpourian et al., 2020; Rezaeinejad & Khaniwadekar, 2021). Cherkaoui et al. (2020) argued that Moroccan ecotourism has been severely damaged due to deforestation, smuggling of wildlife, and illegal hunting amid loss of income in rural communities. In addition, Amador-Jiménez et al. (2020) claimed that in Colombia, the presence of armed groups and several fires in the forests have impacted ecotourism in the region. The impact of human activity can be crucial to the maintenance of natural biodiversity. Nonetheless, there is no conclusive evidence from the existing literature that can offer conclusive details of the types of challenges faced by Iranian ecotourism. Therefore, the present study is an attempt to fill the indicated research gap and answer the proposed questions related to sustainable ecotourism, particularly in Iran.

As per Pourasghari and Amar (2018), Iran's natural attractiveness, tourist opportunities, natural favourable climate, and unspoiled landscapes reinforce the possibility for the development of ecotourism. Iran is a predominantly arid country, a quarter (three-fourths or 3/4) is covered by rangelands, approximately 20% by arid deserts and less than 10% by forests, with salt marshes (Dabiri et al., 2016). Moreover, Iran's biodiversity, distinguishing climate, and beautiful and varied natural landscapes have contributed to its wealth of ecotourism. (Hosseinalizadeh et al., 2018). Though the ecotourism industry in Iran is comparatively new, it has a significant potential for growth due to the various natural attractions in different parts of the country. Moreover, many individuals are attracted to visit Iran; however, the country accounts for less than 1% of the ecotourism market of the Middle East's 5.2% (Financial Tribune, 2017). Moreover, there is a lack of official categorization of ecotourism activities from official organizations in Iran. Moreover, there is a lack of clear indication of official stands and policies on ecotourism. It is not stated to any extent in any of the country's upstream documents and is not supported by the government, planners, and policymakers (Veicy, 2018). Iranian ecotourism activities consist of nature excursions, hunting, winter sports, fishing, desert excursions, water sports, climbing, caving, Moreover, activities such as hiking, trekking, visiting national parks, village tours, and geomorphological attractions can be visited to experience the true essence of Iran's beauty and diverse landscape.

In 1970, for the first time, the term sustainable development was used in the Declaration on the Environment and Development. Fundamental changes in manipulating the resources, investments, and technology development are well-defined as the probability for existing and future resources to meet the human needs. In other words, it can be defined as a process of designing social, natural, physical, financial, economic, trade, energy, agriculture, energy, industry, and various other policies are considered that encourages development that is sustainable both socially and economically.

In 1980, the environmental quality gave an emergence to the concept of sustainable development theory in the form of environmental quality. The theory supports natural resources. The sustainable development ensures meeting the needs of the present without compromising the needs of the future supply. In other words, sustainable development is an expansion that is based on human beings and grounds human happiness and growth. The principal rationale for sustainable development is to enhance the people's living standards and the incredible well-being of those who are part of and enjoy the benefits of society while evading unnecessary costs. Consequently, the foremost issue of sustainable development is how to attain unremitting development, regard nature and human beings short of injustice, and for all human generations. The theoretical fundamentals of land conservation arrangement consist of balanced density, an urban sustainable development pattern, and an efficient land use; attention to the network is constant in the green spaces of the district and city. This theory advocates for a holistic and interdisciplinary approach to land conservation planning that considers both ecological and social factors. A sustainable city is a city that has minimum waste, lowest consumption of renewable energies, and negligible impact on the environment and can withstand its current function in the future.

Sustainable tourism is a form of tourism that is environmentally responsible, economically viable, and socially acceptable. Ecotourism, a form of tourism, consists of responsible travel to natural areas, preserving the environment, and refining the well-being of the local people. Since the 1980s, ecotourism significance has been considered by environmentalists for future generations to experience destinations comparatively untouched by human intervention. Responsible ecotourism programmes comprise minimizing the negative aspects of conventional tourism on the environment and improving cultural integrity of local people. Consequently, evaluating cultural and environmental aspects as an essential part of ecotourism is promoting energy efficiency, recycling, water conservation, and creating economic opportunities for local communities. Therefore, ecotourism repeatedly appeals to promote environmental and social responsibility.

3 Research Methodology

The focus of qualitative analysis is to gain a deeper understanding of the phenomenon (Haque & Yamoah, 2021); thus the focus remains on useful truth rather than factual truth (Yamoah & Haque, 2022). This study's objective is to present an overview and in-depth understanding of the challenges of ecotourism development in Iran in the context of sustainable ecotourism. The exploration of the present challenges to ecotourism development in Iran is based on the critical review of the existing literature. The study approach is an analytical-descriptive method. The data gathering method consists of books, magazines, papers, library study, and electronic resources. Below is the detail of the content analysis to form thematic analysis (Table 1):

Table 1 Thematic categorization based on systematic review of the literature at hand

Paper	Author	Thematic categorization
Planning for ecotourism in the protected area of Manesht and Ghelarang, Ilam Province, Iran	Ahmadi et al. (2018)	Governance and planning challenges Political, socio-economic, and cultural context Infrastructural challenges
Strategies for Iran ecotourism	Asadi (2012)	Political, socio-economic, and cultural context Infrastructural challenges Community awareness and knowledge towards ecotourism Environmental challenges
Environmental and strategic assessment of ecotourism potential in Anzali wetland using SWOT analysis	Ganjali et al. (2014)	Governance and planning challenges Political, socio-economic, and cultural context Legal aspects Environmental challenges
Ecotourism sustainable development strategies using SWOT and QSPM model: A case study of Kaji Namakzar Wetland, South Khorasan Province, Iran	Ghorbani et al. (2015)	Infrastructural challenges
Evaluating ecotourism potential development in Dena County using multi-criteria evaluation of specific hybrid indices	Ghorbani nia et al. (2018)	Governance and planning challenges
Analysis and evaluation of potential and strategies for ecotourism development in lake of Dez dam using Freeman's method	Shomalizade et al. (2015)	Governance and planning challenges Political, socio-economic, and cultural context

(*continued*)

Table 1 (continued)

Paper	Author	Thematic categorization
Environmental vulnerability assessment of Tourism in Anzali Coastal using SWOT.	Ramezani Gourabi and Rajabi (2015)	Infrastructural challenges
Challenges and opportunities of ecotourism development in Iran	Rakhshan Nasab and Zarabi (2010)	Infrastructural challenges
Assessment of sustainable ecotourism development in Kermanshah city	Zarabi and Safarabadi (2014)	Governance and planning challenges Legal aspects Community awareness and knowledge toward ecotourism

Own illustration of content analysis reflecting major themes depicted from literature review

4 Findings and Discussions

Ecotourism can have both positive and negative impacts on the environment, depending on how it is managed and practised. While ecotourism activities can contribute to the conservation of natural resources and promote environmental education and awareness, they can also have adverse effects on the environment if not properly planned and managed. In 2015, after the sanctions were lifted, Iran had tried to be on the Tourist travel list, which has contributed to the inclined ecotourism travels in the country. Moreover, tourists have been finding Iran's pristine and relatively untouched natural areas very attractive. Though the country is striving to make its mark on the world of travel; however, its potential is still untapped.

Based on the systematic review and thematic analysis, the following are the major challenges faced by the Iranian ecosystem in ranking order (Table 2):

From the above ranking table, it is confirmed that this study supports the existing work of Rakhshan Nasab and Zarabi (2010), Asadi (2012), Ganjali et al. (2014), Zarabi and Safarabadi (2014), Ghorbani et al.

Table 2 Ranking of Iranian ecotourism challenges

Rank	Challenges for Iranian ecotourism
1st	Governance and planning challenges
2nd	Infrastructure challenges
3rd	Political, socio-economic, and cultural context
4th	Legal aspects
5th	Environmental challenges
6th	Community awareness and knowledge towards ecotourism

(2015), Ramezani Gourabi and Rajabi (2015), Shomalizade et al. (2015), Ahmadi et al. (2018), and Ghorbani nia et al. (2018). Despite, Iran's ecotourism's potential and beautiful attractions, the country is facing various challenges in developing such type of tourism. One of the significant challenges of ecotourism in Iran is governance and planning challenge. However, the infrastructural challenges, coupled with political, socio-economic, and cultural context with the extent of diversity, are that these have not yet been recognized and amassed, and due to these shortcomings, they cannot be promoted effectively. Effective advertising and promotion are crucial in attracting tourists to a region. However, it is equally important to ensure that the influx of tourists does not harm the environment or the natural and cultural attractions of the region. For ecotourism to thrive in Iran, there needs to be comprehensive macro planning and systematic advertising to attract tourists and ensure the sustainable development of the industry. Therefore, ecotourism in Iran seems to have a slight attention that has the weakness points and threats mentioned (Table 3).

In Iran, the cost of travelling with a tour is views above of personal journey. It is observed that people spend additional money on foreign trips. One of the reasons is that Iranian people do not pay sufficiently to see the sights and values of their communities as they are not familiar with them. The balance of the tourism statistics will be negative if Iranian people do not comprehend the value of their country's attractions. The modification of these perspectives requires deep culture and curriculum understanding from Iranian people. Therefore, ecotourism could be viewed as an opportunity for local people to connect with nature, learn about their natural heritage, and develop a greater appreciation for the

Table 3 Weaknesses and threats for Iranian ecotourism

Weaknesses	Threats
Lack of comprehensive strategic programmes	Tension, unrest, insecurity in the Middle East
Lack of skill and human resources in ecotourism major	Competition among world countries to attract tourists
Weakness in marketing and introduction of Iranian ecosystems	Showing the negative image of Iran in international media
Lack of attention to ecotourism attractions and lack of responsibility for the environment	The global economic downturn, which has led to a decline in large numbers of tourists
Weakness and lack of social security, especially in some remote areas	Environmental degradation, drought, and natural disasters
Unsuitable transportation system to visit specific areas	Non-promotion and exclusion of Iran except for some attractive areas by Westerners
Weakness in health care in some destination areas	
Inadequate or non-access to technologies such as the Internet in some destination areas	
Weakness and lack of hotels and suitable residences for tourists in ecotourism areas	
High inflation rate and economic problems in the country	
Cultural problems	

importance of environmental protection. This can help to build a sense of stewardship among local communities and tourists alike, encouraging them to take an active role in protecting the natural resources of the region. Moreover, there is a need for the appropriate use of natural resources (Bazm Ara et al., 2017). There is a lack of management and plans for environmental conservation (Abdolahi, 2007; Kolahi et al., 2014). Moreover, there is an evident absence of giving priority to ecotourism development projects within the country. As per Shomalizade et al. (2015), there is an absence of ecotourism promotion strategies and the presentation of natural attractions. According to Zarabi and Safarabadi (2014), without taking into consideration the principles of responsible tourism, it becomes evident that Iran is facing challenges associated with governance and the planning of ecotourism development.

In Iran, an extensive number of laws and policies are indirectly or directly are related to the work loss against biodiversity conservation. Furthermore, there is an evidently poor association between as there is a poor connection between environmental laws and tourism within ecotourism. The country's legislators do not adequately address tourism, especially ecotourism, to protect natural attractions because of the weak governance we face in developing tourism in Iran. While the government's role in development has shifted to addressing issues such as economic and socio-cultural impacts, political responsibilities, power relations, and environmental awareness. Promoting ecotourism in Iran requires a comprehensive approach that addresses cultural, educational, environmental, and economic aspects. By raising awareness, improving infrastructure, and adopting sustainable practices, ecotourism can become a significant contributor to Iran's sustainable development and help to preserve its natural and cultural heritage.

Moreover, environmental influence challenges have received minimal attention. In contrast, environmental calamities are the foremost threats to Iran's natural resources (Atlantic Council, 2018). Emerging economies face many challenges in protecting their natural resources while also promoting economic development. Ecotourism can be an effective way for these countries to protect their natural attractions and promote sustainable development at the same time. Therefore, it is important to carefully plan and manage ecotourism activities to ensure that they are sustainable and environmentally responsible and do not cause long-term harm to the natural and cultural resources of the region.

5 Conclusion and Recommendations

Ecotourism has various effects on the region, including social, cultural, economic, and environmental impacts. The development of ecotourism is often viewed as a central pillar of sustainable development because it involves transforming the relationships between social, economic, and natural systems. Natural environmental factors, such as geology, topography, flora, and fauna, are critical in attracting tourists to a region. However, it is essential to recognize that the development of ecotourism can also have negative impacts. For instance, an increase in the number of tourists can lead to overcrowding, increased pollution, and degradation of natural habitats. It can also lead to the exploitation of local communities and cultures, which can result in social and cultural tensions. Iran must improve its cordial relationship with other countries in the Middle East. One of the positive steps taken by Iran's government is to improve relations with Saudi Arabia. This could help them improve their infrastructure and strategic planning with assistance from other Middle Eastern countries.

It is crucial to adopt a sustainable approach to ecotourism development that considers the long-term impacts on the environment, local communities, and the economy. The ecotourism industry has gained significant momentum globally, and many countries have experienced economic, social, and cultural development as a result. The development of ecotourism has created job opportunities in various sectors, such as hospitality, transportation, and tour operations. Therefore, it is crucial to adopt a sustainable approach to ecotourism development that considers the needs and aspirations of local communities and the long-term impacts on the environment. Iran must improve the infrastructural challenges by promoting sustainable programmes and rebates on eco-friendly development in the region.

One of the primary obstacles to ecotourism development in Iran is the lack of suitable communication channels between cities. This can make it difficult for tourists to access remote areas and natural attractions. In addition, there is a shortage of residential, service, and welfare facilities for passengers, which can affect their comfort and safety. Hence, Iran shall improve its communication channels and must adopt digital mechanisms for improving the communication with different stakeholders involved in the planning and operations related to ecotourism.

Another significant challenge is the weakness of advertising, which can limit the visibility of Iran's ecotourism offerings to potential tourists. Furthermore, there is a lack of people willing to invest in the industry, which can limit the availability of funds for ecotourism development projects. To overcome these obstacles, policymakers and tourism stakeholders in Iran should work together to develop effective communication channels, improve the availability of residential, service, and welfare facilities, and invest in advertising campaigns to promote Iran's ecotourism potential.

Iran's diverse attractions and natural landscapes make it a potential ecotourism destination. Ecotourism can bring economic prosperity to rural areas by creating employment opportunities, promoting local businesses, and generating income from tourism activities. Planning is a critical aspect of ecotourism development and can help ensure that the industry's growth is sustainable and contributes to the long-term well-being of local communities and the environment. By adopting a sustainable approach to ecotourism development, Iran can promote the growth of the industry while preserving its natural and cultural heritage, promoting social and economic development, and contributing to the overall sustainability of the country's tourism industry.

Ecotourism can reduce threats through local practices, monitoring, educated people, environmental education, and protected areas. Ecotourism needs complete planning and management along with an understanding of its potential. A district vision for ecotourism development planning must recognize and endorse a range of unique tourist experiences that can be ecologically, socially, and economically maintainable while meeting the needs of visitors and locals alike. Furthermore, for sustainable ecotourism, such as diminishing the negative environmental impact, generating environmental awareness, forming constructive experiences, empowering local people, and creating awareness regarding the social, political, and environmental situation is vital to educate the local communities and those who participate in ecotourism activities. To establish and develop sustainable use of attractions and Iran's natural resources, there is an essential need for understanding the depth of challenges associated with ecotourism in the region as one of the fundamental foundations for ecotourism activities is for tourism authorities to adopt corrective strategies for effective minimization of these negative impacts.

References

Abdolahi, E. (2007). Ecotourism compatible with environmental protection and sustainability of natural resources. In *Presented at the Sixth Iranian Agriculture Economics Conference*, Mashhad, Iran.

Ahmadi, M., Khodadadi, M., & Shahabi, H. (2018). Planning for ecotourism in the protected area of Manesht and Ghelarang, Ilam Province, Iran. *Journal of Quality Assurance in Hospitality & Tourism, 19*(2), 243–268. https://doi.org/10.1080/1528008X.2017.1394956

Amador-Jiménez, M., Millner, N., Palmer, C., Pennington, R. T., & Sileci, L. (2020). The unintended impact of Colombia's COVID-19 lockdown on forest fires. *Environmental Research Economy, 76*, 1081–1105. https://doi.org/10.1007/s10640-020-00501-5

Asadi, R. (2012). Strategies for Iran ecotourism. *World Applied Sciences Journal, 18*(3), 414–424. https://doi.org/10.5829/idosi.wasj.2012.18.03.1710

Asadpourian, Z., Rahimian, M., & Gholamrezai, S. (2020). SWOT-AHP-TOWS analysis for sustainable ecotourism development in the best area in Lorestan Province, Iran. *Social Indicators Research, 152*(1), 289–315. https://doi.org/10.1007/s11205-020-02438-0

Atlantic Council. (2018). *Iran's environmental impasse*. Accessed from https://www.atlanticcouncil.org/commentary/event-recap/iran-s-environmental-impasse/

Bazm Ara, M., Tavakoli, M., & Kaveh, J. (2017). Assessing appropriate areas for ecotourism development of protected areas. Case study: Khaeez protected area. *The Journal of Spatial Planning, 21*(3), 95–118.

Bego, F., & Malltezi, J. (2011). Ecotourism opportunities and challenges in Butrint, Albania, a unique UNESCO and Ramsar site. *Journal of Coastal Research, 61*, 150–157. https://doi.org/10.2112/SI61-001.9

Carson, D. B., & Taylor, A. J. (2008). Sustaining four wheel drive tourism in desert Australia: Exploring the evidence from a demand perspective. *The Rangeland Journal, 30*(1), 77. https://doi.org/10.1071/rj07036

Carvache-Franco, M., Segarra-Oña, M., & Carrascosa-López, C. (2019). Segmentation by motivation in ecotourism: Application to protected areas in Guayas, Ecuador. *Sustainability, 11*(1), 1–19. https://doi.org/10.3390/su11010240

Cetinkaya, G. (2004). Challenges for ecotourism development in Çukurova delta Biosphere Reserve, Turkey. *Budownictwo, 16*, 89–96.

Cherkaoui, S., Boukherouk, M., Lakhal, T., Aghzar, A. E., & El Youssfi, L. (2020). Conservation amid COVID-19 pandemic: Ecotourism collapse threatens communities and wildlife in Morocco. In *Paper Present E3S Web Conference* (Vol. 3, p. 003). https://doi.org/10.1051/e3sconf/202018301003

Dabiri, F., Fazel, A. M., Moghaddasi, N., & Mehrdadi, M. (2016). *Revised National Biodiversity Strategies and Action Plan (NBSAP2) of Islamic Republic of Iran*. Accessed from https://doi.org/10.13140/RG.2.2.17561.62567

Das, M., & Chatterjee, B. (2015). Ecotourism: A panacea or a predicament? *Tourism Management Perspectives, 14*, 3–16. https://doi.org/10.1016/j.tmp.2015.01.002

Fernando, S. L. J., & Shariff, N. M. (2017). Wetland ecotourism in Sri Lanka: Issues and challenges. *Geografia-Malaysian Journal of Society and Space, 9*(4), 99–105.

Financial Tribune. (2017). *Iran ecotourism untapped.* Accessed from https://financialtribune.com/articles/travel/65072/iran-ecotourism_untapped

Ganjali, S., Shayesteh, K., Ghasemi, A., & Mohammadi, H. (2014). Environmental and strategic assessment of ecotourism potential in Anzali wetland using SWOT analysis. *Caspian Journal of Environmental Sciences-University of Guilan, 22*(1), 155–164.

Ghorbani nia, V., Mirsanjari, M., & Liaghati, H. (2018). Evaluating ecotourism potential development in Dena County using multi-criteria evaluation of specific hybrid indices. *Journal of Rangeland, 12*(3), 316–329.

Ghorbani, A., Raufirad, V., Rafiaani, P., & Azadi, H. (2015). Ecotourism sustainable development strategies using SWOT and QSPM model: A case study of Kaji Namakzar Wetland, South Khorasan Province, Iran. *Tourism Management Perspectives, 16*, 290–297. https://doi.org/10.1016/j.tmp.2015.09.005

Goharipour, H., & Hajiluie, M. M. (2016). A study on river ecotourism development: Case study: Karaj River. *International Journal of Geography and Geology, 5*(4), 73–85. https://doi.org/10.18488/journal.10/2016.5.4/10.4.73.85

González Fonseca, F. (2012). Challenges and opportunities in the world of tourism from the point of view of ecotourism. *Higher Learning Research Communications, 2*(4), 5–22. https://doi.org/10.18870/hlrc.v2i4.82

Hadizadeh Zargar, S. (2016). Tourism environmental zoning powers of Mazandaran Province to develop ecotourism. *Journal of Urban Economics and Management, 5*(1), 31–46.

Haque, A. U., & Yamoah, F. A. (2021). The role of ethical leadership in managing occupational stress to promote innovative work behaviour: A cross-cultural management perspective. *Sustainability, 13*, 9608. https://doi.org/10.3390/su13179608

Harrison, D., & Schipani, L. (2007). Tourism and poverty alleviation: Community-based tourism and the private sector. In *Pro-poor Tourism: Who benefits?* 84.

Hosseinalizadeh, S., Jabbari, S., & Haghlesan, M. (2018). Assessment of eco-tourism from the perspective of the sustainable development based on SWOT model (Case: Azerbaijan Region of Iran). *European Journal of Sustainable Development, 7*(1), 163–174. https://doi.org/10.14207/ejsd.2018.v7n1p163

Ijeomah, H. M., & Okoli, C. I. C. (2016). Challenges of ecotourism in selected destinations of Nigeria. *International Journal of Agriculture and Rural Development, 19*(2), 2655–2668.

Kamyabi, S., & Rajaee Rizi, M. A. (2018). Ecotourism development strategies in Chahardangeh District of Sari County. *Journal of Research and Rural Planning, 6*(4), 107–126.

Khalili, S., Moridsadat, P., & Soltaninejad, H. (2020). Toward sustainable rural ecotourism evolution: The case of Kiskan, Iran. *Geography, Environment, Sustainability, 13*(3), 39–48. https://doi.org/10.24057/2071-9388-2019-133

Kolahi, M., Moriya, K., Sakai, T., Khosrojerdi, E., & Etemad, V. (2014). Introduction of participatory conservation in Iran: Case study of the rural communities' perspectives in Khojir National Park. *International Journal of Environmental Research, 8*(4), 913–930. https://doi.org/10.22059/ijer.2014.784

Makian, S., & Hanifezadeh, F. (2021). Current challenges facing ecotourism development in Iran. *Journal of Tourismology, 7*(1), 123–140. https://doi.org/10.26650/jot.2021.7.1.0007

Malkina-Pykh, I. (2002). Integrated assessment models and response function models: Pros and cons for sustainable development indices design. *Ecological Indicators, 2*(1–2), 93–108. https://doi.org/10.1016/s1470-160x(02)00048-1

Mansoori, S., Behzad, R., & Jaybhaye, R. G. (2014). The role of ecotourism in the prosperity of local people in the Tandooreh National Park and the Shir-Ahmad wildlife refuge-Iran. *The International Journal of Humanities & Social Studies, 2*(8), 111–114.

Mgonja, J. T., Sirima, A., & Mkumbo, P. J. (2015). A review of ecotourism in Tanzania: Magnitude, challenges, and prospects for sustainability. *Journal of Ecotourism, 14*(2–3), 264–277. https://doi.org/10.1080/14724049.2015.1114623

Mobaraki, O., Abdollahzadeh, M., & Kamelifar, Z. (2014). Site suitability evaluation for ecotourism using GIS and AHP: A case study of Isfahan townships, Iran. *Management Science Letters, 4*(8), 1893–1898. https://doi.org/10.5267/j.msl.2014.6.038

Moghimehfar, F., Halpenny, E. A., & Ziaee, M. (2014). How big is the gap? Comparing the behaviours and knowledge of mountain hikers with ecotourism ideals: A case study of Iran. *Journal of Ecotourism, 13*(1), 1–15. https://doi.org/10.1080/14724049.2014.925466

Nee, I., & Beckmann, I. (2011). Ecotourism: The growth, its implications and trends. In A. Papathanassis (Ed.), *The long tail of tourism* (pp. 115–127). Gabler. https://doi.org/10.1007/978-3-8349-6231-7_13

Otago, G. S. (2014). Planning for sustainable tourism: Challenges and opportunities for ecotourism development in Addis Ababa, Ethiopia. *American Journal of Human Ecology, 3*(2), 20–26.

Pourasghari, M., & Amar, T. (2018). Feasibility of ecotourism development in Anzali wetland: An emphasis on bird watching stations. *Journal of Tourism & Hospitality Research, 6*(1), 59–77.

Rakhshan Nasab, H., & Zarabi, A. (2010). Challenges and opportunities of ecotourism development in Iran. *Journal of Geographic Space, 9*(28), 41–55.

Ramezani Gourabi, B., & Rajabi, R. (2015). Environmental vulnerability assessment of tourism in Anzali coastal using SWOT. *Journal of Environmental Science and Technology, 16*(1), 245–256.

Rezaeinejad, I., & Khaniwadekar, A. (2021). The role of eco-tourism in sustainable development: Case study eco-tourism challenges in Iran. *E3S Web of Conferences, 311*, 02004. https://doi.org/10.1051/e3sconf/202131102004

Shomalizade, F., Dashti, S., & Hemadi, K. (2015). Analysis and evaluation of potential and strategies for ecotourism development in lake of Dez dam using Freeman's method. *Journal of Wetland Ecobiology, 7*(3), 5–20.

Teressa, D. K. (2015). Development of community-based ecotourism in Wenchi crater Lake, Ethiopia: Challenges and prospects. *Journal of Hospitality Management and Tourism, 6*(4), 39–46. https://doi.org/10.5897/JHMT2014.0133

Tripathi, U. N., & Jain, A. K. (2017). Opportunities and challenges of ecotourism with reference to its employability potential: Uttar Pradesh, India. *Journal for Interdisciplinary Studies, 4*(37), 8872–8882.

Veicy, H. (2018). The study of tourism industry in National Basic Laws of Islamic Republic of Iran. *Strategic Studies of public policy, 7*(25), 93–112.

Yamoah, F. A., & Haque, A. U. (2022). Strategic management through digital platforms for remote working in the higher education industry during and after the COVID-19 pandemic. *Forum Scientiae Oeconomia, 10*(2), 111–128. https://doi.org/10.23762/FSO_VOL10_NO2_6

Zarabi, A., & Safarabadi, A. (2014). Assessment of sustainable ecotourism development in the Kermanshah city. *Journal of Geography and Planning, 17*(46), 147–170.

Emerging Economies in Eastern Europe: Corporate Social Responsibility

Maxim Rakov and Adnan ul Haque

1 Introduction

Corporate Social Responsibility (CSR) has been ubiquitous in contemporary corporate management ecosystems (Aslaksen et al., 2021), but its precise definition remains elusive. Despite the proliferation of CSR initiatives across the corporate landscape, scholars and practitioners have yet to agree on what constitutes CSR (Gorova & Deng, 2021; Maon et al., 2017). Since the mid-twentieth century, CSR has become a distinct and meaningful idea. During this period, several influential writers, scholars, and activists began to articulate a vision of corporate responsibility that emphasised the importance of corporate ethics, justice, and dignity in

M. Rakov • A. ul Haque (✉)
Faculty of Business, Yorkville University, Toronto, ON, Canada
e-mail: ahaque@yorkvilleu.ca

F. A. Yamoah, A. ul Haque (eds.), *Corporate Management Ecosystem in Emerging Economies*, https://doi.org/10.1007/978-3-031-41578-4_16

business practices (Nekhoda et al., 2015). For example, CSR has been defined by Fitch (1976) as a conglomeration of endeavours aimed at addressing societal issues brought about, either entirely or partially, by corporations. However, the original idea behind CSR has evolved significantly over time, encompassing more comprehensive strategic and tactical initiatives that address a wide range of social and environmental issues.

Carroll's earlier proposal (1979) of the definition of corporate trust responsibility has proven to be a valuable framework for contemplating the duties of businesses to society. This framework has also served as an adequate foundation for theoretical advancement and research on the topic. The four-part definition stipulates that corporations must fulfil four responsibilities towards society: economic, legal, ethical, and philanthropic (Carroll, 2000, pp. 33–42).

With the change of millennia, the concept of CSR has become increasingly prevalent in contemporary discourse as companies are compelled to consider their impact on society beyond their financial bottom line (Argandoña & von Weltzien Hoivik, 2009). The discourse surrounding CSR has undergone a paradigm shift, moving away from inquiries into the fundamental nature of the organisational mission and shareholder value and towards an examination of how corporations conceptualise, and potentially deliver, their societal obligations (Wang et al., 2016). This shift has given rise to a fresh wave of perspectives and definitions. It is noteworthy to acknowledge the significance of the concept of CSR, particularly considering its growing importance. For instance, Sheehy (2015) suggests that CSR is a form of regulation for international enterprises. This idea is based on the notion that political agendas play a crucial role in shaping the substance of CSR obligations, which makes establishing a precise definition challenging (Sheehy, 2015).

Drawing upon the aforementioned ideas and perspectives, it can be inferred that CSR is a multifaceted and ever-evolving concept (Argandoña & von Weltzien Hoivik, 2009). It is subject to alterations and transformations over time, and its interpretation and implementation vary significantly across different organisational settings. The specifics of CSR within each organisation are also unique. It is influenced by internal and external factors such as local laws and regulations, organisational nature and structure, and its focus on internal and external stakeholders (Rutkowska & Pakulska, 2021, p. 347).

The analysis above underscores the dynamic nature of CSR as an ever-evolving and multifaceted phenomenon impacted by institutional and socio-political factors that need to be studied further (Argandoña & von Weltzien Hoivik, 2009; Maon et al., 2017, p. 406). Therefore, the dynamic nature of CSR and its role within contemporary corporate management ecosystems in emerging economies necessitate a broader analysis of its intricacies and implications.

This chapter explores the role within the contemporary corporate management ecosystems in emerging economies, focusing on a specific region—Eastern Europe. Europe in general, and Eastern Europe in particular, is not a singular, homogenous entity when examined from an institutional or CSR perspective (Maon et al., 2017, pp. 407–408). Eastern Europe is a complex region with unique political, economic, and social challenges that require careful consideration and attention (Kuti, 1999).

In this chapter, we narrow our analysis down to countries characterised as, and have features of, emerging economies in Eastern Europe—Poland and Russia. While both countries share several historic and cultural similarities, their economic and political development has taken different trajectories, creating unique and distinct environments for CSR practices (Maon et al., 2017).

2 Literature Review

The Growing Role of CSR in Emerging Economies

Recent research indicates that CSR is increasingly perceived as a significant catalyst for achieving organisational goals and driving social value. Chavda (2022) suggests that organisations started realising that their role goes beyond profitability and that they should account for direct or indirect measures required for the survival of society. In their recent study, Lu et al. (2019) suggested that CSR is an increasingly valued facet of modern business practices. Implementing ethical, environmental, and social considerations within a company's operations has been shown to positively correlate with favourable impact on brand loyalty and image. By prioritizing CSR initiatives, companies can bolster their reputation, strengthen their competitive advantage, and ultimately enhance their business opportunities (Lu et al., 2019). These and other potential benefits of CSR for organizational success warrant further investigation. Firstly, multiple research studies have provided more comprehensive data on the positive correlation between CSR and organisational profitability. In works by Cho et al. (2019), the authors confirmed that CSR activities are partially linked to organisational value and profitability, supporting earlier studies conducted by Charles Nwaneri (2015) that show CSR investments positively correlate with organisational profitability in Nigeria. Based on his research, Charles Nwaneri (2015) has concluded that organisational management should formulate and implement its CSR programme in consultation with its stakeholders. In works by Hategan et al. (2018), aimed at establishing the relationships between CSR and profit in Romanian companies, the authors discussed their conclusion that companies with CSR activities in place are more profitable in economic terms. Another study from India has concluded that CSR disclosures lead to better financial performance of a company and vice-versa (Gautam et al., 2016). These novel studies have emphasised the potential for CSR to promote ethical behaviour and drive economic success.

CSR may be a factor in the success of emerging market enterprises in gaining legitimacy among global stakeholders. Tashman et al. (2019) suggest that a correlation exists between emerging market enterprises' global challenges in achieving success and recognition and the negative stereotypes associated with institutional gaps and economic and political issues that often persist in emerging economies. Those stereotypes can be internalised by companies created within the emerging economies themselves and their potential clients on a global scale. Tashman et al. (2019) also referred to numerous studies demonstrating that companies' CSR engagement positively correlated with favourable product evaluations, effective customer relationship management, and conducive treatment from regulatory agencies (Tashman et al., 2019).

CSR Outlook in Emerging Economies of Eastern Europe

This section aims to scrutinise the outlook of CSR in emerging economies, particularly the key players in the Eastern European region—Poland and Russia. Despite the existence of certain similarities in the manner in which corporate entities in these countries administer their CSR activities, discernible distinctions also exist. We will investigate and evaluate the similarities and differences in CSR activities between the two countries.

Similarities Between Poland and Russia in Implementing and Promoting CSR Practices

Numerous studies have also consistently demonstrated that corporate entities in Poland and Russia show a shortage of long-term strategies concerning their CSR programmes, potentially due to a lack of integration of CSR practices and concerns into their operations and strategy, in addition to a tendency among corporate actors in emerging markets to view CSR as a community-oriented activity rather than an integral part of core business processes and strategic planning (Maon et al., 2017; Elms, 2006; Kadnikova & Lobkov, 2018).

Furthermore, the development of CSR reporting practices in Poland and Russia is still early. Compared to developed European economies, a relatively smaller percentage of local corporate entities in Poland and Russia prepare CSR reports or actively engage in CSR activities (Kadnikova & Lobkov, 2018; Kudłak, 2020; Macuda et al., 2015; Wołczek, 2015). CSR reports produced by corporate actors in those emerging economies still have areas for improvement (Hąbek, 2017; Kadnikova & Lobkov, 2018). However, more recent studies suggest that the stakeholder demands towards CSR compliance are increasing, and companies are attempting to improve the reporting standards (Cherkasova & Nenuzhenko, 2022, pp. 54–58). The most evident similarity between these two Eastern European emerging economies is in the focus of the corporate players on their social responsibility agendas. Their focus revolves around community activities and philanthropy projects directed at society at large. Corporate actors in Eastern Europe are less likely to integrate CSR into their business processes and operations. Instead, they are more likely to prioritise philanthropy and charity in collaboration with communities and non-profit organisations (Kadnikova & Lobkov, 2018; Maon et al., 2017).

However, the two emerging economies studied in this review have growing differences associated with their distinct economic and political developments. Crotty (2016) found that, while the market is driving conventional forms of CSR within some Russian corporate actors, the historical legacy of both the Soviet Union and the more recent political developments strongly influence the type and nature of CSR undertaken. At the same time, the CSR approach in Poland is following a different course, as part of the country's integration within the European Union (EU), in addition to the influence of transnational corporations and foreign investors (Hąbek, 2017). Those differences will be examined further to better understand countries' unique approaches to CSR and formulate an outlook for future corporate responsibilities in these two emerging economies.

3 Research Methodology

This chapter is a systematic review of CSR implementation and promotion strategies in the comparative emerging economies. Thus, it falls in the socio-anthropologic paradigm (Haque, 2020). The ontological stance is to gain critical realism through exploring the reality of current corporate social responsibility. The epistemological stance is to know about the knowledge of truth (Haque, 2020); thus, this paper is a running commentary on the extensive literature to understand how the two emerging economies differ in their approaches. As a result, the critical approach is employed to avail the details from the existing body of knowledge. The chapter also employed the funnel approach technique (Faizan et al., 2019) for selection of the papers. Moreover, the content analysis coupled with the thematic analysis was carried out to screen and shortlist the papers using key terminologies such as CSR, implementation strategies, promotion, social factors, and political and social developments.

Since the chapter is based on the existing literature, it uses content validity and reliability. The primary data is not used in the study; thus, it was ensured that only reliable secondary sources are incorporated in this paper. Moreover, a special attention was given to the extraction of information and selection of papers by considering only the peer-reviewed journal articles.

4 Findings and Discussions

The Russian Approach in CSR Implementation and Promotion

Amidst the significant role played by Russia as a supplier of raw materials, it remains an inadequately explored business environment overall. The CSR topic in Russia has also been under-researched (Rogerson, 2023). Recent studies posit that the COVID-19 pandemic has catalysed CSR development in Russia by changing a societal perspective on the contribution of business to social development (Markova, 2021). Furthermore, studies argue that CSR will be further developed in Russia under the influence of three key factors: limited resources, growing qualifications of CSR professionals, and growing expectations from key business stakeholders (Markova, 2021; Tikhomirov, 2022). Nevertheless, most researchers agree that the development of CSR practices in Russia is still in its early stages (Shumilina & Ostapenko, 2022, pp. 156–158; Tikhomirov, 2022). Corporate players face several factors that inevitably impact the development of CSR practices. Those factors can be divided into two groups: historic-geographical and socio-political.

Historic-geographical factors include the considerable territory of the Russian Federation, the significant distance between cities, the predominance of single-industry municipalities, Soviet-era attitudes towards business (Crotty, 2016), and the lack of independent media that can objectively assess corporate activities. On the other hand, socio-political factors include low-income levels, a wide range of social problems, pressure from the authorities, and an insufficient regulatory framework (Shumilina & Ostapenko, 2022, pp. 156–158).

The Russian business model can be aptly described as oligarchic, where companies determine the extent of their social responsibility. This approach leads to an inadequacy in upholding ethical principles and disregards the well-being of society at large (Tikhomirov, 2022). This leads us to an assumption that corporate players in Russia should be held accountable not just for their financial performance but also for their social and environmental impact, and the government should play an active role in it. However, the relationship between the Russian government and the local businesses does not provide a solid foundation for a clear regulatory and taxation framework for CSR activities (Rogerson, 2023, pp. 7–8).

This leads us to one of the key challenges experienced by corporate players looking to implement CSR practices in Russia—the need for more clarity and consistency in the country's perspective on the regulatory environment in CSR (Rogerson, 2023, pp. 7–8). Although the government has taken steps to promote CSR through initiatives, the absence of clear guidelines and regulations from the government remains a critical issue (Rudneva, 2022). CSR disclosure by Russian companies has been a topic of concern in literature, revealing a lack of transparency and involvement (Rogerson, 2023, p. 8; Kadnikova & Lobkov, 2018). A major contributing factor is the absence of a legal benchmark for CSR activity disclosure, which exacerbates the difficulty of monitoring and evaluating CSR practices in local business activities (Rogerson, 2023, p. 8). Although the government has taken active measures in order to address CSR reporting to some extent, smaller companies without close ties to the government are left to set their own priorities with respect to CSR, often leading to a complete disregard for CSR practices (Rogerson, 2023, p. 3).

In addition, CSR suffers from inconsistent reporting in Russia. Some Russian companies follow international standards such as ISO 26000 for reporting, and some use local standards developed by the Russian government, for example, the Social Charter of Russian Business introduced in 2004 (Nekhoda et al., 2015, pp. 187–198). The Social Charter of Russian Business is a set of fundamental principles of responsible business practice, which outline the relationships between employees and employers, civil society institutions, authorities, the local community, and the environment. In the same period of time when the Social Charter of Russian Business was developed, the standard of the Chamber of Commerce of the Russian Federation, "Social reporting of enterprises and organisations registered in the Russian Federation," was developed. Other standards are available (i.e., ICCSR-08260008000a); however, only some companies use them to produce CSR reporting (Nekhoda et al., 2015, pp. 187–198).

The Polish Approach in CSR Implementation and Promotion

CSR is a relatively nascent concept in Poland, with limited research on the subject. This lack is evident in the absence of a unified and exhaustive data source on the scope of companies engaged in voluntary responsible practices (Kudłak, 2020). Kudłak (2020) argues that CSR has gained significant attention in Poland over the past few years. Implementing CSR practices has become increasingly important for companies operating in Poland. However, the practices are still mainly adopted by large corporations. The preponderance of such entities can be identified as subsidiaries of multinational corporations. While earlier studies have suggested that companies in Poland focus on CSR initiatives to promote social and community development (Maon et al., 2017), more recent studies indicate a growing interest among Polish organisations to improve working conditions and protect the natural environment (Kudłak, 2020). However, it is essential to recognise that the COVID-19 pandemic and the ongoing war in Ukraine might further impact the global landscape. There is potential for significant consequences that could necessitate a shift in CSR priorities among corporate actors operating in Eastern Europe. The precise nature of these consequences cannot be reliably predicted at present (Lecka et al., 2022, p. 6).

One of Poland's main drivers of CSR is the country's integration into the EU. As a member state, Poland is subject to EU regulations and standards, including those related to CSR. In fact, the European Commission has played a significant role in the development of CSR reporting in Poland through key documents, including:

1. Green Paper: Promoting a European Framework for Corporate Social Responsibility (2001)
2. White Paper: Communication from the Commission Concerning CSR: A Business Contribution to Sustainable Development (2002)
3. "A Renewed EU Strategy 2011-14 for Corporate Social Responsibility" (European Commission, 2011)

These regulations and standards have led to improvements in CSR reporting, driven by both voluntary commitments and actions by companies, and mandatory requirements established by the EU and implemented into Polish law, further emphasising the importance of CSR reporting in modern business practices (Lecka et al., 2022).

However, despite regulatory measures being implemented, some studies suggest that Polish business organisations encounter challenges in implementing CSR as its impact on businesses remains unclear to companies, leading to misperceptions (Dyczkowska et al., 2016). The content and quality of CSR reports also vary significantly, indicating a further need for improvement. Moreover, it has been observed that, similar to Russia, CSR disclosures in Poland are rare, even though the country is making significant progress in implementing EU regulations and standards (Fijałkowska & Macuda, 2018).

5 Conclusion

In conclusion, Russian firms' lack of CSR disclosure and regulatory measures poses a significant challenge to achieving sustainable development in the country (Rogerson, 2023, pp. 7–8). However, more companies are interested in promoting CSR practices in post-pandemic Russia, which creates an opportunity for the government to institute a conducive environment to match that growing interest with proactive measures (Markova, 2021; Tikhomirov, 2022). On the other hand, the growing interest in CSR initiatives in Poland is a positive development that has the potential to create significant social, environmental, and economic benefits. Additionally, the emergence of CSR professionals and associations will contribute to further institutionalising CSR reporting and to standardising CSR practices (Kudłak, 2020).

References

Argandoña, A., & von Weltzien Hoivik, H. (2009). Corporate social responsibility: One size does not fit all. Collecting evidence from Europe. *Journal of Business Ethics, 89*(3), 221–234. https://doi.org/10.1007/s10551-010-0394-4

Aslaksen, H. M., Hildebrandt, C., & Johnsen, H. C. G. (2021). The long-term transformation of the concept of CSR: Towards a more comprehensive emphasis on sustainability. *International Journal of Corporate Social Responsibility, 6*(1), 11. https://doi.org/10.1186/s40991-021-00063-9

Carroll, A. B. (1979). A three-dimensional conceptual model of corporate performance. *The Academy of Management Review, 4*(4), 497–505. https://doi.org/10.2307/257850

Carroll, A. B. (2000). Ethical challenges for business in the new millennium: Corporate social responsibility and models of management morality. *Business Ethics Quarterly, 10*(1), 33–42. https://doi.org/10.2307/3857692

Charles Nwaneri, E. (2015). The impact of corporate social responsibility (CSR) on organization profitability. *International Journal of Business and Management, 10*(9). https://doi.org/10.5539/ijbm.v10n9p60

Chavda, D., Acharya, M., & Patel, H. (2022). A study on CSR activities in banking sector as a factor of economic growth. *International Journal of Management, Public Policy and Research, 1*(2), 88–93. https://doi.org/10.55829/ijmpr.v1i2.75

Cherkasova, V., & Nenuzhenko, I. (2022). Investment in ESG projects and corporate performance of multinational companies. *Journal of Economic Integration, 37*(1), 54–92. Accessed from https://www.e-jei.org/journal/view.php?doi=10.11130/jei.2022.37.1.54

Cho, S. J., Chung, C. Y., & Young, J. (2019). Study on the relationship between CSR and financial performance. *Sustainability, 11*(2), 343. https://doi.org/10.3390/su11020343

Crotty, J. (2016). Corporate social responsibility in the Russian Federation: A contextualized approach. *Business & Society, 55*(6), 825–853. https://doi.org/10.1177/0007650314561965

Dyczkowska, J., Krasodomska, J., & Michalak, J. (2016). CSR in Poland: Institutional context, legal framework and voluntary initiatives. *Journal of Accounting and Management Information Systems, 15*(2), 206–254. Accessed from https://ideas.repec.org/a/ami/journl/v15y2016i2p206-254.html

Elms, H. (2006). Corporate (and stakeholder) responsibility in central and Eastern Europe. *International Journal of Emerging Markets, 1*(3), 203–211. https://doi.org/10.1108/17468800610674435

European Commission. (2011). *European Commission Communication: A renewed EU strategy 2011-14 for Corporate Social Responsibility*. ENAT Library. Retrieved from: http://ec.europa.eu/enterprise/newsroom/cf/itemlongdetail.cfm?item_id=5511

Faizan, R., Haque, A.U., Cockrill, A., & Aston, J. (2019). Females at Strategic Level affecting Logistics Firms' Competitiveness: Qualitative Comparative Analysis. *Forum Scientiae Oeconomia, 7*(1), 57–71.

Fijałkowska, J., & Macuda, M. (2018). CSR reporting practices in Poland. In *Corporate social responsibility in Poland. Strategies, opportunities and challenges*. Springer.

Fitch, H. G. (1976). Achieving corporate social responsibility. *The Academy of Management Review, 1*(1), 38–46. https://doi.org/10.2307/257357

Gautam, R., Singh, A., & Bhowmick, D. (2016). Demystifying relationship between corporate social responsibility (CSR) and financial performance: An Indian business perspective. *Independent Journal of Management & Production, 7*(4), 1034–1062. Accessed from http://www.redalyc.org/articulo.oa?id=449549377003

Gorova, K., & Deng, Q. (2021). Definition of the concept of corporate social responsibility in modern conditions. *Kharkiv Polytechnic University, 87*(2), 26–29. https://doi.org/10.32782/2304-0920/2-87-4

Hąbek, P. (2017). CSR reporting practices in Visegrad group countries and the quality of disclosure. *Sustainability, 9*(12), 2322. https://doi.org/10.3390/su9122322

Haque, A. U. (2020). *Varying occupational stress and organisational commitment within the university staff of contrasting economies (Cross-sectional comparative study of middle range public universities in Pakistan and the UK)*. Published DBA Thesis, UWTSD Repository. Accessed from https://repository.uwtsd.ac.uk/id/eprint/1570/

Hategan, C.-D., Sirghi, N., Curea-Pitorac, R.-I., & Hategan, V.-P. (2018). Doing well or doing good: The relationship between corporate social responsibility and profit in Romanian companies. *Sustainability, 10*(4), 1041. https://doi.org/10.3390/su10041041

Kadnikova, O. V., & Lobkov, G. (2018). Современное состояние корпоративной социальной ответственности в России и Германии (Current state of corporate social responsibility in Russia and Germany). *Leadership and Management, 5*, 105. https://doi.org/10.18334/lim.5.3.39513

Kudłak, R. (2020). CSR in Poland: The rise and development of corporate social responsibility. In *Rethinking business responsibility in a global context* (pp. 135–146). Springer. https://doi.org/10.1007/978-3-030-34261-6_9

Kuti, É. (1999). Different eastern European countries at different crossroads. *Voluntas: International Journal of Voluntary and Nonprofit Organizations, 10*(1), 51–60. Accessed from http://www.jstor.org/stable/27927634

Lecka, I., Gudowski, J., & Wołowiec, T. (2022). CSR in Poland and the implementation of sustainable development goals in the energy Sector during the COVID-19 pandemic. *Energies, 15*(19), 1–25. https://doi.org/10.3390/en15197057

Lu, J., Ren, L., Lin, W., He, Y., & Streimikis, J. (2019). Policies to promote corporate social responsibility (CSR) and assessment of CSR impacts. *E a M: Ekonomie a Management, 22*(1), 82–98. https://doi.org/10.15240/tul/001/2019-1-006

Macuda, M., Matuszak, Ł., & Różańska, E. (2015). The concept of CSR in accounting theory and practice in Poland: An empirical study. *Zeszyty Teoretyczne Rachunkowości, 84*(140), 115–137. https://doi.org/10.5604/16414381.1173808

Maon, F., Swaen, V., & Lindgreen, A. (2017). One vision, different paths: An investigation of corporate social responsibility initiatives in Europe. *Journal of Business Ethics, 143*(2), 405–422. https://doi.org/10.1007/s10551-015-2810-2

Markova, O. V. (2021). Development of corporate social responsibility in Russia in the post-pandemic period. In *Актуальные тренды в экономике и финансах [Current trends in economics and finance]* (pp. 75–77). Moscow International University.

Nekhoda, Y., Grishina, K., Ziganshina, Y., Golovanov, A., Redchikova, N., & Rakovskaya, V. (2015). *Corporate social responsibility: Theory and practice*. Tomsk State University. Accessed from https://core.ac.uk/download/pdf/287487615.pdf

Rogerson, M. (2023). Business and human rights in Russia: Emerging or merging? *Business and Human Rights Journal, 2023*, 1–26. https://doi.org/10.1017/bhj.2022.29

Rudneva, L. E. (2022). Formation of a comprehensive model of corporate social responsibility. In *Materials of scientific conferences*.

Rutkowska, M., & Pakulska, J. (2021). The corporate social responsibility (CSR) as the modern trend in management and sustainable economy. *European Research Studies Journal, XXIV*(2), 346–357. https://doi.org/10.35808/ersj/2130

Sheehy, B. (2015). Defining CSR: Problems and solutions. *Journal of Business Ethics, 131*(3), 625–648. Accessed from https://papers.ssrn.com/sol3/papers.cfm?abstract_id=2156655

Shumilina, A. A., & Ostapenko, A. V. (2022). Корпоративная социальная ответственность: особенности развития в России и за рубежом [Corporate social responsibility: Peculiarities of development in Russia and abroad]. In *Collection of scientific articles for VIII Russian National Scientific Conference "current management problems"*, pp. 156–158.

Tashman, P., Marano, V., & Kostova, T. (2019). Walking the walk or talking the talk? Corporate social responsibility decoupling in emerging market multinationals. *Journal of International Business Studies, 50*(2), 153–171. https://doi.org/10.1057/s41267-018-0171-7

Tikhomirov, A. S. (2022). Modern trends of corporate social responsibility on the example of Russian and foreign companies. *Interactive Science, 1*(66), 43–45. https://doi.org/10.21661/r-555864

Wang, H., Tong, L., Takeuchi, R., & George, G. (2016). Corporate social responsibility: An overview and new research directions. *The Academy of Management Journal, 59*, 534–544. https://doi.org/10.5465/amj.2016.5001

Wołczek, P. (2015). Development of the CSR concept in Poland – Progress or stagnation? *Prace Naukowe Uniwersytetu Ekonomicznego We Wrocławiu*. https://doi.org/10.15611/pn.2015.387.17

Turkey's Ecotourism: Pre- and Post-pandemic Challenges

Adnan ul Haque, Riffat Faizan, and Fred A. Yamoah

1 Introduction

This exploratory study aims to understand the ecotourism situation and interlinked activities in Turkey. Furthermore, the challenges related to ecotourism in Turkey are the prime focus of this study. From the review of the extensive literature at hand, it is evident that the term ecotourism was mentioned by Kenton Miller in 1978 (Rahemtulla & Wellstead, 2001). The initial definition was nature-based travel to comparatively undisturbed areas with an emphasis on education. However, over time, the concept has emerged as scientific-based approach to managing, planning, and developing sustainable tourism products and activities

A. ul Haque (✉) • R. Faizan
Faculty of Business, Yorkville University, Toronto, ON, Canada
e-mail: ahaque@yorkvilleu.ca

F. A. Yamoah
Department of Management, School of Business, Economics and Informatics, Birkbeck, University of London, London, UK

F. A. Yamoah, A. ul Haque (eds.), *Corporate Management Ecosystem in Emerging Economies*, https://doi.org/10.1007/978-3-031-41578-4_17

(Kahveci et al., 2003; Salici, 2018). In broader context, ecotourism's objectives are founded on the notion of ecotourism with an aim of utilizing cultural and natural resources in a sustainable manner that contributes to the economic development of local region, local economy, and local people. Moreover, it enhances social cohesion and environmental awareness conserving cultural and natural heritages along with decreasing undesirable effects originating from prevailing tourism practices. Several researchers defined ecotourism as a sustainable type of tourism resulting from experiencing and learning about nature and ethical aspects and focusing on local resources and their preservation (Goodwin, 1996; Blamey, 2001; Fennell & Weaver, 2005).

The reason behind the selection of Turkey as a case study is because it is an emerging economy that has recently experienced a natural calamity. Pre-pandemic, 3.8% was the total contribution of the tourism industry to the GDP of Turkey (Dierks, 2022); however, the industry suffered a great deal like other industries around the globe. As evident in Fig. 1, post-pandemic Turkey's economy was in a recovery mood when the

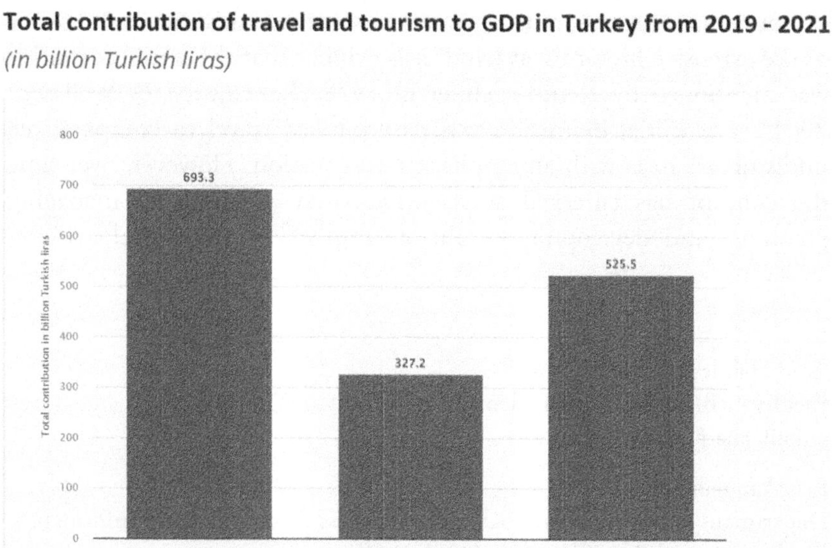

Fig. 1 Pre- and post-pandemic contribution of travel and tourism to GDP. Source: Contribution of travel and tourism of Turkey to GDP, 2019–2021 (Dierks, 2022)

recent earthquake struck Turkey. Thus, this informative research attempts to understand the challenges for Turkey's ecotourism in the face of different types of crises.

In contrast to other countries globally, Turkey has rich natural assets such as forests, highlands, fascinating geographical landscape with caves and canyons, lakes, mountains, 8000 km long coasts, and 9000 species of flora, fauna, and birds (Rahemtulla & Wellstead, 2001). A naturally wealthy place, Turkey is in a relatively attractive position as the ecotourism capital (Erdoğan, 2015). In 1980, to pursue the neo-liberal strategies of the economics of globalization, Turkey opted to adopt ecotourism as an additional economic growth strategy (Kahveci et al., 2003). Tourism Encouragement Law in 1982 provided numerous upgrades and support to tourism-related institutions (Kahveci et al., 2003). A comprehensive incentive system was announced and extended later (Flyista, 2022). Turkey's government has played a vigorous role in tourism development by means of monetary and fiscal instruments. The nature and scope of planning, promotion, and policymaking in ecotourism are decided by the central government.

Ecotourism is highly attractive for local as well as national government in Turkey. Firstly, it delivers government with an incentive to develop protected areas, whereas for private owners, an opportunity to conserve their lands. Subsequently, for rural communities, ecotourism is an attractive concept as it presents employment opportunities for locals along with tending to operate in marginal regions. Third, its importance to local ownership suggests fewer leakages from the economy. Fourth, it requires minimal investment and development and less cultural and environmental interruptions. Fifth, ecotourism can encourage advantageous associations within various, cohesive economy. And finally, eco-tourists incline to stay longer, employ more per day than the typical tourist, and seek out local goods and services (Rahemtulla & Wellstead, 2001). Unambiguously, successful ecotourism developments must efficiently promote the protection of the entire local ecosystem, not just specific species, sites; be economically feasible to appeal to financing and be sustainable; be well financed, managed, and planned as well as marketed in order to meet the severe recreational and environmental demands of a true ecotourism development (Kahveci et al., 2003).

2 Literature Review

In this study, term sustainability is used as a concept to enable decision-makers in tourism to assess and evaluate the consequences of their actions on local communities, culture, and most importantly nature (Kahveci et al., 2003; Salici, 2018). The impact of ecotourism on a region's values, social structure, and economic opportunities is vital to comprehend for sustainable development (Salici, 2018). There is no usage of the term sustainable development as synonymous of sustainable tourism or alternate. As per McCool (1995), to accept the concept of sustainability in ecotourism for the purpose of tourism and environment, it should consider four key challenges:

- A better understanding of how tourists value and use natural environments;
- Identification of the social and environmental impact of tourism;
- Enhancement of the communities dependent on tourism as an industry; and
- Implementation of systems to manage these impacts.

In general, the ecotourism is not only facing challenges in Turkey. In fact, different authors have reported distinct challenges for different countries. For instance, as per Ijeomah and Okoli (2016), Nigeria's fundamental challenges consist of inadequate facilities, poor infrastructure and financing, and seasonal inaccessibility. On the other hand, Fernando and Shariff (2017) found that Sri Lanka's key challenges in ecotourism are poor management, lack of financial and human resources, and absence of basic infrastructure. According to Okech (2011), Kenya experiences challenges in its ecotourism due to insufficient staff, absence of partnership programs, security problems, and lack of appropriate management plans and guidelines. Furthermore, a lack of national strategies and regulatory frameworks and inappropriate use of ecosystems by the inhabitants pose challenges to Ethiopia's ecotourism (Teressa, 2015). Similarly, different challenges related to ecotourism development are evident in Turkey including the absence of responsible organizations, lack of an operating plan, and lack of adequate services along with qualified staff (Cetinkaya, 2004). However, the literature is outdated because there has been significant growth and development in travel and tourism in Turkey. Yet, the recent natural calamity and pandemic impact are not traced in the literature at hand.

In Turkey, there is an evident absence of the meaningful ecotourism establishments and eloquent critical or humane assessment of policies, services, and related industries (Salici, 2018). Moreover, there is no significant data from past researchers or academics, decision-makers, or planners on the ecotourism development. Though there is a makeshift portal of ecotourism, it plays the role of conserving local culture and heritage, helping local community, understanding social, historical, and cultural values, providing knowledge, information, and education, and building understanding, awareness, appreciation, and respect for local culture. As per Datta and Banerji (2015), responsible practices and some corrective measures are necessary to overcome unwanted outcomes of ecotourism activities. This research does acknowledge that there is still an absence of attainment of desirable outcomes from the ecotourism enhancing equal financial gains to all areas of the local communities and there is an evident lack of proper and efficient long-term planning which is essential for sustainable ecotourism in Turkey. A plethora of research has used alternate theoretical and methodological approaches, leading to the questioning of the assumptions and practices related to ecotourism's nature and benefits (Erdogan & Erdogan, 2016; Duffy, 2002; Cater, 2006; Burns & Novelli, 2008; Bianchi, 2009; Fletcher, 2011). This has further led to the insight of ecotourism industry contributing to the economic standby and obliteration of historical economic development of local areas, contributing to unemployment, under-paid work force, and seasonal employment, and therefore contributing to local poverty in contrast to wealth generation.

Failure of proper ecotourism policies and planning such as revenue leakages, inequitable distribution of income, significant loss of land on larger scale, prostitution, homelessness., violence, destruction of local culture, gradual or fast loss of historical livelihood, incline in hopelessness morbidity, alienation, and more importantly damages to flora and fauna (Cetinkaya, 2004; Salici, 2018). Conventional solutions to environmental problems are entirely diverse than solutions provided by alternative approaches. Essentially, some deal with issues as mechanical solutions to an outcome of ecotourism practices and processes. However, the need for substantial changes or revisions in the industrial structures and practices that cause social, economic, cultural, and environmental problems is still to be explored and employed (Cetinkaya, 2004).

3 Research Methodology

This exploratory research employed qualitative analysis of the extensive literature to identify the involvement of ecotourism in sustainable development. Moreover, ecotourism opportunity spectrum (ECOS) methodology comprised of three stages was used in this study. The initial stage was to evaluate the areas that can assist as ecotourism focuses through research papers. In the second stage, ECOS method has been applied to the identified ecotourism focus through paper and field information analysis. To determine the level of suitability for identifying an ecotourism impact, ecotourism opportunity spectrum value was used. Action plan report and maps obtained from the local administrations related with the study area have been accepted as ecotourism focuses.

4 Findings and Discussions

The term ecotourism denotes closely interacting and interrelated specialized activities of business initiatives. The ecotourism sector's structure is complicated since it consists of various interrelated fragments that incorporate nearly every economic, industrial, political, administrative, and cultural structure. Though predominantly, it includes travel agencies, tour operators, tour guides, local, national, and international transportation, and accommodation, catering and recreation services with varying power and size.

In Turkey, the local tourism enterprises are mostly hindered as there is an evident reflection of two main organizational trends within the tourism accommodations, various small firms with horizontal and vertical integration. In vertical integration, the multinational firms have individual extensions and branch offices along with their parent companies at all significant Turkish destinations. Thus, it reflects that the foremost development in Turkish tourism has been the internationalization of firms and their operations in the key European generating markets. Moreover, to capture the European market, e-Turkish-owned tour operators have their own private airline investments, such as Öger Tour with Atlas Jet, Bentour with MNG Airlines, and GTI Tours with Sky Airlines (Turkish Financial Times – Turkish Lira, 2022). In Turkey, it is tough to differentiate the tour operators and travel agencies due to the travel agencies operating as tour operators and visa service providers. Interestingly, they offer guided itineraries for various destinations, including ground transportation, air tickets, hotels, and other services. Moreover, they promote themselves as one-stop shop for all the tourist needs by providing sim card services, flight tickets, transfers (from airport to hotel), comprehensive holiday trip organizations, daily environment tours, outdoor activities, special flights, and tours, customize tours or package tours, insurance, car rental, and visa attainment. As per Erdoğan (2009), though their claims to deliver every service don't mean they essentially provide these services, they limit services in terms of variability in ecotourism.

In Turkey, ecotourism development has given rise to the expectation that local services and handicrafts of region will be recognized globally. However, these success stories in Turkey are partially due to the stories of ecotourism investors and service providers. There is no evidence to collaborate that in Turkey, locals are included or provided access to the resources to generate their own wealth. Moreover, there is an evident absence of affirmation that locals are given inclusion to participate in the decision-making or planning process of Turkey's ecotourism but, most importantly, to be given the rein to access resources for sustainable ecotourism and generate their own wealth. Ecotourism generates momentous opportunities for the protection, conservation, and sustainable usage of natural areas and biodiversity through local empowerment. There is an evident need for education to foster and empower the local community to respect its natural heritage and respect for culture.

There is a lack of critical and humane assessment of ecotourism policies and practices in Turkey. It is important for academics, planners, and decision-makers to engage in open and honest discussions about the benefits and potential negative impacts of ecotourism, as well as the ways in which it can be implemented in a way that benefits both the environment and the local community. While ecotourism can certainly play a role in preserving local heritage and culture, it is important to recognize that it is not a one-size-fits-all solution. Different regions have different ecological, cultural, and social contexts that must be considered when developing ecotourism policies and practices.

Systematic review also revealed that it is important to move beyond superficial portrayals of ecotourism as a panacea for preserving local heritage and culture, and to engage in meaningful discussions and assessments of its potential benefits and drawbacks for both the environment and the local community. Though Turkey has put in place a regulatory framework for protecting sensitive areas and promoting sustainable tourism development, the state and state institutions play a crucial role in developing and implementing policies and regulations that support ecotourism, as well as in enforcing those regulations to ensure compliance. It is also important for Turkey to continue to align its tourism policies with international environmental policy initiatives and standards, such as those set forth by the EU. This can help to ensure that Turkey's tourism industry is sustainable and responsible, and that it meets the expectations of international tourists who are increasingly interested in environmentally and socially responsible tourism. In Turkey, the linkage between ecotourism and sustainable development, especially for small businesses aiming for sustainability, has potential. However, those business ventures lack a rational and systematic approach to develop sustainable local communities. There are some individual efforts, but they lack the support from the local government and administration. Unfortunately, the independent associations with overstated benefits are impractical in Turkey (Agrawal & Redford, 2006; Coria & Calfucura, 2012; Das & Chatterjee, 2015; Carter et al., 2015).

5 Conclusion and Recommendations

Despite the region or country, it is vital to have an in-depth understanding of ecotourism issues as ecotourism venture does not inevitably imply conservation or development. In Turkey, there is indeed a need to comprehend that delinking is required for conservation by not only local people but also tourism industry and allied investors through effective use of natural resources. Moreover, there should be a clear understanding that ecotourism does provide economic incentives for locals and contribute to national development and conservation of natural areas if the generated revenues are large enough and accessible to the local populations (Fennell, 2008). In addition, ecotourism in Turkey should not be viewed a sole source of development of local communities, it should be viewed as a part of process that provides real, long-term, and sustainable development for the entire community outside of few local investors. To ensure that the benefits of ecotourism are distributed more equitably, it is important to involve the local community in the planning and decision-making process from the outset. This can include providing training and support for local entrepreneurs to start their own businesses, promoting sustainable practices that support the local economy and environment, and ensuring that the local community has a say in how tourism development takes place in their area. Ultimately, the success of ecotourism should be measured not only by its ability to generate revenue but also by its ability to support the local economy and culture, while protecting the natural environment for future generations.

The association between ecotourism and sustainable development, particularly for the business venture's sustainability, might be possible; however, it lacks rationality in terms of sustaining local communities. Unfortunately, such an interdependent association with extremely overstated benefits to local communities is impractical in practice in Turkey (e.g., Agrawal & Redford, 2006, Coria & Calfucura, 2012, Das & Chatterjee, 2015, Carter et al., 2015). In Turkey, the ecotourism's potential to expand local livelihood potentials is obliterated due to the greatly irregular distribution of power relations, power itself and therefore causing unbalance distribution of economic benefits. In addition, in Turkey, there is a lack of empirical evidence invalidating the criticism that ecotourism contributes to success only in terms of generating income for tourism institutions and connected industries. However, it spells failure in terms of meeting the promises made to local communities, due to the very nature of the organization and practice of ecotourism and related structures.

Turkey has various opportunities to effectively utilize ecotourism activities to its advantage. The use of natural resources should be in accordance with the principle of sustainability with proper education being provided to the locals. Turkey's rich forests have a vast variety of flora and fauna species. There is an evident need for conserving biodiversity of forest ecosystems along with the genetic diversity of native species which should play dynamic economic and environmental roles. Turkey's population structure has been altering, leading to an incline in urban population; this trend is not unique to Turkey, as it is also happening in many other countries around the world. Urbanization can have both positive and negative impacts on the environment and sustainable tourism development. On the one hand, urbanization can lead to increased economic opportunities and improved infrastructure, which can support the development of sustainable tourism. On the other hand, urbanization can also lead to environmental degradation and loss of natural habitats, as well as increased pollution and traffic congestion. To address these challenges, it is important to adopt a holistic and integrated approach to sustainable tourism development, which takes into account the social, economic, and environmental impacts of tourism on both urban and rural areas. This can involve strategies such as promoting sustainable transportation options, protecting natural habitats and cultural heritage sites, and involving local communities in decision-making processes related to tourism development.

Turkey could effectively use ecotourism activities such as home-boarding businesses which can be attained through restoration of village houses. The idea of promoting home-boarding businesses in restored village houses is a promising one for promoting ecotourism in Turkey. This type of accommodation can provide a unique and authentic experience for tourists, allowing them to immerse themselves in the local culture and way of life. It can also help to support the local economy by providing income and employment opportunities for residents of rural areas. At the same time, this will allow for encouraging greater number of tourists to be enchanted and drawn by the beauty of the natural environment and rural life.

However, it is important to ensure that the restoration of village houses is done in a sustainable and responsible manner, considering the environmental and cultural impacts of such activities. This can involve using local and traditional building materials and techniques, as well as incorporating sustainable design features such as solar panels and rainwater harvesting systems. Effective marketing and promotion of handicrafts to tourists will make it conceivable to attract a greater number of tourists. In addition, the utilization of urban tourists through offering of various sporting activities will open doors for sustainable utilization of the natural environment and enhance the living standards of locals.

References

Agrawal, A., & Redford, K. (2006). *Poverty, development, and biodiversity conservation: Shooting in the dark?* Working paper no 26, Wildlife Conservation Society.

Bianchi, R. V. (2009). The 'critical turn' in tourism studies: A radical critique. *Tourism Geographies, 11*(4), 484–504.

Blamey, R. K. (2001). Principles of ecotourism. In D. Weaver (Ed.), *Encyclopedia of ecotourism* (pp. 5–22). CAB International.

Burns, P., & Novelli, M. (Eds.). (2008). *Tourism development: Growth, myths, and inequalities*. CABI.

Carter, A. H., William, H. D., Driscoll, L., & Honey, M. (2015). Can ecotourism deliver real economic, social, and environmental benefits? A study of the Osa peninsula Costa Rica. *Journal of Sustainable Tourism, 23*(3), 339–357.

Cater, E. (2006). Ecotourism as a western construct. *Journal of Ecotourism, l5*(1–2), 23–39.

Cetinkaya, G. (2004). Challenges for ecotourism development in Çukurova delta Biosphere Reserve, Turkey. *Budownictwo, 16*, 89–96.

Coria, J., & Calfucura, E. (2012). Ecotourism and the development of indigenous communities: The good, the bad, and the ugly. *Ecological Economics, 73*(15), 47–55.

Das, M., & Chatterjee, B. (2015). Ecotourism: A panacea or a predicament? *Tourism Management Perspectives, 14*, 3–16.

Datta, D., & Banerji, S. (2015). In D. Szymańska & K. Rogatka (Eds.), *Bulletin of geography. Socio-economic series, No. 27 Local tourism initiative in an eastern Himalayan village: Sustainable ecotourism or small-scale nature exploitation?* (pp. 33–49). Nicolaus Copernicus University.

Dierks, Z. (2022). *Topic: Travel and tourism in Turkey. Statista*. Accessed April 15, 2023, from https://www.statista.com/topics/9676/travel-and-tourism-in-turkey/

Duffy, R. (2002). *A trip too far: Ecotourism, politics and exploitation*. Earthscan.

Erdoğan, N. (2009). Turkey's tourism policy and environmental performance of tourism enterprises and sustainable development. In L. David (Ed.), *International perspectives on responses to the sustainability agenda* (pp. 194–208). Routledge.

Erdoğan, N. (2015). *Ecotourism: Conceptual and critical approaches* (Vol. IV, pp. 15–29). Centre for Policy and Research on Turkey (Research Turkey).

Erdogan, N., & Erdogan, I. (2016). An alternative view of ecotourism with a specific reference to Turkey. In I. Egresi (Ed.), *Alternative tourism in Turkey: Role, potential development and sustainability*. Springer.

Fennell, D. (2008), Ecotourism, 3rd Edition, Routledge, London.

Fennell, D., & Weaver, D. (2005). The ecotourism concept and tourism-conservation symbiosis. *Journal of Sustainable Tourism, 13*(4), 373–390.

Fernando, S. L. J., & Shariff, N. M. (2017). Wetland ecotourism in Sri Lanka: Issues and challenges. *Geografia-Malaysian Journal of Society and Space, 9*(4), 99–105.

Fletcher, R. (2011). Sustaining tourism, sustaining capitalism? The tourism industry's role in global capitalist expansion. *Tourism Geographies, 13*(3), 443–461.

Flyista. (2022). *Ecotourism routes in Turkey*. Accessed from https://flyista.com/en/blog/ecotourism-routes-turkey

Goodwin, H. (1996). In pursuit of ecotourism. *Biodiversity and Conservation, 5*(3), 277–291.

Ijeomah, H. M., & Okoli, C. I. C. (2016). Challenges of ecotourism in selected destinations of Nigeria. *International Journal of Agriculture and Rural Development, 19*(2), 2655–2668.

Kahveci, G., Ok, K., & Yilmaz, E. (2003). *Ecotourism and sustainable development of forest and forest villagers in Turkey*. Conference Paper.

Mccool, F. S. (1995). *Linking tourism, the environment, and concepts of sustainability: Setting the stage.* USDA Forest Service General Technical Report INT-GTR-323.

Okech, R. N. (2011). Promoting sustainable festival events tourism: A case study of Lamu Kenya. *Worldwide Hospitality and Tourism Themes, 3*(3), 193–202.

Rahemtulla, Y. G. & Wellstead, A. M. (2001). *Ecotourism: Understanding expert and academic definitions.* Northern Forestry Centre Information Report NOT-X-380 Canada.

Salici, A. (2018). Application of ecotourism opportunities Spectrum method in ecotourism resources: A case study of Samandağ coastal areas in Southern Turkey. *Applied Ecology and Environmental Research, 16*(3), 2701–2715.

Teressa, D. K. (2015). Development of community-based ecotourism in Wenchi crater Lake, Ethiopia: Challenges and prospects. *Journal of Hospitality Management and Tourism, 6*(4), 39–46. https://doi.org/10.5897/JHMT2014.0133

Turkish Financial Times – Turkish Lira. (2022). *Teaching cases award: A world of eco-dilemmas.* Accessed from https://www.ft.com/content/d0e069bc-5b06-4003-9f86-5ca286615936

Investigating the Demand of Asian Countries on Malaysian Public Universities: An Application of Panel Generalised Methods of Moments (GMM) Estimation

Fadli Fizari Abu Hassan Asari, Suriyani Muhamad, Mahyudin Ahmad, Jumadil Saputra, and Salwani Affandi

1 Introduction

The World Bank and the Organisation for Economic Co-operation and Development (OECD) apply the same description for cross-border higher education, where "it refers to the movement of people, programmes, providers, curricula, projects, research and services in tertiary

F. F. A. H. Asari • M. Ahmad
Faculty of Business and Management, Universiti Teknologi MARA Perlis Branch, Perlis, Malaysia

S. Muhamad • J. Saputra (✉)
Faculty of Business, Economics and Social Development, Universiti Malaysia Terengganu, Kuala Terengganu, Malaysia
e-mail: jumadil.saputra@umt.edu.my

F. A. Yamoah, A. ul Haque (eds.), *Corporate Management Ecosystem in Emerging Economies*, https://doi.org/10.1007/978-3-031-41578-4_18

(or higher) education across national jurisdictional borders" (Vincent-Lancrin, 2007). The General Agreement on Trade in Services (GATS), signed in 1994 by 128 member countries and enacted in 1995, is a catalyser for the higher education industry (Munadi, 2020; Putra et al., 2021). According to the guideline issued by UNESCO known as "Trade in Higher Education and GATS Basics", the higher education industry is a component of the education sector that can be liberalised in four ways, either individually or collectively.

At the beginning of the agreement, the education industry was the least liberalised compared to tourism. However, the situation changed. More and more countries are opening their higher education to global students following the increase in demand for trans-border education. Besides, higher education, which is a part of quality education, is among the 17 sustainable development goals outlined by the United Nations to transform the world for betterment in 2030 on the principle of "leaving no one behind" (United Nations, 2020). Therefore, more tertiary seats for quality and affordable higher education, though cross-border, need to be offered. The same thing happened to Malaysia, when this country, which became a tertiary education consumer country, is now becoming a country that provides higher education to tertiary students worldwide.

However, most studies on demand for Malaysian higher education are limited to a micro perspective and primarily focus on the background, course, and surroundings of a particular student, including Sidin et al. (2003), Dora et al. (2009), Fernandez (2010), Padlee et al. (2010), Baharun et al. (2011), Wai et al. (2012), Migin et al. (2015), Munisamy et al. (2014), Jaafar (2016), Yusuf et al. (2017), Foo et al. (2019), and Daud et al. (2019). All these studies are also primary-based research and are limited to specific samples, institutions, and areas. In other words, too little attention is given to the macro perspective. This perspective is another essential component in analysing the higher education demand. As highlighted by Chen and Barnett (2000) and Zheng (2014), failure to

---

S. Affandi
Faculty of Business and Management, Universiti Teknologi MARA Terengganu Branch, Terengganu, Malaysia

examine the macro perspective, may lead to an imbalanced analysis and limit the scope of studies. Thus, macro factors at the national level need to be addressed in explaining the demand for these educational services.

On the other hand, although Malaysia welcomes thousands of international enrolments, public universities become the second choice after the private institutions, with only 40% of the total enrolments (MoHE, 2021). It is crucial, considering that these 20 public universities are highly capable in various fields. As detailed in Sheriff and Abdullah (2017), 5 are known as research universities, 11 are considered comprehensive universities, and 4 are listed as specialised technical universities. In unison, all these universities increasingly need to be financially independent by generating around 30% of their own sources of income by 2025 ("Menteri: Jana pendapatan sendiri (Minister: Generate your own income)", 2016). For that reason, welcoming more international students is among the major choices in funding public universities, as these students pay more fees than local students, as implemented in the United States and the United Kingdom (Mitropoulos, 2020).

In addressing the gaps, the macro perspective has been chosen. Besides, the international demand for higher education in public universities by Asian students is the primary focus of this study. Thus, this study is made to cater to one specific objective: to analyse the impacts of macro factors in determining the enrolments of Asian tertiary students in Malaysian public universities.

2 Literature Review

In Psacharopoulos and Patrinos (2018), the rate of return theory is most widely used by economists in determining the demand for education. One of the earliest examples is a study by Campbell and Siegel (1967). It highlights that people will bear the cost of education if the expected rate of return (benefit) is more than the interest rate (cost). The maximum benefit will then be obtained when the marginal benefit equals the marginal cost. In other words, humans are not just a kind of production input but also one of the capitals that must be enriched from time to time (Drylie, 2021). In Blanchard and Olney (2017), human capital ranks high in income accumulation and growth determination. This can only be supported through minimal education at the tertiary level, as secondary education is no longer sufficient in producing competent human capital, especially in the knowledge-based era (Faggian et al., 2019).

The gravity model is rooted in Newton's law of universal gravitation before it is widely used in the field of international trade (Maciejewski & Wach, 2019). It aims to explain the trade flows (F_{ij}) between the two countries. In detail, international trade flows are directly influenced by both countries' economic size (exporters and importers), while distance has the opposite impact on those international trade flows (Tinbergen, 1962). In demand for higher education, Kelley (1921) is possibly the initial study that applied the gravity concept, as emphasised in Schofer (1975). The paper concludes that shorter distance gravitates enrolments in most American colleges. In Didisse et al. (2019), the pushing factors in the origin country and the pulling factors in the destination country are equally important in increasing tertiary students' enrolment in Europe.

Panel data can be defined as repeated cross-sectional studies throughout time, also known as cross-sectional time-series or longitudinal data (Frees, 2004). Andreß (2017) explains that the use of panel data has started since the early 1940s, especially in areas involving public opinion. He argues that the data panel is cost-effective and efficient in terms of data collection, making it easier for researchers to observe changes in patterns over time. Meanwhile, Hsiao (2007) highlights three key benefits of using data in panels. Firstly, higher efficiency in econometric estimations; secondly, greater ability to analyse complex human behaviour; and finally, easier computational and statistical analysis. These three conclusions are made based on using data panels instead of cross-sectional and time-series alone.

Tertiary student enrolments have been used in most studies on demand for higher education, including Campbell and Siegel (1967). The findings reveal that income relates positively to enrolment, while price works negatively on local enrolment. Both variables successfully explain 87% of the variation. This major study is inspired by Schultz (1961) and Becker (1964), which both emphasise on the theory of human capital investment. On the opposite view, international students are part of the proposal to manage a decrease in local demand. The study concludes that cost discourages students from studying in the United States, while per capita income and financial aid impact the right way (Agarwal, 1983). At the same time, this is the earliest study of cross-border higher education demand. In Paulino and Castaño (2019), all micro and macro factors contributing to international enrolment must be given equal attention. In another conclusion, students from developing countries prioritise economic factors in pursuing studies in developed countries compared to their counterparts.

Income and price are the essential explanatory variables applied by Campbell and Siegel (1967). Income represents a student's ability to 'purchase' a type of higher education, while the price is the burden that must be 'borne' by every student when pursuing studies. The same concept is suggested in this study. Two types of variables have been proposed for representing income: the wage and the per capita income. Meanwhile, two proxies have been suggested for the cost, the consumer price index, and the exchange rate, representing the price/cost of demand in the higher education industry. The third aspect in this study is represented by a sole independent variable, distance, as the variable is a fundamental element in the gravity model.

Generally, micro-studies focus on the individual selection of a tertiary institution. Thus, the proxy selection of income is also dependent on an individual source of income. Earlier, family or household income was used, as most tertiary students are full-time students, unemployed, and funded by their family (Hoenack, 1967; Hight, 1975). For Chao et al. (2019), among the reasons, China monopolises the trans-border education, likely from the one-family one-child policy. The policy makes all expenses from family income, centred only on this child, including tertiary education expenses. In contrast, the wage is described as an opportunity cost for studying at tertiary institutions. In Schanzenbach et al. (2017), there is a difference in opportunity cost for those working and those not working. In detail, the opportunity cost may be higher for those who work, as they already have high skills and fixed income.

Naidoo (2007) proposes economics as one of the key reasons for attracting international students to the United Kingdom's tertiary institutions. Origin country's per capita income has been chosen as a proxy for economic reasons. The model is further expanded in Chadee and

Naidoo (2009). In their conclusion, an increase in the origin country's per capita income boosts international students' number to the United Kingdom, especially for Asian students. For Kritz (2015), all four models recorded a positive relationship between the per capita income variable and African students' enrolment abroad. In Arif et al. (2019), not only financial capability, even access to financial resources, especially on money remittance, should be simplified so that financial issues throughout the study period can be resolved immediately.

The price, further described as the cost of continuing studies, is the second variable implied in the model by Campbell and Siegel (1967). However, it was limited only to the tuition fee. Along the way, this variable has been developed by including relevant costs such as living, transportation, and learning equipment costs. Hsing and Chang (1996) highlight the use of CPI in obtaining real economic values. Real wage enters the model, along with the real per capita income and tuition rate. As a result, income is directly proportional to student enrolment, while tuition and wage rates negatively affect enrolment. In Khan et al. (2018), the two countries' CPI (destination and origin) are explored together. As high CPI in the origin country is a pushing factor for international students' mobility, low CPI in the destination country is a pulling factor in attracting trans-border students.

Since higher education is also part of international trade commodity, albeit in the form of services, the exchange rate has been chosen as a proxy for economic reasons (Naidoo, 2007). The same view is also shared by Hearps (2016). Although the United Kingdom and the United States are preferred destinations for pursuing tertiary education, the high currency values of both countries have forced most students, especially from Africa and Southeast Asia, to switch to other major English-speaking destination countries (MESDC) such as Australia, Canada, and New Zealand. A substantial difference between the US Dollar and the home currency also forces trans-border students to shift their destination country from the United States to other European countries (Holden, 2017). Plus, those who come from a country with a weak currency, must do side jobs to accommodate the host country's high currency rate.

Distance is described as a bilateral trade barrier between two entities in the gravity model (Wiseman & Walker, 2017). It can be categorised in numerous ways, such as the physical mileage (airway, railway, roadway, and waterway) or the fuel quantity utilised by a vehicle, as detailed out in Isard (1960). In higher education, Kelley (1921) first uses distance as the basis of demand. It is concluded that half of the demand for colleges in the United States is made by those who reside within a 50-mile radius. In the context of trans-border education, distance is a crucial element that needs to be included (Kaushal & Lanati, 2019; Hou & Du, 2020; Yousaf et al., 2020). For Türk (2019), distance also reflects a student's sacrifice to be away from their families, as well as an indirect cost borne by the student throughout the study period. Nevertheless, distance can be treated by various methods, including the development of the offshore campus (Bennell, 2019).

The international demand for higher education in Malaysian public universities among Asian tertiary students is the primary focus of the study. Three different aspects were selected to evaluate the demand. The first two aspects were income and cost. The income that explains a student's financial ability to pursue higher education in a foreign country is represented by per capita income and wages. Meanwhile, the cost which is a burden on the study abroad is explained through the consumer price index and exchange rate. Both aspects—income and cost—are fundamental to higher education demand (Campbell & Siegel, 1967). Distance between the home and the host countries is the third aspect. It is a crucial property in the gravity model (Tinbergen, 1962) that also forms the basis for this framework. The Rate of Return Theory too supports the selection of all these variables. Specifically, one will continue to study anywhere, even abroad, if the expected rate of return is more than the interest rate.

The theoretical relationship between these five independent variables and a dependent variable is portrayed in Fig. 1. The figure's left side represents the independent variables, per capita income, wage, consumer price index, exchange rate, and distance. In contrast, the enrolment of Asian tertiary students in Malaysian public universities, which is the dependent variable in this study, is on the figure's right side. There are also five arrows pointing from each independent variable to the dependent variable, representing the variables' causal relationship.

For the hypotheses, the *Income* variables ($GNIpc_{AM}$ and $Wage_{AM}$) are expected to affect enrolment positively since higher per capita income

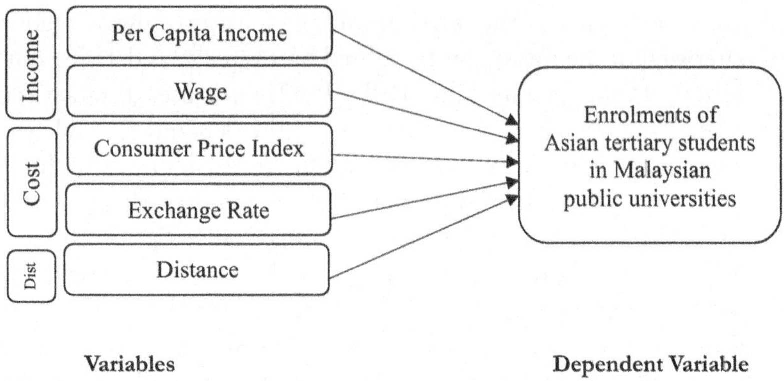

Fig. 1 Theoretical framework

and better wage level in sending countries would show high affordability to send more students abroad (in this study, to Malaysia). Thus, the priori sign of *Income* variables is positive. Secondly, the *Cost* variables, CPI_{AM} and ER_{AM}, are also expected to correlate to enrolment positively. Lower costs in the host country (Malaysia) would be a pull factor in enrolling more Asian students in Malaysian public universities. Simultaneously, the weaker currency in the host country might reduce the financial burden during the study period compared to the home country. Thus, the a priori sign of the *Cost* variable is positive. On the other hand, the negative priori sign is expected for the $Dist_{AM}$ variable. The *Distance* aspect is expected to influence enrolment negatively, as higher distance contributes directly to greater air transportation costs, which will distract enrolment.

3 Material and Methods

The population of the study is 49 out of 50 Asian countries in five different sub-continents: Central Asia, Eastern Asia, South-Eastern Asia, Southern Asia, and Western Asia. Malaysia as the host country was taken out earlier. The sample was then limited to the 44 sending countries that sent their tertiary students to Malaysian public universities from 2008 to 2016, as shown in Table 1. Meanwhile, five countries have been dropped

Table 1 List of the Asian sending countries (sample and sub-samples)

Region	Sending country	Total
Sample (Asia)	Kazakhstan, Kyrgyzstan, Tajikistan, Turkmenistan, Uzbekistan, China, China Hong Kong SAR (Hong Kong), DPR of Korea (North Korea), Japan, Mongolia, Republic of Korea (South Korea), Brunei Darussalam, Cambodia, Indonesia, Lao PDR (Laos), Myanmar, Philippines, Singapore, Thailand, Timor-Leste, Vietnam, Afghanistan, Bangladesh, Bhutan, India, Iran (IRI) (Iran), Maldives, Nepal, Pakistan, Sri Lanka, Azerbaijan, Bahrain, Iraq, Jordan, Kuwait, Lebanon, Oman, Qatar, Saudi Arabia, State of Palestine, Syrian Arab Republic, Turkey, United Arab Emirates, Yemen	44
Sub-sample 1 (Central Asia)	Kazakhstan, Kyrgyzstan, Tajikistan, Turkmenistan, Uzbekistan.	5
Sub-sample 2 (Eastern Asia)	China, China Hong Kong SAR (Hong Kong), DPR of Korea (North Korea), Japan, Mongolia, Republic of Korea (South Korea)	6
Sub-sample 3 (South-eastern Asia)	Brunei Darussalam, Cambodia, Indonesia, Lao PDR (Laos), Myanmar, Philippines, Singapore, Thailand, Timor-Leste, Vietnam	10
Sub-sample 4 (Southern Asia)	Afghanistan, Bangladesh, Bhutan, India, Iran (IRI) (Iran), Maldives, Nepal, Pakistan, Sri Lanka	9
Sub-sample 5 (Western Asia)	Azerbaijan, Bahrain, Iraq, Jordan, Kuwait, Lebanon, Oman, Qatar, Saudi Arabia, State of Palestine, Syrian Arab Republic, Turkey, United Arab Emirates, Yemen	14

Analysis made based on data released by the MoHE (2018)

from the list—China, Macao Special Administrative Region (SAR) or Macao, Armenia, Cyprus, Georgia, and Israel—since these countries have never sent their tertiary students to Malaysia during the same period.

The data set of international enrolments was provided by the Planning, Research & Policy Coordination Division, Ministry of Higher Education Malaysia (MoHE, 2018). Gross National Income (GNI) per capita was downloaded from the World Bank Open Data website.[1] In proxying wage, the wage and salaried workers, total (% of total employment) was

[1] URL: https://data.worldbank.org/indicator/NY.GNP.PCAP.CD

retrieved from the World Bank Open Data website.[2] The Consumer Price Index (CPI) data set was downloaded from the IMF Data—International Monetary Fund website.[3] The annual exchange rate data was obtained from fxtop.com.[4] The distance between Kuala Lumpur International Airport and the primary airport in the sending country was taken from Google Maps[5] and multiplied by the annual price of jet oil obtained from Index Mundi's website.[6] The value was then multiplied for the second time with the average value of usage per kilometre for each jumbo jet (Boeing 747-400) suggested on the flightdeckfriend[7] website.

Generalised Method of Moments (GMM) is strongly proposed due to the dynamic characteristics of the enrolment data, as it is a type of data directly influenced by its past values. It is also known as the pre-determined variable, one of the criteria for dynamic analysis (Lewis-Beck et al., 2003). In addition, most of the regressors used, including per capita income, wage, consumer price index, and exchange rate, are endogenous in type. At the same time, this study's sample (n) of 44 countries is much larger than the timeline (t) nine years. All these are detailed in Roodman (2009). The basic equation for the study is written in Eq. (1).

$$\text{Total}_{i,t} = f\left(\text{GNIpc}_{\text{AM}\,i,t}, \text{Wage}_{\text{AM}\,i,t}, \text{CPI}_{\text{AM}\,i,t}, \text{ER}_{\text{AM}\,i,t}, \text{Dist}_{\text{AM}\,i,t}\right) \tag{1}$$

This basic equation is then transformed into an econometric equation in Eq. (2) for empirical analysis purposes. In addition, the lagged dependent variable is added, as it is one of the properties in the dynamic panel data analysis.

$$\begin{aligned} \ln \text{Total}_{\text{All}\,i,t} = {} & \alpha + \beta_1\, \text{GNIpc}_{\text{AM}\,i,t} + \beta_2\, \text{Wage}_{\text{AM}\,i,t} + \beta_3\, \text{CPI}_{\text{AM}\,i,t} \\ & + \beta_4\, \text{ER}_{\text{AM}\,i,t} + \beta_5 \ln \text{Dist}_{\text{AM}\,i,t} + \beta_6 \ln \text{Total}_{\text{All}\,i,t-1} + u_{i,t} \end{aligned} \tag{2}$$

[2] URL: https://data.worldbank.org/indicator/SL.EMP.WORK.ZS

[3] URL: http://data.imf.org/regular.aspx?key=61015892

[4] URL: https://fxtop.com/en/historical-exchange-rates.php?MA=1

[5] URL: https://www.google.com.my/maps/

[6] URL: https://www.indexmundi.com/commodities/?commodity=jet-fuel

[7] URL: https://www.flightdeckfriend.com/ask-a-captain/how-much-fuel-does-a-jumbo-jet-burn/

The same model is subsequently divided into gender: *Male* and *Female*. Each model is also divided into three levels of study—*PhD*, *Master*, and *Degree*. The definition for each symbol is shown in Table 2.

Table 2 List of symbols and definitions

Symbol	Definition
$\ln Total_{Male}$	Enrolments of Asian students in Malaysian public universities at tertiary level (total male students) in natural logarithmic form
$\ln Total_{Female}$	Enrolments of Asian students in Malaysian public universities at tertiary level (total female students) in natural logarithmic form
$\ln Total_{All}$	Enrolments of Asian students in Malaysian public universities at tertiary level (total students) in natural logarithmic form
$\ln PhD_{Male}$	Enrolments of Asian students in Malaysian public universities at PhD level (total male students) in natural logarithmic form
$\ln PhD_{Female}$	Enrolments of Asian students in Malaysian public universities at PhD level (total female students) in natural logarithmic form
$\ln PhD_{All}$	Enrolments of Asian students in Malaysian public universities at PhD level (total students) in natural logarithmic form
$\ln Master_{Male}$	Enrolments of Asian students in Malaysian public universities at Master level (total male students) in natural logarithmic form
$\ln Master_{Female}$	Enrolments of Asian students in Malaysian public universities at Master level (total female students) in natural logarithmic form
$\ln Master_{All}$	Enrolments of Asian students in Malaysian public universities at Master level (total students) in natural logarithmic form
$\ln Degree_{Male}$	Enrolments of Asian students in Malaysian public universities at Degree level (total male students) in natural logarithmic form
$\ln Degree_{Female}$	Enrolments of Asian students in Malaysian public universities at Degree level (total female students) in natural logarithmic form
$\ln Degree_{All}$	Enrolments of Asian students in Malaysian public universities at Degree level (total students) in natural logarithmic form
$GNIpc_{AM}$	Per capita income ratio of the sending country (Asia) over the receiving country (Malaysia)
$Wage_{AM}$	Wage ratio of the sending country (Asia) over the receiving country (Malaysia)
CPI_{AM}	Consumer price index ratio of the sending country (Asia) over the receiving country (Malaysia)
ER_{AM}	Exchange rate ratio of the sending country (Asia) over the receiving country (Malaysia)
$\ln Dist$	Transportation cost between the sending country (Asia) and the receiving country (Malaysia) in natural logarithmic form
α	Constant term
β	Coefficient term
u	Random error term
i,t	Cross-section time-series

Two diagnostic tests are proposed to maintain the validity of the instruments in both Difference GMM and System GMM for this study. Firstly, the Hansen test. It is verifying the overall validity of the instruments. Secondly, the Arellano-Bond test for AR (2). It is for detecting the serial correlation at the second-order error term. Plus, the number of instruments should not exceed the number of observations, as is the rule of thumb for dynamic panel data analysis. In terms of model significance, the F-test is applied. Simultaneously, the t-test is applied to test the hypothesis for the relationship between each independent variable and the dependent variable.

Employing two generalised methods of moments (GMM) estimations, Difference GMM and System GMM, via xtabond2 command. In avoiding heteroscedasticity and autocorrelation, robust command is inserted. Command small is to generate t-test values. Command nondisparaging is included to avoid reporting certain differences in the statistics of Hansen test. Meanwhile, to estimate the Difference GMM model, nolevel command existed but omitted when estimating the System GMM. All the statistical figures—including number of observations, number of instruments, probability value of F-test, probability value of Arellano-Bond AR (2) test, and probability value of Hansen test—are available through stats(N j p ar2p hansenp) command. To generate * symbol for differentiating between different significance levels for the independent variables, command nogap star (* 0.1 ** 0.05 *** 0.01) is typed in the Stata 14.0 command box. Also, to allow the regressions from the same GMM method to be compiled in the same result table, the eststo and esttab commands are applied.

4 Results, Findings, and Discussions

All macro factors in both models, Difference GMM and System GMM, are significant. The only difference is in the number of significant items. A negative sign is recorded for most items in $GNIpc_{AM}$, with 21 items in Difference GMM and 13 using System GMM. For $Wage_{AM}$, this macro factor recorded more positive signs, with 9 in Difference GMM and 10 in System GMM. Conversely, most signs obtained are negative for

Table 3 Summary of significant macro factors using Difference GMM and System GMM

Region		$GNIpc_{AM}$		$Wage_{AM}$		CPI_{AM}		ER_{AM}		$Dist_{AM}$		Total		
		D	S	D	S	D	S	D	S	D	S	D	S	Total
Significance	1%	11	6	3	1	1	12	2	1	4	0	21	20	41
	5%	10	5	3	9	1	12	7	6	6	0	27	32	59
	10%	3	7	5	6	7	6	5	12	4	3	24	34	58
Sign	+	3	5	9	10	1	0	4	16	14	3	31	34	65
	–	21	13	2	6	8	30	10	3	0	0	41	52	93
Total		24	18	11	16	9	30	14	19	14	3	72	86	158

Notes: (1) D = Difference GMM. (2) S = System GMM. (3) Significance = Significance level. (4) + = Positive relationship. (5) - = Negative relationship

CPI_{AM}, as Difference GMM recorded 8 significant items, while System GMM reported 30. The total positive signs are still more than the negative for ER_{AM}, where the positive value recorded is 20, compared to the opposite sign by 13. For $Dist_{AM}$, Difference GMM recorded 14 items, while System GMM reported three items, all in a positive sign. All these are shown in Table 3.

A negative relationship is recorded in most items for this $GNIpc_{AM}$. This statement is contrary to the earlier hypothesis. This, however, can be accepted as most international demands for Malaysian public universities come from sending countries with smaller economic sizes than Malaysia. This is in line with Gündüz (2018), Yang and Wang (2016), and Perkins and Neumayer (2014), when higher income in the host country attracts more enrolments of trans-border students. Yet, the imbalance in terms of per capita income can be compensated by financial assistance provided to them throughout their study period in the host country (Falcone, 2017). On the other hand, Clark (2010) highlights that the lack of tertiary seats at a national level, coupled with the government's urgency to increase the number of scholars, forced the government to send their students abroad, especially in socio-economically advanced countries.

The negative pattern is further supported by a comparison between the sending blocs, as displayed in Fig. 2. Malaysia was classified as an upper-middle-income country for the period of 2008–2016 by the World Bank. Most demands are dominated by sending countries from the lower-middle-income bloc, with the biggest number in 2016 with 20 sending

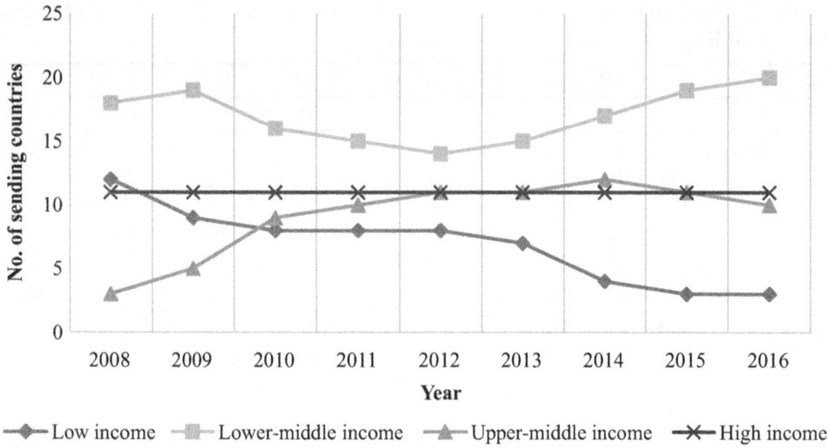

Fig. 2 Classifications by income level of sending countries. Analysis made based on data released by the World Bank (2018) and MoHE (2018)

countries. In 2012, even though only 14 sending countries from the same lower-middle-income bloc were recorded, it was still higher than the other three income blocs, such as low-income and upper-middle-income countries. Apart from that, economic prosperity in the host country also promises prospects for furthering the next level of tertiary education and better future employment opportunities, as compared to the origin country (Vögtle & Windzio, 2020; Ramos & Royuela, 2017).

Wage_{AM} is the next component for the *Income* aspect, and this macro factor recorded more positive relationships, similar to Chao et al. (2019), Ibrahim (2011), and Parish and Willis (1993). Thus, this statement is in line with the earlier hypothesis, where an increase in the wage ratio of the sending country (Asia) to the receiving country (Malaysia) will increase the enrolment of Asian students in Malaysian public universities. From a different perspective, a wage not only represents income from work but also acts as an opportunity cost. In detail, forgone earning is the opportunity cost in return for not working throughout the study period (Schanzenbach et al., 2017). It is also an essential consideration for school leavers, to work or pursue higher education after completing the secondary period (Potelienė & Tamašauskienė, 2014).

Thus, a positive sign proves that Asian tertiary students are willing to sacrifice a higher current wage in origin country, to further their studies in Malaysian public educational institutions. This statement is parallel to what has been discussed in Arshad and Baharuddin (2019). In detail, the current high wage rate, though able to divert interest in furthering studies, is merely temporary in nature. Moreover, the study period for each tertiary level in Malaysia usually takes around two to three years only. For the undergraduate level, a bachelor's degree takes an average of about three years, as shown in Table 4. Meanwhile, countries such as the United States require undergraduate studies to be completed within four years (KIP, 2021). However, the shorter period in Malaysian educational institutions is not offset by the quality of education offered when it is still necessary to fulfil the required credit hours, and the implementation is closely monitored by the Malaysian Qualification Agency.

The second aspect, *cost*, is represented by two macro factors, CPI_{AM} and ER_{AM}. For CPI_{AM}, the majority of signs obtained are negative. In terms of interpretation, the lower the cost of living in the origin country than Malaysia, the higher the enrolment of Asian students in Malaysian educational institutions. This negative relationship contradicts the proposed hypothesis. In other words, the higher cost of living in Malaysia as a country host, compared to the country of origin, does not stop these Asian students from furthering their studies at Malaysian public universities. This statement is similar to Frawley et al. (2019) and Min and Falvey (2018). From another perspective, there are also people who focus on

Table 4 Types of tertiary courses, learning years, and minimum credits

Type	Minimum duration of study (year)	Minimum credit
Certificate	1¼	60
Diploma	2	90
Advanced Diploma	1	40
Bachelor	3	120
Master (Coursework)	1	40
Master (Research)	2	No given credit value.
Doctoral	3	No given credit value.

Source: Malaysian Qualification Statement (MQS) (2015)

future employment in the host country as compared to their home country, as they are already familiar with the new culture and life throughout the study period (Gesing & Glass, 2019).

Although these Asian tertiary students bear a higher cost of living while pursuing their studies in Malaysia, it is still much lower than other higher education destination countries, as shown in Table 5. Singapore, for example, is far ahead, ranked at 47, compared to Kuala Lumpur, Malaysia's capital, at the rank of 356 out of 496 major cities worldwide. Thus, despite sharing the same region, significant differences in the cost of living make it possible for countries with lower living costs, like Malaysia, to enjoy a more considerable portion of international students (Ahmad & Buchanan, 2016). The difference is even more remarkable when Kuala Lumpur is compared to the capital city of the ten best countries for national higher education systems, as issued in the QS Higher Education System Strength Rankings 2016. In conclusion, Malaysia,

Table 5 Ranking for different costs of living for selected capital cities in higher education exporting countries 2016

Rank	City	Cost of living index	Rent index	Groceries index	Restaurant price index
20	Washington, DC, United States	96.18	72.17	89.47	90.03
22	London, United Kingdom	94.82	85.48	73.37	101.34
39	Tokyo, Japan	85.09	49.63	91.08	53.33
47	Singapore, Singapore	83.67	73.88	75.83	53.75
59	Paris, France	81.61	45.98	77.34	80.31
93	Seoul, South Korea	78.33	47.75	91.92	44.74
115	Amsterdam, Netherlands	76.29	46.95	59.18	84.79
118	Canberra, Australia	76.2	43.28	75.53	72.67
229	Berlin, Germany	66.34	25.97	56.71	55.46
246	Ottawa, Canada	63.75	27.48	61.9	63.82
301	Beijing, China	51.39	43.64	53.75	32.85
356	Kuala Lumpur, Malaysia	42.32	17.11	44.64	22.88

Source: Cost of living index by city 2016 (Numbeo, 2017)

despite offering a higher cost of living than the home country, its cost is still competitive and well-received by the Asian tertiary students.

Meanwhile, ER_{AM} exhibits more positive sign and is in parallel with the earlier hypothesis. In detail, appreciation in their home country's currency allows these Asian students to spend more on studies items and non-studies items in Malaysia, using the same amount of money compared to the past. This also allows the sending country to multiply their student enrolments in Malaysian public universities. Thus, the fall in the value of a country's currency cannot be seen from a purely negative perspective, as it can provide profitable returns to an export-based industry, like the Malaysian higher education industry. The lower value of the Malaysian Ringgit is also considered lucrative for most international tertiary students in Malaysia (Chin & Menon, 2020). In addition, most Asian countries are developing countries, and the exchange rate is a significant factor in determining the sending of local students abroad (Zheng, 2014).

The depreciation of the Malaysian Ringgit against major world currencies is closely linked to the 1997/98 East Asian financial crisis. The exchange rate was around MYR2.50/USD to MYR3.00/USD for a period of ten years, starting in 1987. However, it depreciated to around MYR4.00/USD in September 1998. Until today, this effect persists when the value has not returned to the same range before the crisis, with the nearest value, around MYR3.00/USD, recorded only in 2012, as shown in Fig. 3. On the positive side, this depreciation may also be Malaysia's strength in attracting more international students, including from the Asian continent (Chelliah et al., 2019). Besides, the smaller value of the host country's currency, coupled with a quality education system and friendly environment, can attract more demand from developed and rich countries (Lawrence & Yoon, 2016).

The third component, *Distance*, displays a clear positive relationship and contradicts the proposed hypothesis. However, the positively shaped sign can be supported by the geographical distribution of the tertiary students across Asia. Although Malaysia is located in the sub-continent of South-Eastern Asia and is bordered by land, air, and water with almost half of those country members, such as Brunei, the Philippines, Indonesia, Singapore, and Thailand, tertiary enrolment from the same sub-continent

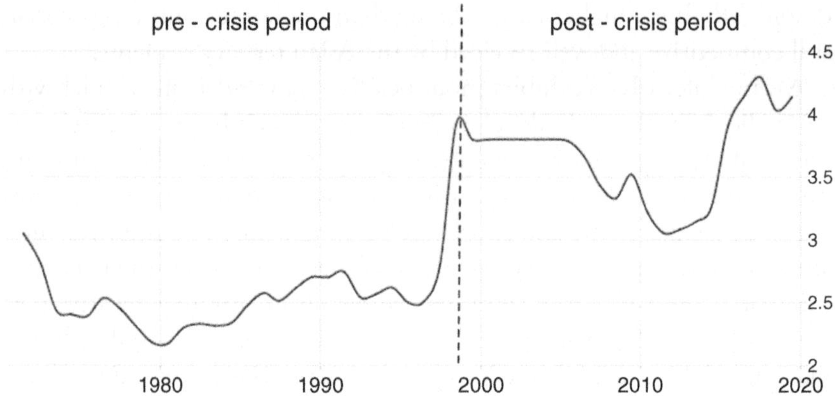

Fig. 3 Exchange rate of Malaysian Ringgit against US Dollar (1970–2020). Adapted from the Trading Economics (2020)

Table 6 Distance range and percentage of enrolment in 2016

Sub-continent	Distance between the major airport of the sending country and Kuala Lumpur International Airport (in kilometres)			Percentage of Asian enrolment in Malaysian public universities
	Minimum	Maximum	Average	
Central Asia	5207	6076	5560	1%
Eastern Asia	2517	5412	4184	10%
South-eastern Asia	298	2937	1383	24%
Southern Asia	2475	6329	3800	31%
Western Asia	5224	8389	6918	34%

Analysis made based on data retrieved from the Google Maps (2018) and MoHE (2018)

was only around 24% in 2016. The opposite is true for sub-continents far away from Malaysia, such as Southern Asia with 31% of students, and Western Asia, which was the largest contributor to enrolment in Malaysian public universities with 34% in the same year. The distance range and percentage of enrolment in the year 2016 are shown in Table 6.

Among the key factors is the fact that most countries in Southern Asia and Western Asia are countries with a Muslim-majority population. Islamophobia, which caused bad prejudice against Muslim students, especially after the 9/11 incident, made them change their direction from Western countries to more Muslim-friendly countries like Malaysia (Seppy, 2018). It is an added value to Malaysia's higher education, as it practises Islam as the official religion and the majority of its population is Muslim, compared to other major destinations for higher education. It is also possible that the reputation of the Malaysian public education institution and the positive image of Malaysia as a whole, coupled with the quality of programme and the availability of facilities, are among the other factors that attract students primarily from Western Asia. The combination offsets the high transportation cost and low frequency of returning home country as explained in Migin et al. (2015) and Rahman and Islam (2016).

5 Conclusion and Policy Implications

The objective of the study is successfully achieved. It is exhibited through empirical analysis of the entire Asian continent and its five sub-continents. This study allows the international demand for Malaysian higher education to be realised more holistically and complements previous macro studies limited to only a few Asian countries, including Ibrahim (2011) and Asari et al. (2011). The results of inferential statistics analysis in this objective also prove that the demand for Malaysian higher education can also be macro measured similarly as exhibited in other countries and blocs such as Agarwal (1983), Cummings (1984), Bessey (2012), Zheng (2014), David et al. (2017), Gündüz (2018), and Paulino & Castaño (2019).

This macro-nature study also complements other studies on international enrolment in Malaysia that are more focused on micro factors, such as Padlee et al. (2010), Baharun et al. (2011), Migin et al. (2015), Jaafar (2016), Daud et al. (2019), and Foo et al. (2019). All these conclusions are made based on the ability of the generalised method of moments (GMM) in analysing the three proposed aspects, *Income, Cost,* and *Aspect* through the five macro factors selected. At the same time, the diversity in terms of tertiary demand in each sample and sub-sample is something unique. It is due to the disparities in socioeconomic conditions and geographical locations in each region of origin and also based on differences in the level of study and type of gender.

Thus, two policies are strongly proposed. Firstly, on the offerings of tertiary programmes based on the macro factors discussed in the second objective. In detail, for international demand coming from lower-income blocs, selective monetary practises can be introduced, such as financial assistance and fee reduction. This approach is more prudent than providing subsidised fees in general without looking at the financial status of each student. This targeted approach allows more savings to be made by the Malaysian government and the Malaysian public universities. Simultaneously, more offerings need to be made at the undergraduate level, as this is the most basic level in the higher education industry and is less elastic for international students from the lower-income bloc.

Contrariwise, for students from the higher-income bloc, more efforts need to be made to ensure that they pursue their studies up to the highest level, PhD. The approach allows these international students to stay longer in Malaysia and spend more throughout the study period, whether for education, need, or even leisure. This idea is practical as most students from this bloc are self-funded. Furthermore, if they stay with their family members, the amount of expenditure is multiplied and generates more income for Malaysia's economy.

Secondly, a different approach needs to be taken for each of the Asian sub-continents involved. For example, for students from Western Asia and Southern Asia, more reductions should be given to the price of airline tickets. The long distance between this sub-continent and Malaysia requires a reduction in air transport costs. Also, special combo packages can be offered to enable airlines to acquire many passengers at once. This promotion also gives a comparative advantage to Malaysia in attracting more students from Western Asia. It should be noted that this sub-continent is located closer to the continent of Europe, which is undoubtedly full of renowned tertiary institutions. Thus, the cost-saving strategy, especially involving air transportation, is something to consider.

On the other hand, proximity does not guarantee higher enrolment for nearby sub-continents such as Eastern Asia. Therefore, more niche areas owned by Malaysia like Islamic banking and finance programmes need to be marketed and known globally. This approach allows nearby students to choose to further their studies in Malaysia compared to other provider countries. For countries in the same sub-continent as Malaysia, despite having similar cultures and lifestyles, the minor differences still need to be celebrated. More student and staff exchange programmes need to be done. In addition to understanding these minor differences, close distances save costs. Also, more exchange of knowledge and skills can be done. These exchanges, in turn, strengthen regional educational cooperation.

References

Agarwal, V. B. (1983). Foreign students' demand for United States higher education. *Eastern Economic Journal, 9*(4), 309–323. Accessed from http://www.jstor.org/stable/40325124

Ahmad, S. Z., & Buchanan, F. R. (2016). Choices of destination for transnational higher education: "Pull" factors in an Asia Pacific market. *Educational Studies, 42*(2), 163–180. https://doi.org/10.1080/03055698.2016.1152171

Andreß, H. J. (2017). The need for and use of panel data. *IZA World of Labor, 352*, 1–10. https://doi.org/10.15185/izawol.352

Arif, I., Raza, S. A., Friemann, A., & Suleman, M. T. (2019). The role of remittances in the development of higher education: Evidence from top remittance receiving countries. *Social Indicators Research, 141*(3), 1233–1243. https://doi.org/10.1007/s11205-018-1857-8

Arshad, M. N. M., & Baharuddin, N. N. (2019). The economic benefits of Malaysian university degrees. *IIUM Journal of Educational Studies, 7*(1), 15–25. https://doi.org/10.31436/ijes.v7i1.197

Asari, F. F. A. H., Idris, A. R., & Daud, N. M. (2011). Modelling education tourism using Gravity Model in Malaysian public higher education institutions. *Australian Journal of Basic and Applied Sciences, 5*(5), 1257–1274. Accessed from http://www.ajbasweb.com/old/ajbas/2011/1257-1274.pdf

Baharun, R., Awang, Z., & Padlee, S. F. (2011). International students' choice criteria for selection of higher learning in Malaysian private universities. *African Journal of Business Management, 5*(12), 4704–4714. https://doi.org/10.5897/AJBM10.422

Becker, G. S. (1964). *Human capital: A theoretical and empirical analysis with special reference to education*. University of Chicago Press. Accessed from http://shorturl.at/nsxHS.

Bennell, P. (2019). The financial returns to onshore and offshore overseas students at British Universities. *International Journal of Educational Development, 70*, 102097. https://doi.org/10.1016/j.ijedudev.2019.102097

Bessey, D. (2012). International student migration to Germany. *Empirical Economics, 42*(1), 345–361. https://doi.org/10.1007/s00181-010-0417-0

Blanchard, E., & Olney, W. W. (2017). Globalisation and human capital investment: Export composition drives educational attainment. *Journal of International Economics, 106*, 165–183. https://doi.org/10.1016/j.jinteco.2017.03.004

Campbell, R., & Siegel, B. N. (1967). The demand for higher education in the United States, 1919-1964. *The American Economic Review, 57*(3), 482–494. Accessed from http://www.jstor.org/stable/1812115

Chadee, D., & Naidoo, V. (2009). Higher educational services exports: Sources of growth of Asian students in US and UK. *Service Business, 3*(2), 173–187. https://doi.org/10.1007/s11628-008-0041-7

Chao, C. N., Hegarty, N., Angelidis, J., & Lu, V. F. (2019). Chinese students' motivations for studying in the United States. *Journal of International Students, 7*(2), 257–269. Accessed from https://www.ojed.org/index.php/jis/article/download/380/299

Chelliah, S., Khan, M. J., Thilagavathy Krishnan, M. E. B. M. K., Goh, N. E., Khan, M. J., Krishnan, T., Kamarulzaman, M. E. B. M., & Goh, N. E. (2019). Factors influencing satisfaction and revisit intention among international exchange students in Malaysia. *Journal of International Education in Business, 12*(1), 111–130. https://doi.org/10.1108/JIEB-07-2018-0026

Chen, T. M., & Barnett, G. A. (2000). Research on international student flows from a macro perspective: A network analysis of 1985, 1989 and 1995. *Higher Education, 39*(4), 435–453. https://doi.org/10.1023/A:1003961327009

Chin, C., & Menon, S. (2020, August 28). *Foreign students waiting for entry*. The Star. Accessed from https://www.thestar.com.my/news/nation/2020/08/28/foreign-students-waiting-for-entry

Clark, N. (2010). Higher education in Vietnam: Student growth, faculty shortages and international partnerships. *World Education News & Reviews*. Accessed from http://wenr.wes.org/2010/08/wenr-julyaugust-2010-practical-information/

Cummings, W. K. (1984). Going overseas for higher education: The Asian experience. *Comparative Education Review, 28*(2), 241–257. Accessed from http://www.jstor.org/stable/1187350

Daud, N., Ali, N. A., & Jantan, A. H. (2019). Influential determinants of international students' satisfaction in higher education. *International Journal of Recent Technology and Engineering, 8*(2S11), 589–597. https://doi.org/10.35940/ijrte.B1091.0982S1119

David, S. A., Taleb, H., Scatolini, S. S., Al-Qallaf, A., Al-Shammari, H. S., & George, M. A. (2017). An exploration into student learning mobility in higher education among the Arabian Gulf Cooperation Council countries. *International Journal of Educational Development, 55*, 41–48. https://doi.org/10.1016/j.ijedudev.2017.05.001

Didisse, J., Nguyen-Huu, T. T., & Tran, T. A. D. (2019). The long walk to knowledge: On the determinants of higher education mobility to Europe. *The Journal of Development Studies, 55*(6), 1099–1120. https://doi.org/10.1080/00220388.2018.1475647

Dora, M. T., Ibrahim, N. R. W., Kasim, S. D. R. A., & Saad, M. S. M. (2009). A study on factors that influence choice of Malaysian institution of higher learning for international graduate students. *Journal of Human Capital Development, 2*(1), 105–114. Accessed from https://journal.utem.edu.my/index.php/jhcd/article/view/2494/1570

Drylie, S. (2021). Adam Smith on schooling: A classical liberal rereading. *Journal of Economic Behavior & Organization, 184*, 748–770. https://doi.org/10.1016/j.jebo.2020.08.032

Faggian, A., Modrego, F., & McCann, P. (2019). Human capital and regional development. In R. Capello & P. Nijkamp (Eds.), *Handbook of regional growth and development theories* (pp. 149–171). Edward Elgar Publishing. https://doi.org/10.4337/9781788970020.00015

Falcone, S. (2017). International student recruitment: Trends and challenges. *Journal of International Students, 7*(2), 246–256. Accessed from https://files.eric.ed.gov/fulltext/EJ1129177.pdf

Fernandez, J. L. (2010). An exploratory study of factors influencing the decision of students to study at Universiti Sains Malaysia. *Kajian Malaysia, 28*(2), 107–136. Accessed from http://web.usm.my/km/28(2)2010/KMART4(107-136).pdf

Foo, C., Ismail, R., Lim, H., Ibrahim, Y., & Sabudin, N. S. (2019). Factors affecting recommendation for higher education destination: The case of Malaysia. *Global Business Management Review, 11*(December), 77–96. Accessed from http://www.e-journal.uum.edu.my/index.php/gbmr/article/view/8666

Frawley, T., Goh, E., & Law, R. (2019). Quality assurance at hotel management tertiary institutions in Australia: An insight into factors behind domestic and international student satisfaction. *Journal of Hospitality & Tourism Education, 31*(1), 1–9. https://doi.org/10.1080/10963758.2018.1480961

Frees, E. W. (2004). *Longitudinal and panel data: Analysis and applications for the social sciences*. Cambridge University Press. https://doi.org/10.1017/CBO9780511790928

Gesing, P., & Glass, C. (2019). STEM student mobility intentions post-graduation and the role of reverse push-pull factors. *International Journal of Educational Development, 65*, 227–236. https://doi.org/10.1016/j.ijedudev.2018.08.008

Google Maps. (2018). *The physical distances between Kuala Lumpur International Airport and the major airports of the Asian sending countries. [Web mapping service]*. Accessed from https://www.google.com.my/maps

Gündüz, F. F. (2018). Analysis of international student mobility from Turkey via Erasmus+ Program. *Ankara Avrupa Çalışmaları Dergisi, 17*(2), 259–278. https://doi.org/10.32450/aacd.511771

Hearps, R. (2016, April 16). *Global trends & disruptors in international student referrals. [PowerPoint slides]*. ANZA Workshop, Melbourne, Australia. Accessed from http://www.icef.com/wp-content/uploads/seminarprogramme/2016/anza__prov_ag__1450__Rod-Hearps__Global-Trends-and-Disruptors-in-International-Student-Mobility%2D%2D-Where-are-International-Students-Going-and-Why.pdf

Hight, J. E. (1975). The demand for higher education in the U.S. 1927-72: The public and private Institutions. *The Journal of Human Resources, 10*(4), 512–520. Accessed from http://www.jstor.org/stable/144988

Hoenack, S. A. (1967). Private demand for higher education in California. *The American Economic Review, 61*(3), 302–311. Accessed from https://www.jstor.org/stable/1813428

Holden, B. L. (2017). *Third country study: The role of degree-seeking international students as study abroad participants* (Publication No. 102541170) [Master's thesis, University of Oregon]. ProQuest Dissertations and Theses Global. Accessed from https://search.proquest.com/openview/9265e769ff9190a4563e8333758760d8/1?pq-origsite=gscholar&cbl=18750&diss=y

Hou, C., & Du, D. (2020). The changing patterns of international student mobility: A network perspective. *Journal of Ethnic and Migration Studies, 2020*, 1–25. https://doi.org/10.1080/1369183X.2020.1797476

Hsiao, C. (2007). Panel data analysis - Advantages and challenges. *TEST, 16*(1), 1–22. https://doi.org/10.1007/s11749-007-0046-x

Hsing, Y., & Chang, H. S. (1996). Testing increasing sensitivity of enrollment at private institutions to tuition and other costs. *The American Economist, 40*(1), 40–45. https://doi.org/10.1177/2F056943459604000106

Ibrahim, F. W. (2011). Determinants of enrolment in higher education in Malaysia and a few selected Asian countries. In *Proceedings of the 1st international conference on accounting, business and economics 2011* (pp. 42–48). Universiti Malaysia Terengganu.

Isard, W. (1960). *Methods of regional analysis: An introduction to regional science.* Wiley. Accessed from http://shorturl.at/jnxDO

Jaafar, N. I. M. (2016). The factors that motivate undergraduates to pursue tertiary education: Employability, expectation, learning or enjoyment. In *Proceedings of the regional conference on science, technology and social sciences 2014* (pp. 353–363). Springer. https://doi.org/10.1007/978-981-10-1458-1_34

Kaushal, N., & Lanati, M. (2019). *International student mobility: Growth and dispersion (NBER Working Paper No. w25921).* National Bureau of Economic Research. https://doi.org/10.3386/w25921

Kelley, R. L. (1921). The preliminary report of the association commission on the distribution of colleges. *Bulletin of the Association of American Colleges, 7*(4), 5–28.

Khan, Y., Hassan, T., Yi, W. M., & Gulzar, R. (2018). A comparative analysis based on economic factors of students' emigration from South Asia. *Asian Journal of Economics and Empirical Research, 5*(2), 201–208. https://doi.org/10.20448/journal.501.2018.52.201.208

KIP (Kaplan International Pathways). (2021). *US higher education explained.* Accessed from https://www.kaplanpathways.com/study-abroad/education-systems-explained/usa/

Kritz, M. M. (2015). International student mobility and tertiary education capacity in Africa. *International Migration, 53*(1), 29–49. https://doi.org/10.1111/imig.12053

Lawrence, R., & Yoon, J. (2016). *The expectations and experiences of Korean International Students in New Zealand tertiary education. [PowerPoint Presentation].* The 4th Korean Studies Association of Australasia Biennial Postgraduate Workshop, University of Auckland, Auckland, New Zealand. Accessed from http://researcharchive.wintec.ac.nz/4481/3/Theexpectations and experiencesofKoreanInternationalStudentsinNewZealandtertiaryeducation.pdf

Lewis-Beck, M., Bryman, A. E., & Liao, T. F. (2003). *The Sage encyclopedia of social science research methods*. Sage. https://doi.org/10.4135/9781412950589.

Maciejewski, M., & Wach, K. (2019). What determines export structure in the EU countries? The use of gravity model in international trade based on the panel data for the years 1995-2015. *Journal of International Studies, 12*(1), 151. https://doi.org/10.14254/2071-8330.2019/12-1/10

Malaysian Qualification Statement (MQS). (2015). *Malaysian qualifications agency*. Accessed from https://www2.mqa.gov.my/qad/garispanduan/GGP-Malaysia%20Qualification%20Statement.pdf

Menteri: Jana pendapatan sendiri, bukan naikkan yuran universiti. (Minister: Generate your own income, not raise university fees). (2016, October 23). *ProjekMM News*. Accessed from https://www.projekmm.com/news/berita/2016/10/23/menteri-jana-pendapatan-sendiri-bukan-naikkan-yuran-universiti/1234033

Migin, M. W., Falahat, M., Yajid, M. S. A., & Khatibi, A. (2015). Impacts of institutional characteristics on international students' choice of private higher education institutions in Malaysia. *Higher Education Studies, 5*(1), 31–42. https://doi.org/10.5539/hes.v5n1p31

Min, B. S., & Falvey, R. (2018). International student flows for university education and the bilateral market integration of Australia. *Higher Education, 75*(5), 871–889. https://doi.org/10.1007/s10734-017-0175-4

Mitropoulos, A. (2020, July 14). *Loss of international students could damage US economy, experts say*. ABC News. Accessed from https://abcnews.go.com/Business/loss-international-students-damage-us-economy-experts/story?id=71754388

MoHE (Malaysia, Ministry of Higher Education). (2018). *Bilangan pelajar antarabangsa di universiti awam tahun 2008-2016 (Number of international students in public universities 2008-2016). [Spreadsheet file]*. MoHE.

MoHE (Malaysia, Ministry of Higher Education). (2021). *Bab 1 - Makro institusi pendidikan tinggi. Statistik Pendidikan Tinggi 2019 (Chapter 1 - Macros of higher education institutions. Higher Education Statistics 2019)*. MoHE. Accessed from https://www.mohe.gov.my/en/downloads/statistics/2021-1/849-statistik-pendidikan-tinggi-2021-03-bab-1-makro-institusi-pendidikan-tinggi/file

Munadi, M. (2020). Systematising internationalisation policy of higher education in state Islamic universities. *International Journal of Higher Education, 9*(6), 96–106. https://doi.org/10.5430/ijhe.v9n6p96

Munisamy, S., Jaafar, N. I. M., & Nagaraj, S. (2014). Does reputation matter? Case study of undergraduate choice at a premier university. *Asia-Pacific Education Researcher, 23*(3), 451–462. https://doi.org/10.1007/s40299-013-0120-y

Naidoo, V. (2007). Research on the flow of international students to UK universities: Determinants and implications. *Journal of Research in International Education, 6*(3), 287–307. https://doi.org/10.1177/2F1475240907083197

Numbeo. (2017). *Cost of living index by city 2016*. Accessed from https://www.numbeo.com/cost-of-living/rankings.jsp?title=2016

Padlee, S. F., Kamaruddin, A. R., & Baharun, R. (2010). International students' choice behavior for higher education at Malaysian private universities. *International Journal of Marketing Studies, 2*(2), 202–211. Accessed from http://www.ccsenet.org/journal/index.php/ijms/article/download/8131/6161

Parish, W. L., & Willis, R. J. (1993). Daughters, education, and family budgets Taiwan experiences. *Journal of Human Resources, 28*, 863–898. Accessed from https://www.jstor.org/stable/146296

Paulino, M. A., & Castaño, M. C. N. (2019). Exploring factors influencing international students' choice. *Review of Integrative Business and Economics Research, 8*(SI3), 131–149. Accessed from http://sibresearch.org/uploads/3/4/0/9/34097180/riber_8-s3_13_t19-136_131-149.pdf

Perkins, R., & Neumayer, E. (2014). Geographies of educational mobilities: Exploring the uneven flows of international students. *Geographical Journal, 180*(3), 246–259. https://doi.org/10.1111/geoj.12045

Potelienė, S., & Tamašauskienė, Z. (2014). The rate of return to investment in education: A case study of Lithuania. *Wroclaw Review of Law, Administration & Economics, 4*(2), 41–55. https://doi.org/10.1515/wrlae-2015-0014

Psacharopoulos, G., & Patrinos, H. A. (2018). Returns to investment in education: a decennial review of the global literature. *Education Economics, 26*(5), 445–458. https://doi.org/10.1080/09645292.2018.1484426

Putra, A. K., Najwan, J., Rahmalia, R., & Daud, S. M. (2021). A normative juridical study of internationalization of Indonesian Higher Education Institution. In *Higher education challenges in South-East Asia* (pp. 74–97). IGI Global. https://doi.org/10.4018/978-1-7998-4489-1.ch004

Rahman, M., & Islam, R. (2016). Selection of institution of higher learning for study abroad: A Malaysian case study. *Malaysian Management Review, 51*(1), 33–48. Accessed from http://www.mim.org.my/wp-content/uploads/2016/08/Pages-from-MMRJan-Jun2016Vol51NO1-Selection of institution-of-higher-learning-for-study-abroad-A-Malaysian-Case-Study-page-49-66-.pdf

Ramos, R., & Royuela, V. (2017). Graduate migration in Spain: The impact of the Great Recession on a low-mobility country. In J. Corcoran & A. Faggian (Eds.), *Graduate migration and regional development*. Edward Elgar Publishing. https://doi.org/10.4337/9781784712167.00012

Roodman, D. (2009). How to do xtabond2: An introduction to difference and system GMM in Stata. *The Stata Journal, 9*(1), 86–136. https://doi.org/10.1177/2F1536867X0900900106

Schanzenbach, D. W., Bauer, L., & Breitwieser, A. (2017, April 26). *Eight economic facts on higher education*. The Hamilton Project. Accessed from http://www.hamiltonproject.org/papers/eight_economic_facts_on_higher_education

Schofer, J. P. (1975). Determining optimal college locations. *Higher Education, 4*(2), 227–232. http://www.jstor.org/stable/3445814

Schultz, T. W. (1961). Investment in human capital. *The American Economic Review, 51*(1), 1–17. Accessed from http://www.jstor.org/stable/1818907

Seppy, D. M. (2018). *Muslim international student and higher education: A qualitative study of students' experiences against a backdrop of Islamophobia* [Doctoral dissertation, University of Maine]. Digital Commons @UMaine. Accessed from https://digitalcommons.library.umaine.edu/etd/2845/

Sheriff, N. M., & Abdullah, N. (2017). Research universities in Malaysia: What beholds? *Asian Journal of University Education, 13*(2), 35–50. Accessed from https://files.eric.ed.gov/fulltext/EJ1207763.pdf

Sidin, S. M., Hussin, S. R., & Soon, T. H. (2003). An exploratory study of factors influencing the college choice decision of undergraduate students in Malaysia. *Asia Pacific Management Review, 8*(3), 259–280. Accessed from http://www.airitilibrary.com/Publication/alDetailedMesh?docid=10293132-200309-8-3-259-280-a

Tinbergen, J. (1962). An analysis of world trade flows. In J. Tinbergen (Ed.), *Shaping the world economy: Suggestions for an international economic policy* (pp. 262–293). Twentieth Century Fund. Accessed from https://repub.eur.nl/pub/16826

Trading Economics. (2020). *Malaysia - Official exchange rate (LCU per US$, period average) [Economics online platform]*. Accessed from https://tradingeconomics.com/malaysia/official-exchange-rate-lcu-per-us-dollar-period-average-wb-data.html

Türk, U. (2019). Socio-economic determinants of student mobility and inequality of access to higher education in Italy. *Networks and Spatial Economics, 19*(1), 125–148. https://doi.org/10.1007/s11067-019-09445-w

United Nations (UN). (2020). *The 17 goals*. UN Department of Economic and Social Affairs Sustainable Development. Accessed from https://sdgs.un.org/goals

Vincent-Lancrin, S. (Ed.). (2007). *Cross border tertiary education: A way towards capacity development*. OECD, World Bank and NUFFIC. Accessed from http://www.oecd.org/education/innovation-education/cross-bordertertiaryeducationawaytowardscapacitydevelopment.htm

Vögtle, E. M., & Windzio, M. (2020). Looking for freedom? Networks of international student mobility and countries' levels of democracy. *The Geographical Journal, 186*(1), 103–115. https://doi.org/10.1111/geoj.12329

Wai, P. S., Ismail, M. T., & Karim, S. A. A. (2012). International students' enrolment in IPTA by using multilevel analysis. In *Proceedings of the International Conference on Fundamental and Applied Sciences 2012* (pp. 15–19). AIP Publishing. https://doi.org/10.1063/1.4757430

Wiseman, T., & Walker, P. (2017). US interstate underground trade flow: A gravity model approach. *Review of Law & Economics, 13*(2), 1–27. https://doi.org/10.1515/rle-2015-0057

World Bank. (2018). *World Bank analytical classifications (presented in World Development Indicators). GNI per capita in US$ (Atlas methodology). [Spreadsheet file]*. Accessed from http://databank.worldbank.org/data/download/site-content/OGHIST.xls

Yang, J., & Wang, Y. (2016). *Tuition fees and student mobility* [Master's thesis, Lund University]. LUP Students Paper. Accessed from https://lup.lub.lu.se/student-papers/search/publication/8619324

Yousaf, S., Fan, X., & Laber, F. (2020). Branding China through the internationalisation of higher education sector: An international students' perspective from China. *Journal of Marketing for Higher Education, 30*(2), 161–179. https://doi.org/10.1080/08841241.2019.1710890

Yusuf, B., Ghazali, M., & Abdullah, M. (2017). Factors influencing local and international students' decision in choosing public higher learning institutions in northern Malaysia. *International Journal of Social Sciences, 48*(1), 29–41. Accessed from https://www.tijoss.com/49th volumetijoss/3.pdf

Zheng, P. (2014). Antecedents to international student inflows to UK higher education: A comparative analysis. *Journal of Business Research, 67*(2), 136–143. https://doi.org/10.1016/j.jbusres.2012.11.003

Factors Affecting the Success of Product/Service Innovation Among SMEs in Ghana: The Moderating Role of Functional Diversity and Strategic Alignment

John Ampontuah Kumah, Fred A. Yamoah, and Adnan ul Haque

1 Introduction

In many economies of the world, small and medium-scale enterprises (SMEs) have undoubtedly played and continue to play a major role. There are a wide range of beliefs among academia and policymakers that SMEs enhance the productivity of countries as well as development

J. A. Kumah
Accra, Ghana

F. A. Yamoah (✉)
Department of Management, School of Business, Economics and Informatics, Birkbeck, University of London, London, UK
e-mail: f.yamoah@bbk.ac.uk

A. ul Haque
Faculty of Business, Yorkville University, Toronto, ON, Canada

F. A. Yamoah, A. ul Haque (eds.), *Corporate Management Ecosystem in Emerging Economies*, https://doi.org/10.1007/978-3-031-41578-4_19

(Al-Mahrouq, 2010). The benefits a country derives from SMEs are overwhelming as, according to Al-Mahrouq (2010), SMEs form the backbone of the private sector globally and account for about 60% of the total labor force in the entire working population. Abor and Quartey (2010) further suggested that the role of SMEs in economic development and growth is very important and strategic. The contribution of SMEs towards economic growth in the Asian continent is enormous too. For instance, in Thailand, Veskaisri et al. (2007) reported that SMEs represent more than 90% of the total number of entrepreneurs in almost all business and accounted for about two-thirds of the labor force and widely contribute to the tax base of the economy (Abor, 2011). Also, SMEs have contributed immensely towards the industrial revolution in China (Schaper, 2002). Data from experts in China show that 60% of China's industrial output is contributed by SMEs employing a total of 75% of its workforce in China's cities and towns (Schaper, 2002). Similarly, SMEs represent the largest percentage of all businesses in North America and contribute about half of the GDP returns in the United States and Canada (Al-Mahrouq, 2010). In Europe, available data from the European Union (EU) revealed that 99% of businesses are SME ventures and have accounted for about 84% of new jobs created between 2002 and 2012 (European Commission, 2012). The above statistics indicate the enormous contribution made by SMEs towards economic growth and reducing poverty. Although the statistics differ in developing economies, available data depicts a positive relationship between SMEs and economic growth. For instance, Okech and Ndagijimana (2014) indicate that about 25% of people employed outside the agricultural sector in the African continent depend on SMEs for their livelihood. Furthermore, statistics from the World Bank (2015) revealed a significant contribution made by SMEs towards economic growth in most developing economies.

In Ghana, SMEs ever since independence have been the mainstay of the Ghanaian economy. According to the Registrar General Department, about 90% of businesses registered in Ghana are SMEs and contribute about 70% of Ghana's Gross Domestic Product (GDP) and account for approximately 85% of employment in the Ghanaian manufacturing sector (Abor & Biekpe, 2006; Adom et al., 2014; Agyapong & Attram,

2019; Peprah et al., 2016). The term SMEs has been ascribed with several definitions. But in Ghana, the number of employees informs how SMEs are defined (Kusi et al., 2015). The Ghana Statistical Service defines businesses with more than ten employees as medium- and large-sized businesses (Cofie, 2012). This study aligns with the definition of the Ghana Statistical Service for SMEs operating in various sectors of the economy (i.e., manufacturing, food and beverages, retail, services, etc.).

In most developing countries, or for that matter, Ghana, studies have focused on identifying the specific factors that affect the success and sustainability of SMEs. Generally, these factors are categorized into endogenous and exogenous factors. The endogenous factors center on specific issues relating to enterprise, such as the skills of management, human resources, financial management, and organizational characteristics. The exogenous factors take into cognizance macroeconomic factors, political and institutional forces, market opportunities, and socio-cultural factors (Olawale & Garwe, 2010; Thandeka, 2008). Al-Mahrouq (2010) asserted that the significance of these factors was country specific. In his study, five key factors were revealed as significant determinants of SMEs' success, which included firm structure, marketing, technical procedures and technology, financial structure, productivity, and human resource structure.

The purpose of the study is to examine the factors affecting the success of product/service innovation in Ghanaian SMEs. This research suggests that the success of products or services is not only dependent on factors such as the characteristics of the product/service, competitive environment, and organizational capabilities, although important but some other essential factors as well.

2 Literature Review

The roles of SMEs have been emphasized in the literature to be significant in many economies, such as the developed and developing economies across the globe. The argument for the relevance of SMEs in the economic development of developed and developing economies is that it has been discovered that national economy is not built by only large businesses but by small businesses as well. According to Cook and Nixson (2000), in both developing and developed countries, SMEs are recognized as key employment generation factor and contribute immensely to the development of entrepreneurial skills. Across these sectors, the development of SMEs is considered a mechanism for facilitating the promotion of equity and sustainability within the Ghanaian economy (Aryeetey & Ahene, 2005). This makes SMEs to be seen as the nursery bed for local entrepreneurship. The significance of SMEs in this context lies in their continuous contribution to the improvement of the efficiency of the local markets and in the utilization of uncommon resources to enhance the long-term economic growth of the country (Aryeetey & Ahene, 2005).

According to the NBSSI, an enterprise is an SME if it employs more than nine workers and has in its possession a number of plants and machinery, worth not more than 10 million Cedis, which is equivalent to USD 9506 at the 1994 exchange rate. According to the NBSSI, buildings, land, and vehicles are excluded from this criterion. However, some researchers such as Osei et al. (1993) asserted SMEs who used the number of employees as a criterion in their definition, further gave four categories of SMEs in Ghana as micro-enterprises, very small enterprises, small enterprises, and medium enterprises as indicated in Table 1.

However, Ghanaian SMEs are said to be without setbacks and challenges. This is common in many developing economies around the world and Ghana is no exception. Notable among these are financial access, raw materials, suitable technology, unreliable power supply, and access to available markets that result in the failure of the SMEs (Mead & Liedholm, 1998; Arthur, 2003; Murphy & Ledwith, 2007; Oladele et al., 2013).

Table 1 Description and categorization of SMEs

Category of SME	Number of employees
Micro-enterprises	Less than 6 employees
Very small enterprises	Between 6 and 9 employees
Small enterprises	Between 10 and 29 employees
Medium enterprises	Between 29 and 50 employees

These notwithstanding, the dynamic environment in which SMEs function proves to be highly competitive as presented through globalization and liberalization of the market as well as the prevalent aggressive competition that comes along with unbridled customer expectations (Webster Jr, 1988).

Product success has been defined in the literature as the contribution of common factors related to market, organizations, consumers, product development process, and product characteristics (Kong, 1998). The notion that innovation develops over time and assumes new forms has become acceptable to researchers and practitioners (Koput, 1997). According to Galbraith (1973) and Schon (1967), product innovation results from the process of creating new technology for use. However, product innovation is categorized as new-to-the-world, line extension, and me-too product.

Functional diversity has been defined by some scholars, in the light of diversity, as the engagement of different partners (Sarpong & Teirlinck, 2017; Van Beers & Zand, 2014). This is seen to focus on the type of partners engaged in the activities of SMEs (Sarpong & Teirlinck, 2017). Some of the scholars have, in this sense, indicated that functional diversity has gained attention in most extant literature in explaining innovation performance including success and failure of innovations (Van Beers & Zand, 2014). Functional diversity assumes that there is heterogeneity among partners in innovation. These partners are identified as competitors, clients or customers, public research centers or government, universities, and research centers or consultants (Sarpong & Teirlinck, 2017). The literature, therefore, suggests that organizations are more likely to adopt functional diversity if they seek to link innovation to the functional capabilities of their partners through their cognitive function or knowledge (Van Beers & Zand, 2014). This involves the activities of sourcing knowledge from clients or customers, universities, competitors, public and private research centers, and consultants. Even though functional diversity underscores the differences in partners, the complementarities of these partners are also recognized by some researchers (Belderbos et al. 2006; Pullen et al., 2012). This reveals the importance of considering both the type and portfolio of the different partners in innovation process (Frenz & Ietto-Gillies, 2009). By exploring functional diversity, Sarpong and Teirlinck (2017) suggested that functional diversity in collaboration fosters innovation by enhancing the introduction of new-to-the-world products. According to Avison et al. (2004), firms become competitive if they can align all their strategies. However, it is revealed in the literature that there is a debate over what constitutes alignment, its relevance, and how the activities of alignment may be carried out. In this case, it is presented that the conceptualization of alignment is problematic due to inadequate agreement on how the concept of alignment may be conceptualized.

Strategic alignment fit, integration, bridge, harmony, fusion, and linkage for easy identification within other contexts by other scholars such as Porter (1996), Smaczny (2001), and Henderson and Venkatramen (1989). However, all these suggest the incorporation of business strategies in the process of planning business.

Collis and Montgomery (1995) have indicated that the definition of organizational capability is commensurate with researchers who have undertaken a study in the area. Collis and Montgomery (1995) explained that the concept has many definitions as its authors abound (Baldwin & Clark, 1994; Henderson & Cockburn, 1994). Specifically, organizational capabilities are viewed to provide a sustainable advantage to organizations.

Based on the review in this study, the application of the RBV to the success of product/service innovation in SMEs suggests that the SMEs operate in a competitive environment where resources and competencies are essential to gain a competitive advantage (Hoopes et al., 2003) (Fig. 1).

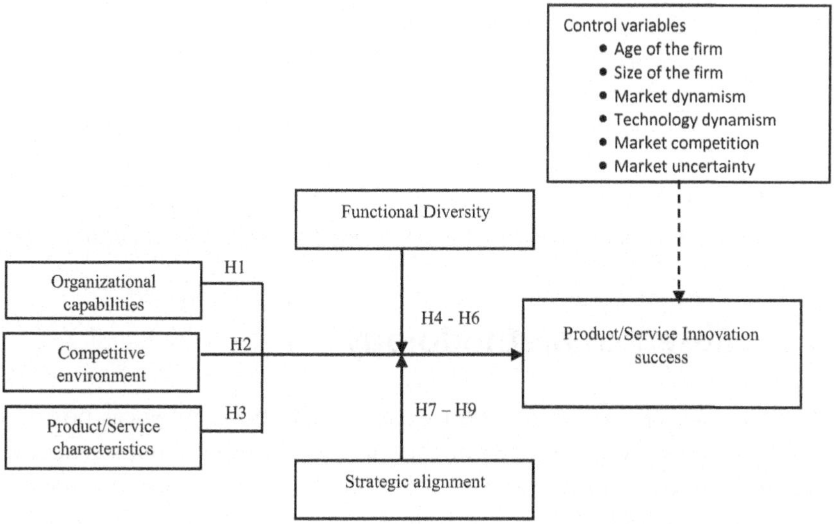

Fig. 1 Conceptual model of factors of product/service innovation success

3 Conceptual Model

Based on the literature review, the following hypotheses have been developed:

H1: Organizational capability positively relates to product/service innovation success.

H2: Competitive environment is negatively related to products/service innovation success in small business.

H3: Product characteristics is positively related to product/service success.

H4: The relationship between organizational capabilities and product/service innovation success would be enhanced when functional diversity is cognitive.

H5: The positive impact of competitive environment on product/service innovation success would be enhanced when functional diversity is cognitive.

H6: The positive effect of product characteristics on product/service innovation success would be higher when functional diversity is cognitive.

H7: The positive effect of organizational capabilities would be enhanced if the level of strategic alignment is high than when it is low.

H8: The negative relationship between competitive environment and product/service innovation success is reduced when strategic alignment high than when it is low.

H9: The positive impact of product characteristics on product/service innovation success would be enhanced with the high strategic alignment than low.

4 Research Methodology

Bryman (2012) asserts that positivism is "an epistemological position that advocates the application of the methods of the natural sciences to the study of social reality and beyond". Our study falls in positivism paradigm. The methods used in research include the utilization of questionnaires in a quantitative study. The deductive approach is more in line with the scientific research of the natural sciences. The deductive approach seeks to test various hypotheses and propositions. Based on a theory, the researcher tests hypothesis to either support or not support a given theory. Surveys are primarily conducted with the aim of quantifying certain information (Haque et al. 2020). The research will obtain data for statistical and quantitative analysis through a sample survey to ascertain the robustness of its findings. The target population for the study comprised selected SMEs in Ghana, mainly situated in the industrial hub of the country. Hair et al. (2010) that in the case where the total number of the population is unknown, to get an adequate sample frame, the respondents should be 5–10 times the number of items used in the questionnaire. The total number of items used in measuring the dependent, independent, and moderating variables in the questionnaire were 55, and therefore, the sample frame was between 275 and 550. Cochran's formula can be deduced if the whole population is relatively small. Thus, we used Cochran's formula in the present study.

The Cochran formula is:

$$n = \frac{Z^2 pq}{e^2}$$

Where:

e is the desired level of precision (i.e., the margin of error),

p is the (estimated) proportion of the population that has the attribute in question,

q is 1 - *p*.

The confidence level corresponds to a *Z*-score. This is a constant value needed for this equation. Here are the *Z*-scores for the most common confidence levels:

- 90%—*Z* Score = 1.645
- 95%—*Z* Score = 1.96
- 99%—*Z* Score = 2.326

The study employed a 95% confidence level with its corresponding Z score and used an error of margin of 0.05. Thus, sample approximation derived is mathematically presented as follows:

$$n = \frac{(1.96)^2 (0.5)(0.5)}{(0.05)^2} = 384$$

Due to the saturated nature of the industry, a total questionnaire of 500 was sent out to respondents, which was deemed adequately representative of the population.

To address content validity in this study, a thorough review of the extant literature and relevant scales used in previous studies were considered. Items covered under the demographic section include: the age and gender of respondents, their education, the average income of the firm, etc. The sources for the measures used in the study are provided in Table 2.

To satisfy the conditions for discriminant validity, the square root of the minimum average variance extracted (AVE) must be higher than the

Table 2 Measurement sources

Construct	No. of items	Source
Organizational capabilities	14	Nasution and Mavondo (2008)
Competitive environment	3	Jaworski and Kohli (1993)
Product/service characteristics	7	Li and Calantone (1998)
Strategic alignment	8	Byrd et al. (2006)
Product/service innovation success	5	Atuahene-Gima et al. (2005)

highest inter-construct correlation (Hair et al., 2010). The criteria were found to be satisfactory. Finally, a hierarchical regression was performed using Aiken and West's (1991) procedure to test the hypothesis of the study. Lastly, the confidentiality of the respondents was maintained.

5 Results, Findings, and Discussions

As reflected in Table 3, the average employee size of the SMEs targeted or involved in the study was approximately eight (8.35). The data revealed that the majority of the respondents were males (69.1%), with females forming about 30.9% of the respondents. The age distribution of the respondents showed that 52% of the respondents surveyed were between 31 and 40 years. This was followed by those between the ages of 41 and 50 years (25.7%), 18–30 years (16.9%), 51–60 years (5.2%), and 61 years and above (0.2%). This may imply that the majority of the respondents involved in this study were adults. In terms of the educational level of respondents, the majority representing more than fifty-five percent (55.2%), have their bachelor's degree, (27.3%) had their higher national diploma (HND), 5.5% were holders of school certificates and (10.6%) had their masters, while (1.4%) had PhD/DBA.

Table 4 shows the independent *t*-test results of the mean differences between strategic alignment and the main construct under study. Clearly the study found significant strategic alignment differences (low and high) among respondents with respect to market dynamism and uncertainty ($t = -0.126, p > 0.10$), environmental dynamism ($t = 0.845, p > 0.10$), technological dynamism ($t = 0.656, p > 0.10$), organizational capability ($t =$

Table 3 Sample characteristics

Variable	Characteristics	Frequency	Percent %
Gender	Male	307	69.1
	Female	137	30.9
Age	18–30 years	75	16.9
	31–40 years	231	52.0
	41–50 years	114	25.7
	51–60 years	23	5.2
	61 years and above	1	0.2
Education	PhD/DBA	6	1.4
	Masters	47	10.6
	Bachelors	245	55.2
	HND	121	27.3
	Other	25	5.6
Position	CEO	124	27.9
	Executive director	35	7.9
	Manager	143	32.2
	Administrative officer	59	13.3
	Head of business unit	15	3.4
	Chief finance officer	18	4.1
	Chief operating officer	43	9.7
	Other	7	1.6
Years of operation	Below 3 years	246	55.4
	4–6 years	163	36.7
	7–9 years	29	6.5
	10–12 years	5	1.1
	16 years and above	1	0.2
Total assets	Less than GHc1 million	330	74.3
	GHc 2–4 million	94	21.2
	GHc 5–7 million	15	3.4
	GHc 8–10million	4	0.9
	GHc 11 million and above	1	0.2

Source: Author's fieldwork (2019)

1.094, $p > 0.10$), product/service characteristics ($t = 1.191, p > 0.01$), and product/service innovation success ($t = -2.717, p < 0.01$). However, the study found no significant strategic alignment differences with respect to competitive environment ($t = -2.717, p < 0.01$) and functional diversity ($t = 2.589, p < 0.01$).

The hierarchical multiple regression, using the entry method was therefore used to assess the relationship between innovation factors and

Table 4 Independent *t*-test results of the mean differences between gender and the factors of bank performance

Gender	Low strategic alignment		High strategic alignment		*t* test	
Variables	Mean	SD	Mean	SD	*t*	*p*-value
1. Market dynamism and uncertainty	2.69	0.651	3.52	0.905	-4.720	0.000
2. Environmental dynamism	2.60	0.954	3.57	0.920	-5.303	0.000
3. Technological dynamism	2.96	0.818	3.98	0.571	-8.737	0.000
4. Organizational capability	3.60	0.875	4.13	0.551	-4.670	0.000
5. Competitive environment	2.77	0.715	3.10	1.135	-1.503	0.133
6. Product/service characteristics	3.61	0.684	3.91	0.607	-2.437	0.015
7. Functional diversity	0.28	0.088	0.23	0.498	0.504	0.615
8. Product/service innovation success	3.38	1.065	3.98	0.634	-4.511	0.000

product/service innovation success. Table 5 presents the results of the relationship between innovation factors and product/service innovation success, moderated by strategic alignment and functional diversity. The control variables explained 23.9% of the variance in product/service innovation success in Model 1. The addition of the independent and moderating variables (organizational capability, competitive environment, product/service characteristics, strategic alignment, and functional diversity) to the control variables in Model 2 increased R^2 by 13.4% ($\Delta F = 15.484$, $p < 0.001$) over the explained variance in product/service innovation success in Model 1. The interaction terms added to the control variables and independent variables in Model 3 increased R^2 by 6.8% ($\Delta F = 7.205$, $p < 0.001$). This lent support to the first hypothesis of the study (H1).

The control variables estimated assets ($b = 0.027$, $t = 0.719$, $p > 0.10$), years of operation ($b = -0.018$, $t = -0.644$, $p > 0.10$) market dynamism and uncertainty ($b = 0.211$, $t = 1.627$, $p > 0.10$), environmental dynamism ($b = 0.030$, $t = 0.752$, $p > 0.10$), were not related to product/service innovation while technological dynamism ($b = 0.116$, $t = 3.490$, $p < 0.10$) and employees ($b = 0.010$, $t = 2.151$, $p < 0.50$) were related to product/service innovation.

Table 5 Regression results of the relationship between innovation factors and product/service innovation success moderated by strategic alignment and functional diversity

	Product/service innovation success		
	Model 1	Model 2	Model 3
Variables	*b* (*t*-values)	*b* (*t*-values)	*b* (*t*-values)
Control variables			
Constant	-0.019 (-0.307)	-0.050 (-0.681)	-0.073 (-0.964)
Employees	0.011 (2.239)*	0.010 (2.119)*	0.010 (2.151)*
Estimated assets	0.041 (1.117)	0.063 (1.661)†	0.027 (0.719)
Years of operation	-0.007 (-0.231)	-0.028 (-0.938)	-0.018 (-0.644)
Market dynamism and uncertainty	0.052 (1.046)	-0.134 (-2.574)**	0.211 (1.627)
Environmental dynamism	0.070 (3.867)***	-0.032 (-1.577)	0.030 (0.752)
Technological dynamism	0.256 (7.768)***	-0.050 (4.102)***	0.116 (3.490)***
Main effects			
Organizational capability		0.097 (3.391)***	0.089 (3.058)**
Competitive environment		0.077 (1.735)†	-0.191 (-1.664)†
Product/service characteristics		0.088 (3.453)***	0.104 (4.261)***
Strategic alignment		0.185 (3.702)***	0.132 (2.696)**
Functional diversity		0.165 (0.998)	0.169 (0.961)
Interaction effects			
Organizational capability × strategic alignment			0.354 (3.619)***
Competitive environment ×			0.064 (1.423)
Product/service characteristics ×			0.179 (2.173)**
Organizational capability × functional diversity			-1.169 (-2.689)**
Competitive environment ×			-0.305 (-2.301)*
Product/service characteristics ×			0.997 (2.580)**
R^2	0.239	0.373	0.441
F value	19.120***	19.531***	16.484***
ΔR^2	0.239	0.134	0.068
Partial *F* value	19.120***	15.484***	7.205***
Degrees of freedom	6/366	11/361	157/355
Durbin Waston test	1.930		

†$p < 0.10$, *$p < 0.05$, **$p < 0.01$, ***$p < 0.001$ (one-tailed test)

Note: Unstandardized regression coefficients were reported with *t*-values for each effect in parentheses

Competitive environment showed a negative relationship with product/service innovation success ($b = -0.191$, $t = -1.664$, $p < 0.10$). This outcome was in sharp contrast to the hypothesis developed for the study, thus not lending support to hypothesis two (H2). Product/service characteristics showed a positive relationship with product/service innovation success ($b = 0.104$, $t = 4.261$, $p < 0.001$). This lent support to the hypothesis three developed for the study (H3). This suggests that if a firm's product/service is superior (i.e., new and improves a customer's work efficiency compared to a competitor's product/services), it leads to product/service innovation success where growth is seen in the profitability of new products/services compared with the firm's business unit objectives. Although not hypothesized, the study found a positive and significant relationship between strategic alignment and product/service innovation success ($b = 0.132$, $t = 2.696$, $p < 0.01$). The results showed that the interaction between organizational capability and strategic alignment positively related product/service innovation success ($b = 0.354$, $t = 3.619$, $p < 0.001$). This suggests that the positive relationship between organizational capability and product/service innovation success is stronger when strategic alignment is high than when it is low. The interaction between strategic alignment and competitive environment positively related product/service innovation success but was insignificant ($b = 0.064$, $t = 1.423$, $p > 0.10$). This did not lend support to the hypothesis suggesting that strategic alignment plays no role in the relationship between competitive environment and product/service innovation. The interaction between strategic alignment and product/service characteristics positively related product/service innovation success ($b = 0.179$, $t = 2.173$, $p < 0.01$). This means that strategic alignment moderates the relationship between product/service characteristics and product/service innovation success.

The results showed that the interaction between functional diversity and organizational capability was negatively related to product/service innovation success ($b = -1.169$, $t = -2.689$, $p < 0.01$). This suggests that the positive relationship between organizational capability and product/service innovation success is weaker when functional diversity is high than when it is low. The interaction between functional diversity and competitive environment negatively related product/service innovation success ($b = -0.305$, $t = -2.301$, $p < 0.05$). This may suggest that an already competitive environment hinders the success of product/service innovation when firms have wider functional diversity. The interaction between functional diversity and product/service characteristics positively related product/service innovation success ($b = 0.997$, $t = 2.580$, $p < 0.01$). This means that functional diversity moderates the relationship between product/service characteristics and product/service innovation success (Tables 6 and 7).

From the extensive literature, SWOT analysis has been developed

Table 6 Summary of hypotheses

Hypothesis	Expected outcome	Empirical conclusions
1. Organizational capability positively relates to product/service innovation success rather than failure	+	Supported
2. Competitive environment is negatively related to products/service innovation success	-	Supported
3. Product characteristics is positively related to product/service success rather than failure.	+	Supported
4. The relationship between organizational capabilities and product/service innovation success would be enhanced when functional diversity is cognitive than when it is affective	+	Not supported
5. The positive impact of competitive environment on product/service innovation success would be enhanced when functional diversity is cognitive than when it is affective	+	Not supported
6. The positive effect of product characteristics on product/service innovation success would be higher when functional diversity is cognitive than when it is affective	+	Not supported
7. The positive effect of organizational capabilities would be enhanced if the level of strategic alignment is high than when it is low	+	Supported
8. The positive relationship between competitive environment and product/service innovation success is enhanced when strategic alignment ensures that firms adopt competitive aggressive strategies	+	Not supported
9. The positive impact of product characteristics on product/service innovation success would be enhanced with the appropriate strategic alignment while poor choice of strategy would lead to failure	+	Supported

Table 7 SWOT analysis of Ghana

Strengths	Opportunities
Drive for innovation	A system of mechanization
Creating value to the production of poultry products	Commercial sale of live birds
Weaknesses	**Threats**
Strong competitors	Threat of disease such as coccidiosis
	Access to finance, fluctuation in the sales price of eggs and meat due to seasonal demand variations

6 Conclusion and Recommendations

The innovation (main) and control variables (factors) for the study were explored through exploratory and confirmatory factor analysis. The study concluded on six main variables and three control variables through the factor analysis process. The main variables included strategic alignment, product/service characteristics, product/service innovation success, organizational capability, and competitive environment. The control variables were market dynamism and uncertainty, environmental dynamism, and technological dynamism. The findings of the study showed a significant positive relationship between organizational capability and product/service innovation success, lending support to the first hypothesis proposed in the study. Product/service characteristics also showed a positive relationship with product/service innovation success, and this lent support to the third hypothesis developed for the study. However, the competitive environment showed a negative relationship with product/service innovation success, also lending support to the second hypothesis developed for the study.

With regard to the moderating role of functional diversity, the findings of the study showed that the interaction between functional diversity and organizational capability was negatively related to product/service innovation success. Also, the interaction between functional diversity and competitive environment was negatively related to product/service innovation success. However, the interaction between functional diversity and product/service characteristics was positively related to product/service innovation success. These findings only lent support to the sixth hypothesis developed for the study. Furthermore, the study observed a positive and significant relationship between strategic alignment and product/service innovation success. With regard to the moderating role of strategic alignment, the interaction between organizational capability and strategic alignment was observed to be positively related to product/service innovation success. Also, the interaction between strategic alignment and competitive environment was positively related to product/service innovation success but was insignificant. In addition, the interaction between strategic alignment and product/service characteristics positively related to product/service innovation success. These findings lent support to the seventh and ninth hypotheses proposed in the study.

Based on the conclusion, we recommend the following:

Strengthen the capabilities of the organization: There is a need for SMEs to make a self-assessment of strengths and weaknesses in how they support their people to innovate (how might we enable our people to innovate?), if their organizational processes are supporting staff to innovate, and assess if they are utilizing the state-of-the-art tools and methods most suited to meet the needs of the workers in the innovation process.

Capitalize on product/service characteristics: SMEs need to aim at meeting the needs of the customers having superiority in terms of specifications that differentiate the product from other products or competitive offerings in the market.

Customize the implementation of best innovation practices to your own organization: The findings of this study showed that the competitive environment has a negative relationship with product/service innovation success when it comes to small enterprises. There is therefore a need for each enterprise to adopt an innovative practice to suit its own operating environment, specific to the industry in which it competes.

References

Abor, J. (2011). Do export status and export intensity increase firm performance? *Thunderbird International Business Review, 53*(1), 9–18.

Abor, J., & Biekpe, N. (2006). Small business financing initiatives in Ghana: Problems and perspectives in management. *Journal of Management Academy, 4*, 69–77.

Abor, J., & Quartey, P. (2010). Issues in SME development in Ghana and South Africa. *International Research Journal of Finance and Economics, 39*, 218–228.

Adom, P. K., Amakye, K., Doh, E., & Anku, R. (2014). SMEs record keeping in Ghana: Has VAT made it better? *International Journal of Economics and Financial Issues, 4*(1), 152.

Agyapong, D., & Attram, A. B. (2019). Effect of owner-manager's financial literacy on the performance of SMEs in the Cape Coast Metropolis in Ghana. *Journal of Global Entrepreneurship Research, 9*(1), 1–13.

Aiken, L. S., & West, S. G. (1991). *Multiple regression: Testing and interpreting interactions*. Sage.

Al-Mahrouq, M. (2010). Success factors of small and medium enterprises: The case of Jordan. *Zagreb International Review of Economics & Business, 13*(2), 89–106.

Arthur, P. (2003). The implications of state policy for micro-enterprise development. In W. P. Tettey (Ed.), *Critical perspectives on politics and socio-economic development in Ghana* (pp. 153–175). Brill.

Aryeetey, E., & Ahene, A. A. (2005). *Changing regulatory environment for small-medium size enterprises and their performance in Ghana (No. 1649-2016-135965)*. Centre on Regulation and Competition, Institute for Development Policy and Management, University of Manchester, Harold Hankins Building, Precinct Centre

Atuahene-Gima, K., Slater, S. F., & Olson, E. M. (2005). The contingent value of responsive and proactive market orientations for new product program performance. *Journal of Product Innovation Management, 22*(6), 464–482.

Avison, D., Jones, J., Powell, P., & Wilson, D. (2004). Using and validating the strategic alignment model. *The Journal of Strategic Information Systems, 13*(3), 223–246.

Baldwin, C. Y., & Clark, K. B. (1994). Capital-budgeting systems and capabilities investments in US companies after the Second World War. *Business History Review, 68*(1), 73–109.

Belderbos, R., Carree, M., & Lokshin, B. (2006). Complementarity in R&D cooperation strategies. *Review of Industrial Organization, 28*(4), 401–426.
Bryman, A. (2012). *Social research methods* (4th ed.). Oxford University Press.
Byrd, T. A., Lewis, B. R., & Bryan, R. W. (2006). The leveraging influence of strategic alignment on IT investment: An empirical examination. *Information & Management, 43*(3), 308–321.
Cofie, A. A. (2012). *The challenges of financing small and medium scale enterprises (SMEs) in the Ashanti region - A case study of Stanbic Bank (Gh) Ltd* (Doctoral dissertation).
Collis, D. J., & Montgomery, C. A. (1995). Competing on resources: Strategy in the 1990s. *Knowledge and Strategy, 1995*, 25–40.
Cook, P., & Nixson, F. (2000). *Finance and small and medium-sized enterprise development*. Finance and Development Research Programme Working Paper Series, 14. Institute for Development Policy and Management, University of Manchester.
European Commission (2012, September). *EU SMEs in 2012: At the crossroads, Annual report on small and medium-sized enterprises in the EU*. Ecory.
Frenz, M., & Ietto-Gillies, G. (2009). The impact on innovation performance of different sources of knowledge: Evidence from the UK Community innovation survey. *Research Policy, 38*(7), 1125–1135.
Galbraith, J. R. (1973). *Designing complex organizations*. Addison-Wesley Longman Publishing.
Hair, J. F., Black, W. C., Babin, B. J., & Anderson, R. E. (2010). *Multivariate data analysis: International version*. Pearson.
Haque, A. U., Sher, A., & Urbański, M. (2020). Is the role of authentic leadership effective in managing occupational stress and psychological capital? *Forum Scientiae Oeconomia, 8*(2), 59–77.
Henderson, R., & Cockburn, I. (1994). Measuring competence? Exploring firm effects in pharmaceutical research. *Strategic Management Journal, 15*(S1), 63–84.
Henderson, J., & Venkatramen, N. (1989). Strategic alignment: A model for organizational transformation. In T. Kochan & M. Unseem (Eds.), *Transforming organizations*. OUP.
Hoopes, D. G., Madsen, T. L., & Walker, G. (2003). Guest editors' introduction to the special issue: Why is there a resource-based view? Toward a theory of competitive heterogeneity. *Strategic Management Journal, 24*(10), 889–902.
Jaworski, B. J., & Kohli, A. K. (1993). Market orientation: Antecedents and consequences. *Journal of Marketing, 57*(3), 53 70.

Kong, L. (1998). *New product success and failure: Factors for new product success and failure in the New Zealand electronics industry*. Massey University.
Koput, K. (1997). A chaotic model of innovative search: Some answers, many questions. *Organization Science, 8*(5), 528–542.
Kusi, A., Opata, C. N., & Narh, T. W. J. (2015). Exploring the factors that hinder the growth and survival of small businesses in Ghana (A case study of small businesses within Kumasi metropolitan area). *American Journal of Industrial and Business Management, 5*(11), 705.
Li, T., & Calantone, R. J. (1998). The impact of market knowledge competence on new product advantage: Conceptualization and empirical examination. *Journal of Marketing, 62*(4), 13–29.
Mead, D. C., & Liedholm, C. (1998). The dynamics of micro and small enterprises in developing countries. *World Development, 26*(1), 61–74.
Murphy, A., & Ledwith, A. (2007). Project management tools and techniques in high-technology SMEs. *Management Research News, 30*(2), 153–166.
Nasution, H. N., & Mavondo, F. T. (2008). Organisational capabilities: Antecedents and implications for customer value. *European Journal of Marketing, 42*, 477.
Okech, T. C., & Ndagijimana, J. P. (2014). *Determinants of working capital management practices in small and medium enterprises in Nairobi. Incomplete.*
Oladele, O. P., Akeke, N. I., Adebisi, O. S., & Adeusi, S. O. (2013). Effects of strategic leadership styles on organisational development in small and medium enterprises (SMEs) in Lagos, Nigeria. *Net Journal of Social Sciences, 1*(2), 54–60.
Olawale, F., & Garwe, D. (2010). Obstacles to the growth of new SMEs in South Africa: A principal component analysis approach. *African Journal of Business Management, 4*(5), 729–738.
Osei, B., Baah-Nuakoh, A., Tutu, K. A., & Sowa, N. K. (1993). Impact of structural adjustment on small-scale enterprises in Ghana. In *Small enterprises and changing policies: Structural adjustment, financial policy and assistance programmes in Africa*. IT Publications.
Peprah, J. A., Mensah, A. O., & Akosah, N. B. (2016). Small and medium sized enterprises (SMEs) accessibility to public procurement: SMEs entity perspective in Ghana. *European Journal of Business and Social Sciences, 4*(11), 25–40.
Porter, M. E. (1996). Competitive advantage, agglomeration economies, and regional policy. *International Regional Science Review, 19*(1–2), 85–90.
Pullen, A. J., de Weerd-Nederhof, P. C., Groen, A. J., & Fisscher, O. A. (2012). Open innovation in practice: Goal complementarity and closed NPD

networks to explain differences in innovation performance for SMEs in the medical devices sector. *Journal of Product Innovation Management, 29*(6), 917–934.

Sarpong, O., & Teirlinck, P. (2017). The influence of functional and geographical diversity in collaboration on product innovation performance in SMEs. *Journal of Technology Transfer*, 1–29.

Schaper, M. (2002). Small firms and environmental management: Predictors of green purchasing in Western Australian pharmacies. *International Small Business Journal, 20*(3), 235–251.

Schon, D. A. (1967). *Technology and change: The new Heraclitus:[the impact of invention and innovation on American social and economic development]*. A Delta book.

Smaczny, T. (2001). Is an alignment between business and information technology the appropriate paradigm to manage IT in today's organisations? *Management Decision, 39*, 797.

Thandeka, R. K. (2008). *SME success in South Africa. A critical analysis of entrepreneurial and business skills in SMEs in the textile and clothing industry in Johannesburg, South Africa*. University of Pretoria.

Van Beers, C., & Zand, F. (2014). R&D cooperation, partner diversity, and innovation performance: An empirical analysis. *Journal of Product Innovation Management, 31*(2), 292–312.

Veskaisri, K., Chan, P., & Pollard, D. (2007). Relationship between strategic planning and SME success: Empirical evidence from Thailand. *Asia and Pacific DSI, 2007*, 1–13.

Webster, F. E., Jr. (1988). The rediscovery of the marketing concept. *Business Horizons, 31*(3), 29–39.

World Bank. (2015). *World development indicators*.

Is Interest Rate an Effective Instrument for Controlling Inflation and Its Effect on Investment Activities in Developing Countries?

Nor Isma Liyana binti Hasran, Jumadil Saputra, and Adnan ul Haque

1 Introduction

High inflation is often associated with lower growth and financial crises (Mishkin, 2008). Rising price levels are also associated with weaker investor confidence, eroding savings incentives, and financial and public sector balance sheets. In addition, the damage from high inflation can hit the poor disproportionately since the poorest households are more dependent on wage income, have less access to interest-bearing accounts,

N. I. L. binti Hasran
Universiti Malaysia Terengganu, Kuala Terengganu, Malaysia

J. Saputra
Faculty of Business, Economics and Social Development, Universiti Malaysia Terengganu, Kuala Terengganu, Malaysia

A. ul Haque (✉)
Faculty of Business, Yorkville University, Toronto, ON, Canada
e-mail: ahaque@yorkvilleu.ca

F. A. Yamoah, A. ul Haque (eds.), *Corporate Management Ecosystem in Emerging Economies*, https://doi.org/10.1007/978-3-031-41578-4_20

and are unlikely to have significant financial or real assets other than money. For these reasons, low and stable inflation is associated with better growth and development outcomes, financial stability, and poverty reduction. Disinflation has been broad-based across all groups of countries in recent decades and is reflected in multiple measures of inflation, including headline and core consumer prices, energy and food prices, producer prices, and the gross domestic product (GDP) deflator.

Disinflation began in the advanced economies in the mid-1980s and in the EMDEs in the mid-1990s and had stabilized at historically low levels. Inflation in the EMDEs fell from a stubborn double-digit in the 1970s, 1980s and most of the 1990s to 3.5% in 2017. By 2017, inflation had been at or below the central bank's target ranges for years, three-quarters of the EMDEs that had introduced inflation targets. As inflation has declined, so has its volatility, most notably in the transition economies of the former Soviet Union and sub-Saharan Africa. Will low inflation persist? One reason for optimism is that the combination of structural and political factors fuelling global disinflation is unlikely to be reversed. The most important was the unprecedented integration of international trade and financial markets. In the middle EMDE, like in the middle-advanced economy, trade has halved since 1970 to 75% of GDP in 2017, and international assets and liabilities have more than tripled (although still only a quarter of the level of advanced economies). Technological changes have also altered production processes in ways that affect pricing (Ha et al., 2019b).

On the policy front, introducing more resilient monetary, exchange rate, and fiscal frameworks by some EMDEs has enabled more effective inflation control (Ha et al., 2019a). Twenty-four EMDEs have introduced inflation-linked monetary policy frameworks since the late 1990s. In some EMDEs, structural reforms of labour and product markets have also supported disinflation by making markets more flexible and competitive. However, there is concern that the factors that have kept inflation in check for the past several decades may be losing momentum or declining. Rogoff (2003) concludes that the greatest threat to today's low inflation would be a reversal of the modern trend towards greater central bank independence, particularly if an economic slowdown drives the growth trend, they say, "a setback in globalization and economic liberalization." The growing protectionist sentiment of recent years and reform fatigue in economies may slow the pace of globalization and improvements in structural policies.

A key feature of the international inflationary experience of the past four or five decades has been the growing importance of a "global inflation cycle" (recorded as a common global factor in 1) to explain country-level inflation (Carney, 2015). Since 2001, this global factor has accounted for a quarter of the median change in inflation in advanced economies and nearly a fifth of the median in EMDEs. The global inflation cycle has been important in more developed countries and more integrated into the world economy.

Several structural and cyclical forces, including globalization, technological advances, changes in the political environment, and a variety of cyclical global shocks, likely drove the emergence of a global inflationary cycle. For example, global demand and oil price shocks have each accounted for 40% of the change in global inflation since 1970. In the median country, three global shocks (global demand, supply, and oil price shocks) have caused about a quarter of the change in domestic inflation since 2001. Of these, the most important were global demand (specifically the 2008–2009 global recession) and oil price shocks (specifically the 2014–2016 crash). However, domestic shocks—domestic supply shocks in particular—have continued to be the main source of fluctuations in domestic inflation.

A strengthening global inflation cycle raises concerns that central banks' control over domestic inflation may have eased. The timing of inflation itself does not require policy intervention (IMF, 2018). However, the heads of the major central banks of advanced economies have recognized the need to consider the global environment when setting monetary policy given the highly synchronized nature of global inflation (Ha et al., 2019b). The greater synchronicity of global inflation could increase the risk of policy errors when there is an appropriate response to undesirably low or high inflation. It differs depending on the underlying inflation shock's origin (domestic or foreign) (Hartmann & McAdam, 2018). In addition, a weakening of the impact of monetary policy on domestic inflation could increase the risk that fiscal policy responds to excessive or insufficient domestic demand.

For policymakers, these observations point to a growing urgency to build resilience to global and national shocks and to develop a deeper understanding of their underlying causes. This is particularly true for EMDEs with fast-growing or deep integration into the global economy or those with weak monetary policy frameworks. Options for protecting economies from the effects of the one global shock include the active use of countercyclical measures, the strengthening of institutions, including through greater independence of central banks, and creation of a fiscal environment resilient enough to contribute to the macroeconomic stabilization effectively. The global inflation cycle could also argue for coordinated monetary policy action to respond to undesirably low or high global inflation. Coordinated actions could increase the impact of the actions implemented by individual countries.

Al-Shammari and Al-Sabaey (2012) identified the main sources of inflation in developed and developing countries. Panel model used with random effects. The model's predictions are tested on annual data from 1970 to 2007. The estimated impact on inflation is examined from four main perspectives: demand-side factors, monetary factors, an external factor, and a supply-side factor. The results indicate that the main determinants of inflation in developed countries differ from those in developing countries.

In developed countries, the main sources of inflation are government spending, money supply growth, world oil prices, the interest rate, the nominal effective exchange rate, and population. Considering that the main sources of inflation for developing countries are public spending, world oil prices, and the nominal effective exchange rate. The surprising finding of money growth can be explained by the role of money in the economy, be it in developing or developed countries. Such an outcome suggests that although the money supply in the economy is growing, it may be the case that the level of inflation is falling. In addition to the empirical insights of the tested model, the results can be used by both monetary authorities and policymakers to specify the country's overall economic policy. A number of policy implications can be derived from the estimates in this paper. First of all, it seems that inflation in developed countries is determined by all the main aspects affecting inflation: demand-side factors (government spending, population), monetary factors (money supply growth, interest rate), supply-side factors (oil prices), and external factors (nominal effective exchange rate). Furthermore, inflation in developing countries is stimulated more by the effects of the demand side (government spending), the supply side (oil prices), and the external factor (effective nominal exchange rate) than by monetary variables. As a result, this also means that inflation in developing countries is not really a monetary phenomenon.

Therefore, the authorities of developing countries can control inflation by effectively using fiscal policy (through government spending), improving their trade position so as not to be heavily dependent on importers, and finally implementing the appropriate exchange rate policy. As in developed countries, price developments in these countries are largely determined by monetary variables, such as the interest rate. Therefore, monetary policy can play an important role in controlling domestic inflation. In addition to monetary variables, other economic factors such as public spending, oil prices, private consumption (as measured by population) and the nominal effective exchange rate influence economic activity in developed countries and, consequently, domestic price movements. In addition, these factors appear to go hand in hand with influencing domestic prices.

Factors that influence the investment activity afford the hobby independence price and go back price graph, in addition to analyses of how the overseas funding boom occurs. An important aspect of the economic system is the investment process. Macroeconomic elements are such situations that are immediately associated with the economic system on a countrywide stage and seize a massive part of its population. When the funding plan is being advanced for the enterprise, the ideas beneath need to be followed: accounting for the dangers and inflation, financial investments justification, and dependable and inexpensive financing methods. Summarizing, each of those factors has a not unusual place to persuade the funding activity, and this already implies an effect on the complete US economic system. In general, they conclude that each element as an entire has a not unusual place aim. This is to persuade funding activity, which already affects the complete US economic system (Anastasiya M. Gladkikh et al., 2023).

Al-Shammari and Al-Sabaey (2012) stated that in developed countries, the main sources of inflation are government spending, money supply growth, world oil prices, the interest rate, the nominal effective exchange rate, and population. Considering that the main sources of inflation for developing countries are public spending, world oil prices, and the nominal effective exchange rate. The surprising finding of money growth can be explained by the role of money in the economy, be it in developing or developed countries. Such an outcome suggests that although the money supply in the economy is growing, it may be the case that the level of inflation is falling.

Anastasiya M. Gladkikh et al. (2023) analyse the factors that affect investment activity, provide the interest independence rate and return rate graph, and analyse how foreign investment growth occurs. An important component of the economy is the investment process. Macroeconomic factors are such conditions that are directly related to the economy at the national level and capture a large part of its population. When the investment plan is being developed at the enterprise, the principles below should be followed: accounting of the risks and inflation, economic investment justification, reliable and cheaper financing methods. Summarizing, we can state that all these factors have a common goal to influence the investment activity, which already impacts the entire country's economy. In general, we can conclude that all these factors have a common goal to influence the investment activity, which already implies an impact on the entire country's economy.

In conjunction with the present issues, this study is written to identify the level of inflation, interest rate, money supply, exchange rate, and foreign direct investment. Also, to examine the effectiveness of interest rates in controlling inflation in developing countries. Besides that, this study aims to investigate the mediating role of interest rate in controlling investment in developing countries.

2 Literature Review

Inflation

The role of inflation targeting as a price signalling mechanism is to reduce price information asymmetry and potentially reduce incentives for corruptive actions through its direct control on the inflation rate, thus simultaneously increasing institutional quality (Stojanovikj, 2022). The obtained evidence suggests that adopting inflation targeting lowers corruption in a sample of 61 developing countries for the period between 1990 and 2018. Countries that have adopted inflation targeting experience lower corruption levels, as measured by the corruption perceptions (CP) index, controlling for other relevant determinants of corruption identified in the empirical literature, such as inflation, level of income, income distribution, trade openness, and the rule of law. This result is sensitive to the type of inflation targeting adopted. Soft (unofficial) inflation targeting has no significant effect on the corruption level, supporting the claim that strong institutional commitment, accompanied by transparency and constant communication regarding inflation targets by the central bank, provides an adequate price signalling mechanism. In addition, the analysis provides evidence that an efficient rule of law reduces corruption levels significantly. However, its effects are rather modest to support the claims that it can solely lessen corruptive behaviour in the sample of developing countries.

Stojanovikj (2022) investigates how government size, as a proxy for fiscal stabilisation policy and inflation targeting, affects the amplitude of the economic cycle and private consumption volatility in a sample of developing nations from 1990 to 2018. Considering these variables' possible endogeneity and controlling for exogenous variance in trade openness, the study shows that government size greatly decreases business cycle volatility while having no effect on private consumption volatility. On the other hand, adopting inflation targeting greatly increases the amplitude of the volatility of real production growth while significantly lowering the volatility of private spending. The adopted inflation targeting regime has no substantial impact on the acquired outcomes.

Chang and Zhang (2022) offer a new explanation for why the literature's claimed growth effect of inflation is a reversed relationship, with lower limit considerations on the rates of lending by banks. We incorporate a non-zero lower interest rate limit in the debate and highlight how inflation affects ideal bank loan contracts. When the lending rate limitation is non-binding, this article contends that informational friction is a cause of the negative link between inflation and growth. Furthermore, it discovers that once this lending rate limitation is enforced, rising inflation can lower the real cost of financing capital investment, hence contributing to growth. This research shows that the non-zero lowest value can be attained only at moderate inflation rates. It suggests emerging nations with low capital conversion efficiency and high transaction costs have a stronger inflation-growth nexus than industrialized countries.

Kalu et al. (2022) reveal that Africa's stock markets are weak and have failed to meet the continent's financial expectations, such as rapid economic development. This chapter investigates the key macroeconomic variables of African growth in stock markets. The study looks at private sector credit, foreign investment, external strategic factors, supply of money, trade openness, per capita GDP, inflation, and interest rates to determine African stock market growth. The study generates a panel data collection of eight African nations from 1994 to 2018 using the pooled mean group estimate technique. According to the report, measures to strengthen African commodity prices should focus on expanding the private market through greater per capita income and better foreign reserve management in order to enhance trust among local and foreign investors.

Alexandrov et al. (2021) examine the impact of household income and money supply on inflation. This study aims to look at the link between inflation, income level, and the money supply by using coefficients for inflation elasticity in relation to household income and the money supply. The authors' premise is that rise in family income and the money supply would affect inflation differently in various national economies. Because of the high inflation elasticity about family income and the money supply in developing economies, the inflationary process is more abrupt and severe, causing substantial harm to the national economy. To analyse the dependency of inflation on income and the money supply, the authors employed their parameters for the inflation elasticity concerning income and the money supply. According to their predictions, the coefficient of inflation in relation to family incomes and the supply of money will be lower in impoverished nations. As a result, poor nations experience more inflation, because in the case of revenue growth and unsecured money issue, all funds gained will be used to fulfil present needs, resulting in an immediate, rapid price increase.

Kartaev and Tubdenov (2021) devoted themselves to investigating the impact of changes in monetary policy transparency on the impact that exchange rates pass-through in consumer pricing. Based on cross-country panel data econometric modelling, it is demonstrated that increasing the disclosure of interaction between the reserve bank and the nation results in a decline in the elasticity of domestic inflation about the exchange rate in countries that target rising prices and adhere to other central bank regimes. The impact is seen in both established and emerging countries, albeit stronger in the latter. The achieved result might be viewed as evidence in support of the Bank of Russia shifting from a vocal explanation of its future activities to a written description.

Chugunov et al. (2021) show that inflation targeting (IT) is a monetary policy regime that has successfully stabilized both inflation and the real economy. Twenty members of the OECD and about 20 developing countries have adopted this monetary regime. This paper aims to evaluate the influence of targeting an inflation regime on economic growth in advanced and developing countries. The results showed that IT had no remarkable impact on the GDP per capita growth rate in the five-year post-inflation targeting period. Empirical research revealed that the inflation level does not significantly influence economic growth in the long run. We observed a positive influence of the IT regime on decreasing the volatility of real output in both advanced and developing countries. After full-fledged IT adoption, consumer inflation and its volatility in the OECD and emerging economies decreased steeply. However, the onward inflation trend existed for "non-IT-targeters," too. The study also describes the Ukrainian experience with monetary-policy strategy. Data showed that IT caused to reduce inflation in Ukraine after its 2014–2015 economic and financial crises.

NGOC (2020) investigates low inflation and sustainable growth as the major macroeconomic goals pursued by every developing country, including Vietnam. The effect of inflation on economic growth has been intensively analysed by a variety of studies, but the empirical evidence often remains controversial and ambiguous. One common hypothesis of previous studies is that they have assumed that the effect of inflation on growth is symmetric. The main purpose of this study is to investigate the asymmetric effect of inflation and money supply on economic growth using the nonlinear autoregressive distributed lag approach introduced by Shin et al. (2013) for Vietnam over the period 1990–2017. Empirical results provide evidence that the effects of inflation on economic growth are negative and asymmetric in the long run. The impact of the money supply on growth is positive in both the short and long run. Accordingly, the impact of the increase in the inflation rate is bigger than the decrease in the long run. This different impact is significant and high inflation will destruct economic activities. As a result, the study provides an empirical evidence for the authorities to plan monetary policies and control the inflation rate to achieve sustainable economic development in the long run.

Monetary Policy

Arsić et al. (2022) examine the macroeconomic performance resulting from adopting an inflation targeting policy in emerging economies of Europe and Central Asia. The research includes 26 countries in the period 1997–2019, with a special focus on the period 2008–2019. Our econometric analysis consists of two approaches: dynamic panel modelling and propensity score matching. The results suggest that macroeconomic performance has improved due to the inflation-targeting monetary framework. We find that a policy of inflation targeting has been effective in reducing the inflation rate, inflation volatility, and GDP volatility. The results are particularly robust for the subperiod that started in 2008. Econometric results suggest that inflation targeting policy did not affect inflation persistence or GDP growth. Our results suggest that inflation targeting improves the macroeconomic performance of developing countries even when they only partially meet the standard requirements for its implementation.

Klutse et al. (2022) show the exchange market pressure index has proven to be a major indicator in identifying exchange rate crises in economies; however, due to the complexities surrounding developing economies, the efficacy of the index has been called to question. Specifically, the selection of an appropriate index and the problem of selecting the appropriate threshold for identifying exchange market pressure. To investigate this issue, this study identifies exchange rate crisis episodes in South Africa and Ghana using ridge regression, a discrete threshold regression, and dynamic ordinary least square (DOLS) models. The results are robust in resolving the problems with an exchange market pressure index. They also point to uneven inflation targeting policy framework implementation in the studied countries.

Sharma et al. (2022) aim to revisit the theme of fiscal-monetary coordination in a general equilibrium setup that allows for unconventional monetary policy, monetary policy transmission, and developing country characteristics. The method uses a calibrated new Keynesian dynamic stochastic general equilibrium (DSGE) model to study fiscal–monetary interaction. Findings: debt sits at the centre of monetary–fiscal interaction. Under high-debt conditions, the inflation-output trade-off rises with an increase in the strictness with which monetary policy targets inflation, undermining the standard prescription of strict inflation targeting. At the same time, the transmission of monetary policy is also impeded, resulting in unconventional monetary policy becoming more appropriate. The need for coordination among the policies gets enhanced in the presence of a borrowing cost channel. While the borrowing cost channel increases the need for policy coordination regardless of the debt situation, features such as higher share of non-Ricardian households and weaker monetary policy transmission affect monetary–fiscal interaction to a greater extent under high-debt environment.

Ghazinoory and Hashemi (2022) suggested that governments can implement monetary and fiscal policies to facilitate the formation and growth of firms, such as tax incentives and direct funding. In developing countries, these incentives are for various purposes, such as to regulate the allocation of resources, support private sector investments through incentives, palliate inequality between income and wealth, control inflation, and create resources for the public sector.

Mhmood et al. (2021) making a comparison to the past, the 2010–2018 global financial crisis has given many developing countries the legitimacy and capabilities to adopt countercyclical policies. It made them better to confront the global downturn and thereby comply with the developing countries. The author analyses the economic situation at home and around the world, evaluates inflationary trends and their viewpoints, and examines the reasons for monetary policy decisions in a straightforward manner. At the international level, in part due to lower oil prices and moderation of economic growth, inflation moderated during the first quarter of the year, in some of the world's leading economies. There is still inflation in advanced economies, which helps them delay their monetary policy mechanism for a while. The implementation of the monetary policy therefore refers to the selection of the inflation target for medium-term reasons and is consolidated by the effectiveness of a flexible rate regime; using financial control tools of indirect value (MSO) and using indicative variables, which favour the decision of the market as well as by reinforcing the monetary policy.

Mbilla et al.'s (2021) study purpose was to examine the effect of monetary policy on key macroeconomic indicators in Ghana. The study used annual time series data from 2002 to 2017, which was sourced from the World Development Indicator (WDI) and the Bank of Ghana (BOG). The data were converted to Quarterly data between 2002Q1 and 2017Q4, which covers a sample period of 16 years. The study employed the autoregressive distributed lagged model (ARDL) for analysing the data. Unit root test was conducted using the augmented Dickey–Fuller (ADF) tests, and the analysis results exhibited a cointegration relationship among the variables of order one (1). Monetary policy changes affected lending rates by (0.32%) compared to the other variables. Overall, the results suggest that monetary policy affects macroeconomic indicators performance in Ghana. Based on the foregoing, the paper recommends the need for policy intervention in determining the stance of fiscal policies, develop financial markets, and liberalize controlled interest rates to enhance the effectiveness of monetary policy.

Bentzen and Tung (2021) find out that Vietnam is an Asian emerging country, which now is ranked in the group of the fastest-growing economies worldwide. However, this economy has faced galloping inflation in recent years. So, the Vietnamese experience is a valuable reference for the policymakers in the developing world to successfully control price volatility. Our study applies the vector autoregressive method, the Johansen cointegration test, and the Granger causality test to examine the impact of fiscal and monetary policy on price volatility in Vietnam with a quarterly data sample collected over the period from 2004 to 2018. The study results confirm the existence of a long-term cointegration relationship between these policies and price volatility in Vietnam. Besides, the variance decomposition and impulse response function also show that the impact of these policies on inflation is clear. However, fiscal policy more strongly affects inflation than monetary policy. Finally, the Granger causality test also indicates one-way causality relationships between the government expenditure as well as the exchange rate to price volatility in the study period.

Nguyen (2020) employs a meta-regression analysis (MRA) to synthesize vector-autoregressive findings of the output effects of tightening monetary policy in 32 emerging and developing countries. The outcomes indicate a publication bias. However, tightening monetary policy has a real negative effect on output. Primary studies, including commodity price variable(s), tend to report stronger negative effects. Output effects are likely to be more negative in an economy with a developed financial system and less effective in an economy with high inflation volatility.

Interest Rate

Serikova et al. (2022) examine the ways to improve and increase the level of efficiency of the tax system based on the analysis of its impact on the performance indicators of socio-economic development of Kazakhstan. The sample for the study is presented according to the financial and statistical data of the Ministry of Finance of the Republic of Kazakhstan. Moreover, secondary data from International Monetary Fund (IMF) reports were used to analyse international trends on the research topic. The additive model is used to analyse the collected data. According to this model, socio-economic development is represented by indicators of the growth rate of real GDP, inflation, unemployment, and the official exchange rate. The study reveals that the absence of link between the growth of real gross domestic product and fiscal instruments indicates low degree of efficiency of the tax system of the analysed country. At the same time, the increase in the level of tax audits burdens business development in the form of extra-transactional production costs. In addition, with the active measures of the state to optimize and simplify tax processes and improve the quality of tax administration, the issues of assessing the economic effect of the implementation of the existing tax policy and its role in sustainable socio-economic development remain relevant.

Sharku et al. (2021) explore the economic factors which stimulate the demand for insurance products in Albania because the insurance industry has a significant effect on the economic development of a country. Albania is a developing country and insurance market has progressed moderately. Considering density insurance as a proxy for life and non-life insurance market development, the authors have examined the economic determinants of the Albanian insurance market from 2009 to 2020 based on quarterly data. The analysis is performed using vector error correction model, designing separate models for each insurance segment: life and non-life. This paper examines the effect of GDP, inflation, real interest rate, and unemployment among several economic variables. According to the empirical results, GDP per capita has the most significant impact, while unemployment is insignificant regarding life and non-life insurance density. The results are mostly in accordance with the empirical research work, and they are valuable to academics and insurance industry experts.

Drobyshevsky et al. (2021) aim to estimate a short-term neutral real interest rate (NRI) in Russia after transition to inflation targeting. The article reviews theoretical factors, demonstrating the difference between short-term and long-term neutral real interest rates. The following analysis of estimates of NRI in different countries shows that its decline in developed and developing countries is due to various factors. Further, the article provides a comparative analysis of the advantages and disadvantages of three main NRI estimation approaches: financial market indicators, statistical methods, and multilevel theoretical models. Based on the multivariate unobserved components model (UCM) for the Russian economy, the article concludes that the short-term NRI decreased from 5 to 1% in 2016–2020, whereas monetary policy was predominantly neutral.

Capasso et al.'s (2019) study aims to analyse the long-term nature of the interrelationship between interest rate and exchange rate. By employing Mexican data, the authors estimate a non-linear autoregressive distributed lags (NARDL) model to investigate the nature of the changes and the interaction between interest rate and exchange rate in response to monetary authorities' actions. The results show that, contrary to simplistic predictions, the real exchange rate causes the real interest rate asymmetrically. The bounds testing approach of the NARDL models suggests the presence of co-integration among the variables, and the exchange rate variations appear to have significant long-run effects on the interest rate. Most importantly, these effects are asymmetric and positive variations in the exchange rate have a lower impact on the interest rate. It is also interesting to report that the reverse is not true: the interest rate in the long run exerts no statistically significant impact on the exchange rate. Under inflation targeting and flexible exchange rate regime, despite central banks pursuing the control of short-term interest rate, in the long run one could observe that the exchange rate influences the interest rate, and this reverse causality is stronger in emerging economies. This paper contributes by analysing the asymmetric relationship between the variables.

Foreign Direct Investment

Four risk dimensions of inward FDI alongside economic growth for 48 developing countries for 2000–2019 using fixed effects and system GMM models (Okafor et al., 2022). After controlling for potential endogeneity issues, the results show that economic growth and currency rate have robust positive effect on FDI inflows. In contrast, the inflation rate and financial risk have negative impacts. Political risk at both the contemporaneous and lagged terms had inconsistent results. The nexus between FDI and risk dimensions emends significantly with the risk cluster analysis that finds a strong interplay among financial and currency risks having economic growth in the centre. Results suggest that countries with stable economic growth can cover an extent ('U' shaped relationship) of inflation, currency, and financial risks. The worst possible countries have unstable political conditions, which cannot be mitigated by higher economic growth. They propose a two-layer FDI decision typology that includes country-specific endogenous and non-country-specific exogenous factors in primary and secondary layers. Using a location-risk typology, they relate our discussions on the locational advantage from the eclectic paradigm with the approaches to risk management in international investment.

McCloud and Delgado (2022) determine some countries have adopted an inflation targeting (IT) regime to reduce inflation and inflation uncertainty: two factors the literature suggests firms put positive weight on when making outlay decisions that may affect aggregate domestic investment. This observation naturally leads to whether domestic investment responds to IT. We apply the synthetic control method to developed and developing IT and non-IT countries to estimate the IT regime's causal effect on domestic investment over time while addressing country heterogeneity. Adopting an IT regime had no short- or long-run effect, at conventional levels of significance, on domestic investment in 21 out of 29 treated countries; this dominant pattern appears consistent with recent works on rational inattentive behaviour of firms. However, IT induced mainly long-run heterogeneous changes in domestic investment prices in nine targeters, suggesting that supply constraints external to firms can also weaken the link between IT and domestic investment.

Imran and Rashid (2022) classify the extreme gross foreign direct investment (FDI) flow episodes into four types. It empirically investigates the determinants of each type by estimating complementary log–log (Clog–log) and probit regressions for 50 developing economies from 1990 to 2018. We document that domestic GDP growth rate, inflation, institutional quality, and human capital are the major empirical drivers of FDI flows. The world uncertainty index (WUI) is negatively associated with FDI inflows toward developing countries. Moreover, we find that the domestic GDP growth rate is positively associated with the probability of having FDI surge and FDI flight. In contrast, inflation is negatively linked with FDI surge episodes. These findings better explain the empirical determinants of FDI flows to and from developing countries. The findings also help to understand the behaviour of extreme FDI movements.

Abdelraouf and Noureldin (2022) study the impact of the exchange rate regime (ERR) on the dispersion of the cross-section distribution of price changes in a large panel of advanced and developing economies. We show that the ERR has an economically and statistically significant nonlinear impact on the dispersion of the price-change distribution. While intermediate regimes are associated with higher dispersion, floating exchange rates deliver lower dispersion. Fixed ERRs are also associated with lower dispersion; however, the impact is only marginally significant. This finding holds after controlling for different types of economic shocks, the characteristics of the monetary policy regime, and structural and institutional variables that impact cross-country variation in the price-change distribution. With few exceptions, the results are robust to controlling for mean inflation, alternative ERR classifications, different country groups, and the use of instruments to address the potential endogeneity of the choice of ERR.

Mukhametov (2021) scrutinizes the relationship between central bank independence and foreign direct investment (FDI) inflows. The relevance of this goal is based on the results of recent studies, which indicate that the inflow of direct investment into the economy depends not only on its indicators of economic development but also on the quality of the institutional environment. The study used a sample of 180 countries covering the period from 1970 to 2012 to model the relationship between the level of central bank independence and foreign direct investment inflows. The primary method used in the study is linear panel regression with country-specific fixed effects. The results of the econometric modelling demonstrate that an increase in the central bank independence index has a statistically significant positive effect on the inflow of foreign investment. This result can serve as the basis for monetary policy reforms, particularly in developing countries, since the expansion of the central bank's independence can become a factor in increasing the investment attractiveness of the economy.

Agudze and Ibhagui (2021) investigate the effects of inflation on FDI in 74 countries clustered into industrialized and developing economies. Contrary to previous studies, we show that the link between inflation and FDI is nonlinear, with evidence of threshold effects in both industrialized and developing economies. The inflation threshold is about five times higher in developing than industrialized economies. Inflation tends to reduce FDI in industrialized economies after exceeding its threshold whereas in developing economies, its impact on FDI is negative even before exceeding its threshold. We propose that the long-standing evidence of mixed relations between inflation and FDI, which is well documented in the literature, may be explained by the existence of previously ignored threshold effects.

Nguyen et al. (2021) analyse the labour force's effect and several other factors on FDI attraction in Vietnam. The empirical model is employed to perform regression and correlation on the impact of the labour force, real gross domestic product, inflation, business freedom index, and investment freedom index on Vietnam's FDI attraction using a secondary time series data set during the period 1995–2018. The empirical results found that both labour force and inflation have a positive influence on FDI at a 5% significance level; index of business freedom has a positive impact on FDI at a 10% significance level; and real gross domestic product and index of investment freedom have a positive impact on FDI at a 1% significance level. From these results, this study proposes several important policy implications for Vietnam in attracting FDI in the future.

Kueh and Soo's (2020) study is to examine the macroeconomic determinants of FDI inflows in Cambodia, Laos, Myanmar, and Vietnam. There are many factors that obstruct the ability in attracting investments into developing countries. The selected macroeconomics determinants are market size, inflation rate, openness, real effective exchange rate, and labour force. This study covered from 2000 to 2016 using annual data. The methods adopted are panel unit root tests, panel cointegration tests, fully-modified ordinary least square (FMOLS) and panel Granger causality. The study findings indicate that all the exogenous variables are cointegrated and significant in influencing FDI inflow. However, in the short run, there is only a unidirectional causal relationship.

Sabir et al. (2019) investigate the impact of institutional quality on foreign direct investment (FDI) inflows using panel data for low, lower-middle, upper-middle, and high-income countries for the sample period of 1996–2016 using the system generalized method of moments (GMM). The empirical results confirm that institutional quality positively impacts FDI in all groups of countries. The magnitude of the coefficients of control of corruption, government effectiveness, political stability, regulatory quality, rule of law, and voice and accountability for FDI inflows are greater in developed countries than in developing countries. We conclude that institutional quality is a more important determinant of FDI in developed countries than in developing countries. However, GDP per capita, agriculture value-added as a percentage of GDP, and inflation influence FDI inflows negatively in developed countries, while GDP per capita, trade openness, agriculture value-added as a percentage of GDP, and infrastructure have positive and statistically significant impacts on FDI inflows in developing countries. Trade openness as a percentage of GDP and infrastructure positively affect FDI in developed countries. From our analysis, we infer that institutional quality is a more important determinant of FDI in developed countries than in developing countries.

3 Materials and Methods

This study adopts a quantitative approach by utilizing secondary data. The data were collected from the World Bank. For empirical analysis, this study uses the unbalanced panel data of 20 countries in Asia Pacific, South America, West Africa, and Middle East, namely, Bangladesh, Brunei, China, India, Indonesia, Laos, Malaysia, Maldives, Mongolia, Myanmar, Pakistan, Philippines, Singapore, Sri Lanka, Thailand, Vietnam, Chile, Colombia, Jordan, and Nigeria from 1991 to 2021, using EViews. This study focuses on interest rate, inflation, and foreign direct investment (FDI). To measure the variables, we use several reliable and prominent proxies. Foreign direct investment (FDI) is reflected by interest rate (IR) and money supply (MS). Broad money is a proxy for the economy's money supply, GDP per capita is a measure of economic growth, and the lending interest rate represents the country's interest rate. The official exchange rate is measured by the exchange rate. All data are presented in logarithmic form for consistency of interpretation and ease of measurement. The panel data regression analysis is used in the study to completely analyse both the direct effect and indirect effect of interest rates to inflation, inflation to FDI and interest rate to FDI. The IS–LM model by John Hicks can help to understand this study. The interest rate has a mediating effect on inflation and FDI.

Definition of Operational Variables

This study uses the World Development Indicator (WDI) from the World Bank from 1991 until 2021. We also utilize reliable and prominent proxies for representing the variables of inflation, interest rate, money supply, exchange rate, and foreign direct investment such as the consumer price index, real interest rate, broad money and real effective exchange rate as a proxy for inflation, interest rate, money supply, and exchange rate and the foreign direct investment involves the foreign direct investment net BOP. The data is unbalanced panel data due to the absence of certain data findings for certain countries. As for foreign direct investment, it is measured by net BOP foreign direct investment. All variables are transformed to the form of the logarithm. Table 1 shows the definitions of the variables.

Data Analysis

All data are presented in logarithmic form for consistency of interpretation and ease of measurement. The Keynesian theory of inflation can help you understand this study. The inflation function was derived using the liquidity preference equation, with inflation as the dependent variable and interest rate as one of the independent variables.

$$Mt / P = \alpha Y \beta 1 + r \beta 2 \qquad (1)$$

where Mt is money demand, P is price level, Y is the national income, and r is the interest rate. The equation simply shows that the level of income in the economy and the interest rate impact total real money demand. As a result, Eq. (2) depicts the ultimate inflation function. These factors influence FDI inflows and are part of a model that may be written as a regression equation after converting FDI inflow and MS to logarithmic form. Converting FDI inflows and MS to logarithmic form reduces the raw data of variables and produces better estimate results:

Table 1 Definitions of operational variables

Variables	Dimension/ proxies	Definition of variables
Independent variables		
Inflation (INFL)	Consumer price index (CPI)	A consumer price index is a price index, the price of a weighted average market basket of consumer goods and services purchased by households. Changes in measured CPI track
Interest rate (IR)	Real interest rate	The real interest rate is the rate of interest an investor, saver or lender receives after allowing for inflation. It can be described more formally by the Fisher equation, which states that the real interest rate is approximately the nominal interest rate minus the inflation rate
Money supply (MS)	Broad money	In economics, broad money is a measure of the amount of money, or money supply, in a national economy including both highly liquid "narrow money" and less liquid forms
Exchange rate (EXC)	Real effective exchange rate	Real effective exchange rate is the nominal effective exchange rate (a measure of the value of a currency against a weighted average of several foreign currencies) divided by a price deflator or index of costs
Dependent variables		
Foreign direct investment (FDI)	Net BOP foreign direct investment	Foreign direct investment are net inflows of investment to acquire a lasting management interest (10% or more of voting stock) in an enterprise operating in an economy other than that of the investor

$$INF = f\left(\mathrm{M2}, Y, r\right) \tag{2}$$

Model Specifications

Equation (2) can be presented in an econometric log form/function as follows:

$$\text{FDIit} = \beta 0 + \beta 1\text{lnMSit} + \beta 2\text{INFLit} + \beta 3\text{IRit} + \beta 4\text{lnEXCit} + uit \quad (3)$$

where FDIit is the foreign direct investment, lnMSit is a log of the money supply, INFLit represents the level of consumer price index, and IRit is the lending interest rate. In addition, we include lnEXCit which is a log of exchange rate as a measure of official exchange rate, βi and δ are parameters/coefficients of the variables and time trend, *i* is the developing countries signifies data to check the effect of inflation, *t* is the time signifies time series data to check the effect of time on inflation (time trend), and *u* is the error term. Using final prediction error (FPE), sequential modified LR test statistic (each test at 5% level), Akaike information criterion (AIC), Hannan–Quinn criteria (HQ), and Schwarz criterion (SC) information criteria revealed that auto lag should be selected. Auto regressive distributive lag (ARDL) test result, estimates the variables log of log of money supply (lnMSt), and the log of exchange rate (lnEXCt) was conducted using maximum lags 2.

4 Results

Descriptive Statistics

This study presents the results using descriptive statistics, correlations, and panel data regression analyses. This section will discuss parallel with this research objective, which will investigate the effectiveness of interest rates in controlling inflation in developing countries and examine the effect of interest rates on investment in developing countries.

Table 2 displays the descriptive statistics for 20 selected countries (Bangladesh, Brunei, China, India, Indonesia, Laos, Malaysia, Maldives,

Table 2 The results of descriptive statistics analysis

Variables	Mean	Standard deviation	Min	Max
Foreign direct investment (FDI)	3.580	4.364	-37.173	43.912
Inflation (INFL)	7.343	10.402	-2.315	125.272
Interest rate (IR)	5.074	7.638	-42.099	50.979
Exchange rate (EXC)	4.275	2.913	-0.344	10.052
Money supply (MS)	4.033	0.645	1.961	5.356

Mongolia, Myanmar, Pakistan, Philippines, Singapore, Sri Lanka, Thailand, Vietnam, Chile, Colombia, Jordan, and Nigeria). The mean of foreign direct investment (FDI) is 3.580, with the standard deviation value being 4.364. Further, the mean value of inflation is 7.343, with a standard deviation equal to 10.402. The interest rate is 5.074 and the standard deviation as much as 7.638. The mean value of exchange rate is 4.275, with the standard deviation value equal to 2913. Lastly, the money supply has a mean value of 4.033 with a standard deviation of 0.645.

The Effectiveness of Interest Rate to Control Inflation in Developing Countries

In addition, this study also examines the multiple correlation analysis among variables to determine the correlation coefficient among them. The results of correlation analysis are seen in Table 3.

Table 3 shows the result that money supply (MS) has a significant positive correlation with foreign direct investment (FDI). The correlation coefficient between money supply (MS) and foreign direct investment (FDI) is 0.127. It indicates that when money supply (MS) increases, then foreign direct investment (FDI) increased as much as 1.27% and conversely. Through this correlation analysis, we found the money supply (MS) is highly correlated to the foreign direct investment (FDI) when compared with the inflation (INFL), interest rate (IR), and exchange rate (EXC).

Further, correlation analysis for other variables involved comprises money supply (MS) and interest rate (IR). We found two interesting

Table 3 The result of correlation analysis

Variables	Coefficient (*r*)
Inflation (INFL)	-0.002
Interest rate (IR)	-0.077
Exchange rate (EXC)	-0.016
Money supply (MS)	0.127

findings. First, the money supply (MS) positively and significantly correlates with foreign direct investment (FDI). Meanwhile, interest rate significantly negatively correlates with foreign direct investment (FDI). Both have a correlation coefficient of 0.1 (MS is 0.127 and IR is -0.077). Based on the correlation result of money supply (MS) and interest rate (IR), the correlation between money supply and foreign direct investment (FDI) can be categorized as high. However, when the money supply (MS) increases as much as 0.127, the foreign direct investment (FDI) decreases to 0.127.

In contrast, the interest rate (IR) decreased to 0.077, then the foreign direct investment (FDI) is 0.077 or 7% and reversely. In order to analyse the relationship between money supply and interest rate on foreign direct investment (FDI), the result of panel regression analysis is presented in Table 4.

The result of the data analysis includes three static panel models, namely, pooled ordinary least square, fixed effect, and random-effect models. Table 4 determines the best model from three static models. Using the Hausman test, we determine the best model between the fixed-effect and random-effect models. The result of the Hausman test shows the significant value is less than 1% ($\alpha < 0.01$). Thus, the null hypothesis is rejected, and we conclude that the fixed-effect model (FEM) is the best. Further, to choose the best model between pooled least square model (POLSM) and FEM, this study uses Breusch and Pagan Lagrangian

Table 4 Result of hypothesis testing

Variables	Model 1 (POLS)	Model 2 (FE)	Model 3 (RE)
Inflation (INFL)	0.515	0.567	0.839
Interest rate (IR)	0.327	0.000	0.001
Exchange rate (EXC)	0.244	0.482	0.596
Money supply (MS)	0.004	0.012	0.020
Constant	0.520	0.438	0.652
R-squared	0.023	0.314	0.0423
F-test		9.96***	
LM test			176.08***
Hausman test			22.080***

Note: ***Significant at the level 1%; **significant at the level 5% and *significant at the level 10%. Dependent variable: foreign direct investment (FDI)

Multiplier test. The result of the Breusch and Pagan Lagrangian Multiplier test shows the significant value prob. > $\chi^2 = 176.08$.

Thus, the null hypothesis was accepted. Based on both Hausman and Breusch and Pagan Lagrangian Multiplier (Breusch–Pagan LM) tests, the best model is the fixed-effect model (FEM). Using the FEM coefficient determination, this study found that interest rate (IR) can explain its relationship to foreign direct investment (FDI) as much as 31.4%. Therefore, there are 68.6% explained by other variables, which are not considered and included in this research.

In other words, there is a country-specific effect in this panel regression. Further, this study tests hypotheses to determine the best model. Table 4 provides the effect of explanatory variables on the dependent variable. The result of hypothesis testing shows that inflation (INFL) has a significant positive effect on interest rate (IR) and interest rate (IR) and has a significant positive effect on foreign direct investment (FDI). Besides, money supply (MS) and exchange rate (EXC) has a significant positive effect on foreign direct investment (FDI). Meanwhile, inflation does not have a significant effect on foreign direct investment (FDI). Thus, following the discussion above, the determinant with the greatest influence on foreign direct investment (FDI) in developing countries is money supply (MS) and the interest rate is a mediating effect that has positive significant to foreign direct investment (FDI). The highest regression coefficient comes from the money supply with 0.004 and significance at 1% ($\alpha < 0.01$).

The Effect of Interest Rate on Investment Activities in Developing Countries

This finding is supported by many theoretical models of foreign direct investment (Faeth, 2009) highlighted the determinants of foreign direct investment. Further, the empirical studies examined by Phillips and Ahmadi-Esfahani (2008) used the exchange rates significant for SE Asia, not Latin America. Also, economic theory indicates that exchange rate and money supply is an important determinant of foreign direct investment and supports the linkage between interest rate and inflation in the developing countries (Nakamura & Oyama, 1998).

Countries that have higher interest rate does not affect the investment activities moderately. Interest rate is a mediating effect in between the inflation and the interest rate. Meanwhile, countries that have higher money supply and exchange rate will have significant positive relationship in the long run with the foreign direct investment. The effect consists of two types which is a direct effect and an indirect effect. For the direct effect, hypothesis tested by pooled least square (POLS) or consistent covariance matrix (CCM) shows that money supply (MS) have significant positive relationship with foreign direct investment (FDI). Besides, fixed effect model to test the hypothesis of the indirect effect shows that inflation (INFL) does not significant relationship to foreign direct investment (FDI) while inflation (INFL) have positive significant relationship to interest rate (IR) and interest rate (IR) have significant positive relationship to foreign direct investment (FDI). In FEM, if the p-value > 0.05, we accept the null hypothesis and conversely. The result of testing shows that the p-value < 0.05, we decide to reject null hypothesis (Table 5).

Path A shows significant positive relationship in between inflation to interest rate and Path B shows significant positive relationship between interest rate to foreign direct investment. Meanwhile, Path C shows no significant relationship in between inflation and foreign direct investment. However, Path D shows significant positive relationship between

Table 5 Testing the direct and indirect effect of studied variables

	Coefficient β	SE	*p*-value	*t*-test
Direct effect				
Inflation (INFL) à foreign direct investment (FDI)	-0.013	0.024*	0.567	-0.572
Money supply (MS) à foreign direct investment (FDI)	1.742	0.688	0.012*	2.534
Indirect effect				
Interest rate (IR) ---> inflation (INFL)	-0.446	0.029*	0.000***	-15.398
Interest rate (IR) ---> foreign direct investment (FDI)	-0.104	0.028*	0.0002***	-3.736

Note: ***Significant at the level 1%; **significant at the level 10% and *significant at the level 5%. Dependent variable: foreign direct investment (FDI)

money supply and foreign direct investment. Inflation and money supply has a direct effect to foreign direct investment while interest rate is a mediating effect in between inflation and foreign direct investment.

5 Findings and Discussions

The primary goal of this research is to examine the influence of interest rates on investment in China's Jiangsu Province. Jiangsu has received the most investment in China. The nexus Johansen Co-integration test is used over the long run. VECM (vector error correction model) is used to find short run connection between 2003 and 2012. The findings suggest that there is a long-term link association between factors. It has a negative relationship in the long run but a favourable relationship in the short term. This research also yields recommendations for interest rate policy and enhancing investment to enhance economic growth in Jiangsu Province (Khurshid, 2015).

What effect do low interest rates have on investor behaviour? We show that when interest rates are low, people "reach for yield," or have a larger appetite for risk. We show that low interest rates lead to considerably larger allocations to hazardous assets among various populations using randomised investment trials with fixed risk premiums and hazards. Traditional portfolio choice theory or institutional frictions cannot explain the behaviour. Then, we suggest and demonstrate processes linked to investor psychology, such as reference dependency and salience. We also report findings from an observational study of household investment decisions (Lian et al., 2019).

The major goal of this research is to examine real interest rates and their influence on investment in Pakistan from 1964 to 2012. The Johansen Cointegration test is primarily used to examine the long-term relationship between income level, interest rate, and investment. The study's premise is that investment in Pakistan has an inverse relationship with the real interest rate. If there is a link, policymakers can make better decisions for Pakistan. The findings support economic theory and a number of previous researches that show investment has a strongly negative relationship with Pakistan's real interest rate (Muhammad et al., 2013).

Besides that, some research conclude that economic growth and interest rate had a positive and significant impact on FDI while INFL had a negative and significant impact on FDI. The recommendation of this research was the governments of ASEAN-6 maintain domestic economy to attract FDI. The domestic economy reflected by economic growth and interest rate. In addition, the governments need to improve the governance of FDI through the empowerment of anticorruption institution (Fazira & Cahyadin, 2018).

Foreign direct investment (FDI) has been seeing as one of the engines that ignite economic growth in recent years in developing countries. This study aims to examine the impact of interest rate on FDI flow in Sierra Leone, as the government of Sierra Leone has made tremendous effort after the civil war ended in 2001 to attract more foreign investment through the implementation of favourable foreign investment policies. Using econometrics techniques to run multiple regression time series data for the period of 1985 to 2012 in which diagnostic test was carried out in order to make the model fit and free from all spuriousness and make result valuable. The main findings were trade openness (TO) and exchange rates (ER) are the key determinants of FDI flow having positive significant signs in Sierra Leone. Other variables, such as inflation, gross domestic products (GDP), and interest rate (IR), were found to be insignificant factors causing the variability of FDI flows. Finally, we accept the null hypothesis that high interest rate has no effect on FDI flow in Sierra Leone. For policy recommendation, government should support the private sector to mobilize domestic resources for productive investment, increase openness to foreign trade, fight corruption, improve the energy and infrastructure to attract foreign investment, maintain single digit inflation figure, promote production through boosting employment to build up GDP, and finally limit exchange rate fluctuation (Faroh & Shen, 2015).

6 Conclusions

The global economy is expected to slow further in the coming year as the massive and historic energy shock triggered by Russia's war of aggression against Ukraine continues to spur inflationary pressures, sapping confidence and household purchasing power, and increasing risks worldwide, according to the OECD's latest economic outlook. The Outlook highlights the unusually imbalanced and fragile prospects for the global economy over the next two years. The global economy is projected to grow well below the outcomes expected before the war—at a modest 3.1% this year, before slowing to 2.2% in 2023 and recovering moderately to a still sub-par 2.7% pace in 2024. Growth in 2023 is strongly dependent on the major Asian emerging market economies, who will account for close to three-quarters of global GDP growth next year, with the United States and Europe decelerating sharply. Persistent inflation, high energy prices, weak real household income growth, falling confidence, and tighter financial conditions are all expected to curtail growth. Higher interest rates, while necessary to moderate inflation, will increase financial challenges for both households and corporate borrowers.

Inflation is projected to remain high in the OECD area, at more than 9% this year. As tighter monetary policy takes effect, demand and energy price pressures diminish and transport costs and delivery times continue to normalise, inflation will gradually moderate to 6.6% in 2023 and 5.1% in 2024. "The global economy is facing serious headwinds. We are dealing with a major energy crisis and risks continue to be titled to the downside with lower global growth, high inflation, weak confidence and high levels of uncertainty making successful navigation of the economy out of this crisis and back toward a sustainable recovery very challenging," OECD Secretary-General Mathias Cormann said during a presentation of the Outlook. "An end to the war and a just peace for Ukraine would be the most impactful way to improve the global economic outlook right now. Until this happens, it is important that governments deploy both short- and medium-term policy measures to confront the crisis, to cushion its impact in the short term while building the foundations for a stronger and sustainable recovery." The OECD points to substantial uncertainty surrounding the economic outlook. Growth may be weaker than projected if energy prices rise further, or if energy supply disruptions affect gas and electricity markets in Europe and Asia. Rising global interest rates may put many households, firms, and governments under greater pressure as debt service burdens rise. Low-income countries will remain particularly vulnerable to high food and energy prices, while tighter global financial conditions may raise the risk of further debt distress. Against this backdrop, the Outlook lays out a series of policy actions that governments should take to confront the crisis. Further monetary policy tightening is needed in most major advanced economies and in many emerging market economies to firmly anchor inflation expectations and lower inflation durably.

Fiscal support that is being provided to help cushion the impact of high energy costs should be increasingly temporary and preserve incentives to reduce energy consumption. Support measures should be designed to minimise fiscal costs and be concentrated on aiding the most vulnerable households and companies. Managing the energy crisis will require more decisive policy support to boost investment in clean technologies, foster energy efficiency, secure alternative supplies, and realign policy with climate mitigation objectives. The cost-of-living crisis also calls for structural reforms that can have a direct effect on household incomes, ease supply constraints, and reduce prices. To this end, countries should focus on policies to improve the functioning of international trade, enhance productivity, tackle gender gaps in the labour market, and boost living standards.

In line with 'Global economy affected by Russia's Ukraine War', this study investigated the relationships of interest rate, inflation, money supply, and exchange rate on the foreign direct investment in 20 selected developing countries (Bangladesh, Brunei, Chile, China, Colombia, India, Indonesia, Jordan, Laos, Malaysia, Maldives, Mongolia, Myanmar, Pakistan, Philippines, Singapore, Sri Lanka, Thailand, and Vietnam). Using the analysis of panel data regression, we found that money supply (MS) and exchange rate (EXC) is reflected by inflation that reflected by Interest rate. So, money supply (MS) and exchange rate (EXC) have a significant positive effect on foreign direct investment (FDI). Meanwhile, interest rate (IR) does not have a significant effect on foreign direct investment (FDI). Interest rate (IR) is a mediating effect to foreign direct investment (FDI). Many developing countries have thus realized that the principal mechanism for developing the money supply (MS) and exchange rate (EXC) is the foreign direct investment (FDI). Therefore, money supply and exchange rate are an important variable to control inflation as well as interest rate in developing countries, not only as an attempt to ensure investment activities goes well to increase the economic growth in developing countries but also to be the developing countries that lead to be in the nation's best developmental interest that investor trust to invest. The countries that succeed in developing and sustaining the inflation capable do well economically, while those that fail tend to fall behind. However, poorer countries find it hard to develop the capabilities and a well-functioning inflation, which is something that is built incrementally over many years. This study only shows the evidence that inflation and interest rate work beautifully to develop individuals and nations, especially developing countries.

Overall, we conclude that inflation and interest rate are crucial elements for measuring foreign direct investment on economic growth. Low inflation rate can contribute significantly to the economic growth and development of the world economy. Developing economies, especially Malaysia, should be more creative and innovative to improve their economy. To answer the objectives of this research, the interest rate have significantly positive relationship to inflation which is an efficient instrument to control inflation meanwhile the interest rate doesn't affect the investment activities moderately, but interest rate is just mediating effect of investment activities in developing countries. To control inflation, we must ensure the interest rate of the countries is stable so that the investment activities will go smoothly as it is because inflation will also affect the money supply and the exchange rate of the countries.

References

Abdelraouf, N., & Noureldin, D. (2022). The impact of the exchange rate regime on the dispersion of the price-change distribution: Evidence from a large panel of countries. *Journal of International Financial Markets, Institutions and Money, 76*, 101462.

Agudze, K., & Ibhagui, O. (2021). Inflation and FDI in industrialized and developing economies. *International Review of Applied Economics, 35*(5), 749–764.

Alexandrov, D. G., Valinurova, L. S., Kostromin, P. A., Zenkina, E., & Egorov, V. G. (2021). Metrics for assessing the effect of household income and the money supply on inflation. *Montenegrin Journal of Economics, 17*(4), 147–154.

Al-Shammari, N., & Al-Sabaey, M. (2012). Inflation sources across developed and developing countries; panel approach. *International Business & Economics Research Journal (IBER), 11*(2), 185–194.

Arsić, M., Mladenović, Z., & Nojković, A. (2022). Inflation targeting and fiscal discipline in selected emerging economies. In *Handbook of banking and finance in emerging markets* (pp. 651–674). Edward Elgar.

Bentzen, J., & Tung, L. T. (2021). A causality test between income, inequality and poverty–empirical evidence from South-East Asia. *Applied Economics Letters, 28*(19), 1682–1685.

Capasso, S., Napolitano, O., & Viveros Jiménez, A. L. (2019). The long-run interrelationship between exchange rate and interest rate: The case of Mexico. *Journal of Economic Studies, 46*(7), 1380–1397.

Carney, M. (2015). Breaking the tragedy of the horizon - climate change and financial stability - speech by Mark Carney, Bank of England, Retrieved from: https://www.bankofengland.co.uk/speech/2015/breaking-the-tragedy-ofthe-horizon-climate-change-and-financial-stability

Chang, F.-H., & Zhang, L. (2022). Revisiting inflation-growth nexus: An endogenous growth model with financial frictions. *Annals of Financial Economics (AFE), 17*(01), 1–13.

Chugunov, I., Pasichnyi, M., Kaneva, T., Nepytaliuk, A., & Koroviy, V. (2021). The influence of inflation targeting on economic growth in the OECD and developing countries. *Montenegrin Journal of Economics, 17*(2), 173–186.

Drobyshevsky, S. M., Trunin, P. V., Sinelnikova-Muryleva, E. V., Makeeva, N. V., & Grebenkina, A. M. (2021). Estimating a neutral real interest rate in Russia during inflation targeting. *Voprosy Ekonomiki, 9*, 5–23.

Faeth, I. (2009). Determinants of foreign direct investment – A tale of nine theoretical models. *Journal of Economic Surveys, 23*(1), 165–196.

Faroh, A., & Shen, H. (2015). Impact of interest rates on foreign direct investment: Case study Sierra Leone economy. *International Journal of Business Management and Economic Research, 6*(1), 124–132.

Fazira, D. R., & Cahyadin, M. (2018). The impact of interest rate, corruption perception index, and economic growth on foreign direct investment in ASEAN-6. *Jurnal Keuangan Dan Perbankan, 22*(4), 707–713.

Ghazinoory, S., & Hashemi, Z. (2022). The impact of government interventions on the performance of biotechnology, information and communications technology, and electrical and electronics firms: Evidence from Iran. *Journal of the Knowledge Economy*, 1–17.

Gladkikh, A., Dedkov, V., Sharova, A., Klyuchnikova, E., Sbarzaglia, V., Kanaeva, O., Arbuzova, T., Tsyganova, N., Popova, A., Ramsay, E., & Totolian, A. (2023). Epidemiological Features of COVID-19 in Northwest Russia in 2021. *Viruses, 15*(5), 1190. https://doi.org/10.3390/v15051190

Ha, J., Kose, M. A., & Ohnsorge, F. (2019a). *Inflation in emerging and developing economies: Evolution, drivers, and policies*. World Bank.

Ha, J., Kose, M. A., & Ohnsorge, F. (2019b). *Understanding inflation in emerging and developing economies*. World Bank Policy Research Working Paper, 8761.

Hartmann, P., & McAdam, P. (2018). *Price and wage-setting in advanced economies: Takeaways from the ECB's 2018 Sintra Forum* (Vol. 6). European Central Bank.

Imran, M., & Rashid, A. (2022). The empirical determinants of foreign direct investment episodes. *Global Journal of Emerging Market Economies, 2022*, 097491012211167.

IMF. (2018). IMF Annual Report 2018 - Building a Shared Future. Retireved from: https://www.imf.org/external/pubs/ft/ar/2018/eng/

Kalu, E. U., Arize, A. C., Ilo, S. O., Ihegboro, I., & Eze, C. G. (2022). Evaluating the interactive effect of domestic and global stock market variables on the depth of the financial system in sub-Saharan African countries: A panel ARDL approach. *Journal of Economic Studies*.

Kartaev, P. S., & Tubdenov, V. G. (2021). The transparency of monetary policy and the effect of exchange rate pass-through. *Voprosy Ekonomiki, 6*, 32–46.

Khurshid, A. (2015). The effect of interest rate on investment; empirical evidence of Jiangsu Province, China. *Journal of International Studies, 8*(1).

Klutse, S. K., Sági, J., & Kiss, G. D. (2022). Exchange rate crisis among inflation targeting countries in sub-Saharan Africa. *Risks, 10*(5), 94.

Kueh, J., & Soo, X.-L. (2020). Macroeconomic determinants of FDI inflows in Cambodia, Laos, Myanmar and Vietnam: Panel data analysis. *Thailand and the World Economy, 38*(1), 54–72.

Lian, C., Ma, Y., & Wang, C. (2019). Low interest rates and risk-taking: Evidence from individual investment decisions. *The Review of Financial Studies, 32*(6), 2107–2148.

Mbilla, S. A. E., Atindaana, P. A., Gadzo, S. G., Adeniyi, A., & Salifu, I. (2021). Monetary policy and macro economic indicators: A review of a developing country's perspectives 2002–2017. *Cogent Economics & Finance, 9*(1), 1935530.

McCloud, N., & Delgado, M. S. (2022). Domestic interest rate, foreign direct investment, and corruption. *Review of World Economics, 158*, 1–25.

Mhmood, M. M., Khalaf, H. H., & Mohammed, O. A. (2021). Monetary policy responses to the global financial crisis: What did emerging economies do differently? *Academy of Entrepreneurship Journal, 27*, 1–13.

Mishkin, F. S. (2008). Challenges for inflation targeting in emerging market countries. *Emerging Markets Finance and Trade, 44*(6), 5–16.

Muhammad, S. D., Lakhan, G. R., Zafar, S., & Noman, M. (2013). Rate of interest and its impact on investment to the extent of Pakistan. *Pakistan Journal of Commerce and Social Sciences (PJCSS), 7*(1), 91–99.

Mukhametov, O. (2021). Relationship between Central Bank independence and foreign direct investment inflows. *Asian Economic and Financial Review, 11*(5), 396–405.

Nakamura, S., & Oyama, T. (1998). *The determinants of foreign direct investment from Japan and the United States to East Asian countries, and the linkage between FDI and trade* (pp. 98–11). Bank of Japan, Working Paper.

Ngoc, B. H. (2020). The asymmetric effect of inflation on economic growth in Vietnam: Evidence by nonlinear ARDL approach. *The Journal of Asian Finance, Economics and Business, 7*(2), 143–149.

Nguyen, T. M. L. (2020). Output effects of monetary policy in emerging and developing countries: Evidence from a meta-analysis. *Emerging Markets Finance and Trade, 56*(1), 68–85.

Nguyen, C. H., Pham, T. T. Q., Tran, T. H., & Nguyen, T. H. (2021). The relationship between foreign capital inflows and economic growth: Empirical evidence from Vietnam. *The Journal of Asian Finance, Economics and Business, 8*(11), 325–332.

Okafor, L. E., Hassan, M. K., Rashid, M., Prabu, D., & Sabit, A. (2022). Risk dimensions, risk clusters, and foreign direct investments in developing countries. *International Review of Economics & Finance, 82*, 636–649.

Phillips, S., & Ahmadi-Esfahani, F. Z. (2008). Exchange rates and foreign direct investment: Theoretical models and empirical evidence. *Australian Journal of Agricultural and Resource Economics, 52*(4), 505–525.

Rogoff, B. (2003). *The Cultural Nature of Human Development*. USA: Oxford University Press.

Sabir, S., Rafique, A., & Abbas, K. (2019). Institutions and FDI: Evidence from developed and developing countries. *Financial Innovation, 5*(1), 1–20.

Serikova, S., Pokrovsky, O. S., Laudon, H., Krickov, I. V., Lim, A. G., Manasypov, R. M., & Karlsson, J. (2022). High carbon emissions from thermokarst lakes of Western Siberia. *Nature Communications, 10*, 1552, https://doi.org/10.1038/s41467-019-09592-1

Sharku, G., Grabova, P., & Vullnetari, D. (2021). Impact of economic factors on life and non-life insurance development in Albania – A VECM analysis. *Universal Journal of Accounting and Finance, 9*, 1280.

Sharma, S., Padhi, I., & Dhal, S. (2022). Monetary-fiscal coordination: When, why and how? *Studies in Economics and Finance.*

Shin, Y., Yu, B., & Greenwood-Nimmo, M. (2013). Modelling asymmetric cointegration and dynamic multipliers in a nonlinear ARDL framework. In W. C. Horrace & R. C. Sickles (Eds.), *Festschrift in honor of P. Schmidt*. Springer.

Stojanovikj, M. (2022). Can inflation targeting reduce price information asymmetry and alleviate corruptive behavior? Evidence from developing countries. *Economic Systems, 46*(3), 100986.

Assessing the impact of customer engagement on brand performance: The Mediating Role of Customer-Based Brand Equity (CBBE)

Ireneus Gundona, Fred A. Yamoah, and Irfan ul Haq

1 Introduction

According to Shariq (2018), brands function as a crucial asset and a differentiator that allows buyers to differentiate among products functionally as well as emotionally. Brands are an essential element for both the consumer and the firm; to the firm, it opens up legal protection, higher financial returns, and competitive advantage, and it also provides easy identification, associations, and symbolism to the consumer (Shariq, 2018). In the process of developing a brand, it requires the addition of

I. Gundona
Consumer Insights Consult Ltd, Accra, Ghana

F. A. Yamoah (✉)
Department of Management, School of Business, Economics and Informatics, Birkbeck, University of London, London, UK
e-mail: f.yamoah@bbk.ac.uk

I. ul Haq
SRIBP, Toronto, ON, Canada

F. A. Yamoah, A. ul Haque (eds.), *Corporate Management Ecosystem in Emerging Economies*, https://doi.org/10.1007/978-3-031-41578-4_21

value in the form of attributes and benefits to define the brand (Ukaj, 2020). However, customers remain the most important form of value to a brand; therefore, retaining and attracting customers to a brand is vital to competitive marketing (Mizani et al., 2018). To attract and retain customers for specific brands, firms do develop unique customer engagement mechanism. The purpose of this engagement mechanism is to retain customers of a specific brand, and this can be done through the customer engagement process. Brands are an essential element for both the consumer and the firm; to the firm, it opens legal protection, higher financial returns, and competitive advantage, and it also provides easy identification, associations, and symbolism to the consumer (Shariq, 2018). In the process of developing a brand, it requires the addition of value in the form of attributes and benefits to define the brand (Ukaj, 2020). However, customers remain the important form of value to a brand, therefore retaining and attracting customers to a brand is vital to competitive marketing (Mizani et al., 2018). To attract and retain customers to specific brands, firms do develop unique customer engagement mechanism. The purpose of this engagement mechanism is to retain customers of a specific brand, and this can be done through the customer engagement process.

Despite the importance of brands, customer engagement, and brand equity in the alcoholic beverage industry in Ghana, there is a lack of research on how these factors impact brand performance in this market. As a result, it is unclear how companies operating in this industry can effectively engage with customers, build strong brand equity, and improve their market performance. Therefore, the problem that this study seeks to address is the lack of understanding of the relationship between customer engagement, brand equity, and brand performance in the alcoholic beverage industry in Ghana. Due to the limited research specifically focused on the alcoholic beverage industry in Ghana. This highlights a gap in the existing literature and further emphasizes the need for research on the relationship between these factors in this particular industry. By studying the relationship between customer engagement, brand equity, and brand performance in the alcoholic beverage industry in Ghana, this research can contribute to a better understanding of how these factors can be leveraged to improve market performance in this industry.

The study aims to explore the role of brand equity in the market performance of different brands in the bitters product category in Ghana, using the consumer-based brand equity (CBBE) model.

The study seeks to provide insights into how companies operating in this industry can build strong brand equity and improve their market performance. This is an important study that contributes to the knowledge of various stakeholders. The study provides assistance to marketers in forming a model for customer engagement and brand equity guided by global best practices with substantial local content to assist industry players in measuring their brands equity. Moreover, the investors and new market entrants benefit from this study as it provides guidance and framework for new entrants and investors alike within West Africa and Ghana. Moreover, with the guide for new entrants to strengthen their brands through best customer engagement measures in face of competition. The academics and researchers benefit by enhancing their knowledge about having the viewpoint of a developing economy where consumers behave differently in terms of how they perceive and relate to products and services. The study's findings can provide valuable insights into how companies can effectively build brand equity and improve market performance in the context of a developing economy such as Ghana.

This study's primary focus is to identify how customer engagement facilitates brand equity using the CBBE construct proposed by Aaker, to impact brand market performance in the bitters industry in Ghana. The study is limited to branded bitters brands sold in Ghana, including both local and imported brands. By focusing on this specific industry and using the CBBE construct, the study aims to provide a comprehensive understanding of the relationship between customer engagement, brand equity, and brand market performance in the context of the bitters industry in Ghana.

2 Literature Review

Aaker's (2009) customer-based brand equity model is one of the most widely used and influential models in the field of brand management. The study uses Aaker's (1991) as the foundation for the conceptual model. Aaker's equity model comprises five distinctive assets, which comprise brand loyalty, brand association, brand awareness, perceived quality, and proprietary brand assets. Though brand loyalty is projected as a forerunner of brand equity, to Nam et al. (2011), it may be perceived as an outcome of brand equity. Moreover, existing studies have affirmed influence of the other equity dimensions, such as associations, perceived quality, and awareness on brand equity (Çifci et al., 2016; Fig. 1).

Current brand equity models do establish a relationship between brand equity and brand performance. However, brand equity scales are principally based on ones developed by Aaker and Keller. Though, these scales are not without challenges. Moreover, the concept of customer engagement has existed over time with leading research interest into the consequences and antecedent's customer engagement. This study contributes to brand performance, customer engagement, brand equity, and discourse from different perspectives.

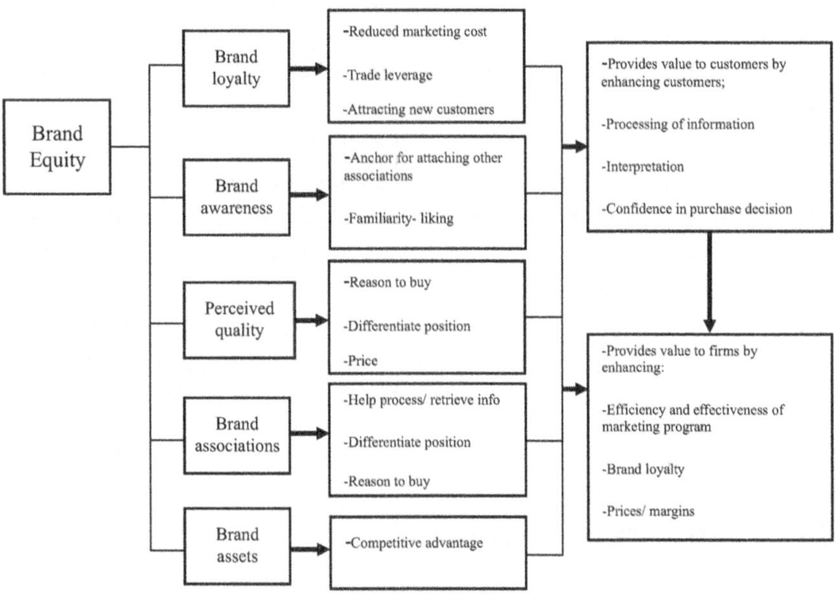

Fig. 1 Aaker's equity model

Conceptual model

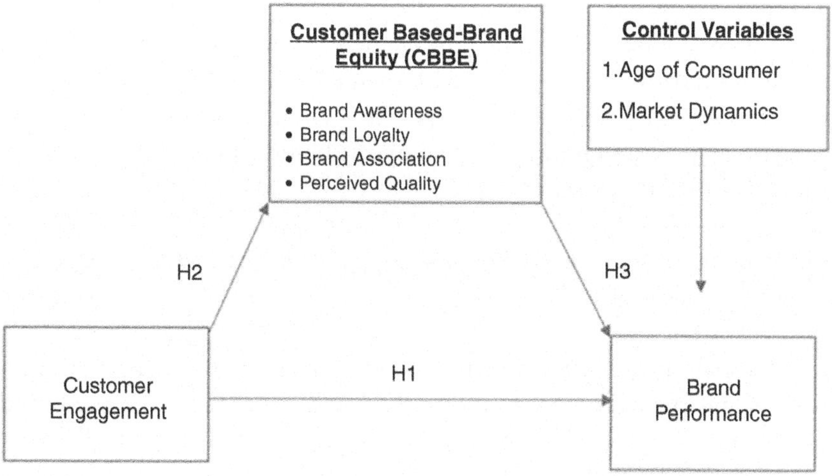

Customer engagement is a broader concept that emphasizes building and maintaining a long-term relationship between a firm and its customers enhancing sales, profitability as well as gaining a competitive advantage (Hollebeek, 2011; Kumar et al., 2010). It goes beyond the traditional transactional relationship of buying and selling products or services and focuses on creating a meaningful and emotional connection with customers. Based on the above justification, the researcher hypothesized that:

Hypothesis 1: *There is a positive relationship between customer engagement and brand performance.*

Customer engagement affects customer behaviour outcomes (Hollebeek et al., 2014). Highly engaged customers tend to be more loyal to a brand, which can ultimately lead to increased sales and revenue for the brand (Xi & Hamari, 2019). On the other hand, unengaged customers are more likely to switch to a competitor's brand, which can negatively impact a brand's market performance. In line with the discussion above, the researcher proposed the second hypothesis:

Hypothesis 2: *Customer engagement has a positive significant impact on brand loyalty.*

Online and offline customer engagement are important for businesses to maintain strong relationships with their customers. Moreover, customers' perception of a company's corporate social responsibility (CSR) initiatives can have a significant impact on the brand equity of the company. The third hypothesis proposed is:

Hypothesis 3: *Customer engagement has a positive significant impact on perceived quality.*

Sponsorship can be an effective way for businesses to engage with customers and promote their brand, raise brand awareness, enhance brand image, and increase sales. Sponsorship engages customers through event experience (Donlan, 2010). The researcher recommends fourth hypothesis:

Hypothesis 4: *Customer engagement has a positive significant impact on brand awareness.*

Customer engagement in the form of reviews can have a significant impact on customers' perceptions of a product and their associations with the brand (Barger et al., 2016). Generated through online engagement, customers' spread of a positive word of mouth also has a positive impact on brand associations (Abdullah & Siraj, 2016).

Hypothesis 5: *Customer engagement has a positive significant impact on brand association.*

Loyalty plays a fundamental role in a company's profitability and future growth. Customer engagement is crucial for brand equity enhancement (Passikoff et al., 2007) and customer loyalty (Bowden, 2009; Patterson et al., 2006). Based on the above, the sixth hypothesis is:

Hypothesis 6: *The positive relationship between customer engagement and brand performance is positively mediated by brand loyalty.*

Quality is determined by the physical attributes of a product or service along with the customers' experiences and perceptions of the brand. A company's knowledge, expertise, and reputation can all influence customers' perceptions of quality (Vera, 2015). Perceived quality can have a significant impact on various aspects of a company's performance, including brand power, market share, brand equity, profit margins, and perceived value. Based on this justification, the researcher proposed that:

Hypothesis 7: *The positive relationship between customer engagement and brand performance is positively mediated by perceived quality.*

Brand awareness is a key factor in building brand loyalty in the long term. When customers are aware of a brand and have knowledge about its products or services, it can influence their purchase decisions and lead to increased brand loyalty. Until a consumer is conscious of a brand, there can be neither trust nor satisfaction (Chaudhuri & Holbrook, 2001). In line with such justification, the researcher suggests the eighth hypothesis:

Hypothesis 8: *The positive relationship between customer engagement and brand performance is positively mediated by brand awareness.*

Brand salience is an important factor in building brand awareness and ultimately driving brand loyalty. As highlighted by Keller, the favorability and uniqueness of brand associations in the mind of the individual determine the strength of brand equity (Schivinski & Dabrowski, 2014). The final hypothesis is proposed on the above justifications:

Hypothesis 9: *The positive relationship between customer engagement and brand performance is positively mediated by brand association.*

3 Research Methodology

Due to the product of interest is an alcoholic-based bitter, consumers aged 18+ (legal age for consumption of alcohol in Ghana), residing in the mentioned geographic regions were considered for this study. Interviews were conducted with consumers from diverse socio-economic strata, thus upper, lower, and mid-income levels (male and female). Survey data collected from 400 consumers, aged 18 (who had bought and consumed any brand of bitters in the last 7 days prior to data collection) was used to test the theoretical model and hypotheses. Statistical software SPSS 22.0. was used for data input and preparation (i.e., checking for missing values). The two-step approach proposed by Anderson and Gerbing (1982) was used to conduct the analysis of structural equation modelling (SEM). In the model, with this approach, the six measurement scales of the constructs were initially subjected to confirmatory factor analysis (CFA), followed by structure model assessment using the statistical software AMOS 22.0.

The study examines the relationship between brand market performance and customer engagement and mediated by brand equity in the alcoholic Bitters industry in Ghana. The relationship between variables was explored through an inductive approach (Bell et al., 2018). This approach assisted in observing patterns founded on the observation to theories or forming an explanation for the patterns through hypothesis. Moreover, a case study approach is applied to expand on the nuances of the beverage industry. This further assisted in testing scientific theories that are well accepted in the field of marketing and management.

The cross-sectional research design was employed to investigate the stated hypotheses, as it delivers a plausible approach to investigate research objectives. It further examines the mediating role of customer engagement in elevating the firm's brand performance within the beverage industry. The quantitative research method is used to collect numerical data that can be analyzed using statistical techniques to test hypotheses. Entire Ghanaian population was the study population. However, the target population, served as a sampling frame used to draw the study sample, was adults aged 18 years and above, within the regional capital of

Ghana. A total sample of 400 respondents was drawn and proportionally distributed across three regional capitals, namely, Accra, Tamale, and Kumasi, based on the region's 'population' size. The sample size of 400 was determined using the formula (Mendenhall et al., 1993):

$$n' = \frac{NZ^2P(1-p)}{d^2(N-1)+Z^2P(1-P)}$$

where

n' represents the sample size to be determined.

N represents the population of adults aged 18 years and above in Ghana which in this case is 13,632,299.

Z denotes the statistics value for a given confidence level, for 95% confidence level Z-statistics = 1.96.

d denotes the margin of error at 95% confidence level.

p denotes an estimated population proportion (0.5).

q denotes the difference between 1 and p that is $q = 1 - p$.

Also, since the exact proportion is not certain, a value of 0.5 (50%) was used (Mendenhall et al., 1993).

This is because the given the level of precision, 'p' of 0.5 has the largest sample size.

Thus,

$q = 1 - p = 0.5$

Pq = Sample proportion variance estimate (maximum 0.5).

Substituting the values in the formula, the sample size was computed as follows:

$$n' = \frac{13{,}632{,}299(1.96)^2\,0.5(1-0.5)}{(0.05)^2(13{,}632{,}299-1)+(1.96)^2\,0.5(1-0.5)} = 384.15$$

The study targets providers, customers, and distributors of herbal-based beverages within alcoholic beverage industry in Ghana. The quality and accuracy of data are guaranteed by soliciting information from critical informants. Moreover, systematic sampling approach was utilized to categorize and request information from consumers of alcoholic beverages, specifically bitters based alcoholic drinks. The objective of the study is the impact of customer brand equity on brand performance of firms in the herbal-based bitters industry. Further evaluating the mediating effect of customer engagement on firms' customer brand equity and brand performance. These measurement scales comprise brand loyalty (Relling et al., 2016), brand awareness (Relling et al., 2016), perceived quality (Liébana-Cabanillas et al., 2017), brand association (Kunkel et al., 2016), brand market share (Huang & Sarigöllü, 2012), and customer engagement (Vivek et al., 2014).

Along with the correlation matrix, confirmatory factor analysis and ANOVA techniques were explored to recognize variations. Empirical analysis such as confirmatory factor analysis, exploratory factor analysis, and structural equation modelling analysis would be conducted. Through these sets of analysis, researcher would be able to draw a casualty relationship amid different constructs under study. Social Science Statistical Package (SPSS version 22) and AMOS package will be used for data analysis. The questionnaire is a precise tool to collect reliable data and information (Haque & Aston, 2016; Haque & Yamoah, 2014). In this study, a questionnaire will be used as measurement scale, on a 5-point Likert scale. Data was collected from consumers of herbal bitters-based alcoholic drinks and collected data is used to evaluate a relationship between firm's brand performance and independent variable (customer engagement). The data was obtained from the consumers and bar managers. The current study controls the method bias by carefully considering concerns with respect to the predictor's measurement and dependent (brand market performance) variables. A pilot study is used to determine the accuracy of data. The pilot study includes 50 respondents entailing 25 enterprises and 25 customers involved in the retailing, production, and distribution of herbal-based bitters alcoholic drinks.

4 Results, Findings, and Discussions

Demographic Description (Table 1)

Above table reflects that majority of the respondents are males (82%) in the age bracket between 25 and 34 (66%) with secondary education (56%) and are employed full time (57%).

Table 1 Demographic characteristics ($N = 410$)

Demographic characteristics	Frequency	Percentage
Gender		
Male	338	82%
Female	72	18%
	Age	
18–24	22	5%
25–34	269	66%
35–44	104	25%
45–54	11	3%
55 years and above	4	1%
	Educational level	
Basic education	59	15%
Secondary education	229	56%
Tertiary education	100	24%
No formal school	22	5%
	Employment status	
Employed full time	232	57%
Employed part-time	151	37%
Unemployed	16	4%
Student	10	2%
	Level of income	
Less than 500	49	12%
GHC500 to GHC1999	313	76%
GHC2000 to GHC3999	45	11%
GHC4000 to GHC5999	3	1%

Source: Author's estimation from field survey, 2020. (* Mean age = 31.9; *Mean income = GHc 1349.56)

KMO and Bartlett's Test

From Table 2, the KMO and Bartlett's test recorded (KMO = 0.950, df = 406, $p < 0.05$) indicating that the adequacy of sampling and applicability of factor analysis (Hair et al., 1998) and Bartlett's test of sphericity (approx.: Chi-Square = 7554.14, df = 406, sig = 0.000). The result, however, confirms the rationale for conducting a factor analysis on the dataset.

Pearson's Correlation Matrix Results

Table 3 shows the customer engagement ($\rho = 0.768$; $p < 0.01$), brand loyalty ($\rho = 0.738$; $p < 0.01$), brand awareness ($\rho = 0.757$; $p < 0.01$), perceived quality ($\rho = 0.657$; $p < 0.01$), and brand association ($\rho = 0.789$; $p < 0.01$) have a strong statistically significant positive relationship with brand performance. Age, on the other hand, also should have a positive statistically significant relationship with brand performance at ($\rho = 0.101$; $p < 0.05$). These results are in line with studies such as Munyau (2017).

The current study examined the impact of customer engagement on brand market performance. The study found that three dimensions that best measure customer engagement include psychological, emotional, and physical affiliation with a brand (Sedley, 2010). This was consistent with the studies of Mollen and Wilson (2010) and Vivek et al. (2014), who identified the validity of these scales to efficiently measure customer engagement.

A good factor loading value estimate was observed by most of the dimensions, above the threshold of 0.5 which specifies that the scales are good indicators for measuring the customer engagement construct. The

Table 2 KMO and Bartlett's test

Kaiser–Meyer–Olkin measure of sampling adequacy		0.950
Bartlett's test of sphericity	Approx. Chi-square	7554.14
	df	406
	Sig.	0.000

Source: Author's estimation from field survey, 2020

Table 3 Pearson's correlation matrix results

Variables	1	2	3	4	5	6	7	8
Brand performance	1							
Age	0.101*	1						
Market dynamic	0.018	-0.075	1					
Customer engagement	0.768**	-0.014	0.049	1				
Brand loyalty	0.738**	0.004	0.055	0.684**	1			
Brand awareness	0.757**	0.088	-0.062	0.618**	0.656**	1		
Perceived quality	0.657**	0.017	-0.023	0.627**	0.719**	0.660**	1	
Brand association	0.789**	0.028	0.017	0.743**	0.799**	0.792**	0.757**	1

Source: Author's estimation from field survey, 2020. $^{+}p < 0.10$, $^{*}p < 0.05$, $^{**}p < 0.01$, $^{***}p < 0.001$

measurement model analysis affirms that the above three dimensions are good indicators of measuring customer engagement within the alcoholic industry.

Moreover, the study results demonstrated a positive impact of customer engagement on brand performance, providing empirical support for the null hypothesis proposed for this study (i.e. H_0: There is a significant positive relationship between customer engagement and brand performance). The result suggests that brand (alcoholic industries) with strong customer engagement among its consumers intensify their overall performance. The findings offer empirical support for theoretical suggestions that customer engagement influences brand performance (Hollebeek et al., 2014). Moreover, the results provide empirical validation for prior studies (Islam et al., 2018) who separately deliver empirical evidence that there is a positive influence of customer engagement on brand performance.

The study recognized the independent variable's (customer engagement) individual effects on the customer-based brand equity (CBBE) variables. Based on the correlation analysis, the findings suggest that positive significant relationship exists between customer engagement and brand loyalty, brand awareness, perceived quality, and brand association.

The result suggests that if brand improves on the brand equity variables, it engages more with customer. This is consistent with prior studies (Bowden, 2009; Hollebeek, 2011) that found that customers engagement has the potential to intensify the brands equity. The final and third objective for this study was to evaluate the mediating role of brand equity on customer engagement and brand market performance. The study reveals that there is a positive and significant mediation of customer engagement by brand loyalty, brand awareness, and brand association.

ANOVA Results (Table 4)

(a) Dependent variable: brand performance
(b) Predictors: (constant) age of respondent, market dynamics
(c) Predictors: (constant) age of respondent, market dynamics, CE, BLTY, BAW, PQLTY, BA
(d) Predictors: (constant) age of respondent, market dynamics, CE, BLTY, BAW, PQTLY, BA, CE-BLTY, CE-BAW, CE-PQTLY, CE-BA

When the brand performance was regressed against the control variables (age of respondent, market dynamics), independent variables (customer engagement, brand loyalty, brand awareness, perceived quality, and brand association), and the mediating variables, the ANOVA results indicated that with the exception of the control variable, the models were significant ($p < 0.01$). The ANOVA results are shown in Table 5.

Table 4 ANOVA results

Model		Sum of squares	*df*	Mean square	*F*	Sig.
1	Regression	0.766	2	0.383	2.232	.109b
	Residual	69.863	407	0.172		
	Total	70.629	409			
2	Regression	53.473	7	7.639	178.999	.000c
	Residual	17.156	402	0.043		
	Total	70.629	409			
3	Regression	52.735	5	10.547	239.697	.000d
	Residual	17.776	404	0.044		
	Total	70.511	409			

Source: Author's estimation from field survey, 2020

Table 5 Hypotheses summary

#	Hypothesis	Expected outcome	Empirical conclusion	Outcome (sign)
1.	The is a positive relationship between customer engagement and brand performance	+	Supported	Significant (+)
2.	Customer engagement has a significant impact on brand loyalty	+	Supported	Significant (+)
3.	Customer engagement has a significant impact on perceived quality	+	Supported	Significant (+)
4.	Customer engagement has a significant impact on brand awareness	+	Supported	Significant (+)
5.	Customer engagement has a significant impact on brand association	+	Supported	Significant (+)
6.	The positive relationship between customer engagement and brand performance is positively mediated by brand loyalty	+	Supported	Significant (+)
7.	The positive relationship between customer engagement and brand performance is positively mediated by perceived quality	+	Not supported	Not significant (-)
8.	The positive relationship between customer engagement and brand performance is positively mediated by brand awareness	+	Supported	Significant (+)
9.	The positive relationship between customer engagement and brand performance is positively mediated by brand association	+	Supported	Significant (+)

Source: Author's estimation from field survey, 2020

However, perceived quality mediates it negatively though it is not statistically significant. From the findings the null hypotheses—H0: "The positive relationship between brand performance and customer engagement mediated by brand loyalty"; H0: "The positive relationship between brand performance and customer engagement is mediated by brand awareness"; and H0: "The positive relationship between brand performance and customer engagement is mediated by brand association"—were accepted; however, the alternate hypothesis, Ha: "The positive relationship between brand performance and customer engagement is negatively mediated by perceived quality" was also accepted.

These results validate empirical studies such as Baldauf et al. (2003), Huang and Sarigöllü (2012), Kim and Kim (2004), Kim et al. (2003), Severi and Ling (2013), and Yoo et al. (2000). The result indicates that with brands who use equity variables such as brand awareness, brand loyalty, and brand association positively enhance their engagement with their customer and in turn enhances the brand performance.

5 Conclusions and Recommendations

The purpose of this study was to evaluate the mediating role of customer-based brand equity on the association between brand performance and customer engagement within alcoholic Bitters industry in Ghana using Kasapreko as the case study. The study specifically examined the relation between performance and customer engagement as well as the relationship between customer engagement and the customer-based brand equity, and lastly assessed the mediation role of the customer-based brand equity on performance and customer engagement and performance. The study revealed that respondents had significantly higher awareness level (91%) for alcoholic Bitters attained generally through the conventional medium (i.e., Billboard advertisements, TV, Radio). Exact 89% of the respondents who are aware of alcoholic bitters have bought it before personally, whereas remaining 11% have their families and friends purchasing it for them. On average, a respondent consumes alcoholic bitters 2–3 times a week.

The study found that customer engagement has a positive impact on brand market performance for alcoholic Bitters in the Ghanaian Bitter industry. Furthermore, the study found that customer-based brand equity variables, such as brand loyalty, brand awareness, perceived quality, and brand association, also have a significant relationship with positive customer engagement. The study found that, except for perceived quality, all other customer-based brand equity variables—brand loyalty, brand awareness, and brand association—play a significant role in positively mediating customer engagement to influence brand market performance in the alcoholic Bitters industry in Ghana.

This finding suggests that firms operating in this industry may want to focus on developing and strengthening these customer-based brand equity variables to better leverage the positive effects of customer engagement on brand market performance. The study revealed fundamental insights on the role of customer-based brand equity in mediating a relationship between brand market performance and customer engagement. In view of the emerging empirical findings of this study, the following recommendations are made.

The study found that brand awareness plays a significant role in positively engaging customers with a brand. To leverage this insight, firms operating in the alcoholic Bitters industry in Ghana may want to focus on building enduring brand awareness and promoting their brands through aggressive recall initiatives such as advertisements on TV, radio, and billboards.

Firms may want to focus on improving the degree of recognizability of their brands through distinctive brand differentiation. Therefore, firms should focus on building strong brand awareness and developing a distinctive brand identity to engage customers with their brands and improve brand market performance in the alcoholic Bitters industry in Ghana. Secondly, brand loyalty is an important element in building customer-based brand equity and contributing to customer engagement and brand performance. To leverage this insight, firms operating in the alcoholic Bitters industry in Ghana may want to focus on pursuing customer engagement as an important element of brand loyalty. Marketing managers may want to operationalize strategies that influence customers to wholeheartedly invest their time, energy, money, and other resources in the brand beyond those expended during the purchase or consumption of the brand. Such strategies may include loyalty programs, personalized communication, and customer service initiatives, among others. These strategies can help foster a stronger emotional connection between customers and the brand, leading to greater customer engagement, brand loyalty, and ultimately, improved brand market performance.

Furthermore, firms should strive to establish strong and positive brand associations as fundamental elements of brand image building. To leverage this insight, firms operating in the alcoholic Bitters industry in Ghana may want to focus on enhancing the positive and favorable primary and secondary associations to their brands to build strong brands. This can be attained through celebrity endorsements, brand partnerships, and sponsorships, to further enhance the positive and favorable associations with their brands.

References

Aaker, D. A. (1991). *Managing Brand Equity New York*. NY: Free Press.

Aaker, D. A. (2009). *Managing brand equity*. The Free Press.

Abdullah, D., & Siraj, S. (2016). Brand equity through customer engagement in social media: A critical review. *IOSR Journal of Business and Management, 18*(8), 38–46.

Anderson, J. C., & Gerbing, D. W. (1982). Some methods for respecifying measurement models to obtain unidimensional construct measurement. *Journal of Marketing Research, 19*(4), 453–460.

Baldauf, A., Cravens, K. S., & Binder, G. (2003). Performance consequences of brand equity management: Evidence from organizations in the value chain. *Journal of Product & Brand Management, 12*(4), 220–236.

Barger, V., Peltier, J. W., & Schultz, D. E. (2016). Social media and consumer engagement: A review and research agenda. *Journal of Research in Interactive Marketing, 10*(4), 268–287.

Bell, E., Bryman, A., & Harley, B. (2018). *Business research methods*. Oxford University Press.

Bowden, J. L. H. (2009). The process of customer engagement: A conceptual framework. *Journal of Marketing Theory and Practice, 17*(1), 63–74.

Chaudhuri, A., & Holbrook, M. B. (2001). The chain of effects from brand trust and brand affect to brand performance: The role of brand loyalty. *Journal of Marketing, 65*(2), 81–93.

Çifci, S., Ekinci, Y., Whyatt, G., Japutra, A., Molinillo, S., & Siala, H. (2016). A cross validation of consumer-based brand equity models: Driving customer equity in retail brands. *Journal of Business Research, 69*(9), 3740–3747. https://doi.org/10.1016/j.jbusres.2015.12.066

Donlan, L. (2010). Sports sponsorship as a tool for customer engagement. *Journal of Marketing Communications, 20*(4), 291–306.

Hair, J. F., Anderson, R. E., & Black, W. C. (1998). Multivariate Analisys 5th ed., Printice Hall International.

Haque, A. U., & Aston, J. (2016). A relationship between occupational stress and organizational commitment of I.T sector's employees in contrasting economies. *Polish Journal of Management Studies, 14*(1), 95–105.

Haque, A. U., & Yamoah, F. (2014). Gender employment longevity: I.T staff response to organisational support programme in Pakistan. *International Journal of Academic Research in Business and Social Science (IJ-ARBSS), 4*(12), 324–347.

Hollebeek, L. (2011). Exploring customer brand engagement: Definition and themes. *Journal of Strategic Marketing, 19*(7), 555–573.

Hollebeek, L. D., Glynn, M. S., & Brodie, R. J. (2014). Consumer brand engagement in social media: Conceptualization, scale development, and validation. *Journal of Interactive Marketing, 28*(2), 149–165.

Huang, R., & Sarigöllü, E. (2012). How brand awareness relates to market outcome, brand equity, and the marketing mix. *Journal of Business Research, 65*(1), 92–99. https://doi.org/10.1016/j.jbusres.2011.02.003

Islam, J. U., Hollebeek, L. D., Rahman, Z., Khan, I., & Rasool, A. (2018). Customer engagement in the service context: An empirical investigation of the construct, its antecedents and consequences. *Journal of Retailing and Consumer Services, 50*(1), 277–285.

Kim, W. G., & Kim, H.-B. (2004). Measuring customer-based restaurant brand equity. Cornell hotel and restaurant. *Administration Quarterly, 45*(2), 115–131.

Kim, H. B., Kim, W. G., & An, J. A. (2003). The effect of consumer-based brand equity on firms' financial performance. *Journal of Consumer Marketing, 20*(4/5), 335–351.

Kumar, V., Aksoy, L., Donkers, B., Venkatesan, R., Wiesel, T., & Tillmanns, S. (2010). Undervalued or overvalued customers: Capturing total customer engagement value. *Journal of Service Research, 13*(3), 297–310.

Kunkel, T., Doyle, J. P., Funk, D. C., Du, J., & McDonald, H. (2016). The development and change of brand associations and their influence on team loyalty over time. *Journal of Sport Management, 30*(2), 117–134.

Liébana-Cabanillas, F., Marinković, V., & Kalinić, Z. (2017). A SEM-neural network approach for predicting antecedents of m-commerce acceptance. *International Journal of Information Management, 37*(2), 14–24.

Mendenhall, C. L., Moritz, T. E., Roselle, G. A., Morgan, T. R., Nemchausky, B. A., Tamburro, C. H., et al. (1993). A study of oral nutritional support with oxandrolone in malnourished patients with alcoholic hepatitis: Results of a department of veterans affairs cooperative study. *Hepatology, 17*(4), 564–576.

Mizani, N., Sheikh, R., Gholami, A., & Sana, S. S. (2018). Attracting and retaining customers by axiomatic design and incomplete rough-set theory. *International Journal of Applied and Computational Mathematics, 4*(2), 75–76.

Mollen, A., & Wilson, H. (2010). Engagement, telepresence and interactivity in online consumer experience: Reconciling scholastic and managerial perspectives. *Journal of Business Research, 63*(9/10), 919–925.

Munyau, P. K. (2017). Role of Customer Based Brand Equity on brand Market Performance in the Banking Service Sector in Kenya (Doctoral dissertation, COHRED, JKUAT).

Nam, J., Ekinci, Y., & Whyatt, G. (2011). Brand equity, brand loyalty and consumer satisfaction. *Annals of Tourism Research, 38*(3), 1009–1030. https://doi.org/10.1016/j.annals.2011.01.015

Passikoff, R., Keys, B., & Schultz, D. E. (2007). *C-MEEs: Cross-media engagement evaluations.*

Patterson, P., Yu, T., & De Ruyter, K. (2006). Understanding customer engagement in services. In *Advancing theory, maintaining relevance, Proceedings of ANZMAC 2006 conference* (pp. 4–6).

Relling, M., Schnittka, O., Ringle, C. M., Sattler, H., & Johnen, M. (2016). Community members' perception of brand community character: Construction and validation of a new scale. *Journal of Interactive Marketing, 36*(11), 107–120.

Schivinski, B., & Dabrowski, D. (2014). *The consumer-based brand equity inventory: Scale construct and validation (No. 4/2014 (22)). GUT FME Working Paper Series A.*

Sedley, R. (2010). *4th Annual online customer engagement report 2010.*

Severi, E., & Ling, K. C. (2013). The mediating effects of brand association, brand loyalty, brand image and perceived quality on brand equity. *Asian Social Science, 9*(3), 125–137.

Shariq, M. A. (2018). Study of brand equity and marketing mix constructs scale invariance in UAE. *International Journal of Scientific and Research Publications, 8*(4), 286–296.

Ukaj, M. (2020). *Start-ups through the lens of marketing: The importance of branding for start-ups and brand awareness* (Doctoral Dissertation).

Vera, J. (2015). Perceived brand quality as a way to superior customer perceived value crossing by moderating effects. *Journal of Product & Brand Management, 24*(2), 147–156.

Vivek, S. D., Beatty, S. E., Vivek, D., & Morgan, R. M. (2014). A generalized multidimensional scale for measuring customer engagement. *Journal of Marketing Theory and Practice, 22*(4), 401–420.

Xi, N., & Hamari, J. (2019). The relationship between gamification, brand engagement and brand equity. In *Proceedings of the 52nd Hawaii International Conference on System Sciences.*

Yoo, B., Donthu, N., & Lee, S. (2000). An examination of selected marketing mix elements and brand equity. *Journal of the Academy of Marketing Science, 28*(2), 195–211.

The Impact of Economy Affirmative to Wealth Distribution Among Ethnic Groups in Malaysia

Muhammad Najit Sukemi, Mohd Nasir Nawawi, Nizam Ahmat, Jumadil Saputra, and Shamsul Amri Baharuddin

1 Introduction

Wealth is often interpreted as equity. Equity means justice, where everyone receives what is his right. "Justice" is defined as "Justice as Fairness" where it does not mean equality, but distribution based on the requirements that have been set (Rawls, 1971). In the field of accounting, equity refers to the value of capital contributed by the owner, while in economics, equity means a condition or situation where everyone gets what is their right (equality of income and wealth) covering equal life

M. N. Sukemi • M. N. Nawawi • N. Ahmat • J. Saputra (✉)
Faculty of Business, Economics and Social Development, Universiti Malaysia Terengganu, Kuala Terengganu, Malaysia
e-mail: jumadil.saputra@umt.edu.my

S. A. Baharuddin
Institut Kajian Etnik, Universiti Kebangsaan Malaysia, Bangi, Malaysia

F. A. Yamoah, A. ul Haque (eds.), *Corporate Management Ecosystem in Emerging Economies*, https://doi.org/10.1007/978-3-031-41578-4_22

opportunities regardless of identity, basic and minimum income, and a commitment to redistribution.

According to Harding (1996), to achieve equality in distribution, equity must be achieved first before equality can be achieved. A balanced distribution between generations will guarantee the equality of distribution of income and wealth for the next generation through higher human capital development and increasing economic growth (Romer, 1986; Alesina & dan Rodrik, 1994; Persson & dan Tabellini, 1994; Perotti, 1996). Unfair and unbalanced distribution of wealth not only results in lower economic growth in the long term but also results in its existence of social conflict, political conflict, division, chaos, and chaos in society (Chua, 2003; OECD, 2008). To create an efficient and fair distribution of income and wealth, government intervention is very important to address and overcome the problem of market failure through the implementation of various policies, including the implementation of affirmative action.

Affirmative action is often conceptualized as a conflict resolution mechanism in situations of ethnic tension and socio-economic imbalance. It is defined as planned measures to correct social and economic injustices and injustices because of governments or policies in the past that have discriminated against certain groups in a multi-ethnic society. It is an intervention policy (direct government intervention) that has the same goal as the "equal opportunity" policy but differs from the approach point of view (Burstein, 1994). Its implementation is one of the strategies to deal with inequality of income and wealth, economic, social, and past injustices between ethnic groups, especially in multi-ethnic countries. It takes the form of positive discrimination by considering various factors such as ethnicity, skin color, religion, gender, sexual orientation, national origin, social class, and disability status to achieve equal opportunity (equal opportunity) in any field, including employment, education, health, and business (public contracts) that are contrary to the effects of historical discrimination.

Affirmative action is implemented in most countries in the world, such as Fiji, India, Malaysia, Northern Ireland, South Africa, Sri Lanka, and the United States, and the number increases from year to year and produces different results that require further proof (Stewart et al., 2007; Gomez & dan Premdas, 2013). This is because there is no one correct method to deal with this problem because each country is faced with different situations and requires different methods of solution. Its implementation aims to address horizontal inequality between ethnic groups through three different methods, namely, direct methods, indirect methods, and integration between the two (Stewart et al., 2007). Malaysia and Northern Ireland are among the best examples of how affirmative action contributes to the reduction of economic and social inequality and subsequently brings harmony in society (Stewart & Brown, 2006).

In Malaysia, the inequality of income and wealth distribution between ethnic groups has been an open issue and has been recognized since the British colonial era. This is proven through the existence of traditional elements in the Federal Constitution (social contract) that give rights and privileges to the Malays/Bumiputras and the people of Sabah and Sarawak through Article 153. To deal with inequality and create fair and equitable distribution, various policies and strategies have been implemented by the government to increase economic growth and improve economic and social imbalances but, it also results in negative impacts such as unbalanced development, widening the inequality gap in the distribution of income and wealth and marginalization between ethnic groups as well as the gap between urban and rural areas and regions (Snodgrass, 1980).

The impact of the bloody tragedy of 13 May 1969, the government has implemented affirmative action through the New Economic Policy (NEB) to address economic imbalances and inequality of income and wealth between ethnic groups through the redistribution of equity, with the goal of 70% equity owned by Malaysians with 30% owned by Bumiputra and 40% owned by other Malaysians. The implementation of affirmative action in Malaysia is quite different compared to other countries where it is implemented explicitly and planned, protected by the constitution, and implemented to help the majority rather than the minority (Stiglitz, 2006). Based on the Second Malaysia Plan (1970), equity holdings in 1970 for Bumiputra were only 2.4% compared to ethnic Chinese holdings of 34.3% and foreign holdings of 63.3%. After the end of DEB (1971–1990), affirmative action continued with modifications in the implementation of further development policies, namely the National Development Policy (1991–2000), the National Vision Policy (2001–2010) and the New Economic Model (2011–2020). The continuation of this goal and spirit exists because the NEP itself is part of the affirmative action that has been implemented in Malaysia.

To create openness and reduce protection, especially the special conditions of an affirmative nature, further increasing the competitiveness and attractiveness of the Malaysian capital market, especially to foreign investors, the government implemented a policy of comprehensive liberalization of the financial sector starting in the capital market sector in 2009. Its implementation resulted in drastic and comprehensive changes in terms of equity ownership, especially the special conditions for bumiputra equity ownership under the guidelines of the Foreign Investment Committee (FIC) that have existed for the past 36 years as part of the strategy to achieve the objective of 30% Bumiputra equity ownership in the DEB.

Along with the implementation of capital market liberalization and the cancellation of FIC requirements, companies that wish to be listed on Bursa Malaysia now only need to meet the basic listing requirements that stipulate a public shareholding of 25%. Under the new FIC conditions, 50% of the 25% public shareholding must be offered to Bumiputra investors (12.5% at the best effort). However, if only 1% of the share allocation is subscribed by Bumiputra investors, it can still be listed without any problems compared to the previous one, which required a subscription of 30% by Bumiputra investors. An "Initial Public Offering (IPO)" can also be listed without making an open offer but through a "private placement" offer to selected investors. This change also officially ended the requirement of 30% Bumiputera equity ownership in a company's equity ownership on Bursa Malaysia and resulted in the role of affirmative action becoming weaker.

As the basis of socio-economic structuring, the implementation of affirmative action has pure values and targets and shows many successes. However, after about 40 years of implementation, the goal of equity distribution still failed to be achieved. Khalid's study (2012) found that the income distribution gap between ethnicities, especially between Bumiputera and ethnic Chinese, widened from 2009 to 2012, thus erasing all the achievements that had been achieved recently. This situation is almost similar to the situation in 1969/1970 where inequality of income, wealth, and poverty converged with ethnic, social, and religious divisions. There is a question: does the implementation of affirmative action affect the distribution of wealth for each ethnic group?

2 Literature Review

Studies on the distribution of income and wealth are among the issues that are often discussed, especially on the wealth gap, injustice in the distribution of income and wealth, and the concentration of wealth. Wolff (1990) found an unbalanced distribution of wealth, where the top 1% of households own an average of 38.9% of wealth and 16.4% of the total household income in the United States (USA) in 1989. Households in the top 10% own nearly 85% of the wealth and receive over 50% of the total household income in the United States. A study by Keister and Moller (2000) found that the concentration of wealth is very high and very unequal among a small part of the population in the United States (USA) since the 1920s where the top 1% of households own an average of 30% of wealth while the top 5% of households own half of the wealth of the US economy. Findings show that economic decline will cause the distribution of wealth to become more balanced.

Chow (2003) argue that unfair and balanced distribution of wealth results in not only lower economic growth in the long term but also social and political conflicts in society. This was confirmed by Noor (2012) where racial conflicts such as the 13 May 1969 incident, the Kampung Rawa incident in 1977, and the Kampung Medan incident in 2001 occurred because of imbalanced development and government governance, inequality between races and national regions, urban poverty, and the marginalization of the people from government service. As such, this imbalance needs to be addressed comprehensively to avoid a more severe impact, and it will take decades to deal with it. Oxfam's study (2016) shows that the wealth of the world's 1% richest households has the same amount of wealth as the total wealth of 80% of the world's population in 2015. The wealth of the world's 62 richest individuals equals the combined wealth of half of the world's poorest. The wealth value of the world's richest 1% controlled 44% of the world's economy in 2010 and increased to 48% in 2014, while the rest of the world's 80% population only controlled 5.5% of the world's wealth.

In Malaysia, studies on wealth distribution and ethnicity are relatively less discussed, especially involving affirmative policies such as DEB. Studies focus more on issues of income inequality (Jomo & Hui, 2014; Khalid, 2014), poverty issues (Jomo, 2004; Rogayah, 2009), issues of development inequality between regions (Khalid, 2012), education issues (Shah, 1995; Lee, 2012), and employment issues (Lee, 2012). Studies also focus more on issues regarding the formation of Bumiputera business and industrial society (Mahmet, 1986; Jesudason, 1989; Searle, 1999). The lack of studies on the issue of inequality of wealth distribution between ethnic groups may be due to the lack of official data where the Malaysian Government classified data related to distribution as "confidential" especially after the end of the implementation of DEB with the argument to avoid abuse, especially the interpretation of data related to distribution between ethnic groups (Shari, 2000; Rogayah, 2009).

Faaland et al.'s (2005) study is one of the comprehensive studies on NEP where it discusses the impact of NEP implementation on Bumiputra economic growth and achievement covering the socio-political background of NEP, contribution of NEP to the Malays, and challenges and opportunities after NEP. After 20 years of implementation, the results showed an increase in income among the population, especially rural residents, eliminating the underemployment rate, and reducing the poverty rate from 49.3% in 1970 to 16.5% in 1990 and to 5.7% in 2005.

3 Methodology

This study examines empirically the influence of affirmative action on the distribution of wealth among ethnic groups in Malaysia using an ARDL approach to determine short-term and long-term asymmetric relationships.

The basic function of this research model is as follows:

$$Y = \alpha + \beta^{*} E + \gamma^{*} X + \varepsilon \tag{1}$$

where Y is the gross domestic product per capita, E is the equity by ethnicity, X is other variables including dummy variables and ε is the error. In this study, we use annual time series data from 1969 to 2012 for ownership by ethnicity, namely, Bumiputra (Bumi), Chinese (Cina), Indian (India) equity, and gross domestic product per capita (Y).

The equity value is the nominal value of the total ownership of the share capital (at par value) of the limited company and obtained from the Economic Planning Unit (EPU) and data published in the Malaysia Plan starting from the 2nd Malaysia Plan (RMKe2), 1970 to the 11th Malaysia Plan (RMKe11), 2011. However, the latest data for equity ownership by ethnicity is categorized as confidential (Shari, 2000; Rogayah, 2009). Data for Gross Domestic Product Per Capita is obtained from the World Development Indicators (World Bank, 2015) while the dummy variable is affirmative action (AA). The measurement value for the variable is Ringgit Malaysia (RM) while all the study variables are processed in logarithmic formation for estimation purposes. Data processing to logarithmic (log) formation is implemented to produce better results and reduce the sharpness of time series data (Shahbaz, 2010).

To achieve the objectives, a series of steps in the ARDL procedure is the investigation of: (i) stationarity, (ii) cointegration, and last but not least (iii) causality. There are other ways to proceed to causality analysis without the first two steps, but this occurs within other methodological frameworks. The first test in ARDL analysis is the unit root analysis to detect the level of stationarity of the time series data before the estimation of the study model is carried out. Two forms of stationarity tests are implemented, namely, the Dickey and Fuller (1981) test and Phillips and Perron (1988) to ensure that all study variables are stationary before being followed up with cointegration analysis. For the cointegration test, the researcher will apply the autoregressive distributed lag (ARDL) approach introduced by Pesaran et al. (2001) and Narayan (2004), where its implementation has advantages over previous cointegration tests in which it is able to help correct serial correlation (Pesaran & dan Shin, 1999). The ARDL approach is appropriate for generating short-run and long-run elasticities for a small sample size at the same time and follows the ordinary least squares (OLS) approach for cointegration between variables (Duasa, 2007). ARDL affords flexibility about the order of integration of the variables. In addition, it can be applied regardless of whether the dependent variable is I(1) or I (0) and is more appropriate to use if the number of study samples is small (Pesaran et al., 2001). Hence, four ARDL models can be specified as:

$$\begin{aligned}\Delta \ln Y = \alpha_0 + \sum_{i=1}^{p}\alpha_1 \Delta \ln Y_{t-i} + \sum_{j=0}^{q}\alpha_2 \Delta\text{lnBumi}_{t-j} + \sum_{k=0}^{r}\alpha_3 \Delta\text{lnCina}_{t-k} \\ + \sum_{l=0}^{s}\alpha_4 \Delta\text{lnIndia}_{t-l} + \sum_{m=0}^{t}\alpha_5 \Delta\text{lnAA}_{t-m} + \pi_1 \ln Y_{t-i} + \pi_2 \ln \text{Bumi}_{t-i} \\ + \pi_3 \ln \text{Cina}_{t-i} + \pi_4 \ln \text{India}_{t-i} + \pi_5 \text{AA}_{t-i} + \varepsilon_t\end{aligned} \tag{2a}$$

$$\begin{aligned}\Delta l\text{nBumi} = \alpha_0 + \sum_{i=1}^{p}\alpha_1 \Delta \text{lnBumi}_{t-i} + \sum_{j=0}^{q}\alpha_2 \Delta \text{lnCina}_{t-j} \\ + \sum_{k=0}^{r}\alpha_3 \Delta \text{lnIndia}_{t-k} + \sum_{l=0}^{s}\alpha_4 \Delta \ln Y_{t-l} + \sum_{m=0}^{t}\alpha_5 \Delta \text{AA}_{t-m} + \pi_1 \text{lnBumi}_{t-i} \\ + \pi_2 \text{lnCina}_{t-i} + \pi_3 \ln \text{India}_{t-i} + \pi_4 \ln Y_{t-i} + \pi_5 \text{AA}_{t-i} + \varepsilon_t\end{aligned} \tag{2b}$$

$$\begin{aligned}\Delta\text{lnCina} = \alpha_0 + \sum_{i=1}^{p}\alpha_1 \Delta\text{lnCina}_{t-i} + \sum_{j=0}^{q}\alpha_2 \Delta\text{lnBumi}_{t-j} \\ + \sum_{k=0}^{r}\alpha_3 \Delta\text{lnIndia}_{t-k} + \sum_{l=0}^{s}\alpha_4 \Delta \ln Y_{t-l} + \sum_{m=0}^{t}\alpha_6 \Delta\text{AA}_{t-m} + \pi_1 \text{lnCina}_{t-i} \\ + \pi_2 \text{lnBumi}_{t-i} + \pi_3 \text{lnIndia}_{t-i} + +\pi_4 \ln Y_{t-i} + \pi_5 \text{AA}_{t-i} + \varepsilon_t\end{aligned} \tag{2c}$$

$$\begin{aligned}\Delta\text{India} = \alpha_0 + \sum_{i=1}^{p}\alpha_1 \Delta\text{lnIndia}_{t-i} + \sum_{j=0}^{q}\alpha_2 \Delta\text{lnBumi}_{t-j} \\ + \sum_{k=0}^{r}\alpha_3 \ln \Delta\text{Cina}_{t-k} + \sum_{l=0}^{s}\alpha_4 \Delta \ln Y_{t-l} + \sum_{m=0}^{t}\alpha_5 \Delta\text{AA}_{t-m} + \pi_1 \Delta\text{lnIndia}_{t-i} \\ + \pi_2 \text{InBumi}_{t-i} + \pi_3 \text{lnCina}_{t-i} + \pi_4 \ln Y_{t-i} + \pi_5 \text{AA}_{t-i} + \varepsilon_t\end{aligned} \tag{2d}$$

where Δ is the level of first differentiation, *Y* represents the gross domestic product per capita, *AA* represents the implementation of affirmative action, and ε, *t* is the residual term in the period "*t*" of the study. The level of lat selection for ARDL model estimation is based on the Akaike Information Criterion (AIC). To determine the "bound" level for ARDL model estimation, the F-statistics test is used, and the value obtained is compared with the critical value introduced by Pesaran et al. (2001). The hypothesis to test the existence of a long-term relationship for Eqs. (2a–2d) is as follows:

$$H_0 : \pi_1 = \pi_2 = \pi_3 = \pi_4 = \pi_5 = 0 \tag{3}$$

$$H_1 : \pi_1 \neq \pi_2 \neq \pi_3 \neq \pi_4 \neq \pi_5 \neq 0 \tag{4}$$

This study also adapted the ARDL-ECM estimation model approach to detect the existence of short-term relationships and the degree of coordination of the study variables. To measure the direction of causality among variables, the Granger causality approach (1969) elaborated in the framework of the ARDL-ECM model is implemented, where it is a combination of χ^2 statistical tests with various lat levels based on the Schwarz information criterion (SBC). The long-term ARDL-ECM Granger causal relationship is determined through the significance level of the error correction coefficient (ECT_{t-1}), while the short-term Granger causal relationship is determined through the χ^2 statistical combination test. The ARDL-ECM Granger model is as follows:

$$\begin{bmatrix} \ln Y_\tau \\ \ln \mathrm{Bumi}_\tau \\ \ln \mathrm{Cina}_\tau \\ \ln \mathrm{India}_\tau \\ \mathrm{AA} \end{bmatrix} = \begin{bmatrix} \delta_1 \\ \delta_2 \\ \delta_3 \\ \delta_4 \\ \delta_5 \end{bmatrix} + \begin{bmatrix} \delta_{11,1} & \delta_{12,1} & \delta_{13,1} & \delta_{14,1} & \delta_{15,1} & \delta_{16,1} & \delta_{17,1} \\ \delta_{21,1} & \delta_{22,1} & \delta_{23,1} & \delta_{24,1} & \delta_{25,1} & \delta_{26,1} & \delta_{27,1} \\ \delta_{31,1} & \delta_{32,1} & \delta_{33,1} & \delta_{34,1} & \delta_{35,1} & \delta_{36,1} & \delta_{37,1} \\ \delta_{41,1} & \delta_{42,1} & \delta_{43,1} & \delta_{44,1} & \delta_{45,1} & \delta_{46,1} & \delta_{47,1} \\ \delta_{51,1} & \delta_{52,1} & \delta_{53,1} & \delta_{54,1} & \delta_{55,1} & \delta_{56,1} & \delta_{57,1} \end{bmatrix} \begin{bmatrix} \ln Y_\tau \\ \ln \mathrm{Bumi}_\tau \\ \ln \mathrm{Cina}_\tau \\ \ln \mathrm{India}_\tau \\ \mathrm{AA} \end{bmatrix}$$

$$+ \ldots \begin{bmatrix} \delta_{11,i} & \delta_{12,i} & \delta_{13,i} & \delta_{14,i} & \delta_{15,i} & \delta_{16,i} & \delta_{17,i} \\ \delta_{21,i} & \delta_{22,i} & \delta_{23,i} & \delta_{24,i} & \delta_{25,i} & \delta_{26,i} & \delta_{27,i} \\ \delta_{31,i} & \delta_{32,i} & \delta_{33,i} & \delta_{34,i} & \delta_{35,i} & \delta_{36,i} & \delta_{37,i} \\ \delta_{41,i} & \delta_{42,i} & \delta_{43,i} & \delta_{44,i} & \delta_{45,i} & \delta_{46,i} & \delta_{47,i} \\ \delta_{51,i} & \delta_{52,i} & \delta_{53,i} & \delta_{54,i} & \delta_{55,i} & \delta_{56,i} & \delta_{57,i} \end{bmatrix} \begin{bmatrix} \Delta \ln Y_{\tau-1} \\ \Delta \ln \mathrm{Bumi}_{\tau-1} \\ \Delta \ln \mathrm{Cina}_{\tau-1} \\ \Delta \ln \mathrm{India}_{\tau-1} \\ \Delta \mathrm{AA} \end{bmatrix} + \begin{bmatrix} \varphi_1 \\ \varphi_2 \\ \varphi_3 \\ \varphi_4 \\ \varphi_5 \end{bmatrix} \times \mathrm{ECT}_{t-1} + \begin{bmatrix} \varepsilon_{1,\tau} \\ \varepsilon_{2,\tau} \\ \varepsilon_{3,\tau} \\ \varepsilon_{4,\tau} \\ \varepsilon_{5,\tau} \end{bmatrix} \tag{5}$$

where Δ represents the variable in the first differential formulation, ε_t represents the error term which is assumed to be independent of estimation disturbances and normally distributed. A positive coefficient indicates divergence, while a negative coefficient indicates convergence. ECT is known as an error correction term which indicates the speed of the adjustment parameter. The ECT shows how much of the disequilibrium is being corrected, that is, the extent to which any disequilibrium in the previous period is being adjusted in the current point. The ECT_{t-1} value, on the other hand, represents the level of short-term coordination until reaching a long-term balance through the estimation of the ARDL model with the condition that the value of the ECT_{t-1} coefficient must be negative and significant to confirm the existence of a long-term relationship between *Y*, Bumi, Chinese, Indian, and AA.

4 Results and Discussions

In performing cointegration analysis, the stationarity test is a basic test that is carried out before further tests in which two forms of stationarity tests are implemented, namely, the augmented Dickey–Fuller (ADF) test and the Phillips–Perron (PP) test. The results of the stationarity test based on ADF and PP are shown in Table 1, where the findings show that all four variables are stationary at the level of significance varying between 1%, 5%, and 10% at the I(0) level. At the first level of differentiation (I(1)), to all stationary variables at the level to mean varying between 1%

Table 1 The result of unit root test

	ADF test	PP test
Variable	*T* statistic	*T* statistic
Panel 1: Level [I(0)]		
lnBumi	-3.2816(0)***	-3.2896 [3]***
lnCina	-4.8270 (1)*	-4.6336 [0]*
lnIndia	-3.7663 (1)**	-3.3205 [3]***
ln*Y*	-3.2384 (5)***	-2.1240 [1]
Panel 2: First difference [I(1)]		
ΔlnBumi	-4.8459 (0)*	-4.7562 [5]*
ΔlnCina	-4.5696 (1)*	-1.8360 [1]***
ΔlnIndia	-3.7027(1)**	-1.9375 [0]***
Δln*Y*	-5.3078 (0)*	-5.3079 [1] *

Notes: *, **, and *** indicate the significance levels of 1%, 5%, and 10%, respectively

Figures in ( ) and [ ] are respectively the optimal lag selected based on Schwarz Information Criteria (SIC) dan *bandwidth* based on Newey–West using Bartlett Kernel and 5%. For the PP stationarity test, the findings show that at the I(0) level, only 3 variables are stationary at the 1% and 10% significance levels while the Y variable is not stationary. However, in the first difference (I(1)), to all stationary variables at varying significance levels at 1% and 10%. The results of this stationary test show that the study can be continued with further tests. The results of the stationary test are in Table 1.

To detect the long-term cointegration relationship among the study variables, the Bounds ARDL test was performed. The selection of the ARDL test because this approach is quite synonymous with the analysis of short time series data, as stated by Pesaran et al. (2001) and Narayan (2004).

Table 2 shows the results of the Bounds ARDL test where the F-statistic value obtained for all the null hypotheses was successfully rejected at the 1% significance level for the Bumiputra variable and at the 10% significance level for the Chinese, Indian, and GDP per capita variables.

A null hypothesis will be rejected if the estimated F-statistic value is greater than the critical value I (0) and I (1) introduced by Pesaran et al. (2001). The results of the test show that there is a long-term relationship between ownership of Bumiputra, Chinese, Indian ethnic equity, GDP per capita, and the implementation of affirmative action. To measure the levels of short-term and long-term relationships between variables, the ARDL-ECM version cointegration test was performed. The research findings obtained can be divided into two periods of time, namely, short term and long term. The results of the short-term ARDL-ECM model cointegration test are shown in Table 3. Findings show that in the short

Table 2 Result of bounds test

Variable	F-Statistic	Hipotesis Nol
ΔlnBumi	8.7202*	Tolak
ΔlnCina	3.1636***	Tolak
ΔlnIndia	2.9648***	Tolak
Δln$Y$	3.9669**	Tolak
Critical value	I (0)	I (1)
1%	2.88	3.99
5%	2.27	3.28
10%	1.99	2.94

Notes: *, **, and *** show the significance levels at 1%, 5%, and 10%, respectively
The critical value of F-Statistics is based on $k = 5$ and $N = 36$ in Pesaran et al. (2001) critical value table

Table 3 Results of the short-term cointegration test

Variables (lag)	Bumi (3,3,4,2,4)	Cina (4,2,2,4,4)	India (3,1,3,4,1,)	*Y* (2,4,3,4,4,4)
$\Delta \ln Bumi_t$		0.3817 (7.6218)*	-0.1023 (-1.5104)	-04140 (-5.7870)*
$\Delta \ln Bumi_{t-1}$	-0.3157 (-3.7411)*	0.3074 (4.519)*	-0.3295 (-3.9612)	-0.2330 (-3.6431)**
$\Delta \ln Bumi_{t-2}$	-0.4298 (-5.2430)*	0.3672 (6.3206)*	-0.3666 (5.1999)*	-0.4909 (-8.0496)*
$\Delta \ln Bumi_{t-3}$		0.4030 (6.3587)*		-0.2276 (-3.4209)**
$\Delta \ln Cina_t$	0.7528 (5.1313)*		-0.2792 (-2.3173)**	0.4808 (3.9674)**
$\Delta \ln Cina_{t-1}$	-0.8216 (-4.0378)*	1.0383 (11.9855)*		-1.1197 (-8.3269)*
$\Delta \ln Cina_{t-2}$	1.7472 (7.0449)*			1.1083 (11.8482)*
$\Delta \ln India_t$	-0.1402 (-1.1563)	-0.0502 (-0.6146)		-0.1083 (-1.3612)
$\Delta \ln India_{t-1}$	1.6358 (8.1119)*	-0.3969 (-3.2471)**	1.0597 (7.4131)*	0.7835 (5.8409)*
$\Delta \ln India_{t-2}$	-0.9495 (-4.3176)*		0.2143 (1.7444)	-0.9221 (-7.8417)*
$\Delta \ln India_{t-3}$	1.1553 (5.6026)*			0.4711 (5.1789)*
$\Delta \ln Y_t$	-0.9789 (-5.2575)*	0.3034 (3.1009)**	-0.4830 (-3.3815)*	
$\Delta \ln Y_{t-1}$	-0.5307 (-4.8461)*	0.3290 (4.2603)*	-0.6874 -4.6658)*	-0.3037 (-3.9787)**
$\Delta \ln Y_{t-2}$		0.0240 (0.2996)	-0.6848 (4.9581)*	
$\Delta \ln Y_{t-3}$		0.2917 (4.1515)*	-0.4302 (-3.777)*	
ΔAA_t	-0.0236 (-0.5916)	-0.0967 (-3.8767)*	-0.1807 (4.2885)*	-0.0483 (-2.0501)
ΔAA_{t-1}	-0.0699 (-1.6999)	-0.0993 (-3.7728)*		0.1645 (4.6818)*
ΔAA_{t-2}	0.0582 (1.5768)	-0.1423 (-5.0697)*		0.1866 (5.7184)*
ΔAA_{t-3}	0.2585 (8.3665)*	-0.1421 (-5.9784)*		0.2277 (6.6580)*
ECT_{t-1}	-0.4302 (-13.8508)*	-0.8338 (-8.7564)*	-0.4611 (-7.8744)*	-0.6883 (-9.3420)*

Notes: *, **, and *** show the significance levels at 1%, 5%, and 10%
The value in () refers to the *t*-test value

term, all variables have a significant relationship with each other. The variable of gross domestic product per capita and Chinese is the variable that has the most dominant positive effect among all the study variables.

For the Bumiputra variable, the findings show that it has a significant relationship with Chinese equity ownership and GDP per capita but relatively weak with the affirmative action and Indian variables. On the other hand, the Chinese variable shows a significant relationship with the Bumiputra variable, GDP per capita, and affirmative action. This supports the findings of Heng and Sieh (2000) who found that the position of the Chinese business community was somewhat compromised during the initial implementation of the NEP following the government's move to pay special attention to Malay/Bumiputra entrepreneurs.

To ensure the continuation and competitiveness of business, ethnic Chinese created a network of cooperation between Chinese businessmen and political elites and Malay entrepreneurs and gave birth to a group known as the "Ali Baba" alliance. This is evidenced by the findings that show Chinese and Indian ethnicities have a significant relationship with the affirmative policies implemented by the government compared to Bumiputra ethnicities.

The negative and significant ECT value for the ARDL-ECM analysis shows that there is at least one direction of causality between all variables and the speed of adjustment towards long-term equilibrium. This reflects that if there is a shock in the market that results in a distortion in equity holdings, then adjustment will be made through the adjustment of equity holdings so that it returns to balance immediately. The ECT value also shows the balance adjustment level, where for the Bumiputra variable, the adjustment value is 0.4302% per year compared to the Chinese variable which enjoys two times the adjustment compared to the Malay ethnicity, which is 0.8338% per year.

The long-term ARDL-ECM model cointegration test results are shown in Table 4. Findings show that in the long run, only Chinese ethnicity has a positive significant relationship with Indian ethnicity and gross domestic product per capita compared to other variables. The results of the study are shown in Table 4.

Table 4 Results of long-term cointegration test

lnBumi		-0.1697 (-0.9980)	0.3410 (1.4079)	0.0567 (0.1532)
lnCina	2.6840 (0.8801)		0.2958 (0.8538)	1.1206 (1.4291)
lnIndia	-1.7754 (-0.8880)	0.6796 (5.8034)*		-0.6152 (-0.9895)
ln*Y*	-0.5503 (0.2423)	0.7573 (3.6553)*	0.6048 (1.4833)	
AA	0.0069 (0.0068)	0.1475 (0.8006)	-0.3972 (-1.6377)	-0.4980 (-1.8395)
C	-8.5138 (2.2545)***	-0.6172 (-0.3755)	-0.6290 (-0.3229)	1.0592 (0.3014)
Adj R^2	0.8590	0.7718	0.5473	0.8174
χ^2 Serial	5.6349 [0.0000]*	11.2298 [0.0000]*	3.6014 [0.0008]*	10.4394 [0.0000]*
χ^2 Hetero	0.8071 [0.4643]	2.2165 [0.3474]	0.5991 [0.6987]	9.2603 [0.2642]
χ^2 Normality	33.3564 [0.0000]*	4.4463 [0.1083)	5.9191 [0.0518]***	0.2335 [0.8897]

Notes: *, **, and *** show the significance at the levels of 1%, 5%, and 10%
The value in () refers to the *t*-test value

To ensure that the estimated ARDL-ECM model is not constrained by basic econometric problems, some diagnostic tests as suggested by Pesaran et al. (2001) were implemented such as serial correlation test, normality test, heteroscedasticity test (Table 4), RESET, and CUSUM diagram (Fig. 1) balance. In general, all the variables do not suffer from any diagnostic problems such as serial correlation and heteroscedasticity in the error of the estimated regression equation and the obtained CUSUM and CUSUMQ diagrams do not provide any situations that indicate that they exceed the equilibrium boundary of the study model estimation. Therefore, it can be concluded that the estimation of the ARDL Model as well as the Lag-Length Selection meet the basic requirements of the econometric model.

To further verify the level of integration among variables, the ARDLECM test of Granger causality is implemented (see Table 5). Findings show the existence of a Granger causal relationship between Chinese and Malay ethnicities and between GDP per capita and all study variables. This shows the existence of interaction between ethnic groups in the

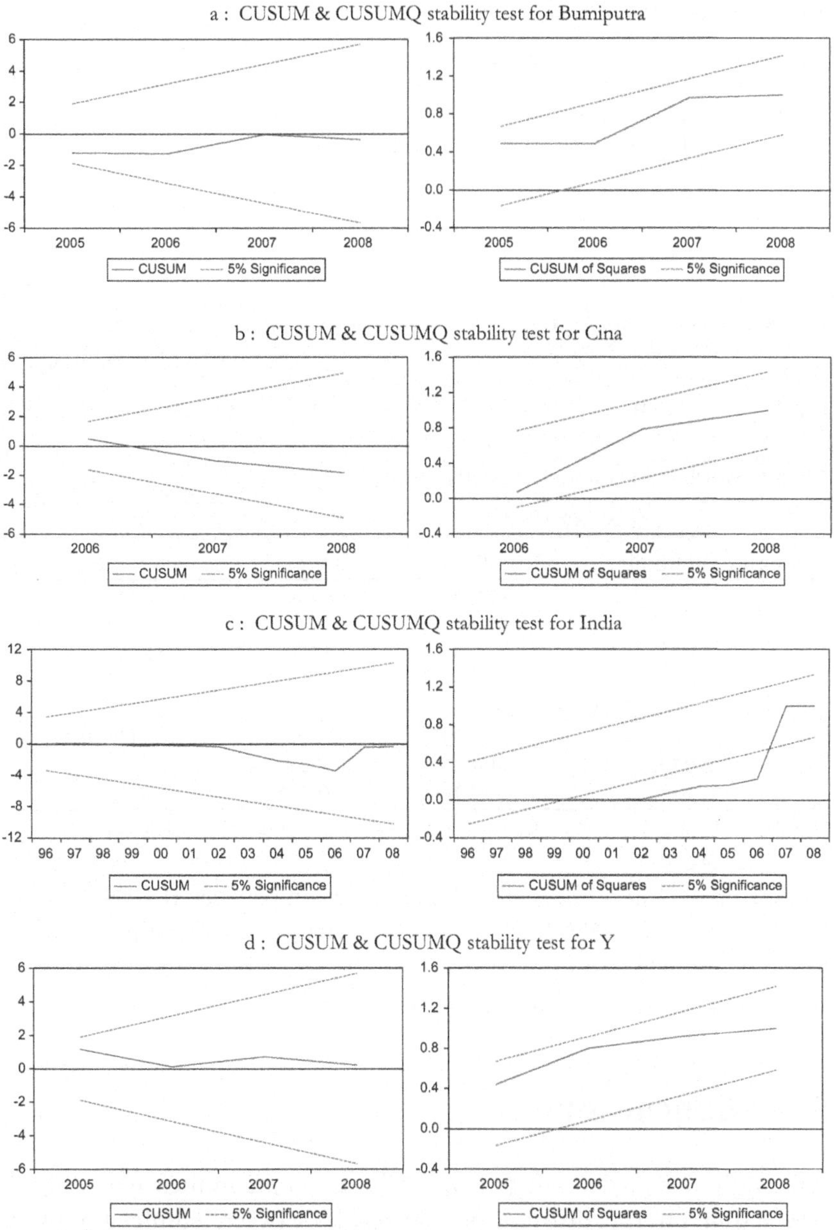

Fig. 1 CUSUM & CUSUMQ stability test. (**a**) CUSUM & CUSUMQ stability test for Bumiputra. (**b**) CUSUM & CUSUMQ stability test for Cina. (**c**) CUSUM & CUSUMQ stability test for India. (**d**) CUSUM & CUSUMQ stability test for Y. (**e**) CUSUM & CUSUMQ stability test for Affirmative Action

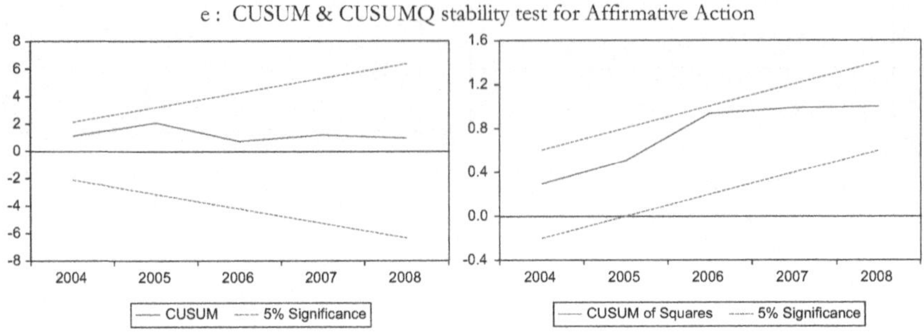

Fig. 1 (continued)

Table 5 ARDL-ECM Granger causality results

	Weak causality effects			
Variables	ΔlnBumi	ΔlnCina	ΔlnIndia	Δln*Y*
ΔlnBumi		1.9372 [0.1747]	1.6769 [0.2119]	4.0464 [0.0393]**
ΔlnCina	4.0715 [0.0282]**		2.4447 [0.1185]	4.5285 [0.0188]**
ΔlnIndia	1.5300 [0.2444]	1.8846 [0.1898]		3.8003 [0.0251]**
Δln*Y*	2.0422 [0.1575]	2.4503 [0.1068]	0.9035 [0.4612]	

Notes: *, **, and *** show the significance at the levels of 1%, 5%, and 10%

ownership of equity, especially the collaboration between traders as found by Heng and Ling (2000). Findings also show that the Bumiputra ethnic group needs help and support from the Chinese ethnic group to increase equity and achieve success in business (Table 5).

5 Conclusions

This study was carried out to empirically assess the influence of affirmative action on the distribution of wealth between ethnic groups in Malaysia. To achieve a fair and equitable distribution of wealth, it is not an easy task and takes a long time compared to the original planning (one generation) and requires careful, comprehensive planning and implementation at the right time. The achievement of equity distribution according to ethnicity, especially Bumiputra ethnicity is still low compared to non-Bumiputra equity, especially after 1990. This is because the role of affirmative action in equity distribution is getting looser and weaker where the conditions of equity ownership are no longer strictly controlled but are given flexibility, especially when the economy is in decline, such as in 1985 (commodity crisis) and the 1997 financial crisis.

Findings show that there is a significant influence of affirmative action on the distribution of wealth between ethnic groups in Malaysia, especially for the Chinese and Indian ethnic groups in the short term but not significant in the long term. This coincides with the findings of Abdullah (2012) who looked at the business dynamism of Chinese companies in Peninsular Malaysia in the era of the New Economic Policy using the Structure, Behavior and Performance Model (SGP) approach which found that even though it had given 30% share ownership to Bumiputra investors, it still did not affecting business achievements and the rapid development of Chinese business the impact of internal dynamism and innovation compared to the aspect of patronage from the Government especially after the implementation of the Coordination Act of 1975 (ICA) as well as the implementation of the Foreign Investment Committee (FIC) guidelines which have required that every company that wants to be listed must allocate 30% equity to Bumiputra investors.

For Bumiputra ethnicity, the influence of affirmative action is not significant in influencing the increase in equity ownership compared to the influence of Chinese ethnicity and GDP per capita. The syndrome of dependence on the government and business in the "Ali Baba" way among the Bumiputra ethnic group is one of the examples of leakage issues in government spending and inefficient use of funds and directed to the practices of those who are known and not based on actual ability (not based on merit). This was confirmed by Heng and Ling (2000), who found that the position of the Chinese business community was somewhat compromised during the implementation of the NEP following the government's move to pay special attention to Malay/Bumiputra entrepreneurs. To ensure the continuation and competitiveness of business, they created a network of cooperation between Chinese businessmen and the Malay political elite and gave birth to a group known as the "Ali Baba" pact.

Findings also prove that the distribution of wealth between ethnic groups through affirmative action is distributed through a growing economy and not through the taking of property rights from other ethnic groups, especially the Chinese ethnic group, and transferred to the Bumiputra ethnic group. This coincides with the basic principle of socio-economic engineering structuring to achieve the target of income and wealth distribution through a growing economy instead of taking the share or rights of non-Bumiputras or other races and transferring them to the Bumiputras (what is distributed is coming from the increase in the size of the economic cake (growth)). This finding supports the findings of Barro R.J. (2000), Forbes K.J (2000) and Chen B.L. (2003) who found the importance of economic growth in solving the imbalance issue. Growth that exists without fair and comprehensive development and structural change will result in a widening gap of inequality among society. The existence of economic growth is very important in efforts to increase people's income and living standards, but it does not guarantee that the benefits can be enjoyed fairly and equitably by all levels of society. This is different compared to Zimbabwe's experience under the leadership of the Mugabe government in implementing affirmative action to achieve income equality through tax strategies and "confiscating" the property and ownership of whites to distribute to blacks. As a result, the economy of Zimbabwe suffered a decline (Sowell, 2004).

Findings also show that the affirmative policy has become the basis of inter-ethnic integration to create a balanced distribution of wealth between ethnic groups. The interaction between ethnicities and the impact of the implementation of affirmative action has successfully driven the development of companies listed on Bursa Malaysia. This is evidenced by the increase in the number of companies listed on Bursa Malaysia compared to when DEB was first implemented. The number of companies listed on Bursa Malaysia has increased to 957 companies in 2015, where 75% of companies are owned by ethnic Chinese, 16% or 136 companies are owned by Bumiputra, and 1% are owned by ethnic Indians compared to only 262 companies in 1973 with 99 companies or 37.8% owned by ethnic Chinese and a company or 0.38% owned by Bumiputra while the rest belonged to foreigners. This certainly supports the structural, behavioral, and performance approach developed by Mason and Bain in the 1940s and 1950s in assessing the development of community businesses. This proves that the implementation of affirmative action has a positive impact in the long term on the Chinese ethnic group compared to the Malay ethnic group.

Findings prove the importance and intervention of the government in dealing with market failure in the economy and the reorganization of society, especially in the short term. Shari (1999) argues that equal development will not be achieved through the market without government intervention in the economy. This is in line with the government's function in determining and implementing national policies and policies, namely, the allocation function, the distribution function, and the stability function (Musgrave, 1996).

To achieve this goal, the country not only needs a high rate of economic growth but also needs to ensure the existence of social justice, share an equitable increase in income, and increase employment opportunities. This coincides with the view of Embong (2003) where development should be holistic and comprehensive so that the results of development can be enjoyed equally among the community and the government has a role to implement fair and equitable development and distribution. The success of this wealth distribution is important as a goal of the reorganization of society to create an economic balance between ethnic groups, reduce the economic and social imbalance gap between ethnic groups at once, and eliminate racial identification according to economic function.

Acknowledgment This study was fully funded by the Universiti Malaysia Terengganu through Talent and Publication Enhancement-Research Grant (TAPE-RG) phase 1/2018.

References

Abdullah, M. A. I. L. (2012). *Kedinamikan perniagaan syarikat Cina Semenanjung Malaysia era Dasar Ekonomi Baru* (Doctoral dissertation, Universiti Utara Malaysia).

Alesina, A., & dan Rodrik, D. (1994). Distributive politics and economic growth. *Quarterly Journal of Economics, 109*(2), 465–490.

Baroo, R. J. (2000). Inequality and growth in a panel of countries. *Journal of Economic Growth. Issues, 5*, 5–32.

Burstein, P. (1994). *Equal employment opportunity: Labor market discrimination and public policy*. De Gruyter Aldine.

Chen, B. L. (2003). An inverted-U relationship between inequality and long-run growth. *Economics Letters, 78*, 205–212.

Chow, E. N. (2003). Gender Matters: Studying Globalization and Social Change in the 21st Century. *International Sociology, 18*(3), 443–460. https://doi.org/10.1177/02685809030183001

Chua, A. (2003). *World on fire: How exporting free-market democracy breeds ethnic hatred and global instability*. William Heinemann.

Dickey, D. A., & Fuller, W. A. (1981). Likelihood ratio statistics for autoregressive time series with a unit root. *Econometrica, 49*, 1057–1072.

Duasa, J. (2007). Determinants of Malaysian trade balance: An ARDL bound testing approach. *Global Economic Review, 36*(1), 89–102. https://doi.org/10.1080/12265080701217405

Embong, A. R. (2003). *Pembangunan dan kesejahteraan agenda kemanusiaan abad ke 21. Syarahan perdana jawatan profesor*. Penerbit Universiti Kebangsaan Malaysia.

Faaland, J., Parkinson, J., & Saniman, D. S. (2005). *Dasar Ekonomi Baru: Pertumbuhan Negara Dan Pencapaian Ekonomi Orang Melayu* (3rd ed.). Utusan Publications & Distributors.

Forbes, K. J. (2000). A reassessment of the relationship between inequality and growth. *American Economic Review, 90*(4), 869–887.

Gomez, E. T., & dan Premdas, R. (Eds.). (2013). *Affirmative action, Ethnicity and conflict* (Routledge Malaysian studies series). Routledge.

Harding, A. J. (1996). *Law, government and the constitution in Malaysia*. Malayan Law, Kuala Lumpur.

Heng, P. K., & Ling, S. M. (2000). The Chinese business Community in Peninsular Malaysia, 1957–1999. In L. K. Hing & T. C. Beng (Eds.), *The Chinese in Malaysia*. Oxford University Press.

Heng, P. K., & Sieh-Lee, M. L. (2000). The Chinese business community in peninsular Malaysia, 1957–1999. In K. H. Lee & C. B. Tan (Eds.), *The Chinese in Malaysia*. Oxford University Press.

Jesudason, J. V. (1989). *Ethnicity and the economy: The states, Chinese business and multinationals in Malaysia*. Oxford University Press.

Jomo, K. S. (2004). *The new economic policy and interethnic relations in Malaysia. Identities, conflict and cohesion programme, paper number 7*. United Nations Research Institute for Social Development.

Jomo, K. S., & Hui, W. C. (2014). *Malaysia @ 50. Economic Development, Distribution, Disparities*. Strategic Information and Research Development Centre.

Keister, L. A., & Moller, S. (2000). Wealth inequality in the United States. *Annual Reviews of Sociology, 26*, 63–81.

Khalid, M. A. (2012). Household wealth in Malaysia: Composition and inequality among ethnic groups. *Jurnal Ekonomi Malaysia, 45*, 71–80.

Khalid, M. A. (2014). *The colour of inequality. Ethnicity, class, income and wealth in Malaysia*. MPH Publishing.

Lee, H.-A. (2012). Affirmative action in Malaysia: Education and employment outcomes since the 1990s. *Journal of Contemporary Asia, 42*(2), 230–254.

Mahmet, O. (1986). *Development in Malaysia: Poverty, wealth and trusteeship*. Croom Helm.

Malaysia. (1970). *Rancangan Malaysia Kedua*. Pencetakan Nasional Berhad.

Musgrave, R. A. (1996). The role of the state in fiscal theory. In *Public finance in a democratic society* (Vol. III, pp. 247–258). Edward Elgar.

Narayan, P. K. (2004). Fiji's tourism demand: The ARDL approach to cointegration. *Tourism Economics, 10*(2), 193–206.

Noor, M. M. (2012). *Kerencaman Sosial Dan Penipisan Batas Etnik*. Penerbit Universiti Kebangsaan Malaysia.

OECD. (2008). *Growing unequal: Income distribution and poverty in OECD countries*. OECD.

Oxfam. (2016). *Oxfam briefing paper.*

Perotti, R. (1996). Growth, income distribution and democracy: What the data say? *Journal of Economic Growth, 1*(2), 149–187.

Persson, T., & dan Tabellini, G. (1994). Is inequality harmful for growth? *The American Economic Review, 84*(3), 600–621.

Pesaran, M. H., & dan Shin, Y. (1999). An autoregressive distributed lag modelling approach to cointegration analysis, Chapter 11. In S. Strom (Ed.),

Econometrics and economic theory in the 20th century the Ragnar Frisch Centennial symposium. Cambridge University Press.
Pesaran, M. H., dan Shin, Y., & Smith, R. J. (2001). Bound testing approaches to the analysis of level relationships. *Journal of Applied Econometrics, 16*, 289–326.
Phillips, P. C. B., & Perron, P. (1988). Testing for a unit root in times series regression. *Biometrica, 75*, 335–446.
Rawls, J. (1971). *A theory of justice*. Belknap Press.
Rogayah, M. Z. (2009). *Pertumbuhan dengan Kesetaraan: Realitu dan Harapan*. Penerbit Universiti Kebangsaan Malaysia.
Romer, P. M. (1986). Increasing returns and long run growth. *Journal of Political Economy, 94*, 1002–1037.
Searle, P. (1999). *The riddle of Malaysian capitalism*. Allen & Unwin and University of Hawai Press.
Shah, I. A. (1995). *Kesedaran Dan Persepsi Pelajar Di luar Bandar Terhadap Pembangunan sumber Manusia Di Sarawak*. Dewan Bahasa Dan Pustaka.
Shahbaz, M. (2010). Income inequality-economic growth and non-linearity: A case of Pakistan. *International Journal of Social Economics., 37*(8), 613–636.
Shari, I. (1999). *Bumi Semua Manusia: Menangani Ketidaksetaraan Ekonomi Dalam arus globalisasi*. Penerbit Universiti Kebangsaan Malaysia.
Shari, I. (2000). Economic growth and income inequality in Malaysia, 1971-95. *Journal of the Asia-Pacific Economy, 5*, 112–124.
Snodgrass, D. R. (1980). *Inequality and economic development in Malaysia*. Oxford University Press.
Sowell, T. (2004). *Affirmative action around the world: An empirical study*. Yale University Press.
Stewart, F., & Brown, G. (2006). *The implications of horizontal inequalities for aid*. Centre for Research on Inequality Human Security and Ethnicity.
Stewart, F., Brown, G., & Langer, A. (2007). *Policies towards horizontal inequalities*. Centre for Research on Inequality Human Security and Ethnicity.
Stiglitz, J. E. (2006). *Making globalization work*. W.W. Norton.
Wolff, E. N. (1990). Wealth holdings and poverty status in the U.S. *Review of Income and Wealth, 26*(2).
World Bank. (2015). *GDP per capita (constant 2015 US$)*. https://data.worldbank.org/indicator/NY.GDP.PCAP.KD

The Reasons Behind Imbalanced Ecosystem of Latin America: A Comprehensive Systematic Review

Irfan ul Haq, Adnan ul Haque, and Fred A. Yamoah

1 Introduction

Tsujimoto et al. (2018) explained that there is no single agreed definition of ecosystem that explains sound theoretical backing. Nonetheless, a plethora of research has confirmed the consistently growing significance of ecosystem in the field of management of technology and innovation (Adner & Kapoor, 2010; Kapoor & Lee, 2012; Meyer et al., 2005; Pierce, 2009; Teece, 2007). In simplest terms, it is defined as "A biological system composed of all the organisms found in a particular physical

I. ul Haq
SRIBP, Toronto, ON, Canada

A. ul Haque
Faculty of Business, Yorkville University, Toronto, ON, Canada

F. A. Yamoah (✉)
Department of Management, School of Business, Economics and Informatics, Birkbeck, University of London, London, UK
e-mail: f.yamoah@bbk.ac.uk

F. A. Yamoah, A. ul Haque (eds.), *Corporate Management Ecosystem in Emerging Economies*, https://doi.org/10.1007/978-3-031-41578-4_23

environment, interacting with it and each other. Also in extended use: a complex system resembling this" (Oxford English Dictionary, 2017). After defining ecosystem, the next step is what is sustainable ecosystem? According to Kanter (2017), any ecosystem that has the capability to strive and prosper without external exertions are regarded as a sustainable ecosystem. In other words, the ability to strive and survive on own accord at a constant gradual rate (sustainability—ability to sustain over the period). Moreover, Kanter (2017) explains that diverse biological components and habitats function together to assist and promote the life within the ecosystem. Within an ideal sustainable ecosystem, all essential resources are pre-existing and available for the survival within the ecosystem without any man-made efforts. In other words, necessary resources exist in natural phenomenon.

After explaining the key concept, the article explains Latin America and its sustainable ecosystem. The reason for selecting Latin America is due to its incomparable natural capital (CEPAL, 2022). Latin American countries have been positioned at the top in regard to natural capital resources. Nonetheless, there is still no conclusive evidence from the literature at hand to examine the comparison of rural ecosystem and urban ecosystem. Moreover, despite having incomparable natural resources in the region, there lies a huge responsibility in terms of fair policies and strategies to ensure there is conservation and protection of natural resources in both rural and urban areas. There is a need for Latin America to ensure that the natural resources in the region are properly appreciated and preserved in a natural manner so that they can be sustained in the long run.

This takes us to consider the Latin American countries that are ranked as per their sustainable operations.

According to the survey of Alves (2023), Costa Rica (77.5) is at the top of the list among the most sustainable countries in Latin America, followed by Uruguay (74.8). Columbia (65.3), Chile (64.1), Paraguay (62.1), Peru (60.6), Brazil (58.7), Mexico (55.2), Argentina (54.3) and, lastly, Ecuador (54.2) (Fig. 1). However, this does not mean that these countries are free from any environmental issues. In fact, the five most critical environmental issues in Latin America, irrespective of the

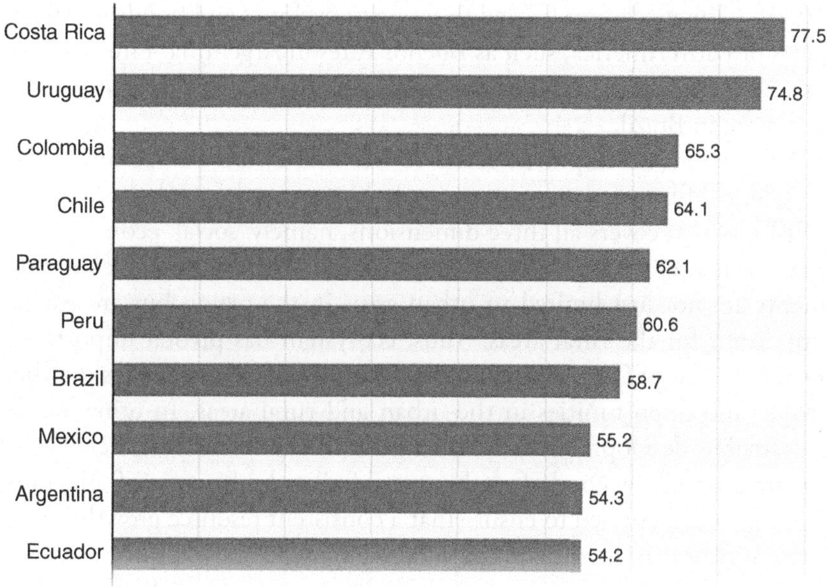

Fig. 1 Sustainability ranking of selected Latin American countries—2021. Source: Sustainability ranking of selected Latin American countries (Alves, 2023)

sustainability ranking include, first, deforestation, especially rampant in Brazil, Bolivia, Peru, Chile and Ecuador (Carvalho, 2023). Second is the soil erosion affecting approximately 60% of the food cultivation in South America specifically, Argentina, Brazil, Paraguay and Mexico are deemed to cultivation (ibid). Third environmental challenge is melting Glaciers. Continued melting, along with rising temperatures, poses a severe challenge to water security among the Andean population (especially Argentinian and Chilian Andes) and ecosystems. "Peru has also lost more than 40% of its glaciers. Lake Palcacocha in the central Peruvian Andes has grown 34 times larges in only four decades, being fed by the melting waters of the Palcaraju ice sheet" (ibid). Water scarcity and water pollution is the fourth environmental issue in Latin America despite being the largest freshwater resource. Overexploitation, wide-scale mismanagement and poor and untreated water distribution are the reasons behind this issue. Lastly, rise in the sea level due to extreme weather events (Carvalho,

2023). Climate change has led to frequent cyclones and floods in various parts of Latin America, such as Buenos Aires in Argentina; Lima in Peru; Santiago in Chile; and Porto Alegre, São Paulo, Rio de Janeiro and Fortaleza in Brazil.

Sustainable development refers to the framework comprising 3Ps—people, profit and planet—commonly known as the triple bottom line (TBL), which covers all three dimensions, namely, social, economic and environmental aspects (Slaper & Hall, 2011). These sustainable developments are not just limited to urban areas in the region but are equally important for the rural areas. Thus, ecosystem has pivotal importance. From the lens of Latin America, this systematic review evaluates the challenges and opportunities in the urban and rural areas. In other words, sustainable development is following the rule of "Pareto Efficiency"—making somebody good of, without making anybody worse of. The same concept when applied to ensure that a consistent resource growth for the present people in the urban and rural region while no compromise made for the future generation would be called sustainable urban and rural development.

2 Literature Review

According to Balasubramanian (2008), the "eco" is a term that refers to the part of the world, whereas the "system" reflects the coordination of different units. Building on the argument of Balasubramanian (2008), it could be narrated that when living organisms interact with each other and surrounding environment, the ecological unit or ecosystem is formed. Moreover, a plethora of research confirmed that ecosystems emerge naturally that assemble the lives of inhabitants and their respective environment (Tansley, 1935; Balasubramanian, 2008; Locatelli et al., 2017; Tsujimoto et al., 2018; Breen et al., 2020; Zulauf & Wagner, 2021; Muñoz-Pacheco & Villaseñor, 2022; Santos et al., 2023). An ecological system (i.e., ecosystem) includes the physical environment (abiotic pools) and types of organisms that interact with each other (Chapin, 2011). In other words, ecosystem comprises everything that exists in that geographic region, such as animals, plants, weather, plans, landscape, and other living creatures and nonliving things. All these resources and components often exist naturally; however, sometimes manmade components are also part of the ecosystem.

Ecosystem interlinks various living mechanisms in biodiverse environment through food supply, reproduction and atmosphere to promote the sustainable growth and consumption of resources in effective and efficient manner. The importance of ecosystem cannot be ignored because of the relationship between biotic and abiotic resources. As per Subramanian (2008), the food chains, circulation and transformation of nutrients and elements, biomass and biodiversity, and natural evolution of ecological system provide resources to the inhabitants. Nevertheless, there is an argument for appropriate and balanced resource distribution. Especially, the existing literature at hand is limited in explaining the challenges of a sustainable ecosystem that could offer a balanced resource distribution between urban and rural regions. Thus, to understand the core challenges and reasons for disparity, we must explain the concept of sustainable development.

Triple bottom line (TPL) reflects sustainable development, and the word was coined by John Elkington in 1994 (Elkington, 2018). This is the framework that comprises three major dimensions, namely, economical, concerning with the profit; social, concerning with the people; and environmental, concerning with the planet (Slaper & Hall, 2011). The progress of the region must be measured in all three dimensions because it enables us to understand the impact of operations. However, the counterargument is that why only three dimensions? The legal dimension is not considered in the existing literature to understand the complexities of the phenomenon. In other words, something that might be social, but may not be aligned with legal factors could be a point of concern. The least negative/adverse impact indicates that the operations in the region are acceptable because it does affect the natural environment in minimal manner. However, the existing literature has primarily focused on the importance of sustainable development in more generic manner. Thus, it only explains the sustainable development approaches, without explaining what the challenges in other regions could be and how it could be dealt. One-fit-all strategy cannot be applied to all emerging countries because the nature and dynamics of every country vary. Thus, an attempt is made to gather the data to find the common themes evident for the

Latin American countries facing shared challenges related to sustainable ecosystem. To understand the challenges, we must give an overview of the Latin American ecosystem.

The extensive review of the literature revealed that despite different countries in Latin America on the list of ranked sustainable countries (Alves, 2023), still no country exceeds to 78% which means there is still a need for adoption of sustainable practices. A plethora of research confirmed that Latin America has one of the world's largest rainforests—Amazon, second largest forest in South America that encompasses Bolivia, Argentina, Brazil and Paraguay (Locatelli et al., 2017; Tsujimoto et al., 2018; Breen et al., 2020; Alves, 2023; Zulauf & Wagner 2021; Muñoz-Pacheco & Villaseñor, 2022; Carvalho, 2023; Santos et al., 2023). Despite that Latin America is facing serious environmental issues, as identified in the literature by Carvalho (2023): (1) deforestation, (2) soil erosion, (3) melting glaciers, (4) water scarcity and water pollution and (5) rise in the Sea level. Nonetheless, the literature has hinted towards wide-scale mismanagement, overexploitation and untreated and inadequate distribution of water coupled with the global warming has increased the vulnerability of the ecosystem in Latin America (Carvalho, 2023).

The major considered literature is presented in Table 1:

3 Research Methodology

This systematic review is based on the secondary data for understanding the challenges and concerns in the urban and rural areas of Latin America. This is an attempt to examine the ecosystem of the emerging Latin American economies. For, this reason, we have considered the axiological stance (authors' preference based on the extensive review of the Scopus indexed papers and chapters) for the selection of the papers. According to Mack (2010), the social science research is categorized into anthropological paradigm. The use of such paradigm also enables the readers to understand the quality of the issue in-depth rather than width, reflecting significance of useful truth rather than factual truth (Haque, 2020; Haque & Yamoah, 2021). Since this study is under the anthropological paradigm, it has critical realism ontological and epistemological stances

Table 1 Summary of the articles examined in this study

Articles	Authors	Indexing	Findings
A Review of the Ecosystem Concept—Towards Coherent Ecosystem Design	Tsujimoto et al. (2018)	Scopus	Viewing the ecosystem as a complex actor network, each actor has a different background and attributes The ecosystem analysis requires the longitudinal observation of the product/service system's dynamic evolution or extinction
Urban Ecosystem Services in South America: A Systematic Review	Muñoz-Pacheco and Villaseñor (2022)	Scopus	Large green areas contribute to many quantitative and qualitative features related to urban ecosystem services, such as temperature control, recreation, and flood control—the most evaluated services in South America
Urban and Rural Sustainability: Divergent concepts and Their Consequences for Marketing	Zulauf and Wagner (2021).	Scopus	Reducing "sustainability" to urban living consumers' conceptualization leaves a significant portion of the population behind, denies and hinders the dynamics of innovation in rural areas of affluent and developed regions of the world, and might even induce innovation resistance

(*continued*)

Table 1 (continued)

Articles	Authors	Indexing	Findings
From "Government to Governance"? A Systematic Literature Review of Research for Urban Green Infrastructure Management in Latin America	Breen et al. (2020).	Scopus	Local government as the principal actor in the management of the urban green initiative and community-run initiatives are equally important. A directional push toward governance practices but significant obstacles in the form of weak local government, divisions driven by a lack of context-sensitive approaches to informal settlements and socioeconomic segregation, and a management discourse
Socioeconomic Urban Environment in Latin America: Towards a Typology of Cities	Santos et al. (2023).	Scopus	Identifying clusters of cities with similar features underscores understanding of the urban social and economic development dynamics and assists in studying how urban features affect health, the environment, and sustainability
Research on Climate Change Policies and Rural Development in Latin America: Scope and gaps	Locatelli et al. (2017).	Scopus	The two complementary types of research considered here, "science for climate policies" and "science of climate policies", should be strengthened in order to better support climate policy development in Latin America

Source: Own illustration of bibliometric analysis

(Mack, 2010). The manuscript is basic research focusing on enhancing the existing knowledge about the research phenomenon. A case study approach is employed to understand the urban and rural sustainable development along with the challenges in those regions of Latin America. Nonetheless, this systematic review primarily relied on bibliometric analysis (Fig. 2).

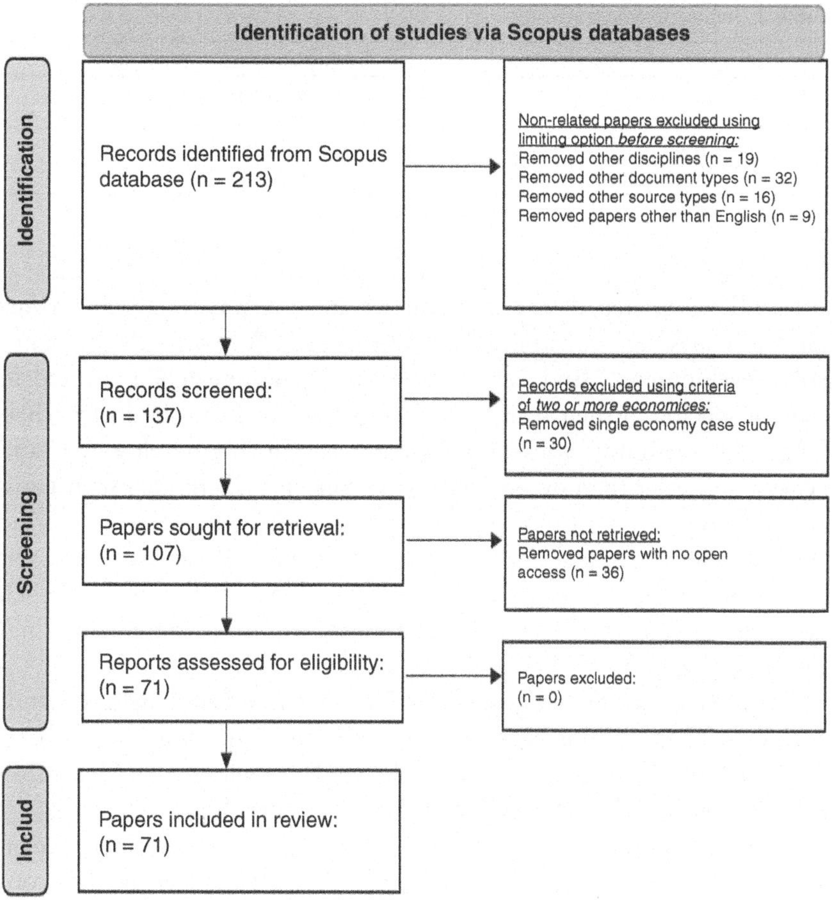

Fig. 2 PRISMA

According to Donthu et al. (2021), the novelty of bibliometric research could not be ignored in social and management sciences. However, the use of bibliometric analysis has enhanced and attained exponential growth more because of the challenges in gathering primary data in the COVID-19 era. It would not be incorrect to state that in existing knowledge and prediction of the future knowledge, the bibliometric analysis is an art of finding greater variations. The researchers used Boolean search for scraping the Scopus database by including the abstract, keywords, and

Table 2 Inclusion and exclusion

Inclusion	Exclusion
Bibliometric analysis	Field research
Basic research	Applied research
Systematic review	Quantitative analysis
Case study approach	Statistical analysis

titles. The first step of the bibliometric analysis was to search for key terms: "issues" or "constraints" or "challenges", "ecosystem*", "sustainable development*" and "Latin America*". The researchers wanted to remain specific in their search for articles that focus on the issues, challenges or constraints for Latin America, sustainable development and ecosystem rather than overpowering the concepts interlinked with Latin America such as political disruptions, poverty, diseases and so on. During the initial search, a total of 213 articles were found. The initial search was further filtered by following the inclusion-and-exclusion criteria (Fig. 1). R-based software—VOSviewer and Biblishiny—drove the key findings by narrowing down to 137 usable articles.

For the case study and general review process, another inclusion-and-exclusion criterion was employed. In this study, the following aspects were included and/or excluded (Table 2). The inclusion and exclusion criteria were set for the determination of the papers:

Primarily, sustainable and environmental concerns have increased in the last one-and-a-half decade; therefore, this systematic review only considered the articles published in last one decade in the Scopus journals. With the strictly only Scopus papers inclusion, the reliability and credibility are confirmed. Since those papers were published through rigorous peer-review process, content validity and reliability were obtained.

4 Findings and Discussions

Based on the systemic review of the literature at hand, SWOT analysis has been developed to give a quick glance at the different aspects of Latin America's ecosystem:

The above SWOT analysis serves as a foundation for understanding the challenges for urban and rural sustainable development in Latin America. Being home to the world's longest mountain range and the second-largest river, Latin America is a true example of rich biological diversity and natural landscapes that breed aquatic life, terrestrial and marine inhabitants (Table 3). We confirm from the literature that the ecosystem of Latin America is highly significant. Based on the systematic review of the literature, below graphs highlight core environmental issues in Latin America through certain selected economies. These fundamental five issues vary in different countries and demonstrate the most severe and the least concern in each selected region (Table 3).

The extensive systematic review of the existing literature confirmed that Latin America has five major challenges, namely, deforestation, soil erosion, melting glaciers, water scarcity and water pollution, and rise in the sea level (Fig. 3). Thus, we support the argument of Carvalho (2023). Many countries on shore of the Pacific Ocean, especially Peru, Chile,

Table 3 SWOT analysis of Latin America's ecosystems

Strengths	**Weaknesses**
• Geography—world's third largest freshwater • Awareness about green initiatives and urban green development • Natural green parks and water preserves • Agricultural areas in close vicinity of urban region	• Lack of optimal distribution of freshwater • Less emphasis on rural green initiatives • Poor infrastructure for resource preservation • Industrial waste and traffic pollution effecting the natural climate
Opportunities	**Threats**
• Wastewater—Only 20% of wastewater has been used however there is future opportunity to increase the utilization of wastewater • Chance for local government to participate in sustainable growth and development • Sustainable tourism in the region could be developed because of the abundance of natural resources	• Deforestation—Alarming high rate • Soil erosion—Effecting food cultivation • Melting glaciers—Meting into freshwater therefore affecting drinkable and useable water • Water pollution—No affective methods for water treatment • Rising sea level—Higher chances of floods and cyclones due to climate change

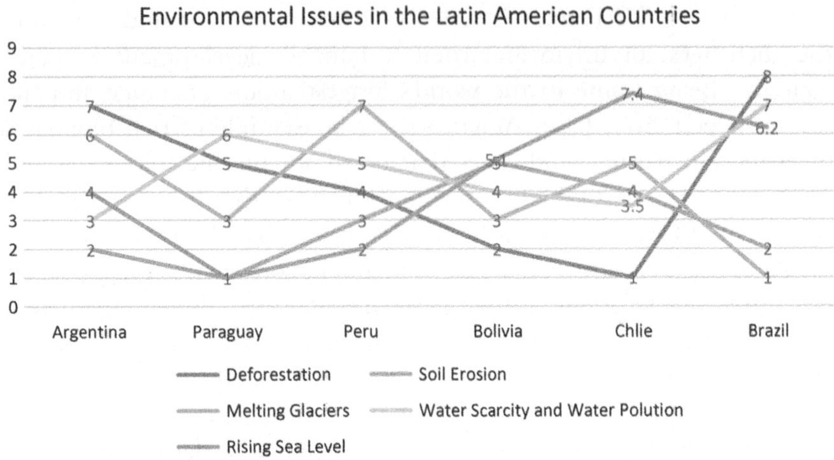

Fig. 3 Environmental Issues in Latin America. Source: own illustration based on the literature at hand

Bolivia and Ecuador, are facing deforestation issue affecting the ecosystem. Nonetheless, Brazil is another country that has the highest deforestation in the Amazon rainforest. The Gran Chaco Forest is the second-largest forest that is the nucleus among several Latin countries (such as Argentina, Paraguay, Brazil and Bolivia). Another pressing issue affecting the ecosystem of Latin America is the soil erosion which threatens 60% of food cultivation in Mexico, Argentina, Paraguay and Brazil. Our findings also stay consistent with the work of Carvalho (2023) by confirming that melting glaciers and rising temperatures have affected the lives of Andean people and ecosystems. Approximately 40% of Peru's glaciers have melted into water, resulting in scarcity of drinkable and useable water. This issue is also interlinked with the fourth issue, that is, water scarcity and water pollution due to wide-scale mismanagement, overexploitation and untreated water distribution. The ecosystem of Latin America is also subject to cyclones and floods.

Moreover, the systematic review of the literature revealed that ecosystem is not an ordinary factor but a very complex actor network where each and every stakeholder has a huge responsibility towards the preservation and promotion of sustainable consumption patterns. Thus, we support the argument of Tsujimoto et al. (2018). We also agree that an ecosystem requires longitudinal observations (covert and overt observations in different time lag), especially in the urban and rural areas where services and product systems are slowly and gradually becoming extinct. Furthermore, the work of Muñoz-Pacheco and Villaseñor (2022) is another important study that explores larger green areas, serving to the urban ecosystem services because of its qualitative and quantitative characteristics. Nonetheless, in Latin America, flood control, recreation and temperature control are vital urban ecosystem services that can ensure sustainable development.

While reviewing the ecosystems of Latin America, we found from the work of Zulauf and Wagner (2021) that there is a disparity in the policies and regulations of different countries which has led to the challenges for maintaining sustainable growth and development in the rural areas. For instance, to ensure sustainable practices for urban area, consumers have left large numbers of population in the rural areas deprived from the innovations and resource allocations. Hence the majority of Latin American countries are facing the issue of innovation resistances and brining a balanced resource distribution between urban and rural areas. Furthermore, we partially disagree with the work of Breen et al. (2020) because of the generic description of local government. According to Haque (2012), there are different types of local government (i.e., decentralization, deconcentration, devolution, delegation and privatization), so the argument of Breen et al. (2020) lacks clarity about the effective type of local government running the community initiatives and urban green initiatives. Furthermore, we agree with Breen et al. (2020) that a directional push towards governance practices is vital for community-run initiatives and urban green initiatives; however, the focus should not only be limited to urban development. The rural sustainable development is equally of greater importance.

We found the argument of Santos et al. (2023) valid that the Latin American countries differ to larger extent when it comes to urban and rural structural development and progress. The clusters of cities in different Latin American countries may appear to have similar features indicating urban and rural development in the region; however, this doesn't reflect the true urban social and economic development in the region. For instance, the health conditions of country A's urban developed city (better developed infrastructure) might be poor as compared to country B's urban developed city (which might be in-progress infrastructure). We found that Locatelli et al.'s (2017) argument valid that in order to understand the urban and rural sustainable development, the chief actors must consider both complementary types of research: 'science for climate policies' and 'science of climate policies' because there will be a comprehensive framework for understanding the sustainable use and natural preservation of ecosystems. Thus, climate policy development in Latin America is important in the long term.

5 Conclusion and Recommendations

From the above discussions, we have drawn the conclusion that Latin America has a rich ecosystem with the potential to do well. The geography and natural resources are key strengths that offer opportunities for sustainable tourism, responsible local government initiative and so on. However, the biggest weaknesses include poor infrastructure and imbalanced resource distribution. The optimal distribution of fresh water is missing despite being the third largest freshwater reserves of the planet. The weaknesses have led to five major challenges (such as deforestation, soil erosion, melting glaciers, water pollution and rising sea level) that hinder the sustainable ecosystem of Latin America.

Due to these challenges, the urban and rural sustainable development in Latin America has suffered to a larger extent. We concluded that Latin America is the true example of rich biological diversity and natural landscapes, but mismanagement and weak infrastructure are causing serious threat to the region. Moreover, the rural and urban sustainable development are not balanced in terms of operations. There is a higher emphasis on the urban green initiative (UGI) and community-run initiative in the urban areas while leaving a very little for the rural sustainability projects. Although the local government is the principal actor, there is no clarity about the type of local government that could be appropriate in ensuring the balanced-and-sustainable development. Interestingly, the triple bottom line (TPL) focuses on three dimensions—social, economical and environmental aspects. However, the legal dimension is missing from the work. This is one of the shortfalls of the current literature that should be explored.

The natural calamity in Latin America is affecting the ecosystem and balanced-sustainable development in the urban and rural regions. There are various complex network actors involved in the process, and they must be considered during the project development and execution stages. Rural sustainable developments are equally important, and special focus should be on the structural improvements. Moreover, the climate policies should be explored more in depth to find more natural modes for the preservation of ecosystems.

Based on the findings, the following recommendations are given:

Legal dimension: Incorporate the legal framework to understand the sustainable ecosystem. Triple bottom line is a good approach. However, the legal framework should be included in the procedures of the sustainable development process, especially in the allocation of resources.

Specificity about the type of local government: The importance of the local government as a principal actor could not be discarded. However, there are different types of local government, and each project must consider the type of local government (such as devolution, decentralization, deconcentration, delegation and privatization). The specificity would be helpful in using the required expertise of the principal actor involved in the process.

Balanced-sustainable development: There should be a mechanism to ensure that the sustainable development in the region should be based on the principle of "Pareto efficiency". Too much over-emphasis on any region (irrespective of urban and/or rural) would adversely impact the underprivileged area. Thus, rather than focusing on sustainable development, the concerned authorities should work on building the proper mechanism of balanced-sustainable development.

References

Adner, R., & Kapoor, R. (2010). Value creation in innovation ecosystems: How the structure of technological interdependence affects firm performance in new technology generations. *Strategic Management Journal, 31*(3), 306–333.

Alves, B. (2023, February 8). *Latin America: Sustainability ranking 2021.* Statista. Retrieved April 7, 2023, from https://www.statista.com/statistics/1107780/latin-america-sustainability-ranking/#:~:text=Costa%20Rica%20was%20considered%20the,in%20third%2C%20with%2065.3%20points

Balasubramanian, A. (2008). *Ecosystem and its components.* Retrieved from https://www.researchgate.net/publication/314213426_ECOSYSTEM_AND_ITS_COMPONENTS

Breen, A., Giannotti, E., Flores Molina, M., & Vásquez, A. (2020). From "government to governance"? A systematic literature review of research for urban green infrastructure Management in Latin America. *Frontiers in Sustainable Cities, 2.* https://doi.org/10.3389/frsc.2020.572360

Carvalho, K. (2023, February 2). *5 environmental issues in South America in 2023.* Earth.Org. Retrieved April 7, 2023, from https://earth.org/environmental-issues-in-south-america/

CEPAL. (2022). *Natural Resources in Latin America and the Caribbean - No.4.* Retrieved from: https://www.cepal.org/en/publications/48131-natural-resources-latin-america-and-caribbean-no4

Chapin, F. S., III. (2011). Chapter 1: The ecosystem concept. In P. A. Matson, P. M. Vitousek, & M. C. Chapin (Eds.), *Principles of terrestrial ecosystem ecology* (2nd ed.). Springer.

Donthu, N., Kumar, S., Mukherjee, D., Pandey, N., & Lim, W. M. (2021). How to conduct a bibliometric analysis: An overview and guidelines. *Journal of Business Research, 133,* 285–296.

Elkington, J. (2018, June 25). 25 years ago I coined the phrase "triple bottom line." Here's why it's time to rethink it. *Harvard Business Review.*

Haque, A. (2012). *Theoretical perspective of local government-literature review.* Munich Personal RePEc Archive Paper (46301).

Haque, A. U. (2020). *Varying occupational stress and organisational commitment within the university staff of contrasting economies (cross-sectional comparative study of middle range public universities in Pakistan and the UK).* Published DBA Thesis, UWTSD Repository. Retrieved from https://repository.uwtsd.ac.uk/id/eprint/1570/

Haque, A. U., & Yamoah, F. A. (2021). The role of ethical leadership in managing occupational stress to promote innovative work behaviour: A cross-cultural management perspective. *Sustainability, 13*(17), 9608.

Kanter, H. (2017). *What is a sustainable ecosystem?* Synonym. Retrieved April 7, 2023, from https://classroom.synonym.com/what-is-a-sustainable-ecosystem-12081802.html

Kapoor, R., & Lee, J. M. (2012). Coordinating and competing in ecosystems: How organizational forms shape new technology investments. *Strategic Management Journal, 34*(3), 274–296. https://doi.org/10.1002/smj.2010

Locatelli, B., Aldunce, P., Fallot, A., Le Coq, J.-F., Sabourin, E., & Tapasco, J. (2017). Research on climate change policies and rural development in Latin America: Scope and gaps. *Sustainability, 9*(10), 1831. https://doi.org/10.3390/su9101831

Mack, L. (2010). The philosophical underpinnings of educational research. *Polyglossia, 19*, 1–10.

Meyer, A. D., Gaba, V., & Colwell, K. A. (2005). Organizing far from equilibrium: Nonlinear change in organizational fields. *Organization Science, 16*(5), 456–473. https://doi.org/10.1287/orsc.1050.0135

Muñoz-Pacheco, C. B., & Villaseñor, N. R. (2022). Urban ecosystem Services in South America: A systematic review. *Sustainability, 14*(17), 10751. https://doi.org/10.3390/su141710751

Oxford English Dictionary. (2017). *Ecosystem.* Retrieved from https://en.oxforddictionaries.com/definition/ecosystem

Pierce, L. (2009). Big losses in ecosystem niches: How core firm decisions drive complementary product shakeouts. *Strategic Management Journal, 30*(3), 323–347. https://doi.org/10.1002/smj.736

Santos, G. F. D., Vergara, A. V., Alburquenque, M. F., de Sousa Filho, J. F., Paiva, A. S., Useche, A. F., Yamada, G., Alfaro, T., Friche, A. A. L., Andrade, R. F. S., Barreto, M. L., Caiaffa, W. T., & Diez-Roux, A. V. (2023). Socioeconomic urban environment in Latin America: Towards a typology of cities. *Sustainability, 15*, 6380. https://doi.org/10.3390/su15086380

Slaper, T. F., and Hall, T. J. (2011). *The triple bottom line: What is it and how does it work?* Retrieved April 7, 2023, from http://www.ibrc.indiana.edu/ibr/2011/spring/article2.html

Tansley, A. G. (1935). The use and abuse of vegetational terms and concepts. *Ecology, 16*(3), 284–307.

Teece, D. J. (2007). Explicating dynamic capabilities: The nature and microfoundations of (sustainable) enterprise performance. *Strategic Management Journal, 28*(13), 1319–1350. https://doi.org/10.1002/smj.640

Tsujimoto, M., Kajikawa, Y., Tomita, J., & Matsumoto, Y. (2018). A review of the ecosystem concept—Towards coherent ecosystem design. *Technological Forecasting and Social Change, 136*, 49–58. https://doi.org/10.1016/j.techfore.2017.06.032

Zulauf, K., & Wagner, R. (2021). Urban and rural sustainability: Divergent concepts and their consequences for marketing. *Frontiers in Sustainability, 2*. https://doi.org/10.3389/frsus.2021.670866

SPRINGER NATURE

GPSR Compliance

The European Union's (EU) General Product Safety Regulation (GPSR) is a set of rules that requires consumer products to be safe and our obligations to ensure this.

If you have any concerns about our products, you can contact us on ProductSafety@springernature.com

In case Publisher is established outside the EU, the EU authorized representative is:

Springer Nature Customer Service Center GmbH
Europaplatz 3
69115 Heidelberg, Germany

The manufacturer's authorised representative in the EU is Springer Nature Customer Service Centre GmbH, Europaplatz 3, 69115 Heidelberg, Germany. If you have any concerns regarding our products, please contact ProductSafety@springernature.com

Printed and bound by CPI Group (UK) Ltd, Croydon, CR0 4YY
28/09/2026
02224060-0010